ABRIDGED EDITION
THE
TEACHING
OF
CHRIST
A CATHOLIC CATECHISM
FOR ADULTS

ABRIDGED EDITION
THE
TEACHING
OF
CHRIST
A CATHOLIC CATECHISM
FOR ADULTS

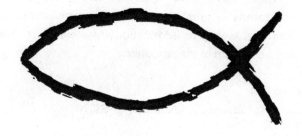

Edited by

RONALD LAWLER, O.F.M.Cap.   **DONALD W. WUERL**
THOMAS COMERFORD LAWLER

Our Sunday Visitor, Inc.
Huntington, Indiana 46750

Nihil Obstat:
Rev. Terry E. Place
Censor Librorum

Imprimatur:
✠William E. McManus
Bishop of Fort Wayne-South Bend
July 2, 1979

The Nihil Obstat and Imprimatur are official declarations that a book or pamphlet is free of doctrinal or moral error. No implication is contained therein that those who have granted the Nihil Obstat and the Imprimatur agree with the contents, opinions, or statements expressed.

Copyright © 1979 by Ronald Lawler, O.F.M. Cap.,
Donald W. Wuerl, and Thomas Comerford Lawler

All rights reserved. No part of this book may be reproduced or copied in any form or by any means — graphic, electronic, or mechanical, including photocopying, recording, taping, or information storage and retrieval systems — without written permission of the publisher.

ISBN: 0-87973-538-4
Library of Congress Catalog Card Number: 79-53070

Published, printed, and bound in the United States of America

538

An abridgment of:
THE TEACHING OF CHRIST
A Catholic Catechism for Adults
by

LORENZO ALBACETE
Archdiocese of Washington

ROMANO STEPHEN ALMAGNO, O.F.M.
Collegio Internazionale S. Bonaventure, Rome

JORDAN AUMANN, O.P.
Angelicum University, Rome

DONALD CONNOLLY
Pastor, Archdiocese of Miami

JOHN FINNIS
University College, Oxford University

GERMAIN GRISEZ
Campion College, University of Regina

JOHN J. HUGO
Worship Commission, Diocese of Pittsburgh

FREDERICK M. JELLY, O.P.
Dominican House of Studies, Washington, D.C.

GEORGE F. KIRWIN
Oblate College, Washington, D.C.

MARY ELISE KRANTZ, S.N.D.
Generalate, S.N.D., Rome

RONALD LAWLER, O.F.M.Cap.
Pontifical College Josephinum

THOMAS COMERFORD LAWLER
Co-editor, Ancient Christian Writers

DAVID M. MALONEY
Bishop of Wichita

JOSEPH MINDLING, O.F.M.Cap.
Washington Theological Coalition

JOHANNES QUASTEN
Catholic University of America

JOHN F. WHEALON
Archbishop of Hartford

DONALD W. WUERL
Angelicum University, Rome

ACKNOWLEDGMENTS

The Scripture quotations in this publication are taken from the Revised Standard Version Bible, Catholic Edition, copyrighted © 1965 and 1966 by the Division of Christian Education of the National Council of the Churches of Christ in the U.S.A., and used by permission. Special permission has been received to use the you-your-yours forms of the personal pronouns in address to God, and to capitalize personal pronouns referring to God.

Quotations from the Constitutions, Decrees, and Declarations of the Second Vatican Council used in this book are from the translation, with some amendments, appearing in *The Documents of Vatican II,* Walter M. Abbott, S.J., General Editor. Reprinted with permission of AMERICA. All Rights Reserved. © 1966 by America Press, 106 W. 56th Street, N.Y., N.Y., 10019.

Excerpts from the English translation of the Roman Missal © 1973, International Committee on English in the Liturgy, Inc. (ICEL); excerpts from the English translation of the Rite of Baptism for Children © 1969, ICEL; excerpts from the English translation of Rite of Christian Initiation of Adults © 1974, ICEL; excerpts from the English translation of the Rite of Confirmation © 1975, ICEL; excerpts from the English translation of the Rite of Penance © 1974, ICEL; excerpts from the English translation of the Rite of Anointing and Pastoral Care of the Sick © 1973, ICEL; excerpts from the English translation of the Rite of Marriage © 1969, ICEL; and excerpts from the English translation of the Ordination of Deacons, Priests, and Bishops © 1969, ICEL. All rights reserved.

Table of Contents

Table of Contents — continued

PART FOUR • *In Christ: Fulfillment of All*

APPENDIXES

Introduction

This is a Catholic catechism for adults. It is a catechism in the sense that it is a comprehensive summary of doctrine. It is Catholic in that the doctrine it presents is the teaching of the Catholic Church.

True, this is an abridgment, prepared by us only after some hesitation. But many friends urged us to proceed. They wished to make more extensive use of the catechism which many critics welcomed as the best to date for catechetical instruction of adults; they felt that *The Teaching of Christ* was sometimes too long for the instruction of converts and for other pastoral needs.

The present text is a response. It retains the spirit, style, and even the language of the original. To make it more useful, study questions, drawn largely from the *Study Guide for The Teaching of Christ,* have been added to each chapter. Obviously deletions were made; and we still recommend use of the larger edition whenever that is feasible. Yet the present text does offer a complete and balanced statement of the Catholic faith.

†

A catechism should not only state Catholic faith, but also gather the testimony of many "witnesses." In declaring the teaching of the Church, a catechism notes how the faith of the Church is rooted in the Scriptures; it points out how councils of the Church in times past have spoken this message. It calls forth as witnesses to the faith the Fathers of the Church, the saints, the popes. The liturgy and life of the Church in the past and the present are cited to show how these too bear testimony to what the Church believes and teaches.

This "witness" form of catechesis is most appropriate here, for a catechism is addressed first of all (though not exclusively) to those who have already found faith in Christ. Though their faith may yet be in need of instruction, they already know that Christ's word is entirely reliable. To them the Church speaks in the voices of those in whom Christ's followers have regularly recognized His voice, and have been led by His Spirit to love. In all the witnesses the Church appeals to, the faithful are invited to hear the voice of Christ and the Father in the light of the Spirit. St. Paul speaks of this mystery of faith in his First Epistle to the Thessalonians; he rejoices that they were able to hear the human witness God had given them, recognize the real source of this teaching, 188* and believe only God. "And we also thank God constantly for this, that when you received the word of God which you heard from us, you accepted it not as the word of men but as what it really is, the word of God, which is at work in you believers" (1 Thess. 2.13).

Although a catechism is addressed primarily to those who have already found faith in Christ, and have recognized His presence in the Church, it is addressed also to those who are weak in faith, or entirely without faith. To them it should speak of the ways that lead toward faith.

God calls men to faith in many ways. But there are certain common patterns. Love inclines people toward faith; intelligence and reflection give support; but faith itself is the free gift of God.

Love stimulates a desire for faith. Perfect love, the love of divine charity, presupposes faith; but there is also a preliminary love. It is the earnest desire to cling to what one begins to see as good. The prospect of finding faith is interesting and appealing only when one begins to grasp the goodness of a life of faith.

169   When Jesus led the apostles toward faith, He first invited them to friendship with Himself. As they came to know Him, they began to realize the richness of a kind of life they had not known before, and they wished to share in its fullness. A catechism should try to show something of the richness of the life to which Christ calls us in faith, and to show how effectively the new life in Christ fulfills the actual desires and longings of the human heart.

When Jesus invited men to faith, He clearly respected their in- 80 telligence. His words were accompanied by signs of their truth, in the wisdom of His teaching, in the goodness of His life, in the power of the deeds He performed.

People normally need good reasons to clear their way toward faith. Certainly there is no conflict between intelligence and faith. Human reasoning alone, however, is not sufficient to establish personal faith. No one can be driven to personal faith by dialectics, for faith involves believing God, not complex argumentation. But intelligence can stimulate the pursuit of personal faith.

A catechism does not give a full and systematic apologetics (that is, a rational defense of the faith), but it does present many of the evi-

---

*See page 12 for explanation of marginal numbers.

dences that have led thoughtful persons toward faith. The whole message of faith is itself a sign of its own truth; for when it is reflected on with care, it is grasped as an astonishingly profound response to the deepest questions men ask. A catechism speaks, of course, of that greatest of signs, the resurrection of Jesus, and the effects this has had on 94-96 history and in the lives of countless millions. It speaks also of the most visible sign of faith, the Church itself, sealed with certain characteristic marks that make it unique in the world and arouse a wonder that can 122 incline one toward faith.

Faith itself is a gift. The Gospels portray the progress of St. Peter 170 toward faith. He had seen Christ's goodness, wisdom, and power. He had come gradually to have more firm views about Christ and who He was. But when the Lord's invitation led Peter from opinion to a ringing profession of faith, Christ told him that his new confident conviction was not the result of merely human insight. "Blessed are you, Simon Bar-Jona! For flesh and blood has not revealed this to you, but My Father who is in heaven" (Matt. 16.17).

Scripture speaks in many ways of the gift of faith. Faith brings one to a new life with a new way of knowing (cf. John 1). It gives vision: faith opens the eyes of one born blind (cf. John 9). God Himself opens the eyes of the heart (cf. Eph. 1.18) and brings one into the freedom of faith. No one can come to faith unless the Father draws him (cf. John 6.44); but one who is drawn by God, and does not resist God's gift, comes to realize that it is God who calls.

For that reason, one who desires strength in personal faith must do more than examine the evidences for Christianity. When one begins to realize personally the reality of God, he begins to realize also that he must call upon the Lord for light. God surely is not pleased by pretense. But He is pleased by the prayers of those who, moved by divine signs and heartened by grace, cry out for a faith they do not have, or have but faintly. He Himself is the Light and source of light for which they long.

†

The general plan and overall outline of this catechism are readily shown by the table of contents.

The sources quoted or cited most frequently in this catechism are Sacred Scripture and the documents of the Second Vatican Council. The references for these are given in parentheses in the running text. The references for other sources are given in footnotes. Abbreviations used in the text and footnotes are listed immediately after this Introduction.

11

Numbers in the margins of the pages of the chapters are references to other pages of the catechism where the same general subject or relat ed material is discussed. It is virtually inevitable in a catechism such as this that some subjects will be discussed under more than one heading and in more than one chapter. The marginal numbers will enable the reader to find the principal places of discussion more easily. Fuller and more detailed references will of course be found in the index at the end of the volume.

Between the chapters and the index are four appendixes. The first three of these provide expanded notes, largely factual, on the Bible, on the general councils of the Church, and on the Fathers and Doctors of the Church. The fourth contains the texts of a number of prayers loved and cherished in the Church.

THE EDITORS

List of Abbreviations

Books of the Bible

Bar. — Baruch
Col. — Colossians
1, 2 Cor. — Corinthians
Dan. — Daniel
Deut. — Deuteronomy
Eccle. — Ecclesiastes
Eph. — Ephesians
Exod. — Exodus
Ezek. — Ezekiel
Gal. — Galatians
Gen. — Genesis
Heb. — Hebrews
Isa. — Isaiah
Jer. — Jeremiah
Jos. — Joshua

Lev. — Leviticus
1, 2 Macc. — Maccabees
Mal. — Malachi
Matt. — Matthew
Phil. — Philippians
Prov. — Proverbs
Ps. — Psalms
Rev. — Revelation
Rom. — Romans
1, 2 Sam. — Samuel
1, 2 Thess. — Thessalonians
1, 2 Tim. — Timothy
Wisd. — Wisdom
Zeph. — Zephaniah

Documents of the Second Vatican Council

AA   Decree on the Apostolate of the Laity *(Apostolicam Actuositatem)*
AG   Decree on the Missionary Activity of the Church *(Ad Gentes)*
CD   Decree on the Bishops' Pastoral Office in the Church *(Christus Dominus)*
DH   Declaration on Religious Freedom *(Dignitatis Humanae)*
DV   Dogmatic Constitution on Divine Revelation *(Dei Verbum)*
GE   Declaration on Christian Education *(Gravissimum Educationis)*
GS   Pastoral Constitution on the Church in the Modern World *(Gaudium et Spes)*
IM   Decree on the Instruments of Social Communication *(Inter Mirifica)*
LG   Dogmatic Constitution on the Church *(Lumen Gentium)*
NA   Declaration on the Relationship of the Church to Non-Christian Religions *(Nostra Aetate)*
OE   Decree on Eastern Catholic Churches *(Orientalium Ecclesiarum)*
OT   Decree on Priestly Formation *(Optatam Totius)*

PC	Decree on the Appropriate Renewal of Religious Life *(Perfectae Caritatis)*
PO	Decree on the Ministry and Life of Priests *(Presbyterorum Ordinis)*
SC	Constitution on the Sacred Liturgy *(Sacrosanctum Concilium)*
UR	Decree on Ecumenism *(Unitatis Redintegratio)*

Other abbreviations

AAS	Acta Apostolicae Sedis
ACW	Ancient Christian Writers
ASS	Acta Sanctae Sedis
DS	H. Denzinger-A. Schönmetzer, Enchiridion Symbolorum Definitionum et Declarationum de Rebus Fidei et Morum
MG	J.P. Migne, ed., Patrologiae cursus completus, series graeca
ML	J.P. Migne, ed., Patrologiae cursus completus, series latina

Part One

THE
INVITATION
TO FAITH

1

The Hope of Our Calling

Christ is our Teacher. "You call Me Teacher and Lord; and you are right, for so I am" (John 13.13).

This chapter speaks of the goodness of the life to which Christ invites us. It shows how Christian hope is realized already in part in this world. It shows how the Christian life is essentially a life of hope, pointing confidently toward perfect fulfillment of the gifts God has already planted in our hearts. Finally, the chapter speaks of the central role of Christ in our hope and in our life.

THE END IS THE BEGINNING

Life is mysterious. It stirs rich hopes in our hearts even as it bears within itself profound tragedies. "Hope and joy, grief and anxiety" (GS 1) are strangely intermingled in the world, and we cannot help asking: Why do we exist? What is the meaning and purpose of our lives?

The "hope and joy" in life are very real. Though the world is wounded by sin, it remains the world God made and found "very good" 34 (Gen. 1.31).

But the "grief and anxiety" in life are also real. Human history is in large part a record of wars and of personal failures and tragedies. 49

What is this life that promises so much and yet so frequently disappoints?

Why are we, and why do we live in a world like this?

Man's Questions Answered in Christ

The answer to man's persistent queries is Christ.

He brought realistic hope to the real world. He, the Crucified, did nothing to gloss over the mystery of evil and pain. He, the Lord of all, tasted suffering, sanctified it, and made it redemptive. He teaches confident hope and intelligent joy even in a world far from its final perfection.

The mystery of life is complex and profound. So also is Christ's an- 169

17

swer to it. Christ's answer is found in His entire life, and in the life He taught and made possible for men. He invites us to act with Him in the gift of the Spirit. "I came that they may have life, and have it abundantly" (John 10.10).

THE END WITHIN TIME

Christ lived on this earth a perfect human life, and He called men to adopt His way of life.

When Christ taught here on earth, men flocked to Him. Indeed, the world has always been drawn toward Christ. Over the centuries He has been loved by countless millions who have known Him only through faith. He has, it is true, been sharply rejected, too. Many reject Him at least partially in ignorance and misunderstanding. Others turn against Christ with deliberate hostility, for they have decided not to abandon the pride and selfishness of their lives.

But those who, touched by grace, come to know Christ, and who wish to lay aside the burden of their sinful and empty lives, have drawn close to Him. For the life He actually lived on earth reveals a goodness so universal that it endlessly attracts the human heart. "He has done all things well" (Mark 7.37).

The Truly Human Life

Christ teaches men how to live on earth in a genuinely human way. The Catholic faith urges men to be faithful to the deepest longings of the human spirit: to be bearers of peace, and to be themselves a blessing to others.

171   Christ teaches a good human life. He makes men more human by enabling them to draw on the resources of God. He who is the most loved of all men is Himself the Son of God, and He lives the life of God as well as the life of man. So also He calls men to become fully human by becoming children of God. Thus we are called to share on earth in the life of God: by faith to share in the light of God's wisdom, and by hope and love to be drawn into the warmth of His life.

Those who have begun to live such a life of faith, hope, and love should pass on to others the good news they have learned, and "spread abroad a living witness to Christ, especially by means of a life of faith and charity" (LG 12).

18

Task of This World

Christ Himself considered this world worth His care. He came into this world to reconcile it with the Father, and He sends those who love Him to continue this work among all the nations.

Christ teaches those who come to Him how to live lives which are fruitful. There is a reign of God, a kingdom of truth and life, of justice, 216 love, and peace, to be built on earth. There are men around us who need 232 to be healed and supported; the unstable world needs the anchor of hope. God offers to men the opportunity to be bearers of a healing that goes beyond all human expectation.

Faith and Human Progress

Because man is called to share in divine life, it is a divine task to humanize the world. Today, especially with the help of science and technology, man "has extended his mastery over nearly the whole of nature, and continues to do so" (GS 33).

But the wisdom which faith and love bring is necessary to control technology itself. Technology can enslave men; technical progress does 47 not guarantee happiness.

The Lord directs His disciples to care about the hungry and the weak. In a complex society, scientific and technological advances are tools by which men can subdue the earth (cf. Gen. 1.28) for the benefit of man and the glory of his Creator. Technical progress is so rich and varied today that it has become possible — and therefore obligatory — for more persons than ever before to be actively concerned with the material and social well-being of their fellowmen. There is also a duty to be concerned about the political and economic structures of the world. Followers of Christ should work for a just society. 225

The social teachings of Christ and His Church encourage a determination to make the world better. For the rebuilding of our broken world glorifies God, and contributes to the coming of the better world of God's eternal kingdom. 353

Those who sincerely try to fulfill their earthly tasks can never entirely fail. At times their efforts may be frustrated and their immediate goals not achieved. But the presence in the world of persons who ceaselessly labor to reshape the world according to the mind of Christ is itself a healing of the earth. A world with a St. Francis of Assisi or a St. Vincent de Paul is already a better world.

19

359   God willed that men should come to their perfect fulfillment in eternal life, but He willed that they come to that perfect life through their own willing cooperation. It was not God's will simply to make men in heaven; nor was it His will to create men for a life of endless struggle. Rather, He made men on earth to know and to love and to serve Him, and one another in His name, and so to arrive at an eternal life which is the fulfillment of a divine life begun in time.

The Longing and Hopes of Time

The gifts God gives us now call out for fulfillment in eternal life. God loves and calls to Himself every person of every time and every place. Moreover, men desire more than that which even a wonderfully developed earth could ever provide.

God plants divine hunger in human hearts. Man longs not only for peace and justice, and for a good share of material things, but for far more: to see God face to face, to understand far more clearly than he

361 now can, and to love and to be loved in ways not possible in the conditions of time.

To Eternal Life through Time

Eternal life, then, is the fulfillment of longings already planted in man. By faith we now know God dimly, but we long for a quality of love and a joy of life that can be had only when one possesses in a new and radically richer way the life of the Lord.

Still, heavenly life is not the only precious life of man. It is a great good also to be able to serve God and one another in darkness and difficulties. Thus it is possible for one to wish to remain in this world for the time that God allots, even when aware that the heavenly life we are called to is "far better" (Phil. 1.23).

For God did not make men simply for heaven, but for coming to

269 heaven through generous and good acts that His grace enables us to perform here and now. God's gift was not to be only the blessed life of heaven, but the further gift of letting men gain blessedness as a merited award.

The Perfect Fulfillment

Heaven is perfect fulfillment, and it is in the light of it that our present life makes sense. When we come to the blessed vision of the Trinity, we shall know ourselves in a better way. When the body has 360 risen to newness of life, the value of earthly things will be more deeply understood. All the sacramental signs and the symbols of faith, all the prophetic words, and all the precepts of life God has given are fully understood only in the light of that fullness of life into which all grace is to blossom.

We live now a pilgrim life, among sacraments and symbols. But one who believes and hopes and loves possesses already the living seeds of that life which is beyond signs. It is our joy to have received the life God gives now, and freely to serve Him now, making His kingdom present even now on earth among men.

"We are God's children now; it does not yet appear what we shall be, but we know that when He appears we shall be like Him, for we shall see Him as He is. And every one who thus hopes in Him purifies himself as He is pure" (1 John 3.2-3).

JESUS CHRIST: TRUE GOD AND ETERNAL LIFE IN TIME

Jesus Christ, our Savior, true man and true God, is the eternal 60 Word. He is "the only Son of God, eternally begotten of the Father, God from God . . ., one in Being with the Father."[1] Remaining God, He came down from heaven and was made man, and lived among men, teaching them and showing them how to live. Our Redeemer, He suffered and died for us, and rose again in glory. In the Church which He founded He continues His saving acts even now, and in the fulfillment of time He will come again, in power and majesty.

Center of Christian Life

The Christian way of life is the way of Christ. He is Himself the Way, the Truth, and the Life (cf. John 14.5). He revealed to us the Fa- 178 ther, and He taught us by words and by example how to live our earthly lives. He draws us to holiness. He is the center of God's entire plan of salvation.

---

[1] Roman Missal, The Order of Mass, Profession of Faith. The creed used in the Mass is essentially the creed of the First Council of Constantinople, 381 (DS 150).

All creation is in, through, and for Christ. "In Him all things were created, in heaven and on earth . . . all things were created through Him" (Col. 1.16). All things were made for Him; He is the One who binds the universe together. He is why we are. Through Him we come to know the Father; with Him we come to new life; in Him we find eternal life. "I am the Alpha and the Omega, the first and the last, the beginning and the end" (Rev. 22.13).

117   The Church teaches only Christ. He is the "fullness of all revelation" (DV 2). To learn Christ is to learn the Father (cf. John 14.9); to know Him is to live in God's Holy Spirit. All that God reveals to men is Jesus, all that God wills for us shines forth in His life and in His words. This is the completion and goal of Catholic teaching: that those who believe may have "all the riches of assured understanding and the knowledge of God's mystery, of Christ, in whom are hid all the treasures of wisdom and knowledge" (Col. 2.2-3).

To know Christ is sufficient. He is not only the Life and the Truth, but also the Way by which men come to these (cf. John 14.6). By words that speak truly of Him and of His Gospel, by sacraments that make His saving power present, by lives that do His work on earth, the Catholic Church teaches the whole message of Christ.

·   ·   ·

Questions related to the material in this chapter:

1. To what sorts of questions might we appropriately seek answers from Christ?

2. Did Christ intend that we should have no concern about the goods to be found and created in this world, and seek only His future kingdom in heaven?

3. How does faith in Christ tend to make His followers more human and more confident in pursuing human values in this world?

4. If I am destined for heaven, what value does my life on earth have and why should I work to make this earth a better place in which to live?

5. Why do we call Christ "the Way"?

6. Why is Christ called the center of Christian life? Why is knowledge of Him the fullness of Christian wisdom?

Part Two

THROUGH CHRIST: COMING TO KNOWLEDGE OF GOD

2

The Father
of Our Lord Jesus Christ

God is. "Before the mountains were brought forth, or ever You had formed the earth and the world, from everlasting to everlasting You are God" (Ps. 90.2). All of creation gives testimony to God; all has reality only from Him.

In this chapter we speak of the mystery of God our Father, of God revealing Himself, and of the ways we come to know God. The chapter notes that human reason can come to a knowledge of the existence of God, and how faith supplies for the limitations of reason. It then discusses attributes of God, something of what the infinite and infinitely perfect God is like.

GOD REVEALS HIMSELF PERSONALLY

God indeed dwells in mystery (cf. 1 Tim. 6.16), but He enables us to know Him, so that He might give us true fullness of life. We are held down by the burden of our sins and our limitations, but God wishes us to be raised up into sharing His life. God wants us to know Him, and 241 He "chose to reveal Himself and to make known the hidden purpose of His will (cf. Eph. 1.9) by which through Christ, the Word made flesh, man has access to the Father in the Holy Spirit and comes to share in the divine nature (cf. Eph. 2.18; 2 Peter 1.4)" (DV 2).

The Content of Revelation

God Himself is the principal reality which is revealed. He who 109 knows us perfectly wishes us to know Him. All else that He reveals — of ourselves, of creation, of commandments and sacraments — is intended to lead us to Him who is our Life. To discover God by reason is the crown of intellectual life. But to know Him by faith is eternal life for us (cf. John 17.3).

Faith is a response to God's revelation of Himself; it begins a personal friendship which leads toward the blessed "vision" of God, that is,

25

a life of perfect intimacy with Him in eternity. All faith is rooted in God. The creeds of the Church begin with "I believe in God." When we say these words we are not only professing our belief that there is a God, but are acknowledging the testimony God gives about Himself.

Faith and Grace

Revelation and faith are personal gifts of a living God. He causes the truth about Himself to be proclaimed, and He makes it possible for the hearer to recognize this truth: "It is the Lord!" (John 21.7).

170　　By the gentle assistance of grace God makes it possible for men to have personal faith. He does not, however, force men to believe in Him. He makes Himself present in the world by His saving deeds and words, and in the hearts of men by His grace, and He invites men to recognize their Lord. One who comes to faith recognizes God in the light of God's own witnessing.

God is Himself the light by which we believe, and is the goal of all our knowing and striving. From God we learn what God is like, and we realize why He is to be believed before all else.

COMING TO KNOW GOD

God is most real, and near to us in many ways (cf. Deut. 4.8). Even without the gift of faith men can know with certainty that God exists. "You have made us for Yourself, and our heart is restless until it rests in You."[1]

The Mystery of Unbelief

Although God has made Himself personally accessible to man in many ways, there yet remains in the world much unbelief (cf. Matt. 17.16). The Church is sensitive to the fact of atheism, and is aware there are many different reasons for the alienation of men from their God (cf. GS 19-21).

Some people reject faith in God because they consider it humiliating for anyone to admit the existence of One far superior to man. Others deny the reality of a good God to express "violent protest against the evil in the world" (GS 19). Others have in effect abandoned hope of

---

[1]St. Augustine, *Confessiones* 1.1.1 (ML 32.661).

knowing God, because their philosophical prejudices have convinced 38
them that only the material things that science explores can be known
by man, or because they simply deny all possibility of absolute truth.
Many put their hearts elsewhere and never really consider the question
of God. Many are also pushed toward unbelief by the pressures of governments committed by policy to atheism and the depersonalization of
the subjects, or by the unbelieving molders of cultures who in greed and
lust have turned from God.

"Undoubtedly, those who willfully try to shut out God from their
hearts and to avoid religious questions are not following the dictates of
their consciences, and hence they are not free of fault" (GS 19).

But the extent of their willfulness is hard to assess. Those who do 163
not know God are often victims of the sins of others as well and "believers themselves often bear some responsibility for this situation" (GS
19). Atheism can be a reaction to the unworthy ways in which some
believers, in their words, attitudes, and behavior, give inadequate
witness to God.

Human Reason and the Existence of God

The Church "holds and teaches that God, the beginning and end of
all things, can by the natural light of human reason be known with certainty from created things, 'for since the creation of the world the invisible things of Him are perceived, being understood through the things
which have been made' (Rom. 1.20)."[2]

Reflection on the moral order of the universe can also lead to a natural knowledge of God. Aware of their human duties to be just and
truthful and temperate, men come to realize that the insistent call to
goodness, which they hear in their conscience, in fact manifests the reality of One who rightfully demands goodness of them.   179

Experience and Limits of Natural Revelation

Over the course of centuries people of various nations and cultures
have in fact come to a knowledge of God by reflection on the physical
and moral orders God has created. The philosophers and sages of many

---

[2]First Vatican Council, Session 3, April 24, 1870, *Dogmatic Constitution on the Catholic
Faith,* ch. 2 (DS 3004). Cf. DV 6.

56 nations have pointed out various paths by which men may come to know Him who is the source of all.

It is certainly possible for man to come to a knowledge of God by rational reflection on things that are. In everyday life, however, emotions, pleasures and problems, the demands of work, and so on, tend to obscure the way to God through finite things. In the actual circumstances of a given human life it might be very difficult to come to a certain knowledge of God in a deliberate, rational way. It could be especially difficult to do so in time to allow one's whole life to be illumined by the knowledge of God. Even more difficult would it be to gain a knowledge free of serious error.

Hence it is only by the gift of God's revelation that even "those religious truths which are by their nature accessible to human reason can, even in the present state of the human race, be known by all men with ease, with solid certitude, and with no trace of error" (DV 6).[3] Reason and the world indeed bear witness to God, but the chief witness to God is God Himself.

GOD MANIFESTS HIS REALITY AND PRESENCE

God reveals Himself more clearly and directly than do His works which speak of Him. He Himself speaks. He personally seeks out the creatures He has made to give them saving knowledge of Himself.

God reveals Himself through the deeds of salvation history and
65 through the words of the prophets. Most of all, He has spoken to us through His Son (cf. Heb. 1.2). But He who made our minds and hearts speaks also within us. He gives those whom He calls to know Him a light by which they can with certainty recognize that it is the Lord of all who calls them to life.

The Free Gift of Faith

The life of faith is built on God. It is His gift. The gift of faith is the beginning of a new life that only God can give.

It was not merely words and visible signs that led Christ's disciples to the fullness of faith. When the apostles began to realize who Christ really was, they cried out in longing to the God they were aware of only

---

[3]The Second Vatican Council is here quoting the First Vatican Council, Session 3, April 24, 1870, *Dogmatic Constitution on the Catholic Faith,* ch. 2 (DS 3005).

obscurely: "Increase our faith" (Luke 17.5). For faith is the living fruit of two freedoms, that of God who freely gives light, and that of man who of his own free will responds to God with the power God's grace gives.

The path of coming to faith, then, is different from that of coming to merely natural knowledge of God. God initiates the series of acts, by 240 causing in the world the presence of witnesses to Himself. In the heart of man He gives grace, and speaks, stimulating the hearer to see the reasonableness of belief and at the same time moving him to prayer, to a burning desire for faith, and to an openness to God that changes everything. Then God causes that transforming recognition in which the hearer realizes, in the light of God's gift, that it is God Himself who is present and inviting him to life. The hearer believes, because God has effectively led him to realize that it is God Himself who bears witness to Himself. Although human freedom is such that one is able to resist the grace of faith, it is indeed most intelligent and right for a creature, brought by God to recognize God, to assent to God's word willingly, joyfully, wholeheartedly.[4]

Faith and Salvation

"Faith is the beginning of human salvation, the foundation and root of all justification, 'without which it is impossible to please God' (Heb. 11.6)."[5]

Knowledge of God growing out of faith is far stronger and more secure than any other knowledge men have. It is based not merely on the strength of human insight and interpretation, but on God Himself. God gives the believer's faith not only a rich content, but also such firmness and certainty that the believer can build his whole life on it (cf. Matt. 7.24-25).

THE GOD OF REVELATION

God reveals Himself to us as a Lord whose greatness exceeds our understanding, but also as a Father who is near to us and truly loves us.

Through events in the history of salvation, and through the divine-

---

[4]Cf. First Vatican Council, Session 3, April 24, 1870, *Dogmatic Constitution on the Catholic Faith,* ch. 3 (DS 3008-3011).
[5]Council of Trent, Session 4, January 13, 1547, *Decree on Justification,* ch. 8 (DS 1532).

ly inspired words accompanying and clarifying those events, He makes
169 Himself and His saving plan known (cf. DV 2).

God is very different from us and from all the things we experience. He is the fountain and source of all being and life. Nothing exists without Him.

Man cannot fully grasp the transcendent mystery of God. He is eternal, perfect, and infinite. We are temporal, flawed, and finite. He is the holy God before whom we stand in awe and sense our smallness. Yet in His bountiful mercy He has willed to be a "God with us" (Matt. 1.23; cf. Rev. 21.3). He makes Himself truly near to us and known to us, so that we may have friendship with Him.

A Personal God

God makes clear the truth that He is a personal God by all the
54 deeds He did for the Israelites. He brought them from slavery, gave them precepts of life, overcame their foes, and brought them to a promised land. He gave them not only external freedom, but he gave them the way to the greater and more personal freedom to know truth and to love what is enduringly good. By His saving work He taught them that "the living God is among you" (Jos. 3.10).

Thus He showed how He who sustains and rules all that is, is a Father who knows and cares. He reveals that it is He, a saving Person, who is the first principle of all that is.

All-knowing

God's knowledge encompasses everyone and everything, all that is, was, and will be. He knows the sorrows of His people and He foresees how He will save them (cf. Exod. 3.19-22). The farthest regions of the universe are familar to Him. Not even the most trivial things escape Him (cf. Matt. 10.30). The future and the most hidden secrets of men's hearts are open to Him (cf. Matt. 24.36; Ps. 139.1-4).

God is, then, truly all-knowing, omniscient. " 'All things are bare and open to His eyes' (Heb. 4.13), even those things which are yet to be by the free action of creatures."[6]

------

[6]First Vatican Council, Session 3, April 24, 1870, *Dogmatic Constitution on the Catholic Faith,* ch. 1 (DS 3003).

Loving

To know God is to know One who loves His people and wishes to save them. "I have loved you with an everlasting love; therefore I have continued My faithfulness to you" (Jer. 31.3). Even in the earliest days of salvation history, He made Himself known as our Father. He is One to be infinitely trusted; He will never fail us. "It is the LORD your God 55 who goes with you; He will not fail you or forsake you" (Deut. 31.6).

Almighty

God's power and majesty are limitless.

To say that God is almighty is to say that He can do all things. He is all-powerful, omnipotent. "With God nothing will be impossible" (Luke 34 1.37). God never lacks the power to keep His promises; His will is never frustrated by those who seek to oppose Him.

Eternal and Changeless

In a restless and changing world, God reveals His own unchanging constancy. "For I the LORD do not change" (Mal. 3.6). In His very being, too, God is unchanging. The many elements in the changing world alter one another, and depend on one another, but the powerful and merciful God is utterly independent and suffers no alteration.

God dwells in an eternity to which every moment of all time is always present, and He watches over all things with unchanging love. His eternal changelessness is not like that of a rock which cannot of itself change, but is that of the utter fullness of life and love that is always totally present to us who depend on Him that we may be.

Spirit and Present Everywhere

God is a spirit. Human minds find it difficult to grasp the meaning of spiritual reality, to understand how something can be real without having spatial and temporal dimensions. Yet God's spiritual reality is more intense and mighty than that of beings encountered in space and time.

God is present to all (cf. Ps. 139.7-10; Acts 17.28). He is everywhere, omnipresent.

Although God is everywhere present, He is in special ways present

31

241 to those who love Him. For God has many other gifts to give us, and He dwells in those who love Him (cf. John 14.23) in a presence of infinite personal concern.

Transcendent and Holy

While God is ever with us and always present to the world He
38 made, He is utterly distinct from the world.

God is transcendent. He is exalted far above the universe, for it exists only at His bidding; before the universe and its time, He is; His changeless and eternal reality is in its perfection entirely distinct from the dependent reality of finite things.

Scripture frequently expresses God's otherness by proclaiming that He is perfectly holy. He is "the Holy One" (Isa. 5.24; cf. Lev. 11.44-45; Jos. 24.19; Isa. 6.3; etc.). His holiness is far more than freedom from any touch of moral evil, for God cannot sin. References to His holiness also express more than His hostility to the moral evil that wounds and
358 bruises creation and calls for punishment by Him (cf. Isa. 42.24-25; Ezek. 28.22). Primarily the references to God's holiness are to His absolute perfection.

The One God

There is only one God. In Him alone is our hope; and he who fears the Lord should fear no one else. His is the one mighty wisdom, the one infinite love, that shapes the world and governs all things; His is the one infinite goodness and beauty for which all hearts long.
360　　　This one God is the blessedness that every man longs for. Everything that is learned in the study of faith speaks of Him. For He is the last goal of every person, the final good that moves and stirs all the longings of all. He is the "Love that moves the sun and other stars."[7]

·　　·　　·

Questions related to the material in this chapter:

1. Why does God reveal Himself to us?
2. How does God enable us to recognize that it is He who reveals?

---

[7]Dante, *Divine Comedy*, Paradise, Canto 33.

3. What ought to be our response to God's self-revelation?

4. Why does the Church teach that faith is a "grace" or "favor" of God?

5. Why do not all persons hear God and believe Him?

6. Can we come to know of God's existence by human reason alone?

7. If reason can lead us to knowledge of God, why do so many people not know Him?

8. God freely chooses to reveal to us what He is like. How does He portray Himself in His self-revelation?

9. What do we mean when we say that God is a spirit, is transcendent, is holy?

10. How should the realization that there is only one God, one Love that is the source of all things, affect our attitude toward all the world?

3

God the Lord
and Creator of All

The Lord God who created all things created all of us. "Have we not all one Father? Has not one God created us?" (Mal. 2.10).

In this chapter we speak of God the Creator. The chapter treats of the meaning of creation, and of the account of creation given us in Scripture; and it shows how there can be no real conflict between Christian faith and human reason, or between the truths of the faith and genuine scientific truth. It notes how the Creator God continues to sustain all things in being, and guides them by His providential care. Finally, the chapter speaks of God's invisible creation and of the reality of angels.

CREATOR OF HEAVEN AND EARTH

God reveals Himself to us as our Creator. To know His grandeur and to know our dignity as persons made in the image of God (cf. Gen. 1.26-27) we must begin to grasp His creative power. To know God truly is to know that He is "Creator of heaven and earth."[1]

The philosophers of antiquity and the pagan nations knew something of God, but they did not know Him as the Creator of all. Even to His chosen people in the Old Testament era God revealed this aspect of His reality only gradually.

The Israelites knew that His power surpassed all their understanding. But it was only little by little that God led them to a full understanding of His limitless power over all that is. Finally, they came to know that nothing whatever could in any way resist Him. To know the creative might of the good God is to know that He "can do all things" (Job 42.2).

DOCTRINE OF CREATION

The Catholic faith speaks clearly of the many facets of the revealed doctrine of creation. "This one and only true God, of His own goodness

---

[1]The Apostles' Creed (DS 30).

34

and 'almighty power,' not in order to increase or to acquire His happiness, but in order to manifest His perfection through the blessings He bestows on His creatures, by a most free decision 'from the very beginning of time created out of nothing both the spiritual and the corporeal creature, that is, the angelic and the earthly, and then the human creature, which is as it were common to both, being composed of spirit and body.' "[2]

"Out of Nothing"

To say that God made all things "out of nothing" is not, of course, to suggest that "nothing" is some kind of existing stuff out of which God fashioned the world. Rather, it means that all things "in their whole substance have been produced by God."[3]

Only God has existed forever. There was a beginning to creation.[4] 51 "In the beginning God created the heavens and the earth" (Gen. 1.1). Before the first moment of creation, there was no earth, no universe, no elements; there was not even time.

When did creation and time begin? We do not know. Things came to be when God chose,[5] and it was from Him they received all their reality.

Created Freely

God is not the name of some impersonal force; He is not merely some dimension or depth of the universe. He is a personal God, a God of knowledge and love. He created freely, out of love.

God needed nothing. There was no poverty in Him calling for fulfillment. Nothing forced Him. But in the rich interpersonal love that is God the Blessed Trinity, God most freely chose to create.

Creation was and is no struggle for God. "For He spoke, and it came to be; He commanded and it stood forth" (Ps. 33.9).

---

[2]First Vatican Council, Session 3, April 24, 1870, *Dogmatic Constitution on the Catholic Faith,* ch. 1 (DS 3002). The inner quotation is from the Fourth Lateran Council, November 1215 (DS 800).

[3]First Vatican Council, Session 3, April 24, 1870, *Dogmatic Constitution on the Catholic Faith,* canon 5 on God the Creator of all things (DS 3025).

[4]Cf. Pope Pius XII, Encyclical, *Humani Generis* (August 12, 1950) (DS 3890).

[5]Cf. Council of Florence, Bull, *Cantate Domino* (February 4, 1442) (DS 1333).

The first two chapters of Genesis describe the creation of the world and of man. They teach us truth about God's mercy, and they do this with great simplicity and poetic beauty, and with reverence and awe. Clearly, however, they are not chapters written in the manner of a scientific textbook; their concern is not with dates and physical processes, but with other truths.

38 A number of important religious truths are taught in the Genesis accounts of creation, but there is nothing in those accounts that rightly understood could ever justify fears of a conflict or confrontation between faith and science. The Bible, to be sure, does not teach evolution; neither does it say anything to oppose scientific theories about bodily evolution.[6] It simply is not concerned with the kinds of questions the scientist deals with.

Interpreting the Genesis Account

369 Scripture always speaks the truth, but it sometimes uses poetic or figurative language, and like all great literature, it speaks the truth in a number of different ways (cf. DV 12).

The structure and literary form of the creation narrative serve the memory and at the same time reinforce other sacred teachings. Some of the important sacred truths taught in the Genesis account touch upon the foundations of Christian religion, such as, for example, the creation of all things by God at the beginning of time, the particular creation of man, the fact of original sin, and so on.

43 Revelation does not discuss the date of man's beginning or the precise manner in which God called him into being; it does not discuss the physiology or psychology of man in his origins. But it does teach that man is of surpassing dignity, essentially different from every material being that preceded him. It does teach that he was created in the full friendship of God.

FAITH AND HUMAN REASON

Philosophers and scholars of every culture have viewed the intricate reality of this world from many different viewpoints, and they

---

[6]Cf. Pope Pius XII, Encyclical, *Humani Generis* (August 12, 1950) (DS 3896).

have gained insights into many important truths. Many, however, have
also fallen into error.

Impossibility of Real Conflict

Men are called both to believe God and, as far as possible, to master the world through the use of their God-given intelligence. Faith and reason are of course fundamentally in harmony, for God is the one source of both. "Although faith is above reason, there can never be any real disagreement between faith and reason, since the same God who reveals mysteries and infuses faith has put the light of reason in the human mind, and God cannot deny Himself, nor can truth ever contradict truth."[7]

In the conflicts and disagreements which do in fact occur among men on these matters, it is never the faith and human wisdom that are opposed. "The false appearance of such a contradiction arises for the most part because the dogmas of faith have not been understood and explained according to the mind of the Church, or because false conjectures are taken for verdicts of reason. Therefore, 'we define that every assertion contrary to a truth of enlightened faith is utterly false.' "[8]

The Sureness of the Faith

It is important to understand what it is the Church teaches. One would be mistaken, for example, if he were to interpret the first chapters of Genesis in a slavishly literal way. On the other hand, one would be even more seriously mistaken if he were to abandon the literal truth of the doctrines which the Church has found in the Genesis account, or if he sought to give a radically different meaning to those doctrines because the philosophy or scientific theories fashionable at a given time might seem to be in conflict with the message of faith.

There is an enduring and meaningful content of faith. One who has 135 recognized a sacred truth as a part of divine revelation will have com-

---

[7]First Vatican Council, Session 3, April 24, 1870, *Dogmatic Constitution on the Catholic Faith,* ch. 4 (DS 3017).
[8]First Vatican Council, Session 3, April 24, 1870, *Dogmatic Constitution on the Catholic Faith,* ch. 4 (DS 3017). The internal quotation is from the Fifth Lateran Council, Session 8, December 19, 1513, Bull, *Apostolici Regiminis* (DS 1441).

plete certainty of its truth. He will not let difficulties turn him aside from a message recognized as divine.

218　　Doctrine can indeed be said to develop and to be more fully comprehended through the assistance of the Holy Spirit over the ages. But that which has been once proclaimed and recognized as the meaningful word of God is enduringly true. Its significance may come to be more fully realized, but what the Church has once infallibly proclaimed as the content of God's message will never be found to be false.

Pluralism

The message of faith can be expressed in more than one way. But whatever the plurality of forms of expression, genuine Christian teaching always expresses the same enduring truth.

160　　There is a kind of "pluralism" acceptable in the expression of the Catholic faith, but this is never a pluralism in which different persons believe different doctrines. So also is there a legitimate and beneficial pluralism of theological research and thought, but the theological speculations and investigations of each must always be subordinate to and in harmony with the faith.

The Church welcomes not only a certain pluralism of expression, but also a certain philosophical pluralism. Indeed, the creative work of many philosophical schools has been found useful in understanding and serving the message of faith.

32　　Faith sometimes completes and heals human philosophies; it is never corrected or altered by them. Any philosophical theory which holds that God is finite, or impersonal, or incomplete and developing, or merely some "depth" in visible things, would of course be entirely unacceptable. On the other hand, if a secular philosophy expresses vividly many truths precious and important to a given culture, and only incidentally teaches some points contrary to the faith, a Christian need not utterly reject it. Rather, he may seek to remedy its defects, and thus to allow this human wisdom also to serve the revealed wisdom of faith.

Science and Faith

Catholic teaching urges all to respect the dignity of human sciences.

It is true that there can be abuses in the pursuit of science. Some persons, for example, tend to put excessive confidence in the so-called

38

"scientific method" and to consider as true, or perhaps even knowable, only that which can be empirically verified. This abuse, however, flows from a philosophical error, not from the nature of science itself.

Cultivation of the sciences is part of our proper service to God as His creatures. Through the arts and sciences we can contribute to fulfillment of the common human duty to "elevate the human family to a more sublime understanding of the true, the good, and the beautiful" (GS 57).

Certainly each of the human arts and sciences is free in its sphere to use its own principles and its own method. Not only does the Church not forbid this, but it asserts its recognition of "this just liberty"[9] and indeed "affirms the legitimate autonomy of human culture and especially of the sciences" (GS 59).

GOD SUSTAINS AND RULES THE WORLD

God did not create the world and then abandon it. Created things not only have their origin in Him but could not continue to exist if He did not continue to keep them in being. "How would anything have endured if You had not willed it?" (Wisd. 11.25).

God cares for the world with great love, ever directing it toward the goal for the sake of which He made all things. All things have been created in Christ, through Christ, and for Christ (cf. Col. 1.16), and the divine plan is "to unite all things in Him, things in heaven and things on earth" (Eph. 1.10).

God in His providence never ceases to care for the world. His providence extends to all His creatures, and in a special way to the persons He has made. "Look at the birds of the air: they neither sow nor reap nor gather into barns, and yet your heavenly Father feeds them. Are you not of more value than they?" (Matt. 6.26).

Predestination

The proper destiny of man is eternal life with God, for God calls 359 and invites all men to Himself and wills all men to be saved (cf. 1 Tim. 2.4).

Men are predestined in the sense that God's merciful gift precedes

---

[9]First Vatican Council, Session 3, April 24, 1870, *Dogmatic Constitution on the Catholic Faith*, ch. 4 (DS 3019). The words are quoted by the Second Vatican Council in GS 59.

and makes possible every mercy, especially that of eternal salvation. Certainly there is no predestination in which God selects certain per351 sons not to attain eternal life with Him and withholds from them the gifts of salvation. At the same time, the predestination of which we speak does not mean that in the past God planned things that would mechanically occur in future time. Rather, it is a predestination that fully respects the freedom that God Himself gives men.

Men can do no saving deeds at all without the God who sustains 245 them in being and who alone enables them to do good. But God also allows men to resist His grace, to refuse the life He offers, to do the things He forbids.

SIGNIFICANCE OF DOCTRINE OF CREATION

God's revelation of Himself as Creator provides a radical foundation for the humility men should have before God, and also for the respect men should have for the dignity of created reality.

Man's Creaturely Status

Clearly it is folly for men to resist the One who has made them and who keeps them in existence. "Shall the axe vaunt itself over him who hews with it, or the saw magnify itself against him who wields it? As if a rod should wield him who lifts it, or as if a staff should lift him who is not wood" (Isa. 10.15).

Men should have a bracing fear of God, founded on the recognition of reality.

Dignity of Creation

God has created a real world. Though He creates out of nothing, He brings into existence enduring realities; He calls to being, and to participation in a plan that has eternal significance.

It is real life, not playacting, that goes on in this real world. The world of creation is crowned by and is to be subdued by free persons, 353 men whose free choices in creation will have significance for all eternity.

Man's duty to salute God as Creator is also the honor of recognizing the sublime dignity of creation, which is indeed the fruit of eternal love.

40

ANGELS

God's creation extends to more than the visible creation. The faith of the Church recognizes the words of Scripture about angels as far more than figurative speech about God's providential care, and it knows that there really are purely spiritual persons made by God who rejoice to know Him and to share His life.[10]

Angels have frequent roles in the history of salvation, in both the Old Testament and the New. 71

The angels are not mere abstractions or beings barely real. They are powerful realities, of whom we in fact know but little, and they are instruments of God's providence for us in mighty but hidden ways. 54

•   •   •

Questions related to the material in this chapter:

1. How do we know that God is our Creator?

2. Does God need creation to be really happy?

3. What did God use for material when He created the universe?

4. Is God actually free in His creation or is He also part of an ongoing creative process?

5. Where in the Bible do we find the story of God's creation?

6. What does the Genesis account of creation teach us?

7. In what way is the Genesis account of creation different from a technical report or a newspaper story?

8. What do we mean when we say that faith and reason both tell us the truth and therefore are not in conflict?

9. Does pluralism in the expression of the Catholic faith mean that Catholics can each believe something different?

10. Did God create the world and then abandon it to run by itself?

11. What is the proper destiny of each of us, and in what sense can I say I am predestined?

12. Are angels real or is our talk about angels just a way of talking about God's presence and inspiration?

---

[10]Cf., e.g., Fourth Lateran Council, November 1215, *The Catholic Faith* (DS 800); First Vatican Council, Session 3, April 24, 1870, *Dogmatic Constitution on the Catholic Faith,* ch. 1 (DS 3002); Pope Paul VI, *Professio Fidei* ("The Credo of the People of God," June 30, 1968).

4

Living Man —
The Glory of God

"What is man that You are mindful of him, and the son of man that You care for him?" (Ps. 8.4).

In this chapter we speak of man as the image of God, wonderful in body and soul, and of God's design in creating man and in giving profound unity to the whole human race. We also speak of man's social nature and personal dignity, of how Christ reveals to man the meaning of his being, and of the tasks to which man is called.

THE IMAGE OF GOD

As the first account of the creation of the world reaches a climax in the first chapter of Genesis, God is portrayed as creating man as the crown and glory of all that He had made. Since man is the "image of God" (cf. Gen. 1.26), what we are told of God helps reveal to us what we are; what we see of humanity, schooled and aided by faith, teaches us of God.

Both in his individual being and in his social reality man mirrors the God who made him.

Physical and Spiritual

Intimately joined in each living human being are physical reality and spiritual reality.

Made of the "dust from the ground" (Gen. 2.7), of the same elements of which the earth is shaped, man is the spokesman and priest of 202 all material reality. Man is essentially a bodily creature, and he is "not allowed to despise his bodily life" (GS 14). As the body of Christ is most holy to Christians, so is there also a sacredness in the bodily dimension of every human life.

But man is God's image more in his specifically human qualities. It is the spiritual principle of each man that makes him the living flesh that 344 he is. It is this spiritual principle, or soul, that makes him open to understanding and love of the infinite Love who called him to life.

Man is not composed of body and soul as though these were distinct beings, for man is not simply a soul which "has" a body. Body and soul make a single living person. Man's soul is not material, but it is created to give human life to a body, the body that with it makes up the living man.

The soul of a man does not exist before his body. God immediately creates each individual soul[1] at the coming to be of the living person. Nor is it man's destiny to live forever as simply a soul when death dissolves the body. The soul continues to exist as a spiritual reality after a person's death. The salvation of a man will be fulfilled only in the resurrection of the body, and in the life of fully living men gathered together 356 in the joy of the Lord.

Human Intelligence and Freedom

Man is like God especially in the capacities that he has as a person.

In his intelligence man is God's image. By his arts and technological skills man has wonderfully transformed the material world which God made and committed to him as its master (cf. Gen. 1.26). It is chiefly through revelation that God illumines the minds of men with the wisdom needed to shape the world wisely (cf. GS 15).

Man's conscience also makes him godlike. Unlike other living things, man has a restless concern for what is truly good and evil, how- 180 ever often he wavers in that concern. "For man has in his heart a law written by God" (GS 16; cf. Rom. 2.15).

Man's freedom, too, makes him like God, who is supremely free. Men are not driven simply by blind forces or instincts. They have responsibility and freedom. Even in his fallen state man retains this freedom to make his own choices, to act or not to act, to do this or to do that.[2]

Human freedom is not full and perfect as God's is. The pressures of 194 circumstances can limit greatly a person's freedom and responsibility. Yet as long as a person has the power to live in a human way, he retains a measure of this freedom.

In creating man God also gave him another freedom, one which is restored to us by Christ. This is the freedom to live in God's friendship,

---

[1]Cf. Pope Pius XII, Encyclical, *Humani Generis* (August 12, 1950) (DS 3896).
[2]Cf. Council of Trent, Session 6, January 13, 1547, *Decree on Justification,* ch. 1 (DS 1521). Cf. also St. Thomas Aquinas, *Summa Theologica* I-II, prologue.

43

and by the aid of grace to do the good things that one's heart longs for, and to fulfill one's divinely implanted longings.

Death and Immortality

No living things made of matter have personal knowledge of God, and none have immortality, except man. Obviously man is mortal. Men do die. But men do not totally die. "It is appointed for men to die once, and after that comes judgment" (Heb. 9.27). What we call death is not a
343 complete ceasing to be. Rather, it is a transition to another state of living. "Lord, for your faithful people life is changed, not ended."[3]

Each man is like God in being destined to live forever. This is one reason why every human person, however young or old, however useless or limited in terms of worldly possibilities, is to be treated with great reverence.

"Saving One's Soul"

In much Catholic pastoral and devotional writing the expression "to save one's soul" is extremely common (cf. Matt. 16.26).
357 "Saving one's soul" has the meaning of saving oneself entirely, saving one's total self for eternal life. One reaches full salvation only when body and soul together are joined in the joy of the resurrection.

SOCIAL NATURE OF MAN

Man is the image of God not merely in his personal and individual being, but also in his social nature, and in the love which binds him to his fellowmen. There is a "certain likeness between the union of the divine Persons and the union of God's sons in truth and charity" (GS 24).
216 What man is, is revealed also in the inclination God has given him to enter into various communities, first the family, and then other forms of community.

Male and Female

The Genesis account of human origins, with much subsequent revelation, proclaims the divine origin and sacredness of human sexuality

---

[3]Roman Missal, Preface I used in Masses for the dead.

and its purposes, the divine institution of marriage, and the dignity and nobility of woman, who had been degraded in so many societies of fallen man.

Scripture stresses the equality and complementarity of man and woman. They complete each other, relieving the loneliness of the human condition. They see each other as equals, so that in marriage they may become deeply one. Marriage ought to be monogamous: one man and one woman are to become one in it. Such is the vision of Genesis (cf. Gen. 2.23-24). Christ the Lord appeals to this when He declares that divorce is wrong, contrary to the will expressed by the Creator from the beginning (cf. Matt. 19.4-9). 220

Man in Society

To become more fully what he is, to develop his powers and his possibilities, man needs to live in social friendship and cooperation with fellow humans. 216

In social life and the pursuit of the common good, the dignity and worth of each person must always be remembered. Individuals must make sacrifices for the common welfare, but the personal dignity of no person may be assailed or violated for any social good whatever. For societies exist to ennoble and enrich persons; persons are not mere means by which societies reach desired ends (cf. GS 75). 202

Created in Harmony

Scripture tells us little about the condition of man in the springtime of his creation.

The purpose of the Genesis account of creation is to tell us certain truths that help us to understand the essentials of the human condition. For example, the evils man knows, revelation instructs us, were not inevitable. Human misery is not to be explained by saying that an evolving world must have deep and mysterious pain. Nor was human misery part of God's original design for man. Rather, much of the discord and pain of man is the fruit of man's own deliberate sin. This is not a pessimistic view. On the contrary, viewed in the light of redemption, it points toward vast hope. 52

Christ and Creation

From the very beginning it was God's plan that men should become His children by adoption and share the richness of the life of the Trinity.

Christ was already foreshadowed at the very beginning of human history. The first parents of our race were created in grace, so sharing in Christ's sonship that the Son "might be the first-born among many brethren" (Rom. 8.29). Christ is the "first-born of all creation" (Col. 1.15), the first in rank in God's plan. It was because of what the world was to become that all things were made. Adam, as the first man, is in one sense a type and image of Christ; but Christ is absolutely first in the divine plan, in dignity, and in the richness of all that men can be.

178

Created in Holiness

The first parents of mankind were created in that grace which made them share in the divine sonship. There is much about the first parents we do not know. They may have been very much underdeveloped in their natural human endowments. But the first parents were made in a certain universal harmony: grace and virtues bound them in peaceful friendship with God; their hearts were at peace, with no inner turmoil, which has been called concupiscence, thrusting them toward evil; they were at peace with the world and possessed special gifts of God that were appropriate to their grace and innocence.[4]

343

By nature, of course, they were as material creatures subject to the dissolution of death and to the pains and afflictions our state suggests. But they were friends of God, and God would have kept man "immune from bodily death had he not sinned" (GS 18).[5] In their innocence, prior to their sin, God guarded them also from the suffering and anxiety that are the fruit of sin. They had a peaceful self-possession that gave them a wisdom suited to their state.

Man and His Creator

Man at peace and in friendship with God has both a grandeur and an awareness of his own status as creature.

212

Nothing is more honorable for a man than to recognize the reality of God and the truth of the relationships he has to God. For God is the source of all he is and possesses. All the possibilities of life and friendship, all the limitless scope of what man can become, depend utterly upon God. But God is generous, and He invites man to the greatest of

---

[4]Cf. Council of Trent, Session 5, June 17, 1546, *Decree on Original Sin* 1 (DS 1511) and 5 (DS 1515); Council of Orange, 529, canons 1 (DS 371) and 19 (DS 389); Pope Paul V, Bull, *Ex Omnibus Afflictionibus* (October 1, 1567) (DS 1926). Cf. also GS 13.

[5]Cf. also Council of Trent, Session 5, June 17, 1546, *Decree on Original Sin* 1 (DS 1511).

hopes. Man is called to share the divine life, to inherit the fullness of everything that is.

THE TASKS OF MAN

Man was created to "have dominion" over the earth and to "subdue it" (Gen. 1.26, 28). As it was not beneath God's dignity to create a material universe, so it is not beneath man to master it with the skills of his science and technology, with the beauty of his art and imagination. Creative work is a glory of man, and man's work should, by those who have power to shape society, be made as human and creative as possible.

All material reality and all human work are to serve the good of persons. Man's task is even more to make human lives that are rich and good, human lives that mirror God on earth. Man is made to serve God and to glorify Him on earth. This does not mean that we are to satisfy God's needs. God has no needs, and certainly we have no resources that would enrich Him. But we can glorify Him by allowing the abundance of 221 His goodness to shine in us and in the life we build.

The task of man is also to prepare himself to enter the blessed vision of God, that is, to live with God in the infinite riches of His life.

God loves freedom; and God loves to give men the glory of being causes of the good things that flow from His own mercy. In our lives He blesses us most of all with the ability to do and to act in ways that are holy and generous. The richest gift He gives men is the gift to do freely what is good — to mirror Him in not merely being good but in causing good.

So God wishes us not merely to enjoy eternal life, but to do the deeds that, by His mercy, merit it. It is His will that when we rejoice before Him in the beatific vision we stand with Jesus in the glory of God's free sons who love Him and love one another because we have chosen to.

Thus part of the vocation of a man is to take responsibility for this 174 world and make it a presence of God's kingdom, and so to become worthy of dwelling with Him forever.

*　*　*

Questions related to the material in this chapter:

1. Where in the Bible do we find the account of the creation of man?
2. When we speak of man's "body" and "soul," what do we mean?

3. In what ways is man an image of God?

4. In what sense can we say that we do not totally die?

5. What does the phrase "saving one's soul" mean?

6. Am I made up of two parts, soul and body, one good and the other bad, both at war with each other?

7. What does Sacred Scripture teach about the equality and complementarity of man and woman?

8. Why did God create me and make me in His own image and likeness? What does He ask of me in return?

5

Fallen Man
and the Faithfulness of God

"And God saw everything that He had made, and behold, it was very good" (Gen. 1.31). Revelation teaches us that God made man rightly (cf. Eccle. 7.30), but that man brought upon himself a multitude of evils.

In this chapter we speak first of the mystery of evil, and of how the personal sins of men and of the fallen angels touch upon it. We then speak of how God promises man a Redeemer, and of how in the old covenant God sustained the hopes for redemption, the redemption which Christ came to work. For it is "through Christ and in Christ" that "the riddle of sorrow and death is illumined" (GS 22).

THE MYSTERY OF EVIL

The history of mankind is heavily marked with suffering and grief. Much of Sacred Scripture itself is a record of human sorrow. Though the books of Scripture recall the vast mercies of God and are the source of 39 boundless hope and confidence in Him, they are also starkly realistic in noting the tragedies and afflictions the flesh is heir to.

But the Scriptures remind us that God does not love human suffering. God does not will any evil at all as such or for its own sake.

God may indeed cause punishments or other purely physical evils for the sake of the greater goods He wills for us, and without His creative and sustaining powers no bad deed could be done; but never does He will or cause any moral evil or sin.[1]

The Reactions of Men

Sensitivity toward the pains and afflictions of others is commonly a sign of a generous heart. Those who share with deep feeling the suffer-

---

[1] Cf. Council of Trent, Session 6, January 13, 1547, *Decree on Justification,* canon 6 (DS 1556).

ings and losses of so many are supported by their confident trust in Him who wishes men to care even in circumstances which may seem at times hopeless.

Not all of us react to ills and sufferings the same way. More than a few persons have cited the presence of evil in this world as their reason 26 for denying the very existence of God (cf. GS 19). Some indeed are so pressed by their sorrows that they feel tragically driven toward rebellion against their Lord. Others, however, use the pain they experience or observe as a facile pretext for unbelief.

The Example of Job

The problem of evil is deeply explored in the Old Testament, above all in the book of Job. There Job is portrayed as an innocent person who suffers great reverses and affliction. He loses all his possessions, his health and his peace, and even all his loved ones. Though friends come to console him, many of their words are shallow and useless.

It is of course foolish to tell each person in great pain that his pain is "all for the best," as though every evil were really directly wanted by God and therefore "secretly a blessing." Revelation does not teach that.

It is also not right to say that those who suffer much are those who have sinned much, and therefore they deserve to suffer (cf. Job 4.7). When Jesus was asked by His disciples about a man who had been blind from birth, whether it was his sin or that of his parents that caused him to be born blind, Jesus answered: "It was not that this man sinned, or his parents, but that the works of God might be made manifest in him" (John 9.3).

Job complains that the evils he bears are a stark mystery, while his friends have easy answers. And the divine response at the end is that it is Job who is right. Or, rather, more nearly right, for Job in his sorrows did not sufficiently reverence God's mysterious ways, assumed too readily that his view of justice was entirely right, and thought he saw some edge of unfairness in God. So God is portrayed as asking Job questions Job had put to Him.

"Who is this that darkens counsel by words without knowledge? Gird up your loins like a man, I will question you, and you shall declare to me. Where were you when I laid the foundation of the earth? . . ." (Job 38.2-4). Job, fundamentally good, sees God's concern and recalls that he really knows God is righteous, though He dwells in mystery, and Job replies to God: "Behold, I am of small account; what shall I an-

50

swer You? . . . I know that You can do all things, and that no purpose of Yours can be thwarted. . . . I have uttered what I did not understand, things too wonderful for me, which I did not know. . . . I had heard of You by the hearing of the ear, but now my eye sees You; therefore I despise myself, and repent in dust and ashes" (Job 40.4, 42.2-6). God then blesses Job for all his sufferings, and He reproaches the false apologists: "You have not spoken of Me what is right, as My servant Job has" (Job 42.7).

Those who complain of God with none of Job's patience, who blaspheme God because of the pain they experience or see, may also be called to account by divine questioning.

God's questions to Job (cf. Job 38-41) are answers to the atheist's exploitation of the mystery of evil. Anyone who would claim to understand the mystery of everything is deluding himself or has lost perspective. There is in fact much that none of us is able to know.

Perhaps some of the good things God wills to be in this world could 226 not be here without a real risk of genuine evils. The God who gives men freedom "neither wills evil to be done nor wills evil not to be done, but He wills to permit evil to be done, and this is a good."[2]

And when evils are brought into creation through abuses of the freedom God gives to men, He promises to turn even this toward good. 274 "We know that in everything God works for good with those who love Him" (Rom. 8.28).

Light from Christ's Life

The problem of evil is a living problem. The evils of the world can be endured with intelligent hope only by those who discover also the mercy of a God great enough to heal the wounds of all.

The problem of evil is illumined by the life of Christ. It is illumined for one thing by His tears and compassion. Many have felt that pains and sorrows are a sign of God's absence. When Jesus came to the tomb of His friend Lazarus, Martha said to Him: "Lord, if You had been here, my brother would not have died" (John 11.21). Jesus did not answer Martha in words. Instead, He, the Lord of all, in the presence of His creatures, revealed His heart: "Jesus wept" (John 11.35).

The life of Jesus, the whole mystery of the incarnation, is the reve-

---

[2]St. Thomas Aquinas, *Summa Theologica* 1, 19, 9 ad 3, quoted in Pope Leo XIII, Encyclical, *Libertas Praestantissimum* (June 20, 1888) (DS 3251).

91 lation of God's earnest will to share and to heal the suffering of all. The Son of God underwent evil to overcome evil. In His passion, Christ in His humanity endured for men humiliation and abuse, loneliness, dread, anguish, and great physical pain. Not only does He wish everyone in pain in some way to have a fellow Sufferer who is able to heal those who turn to Him, but in this, as in all things, He reveals the inner heart of God eternal: God's compassion is always with us.

THE SIN OF MAN

Man was created in a state of holiness, freedom, and peace. But he 45 deliberately sinned, and brought great sorrows on himself and all his descendants.

Original Sin

The account of the fall of man in the book of Genesis (cf. Gen. 3) presents the deep truth of man's first rebellion against God in language somewhat figurative in its details. We do not know the exact nature of the first human sin. Scripture suggests that the malice of that sin lay chiefly in its elements of pride and disobedience (cf. Gen. 3; Sir. 10.15; Rom. 5.12-14).

The sin of Adam was in him an actual sin. He of his own free will did something he knew was in opposition to God's will.

Basing its teaching firmly on Scripture (esp. Rom. 5.12-19), the Church teaches[3] that from Adam original sin has been transmitted to all men. Not only do men tend to imitate the sinfulness that surrounds them, but each individual is born in a condition of sin, and can be freed from that condition only by the merits of Jesus Christ.

193 The original sin each person inherits is not an actual sin he personally commits. Rather, "it is human nature so fallen, stripped of the grace that clothed it, injured in its own natural powers and subjected to the dominion of death, that is transmitted to all men, and it is in this sense that every man is born in sin."[4]

The transmission of original sin means that each descendant of Adam is created without sanctifying grace, and without the special gifts that had accompanied that grace. Thus the entire human race, all mankind, has been wounded by original sin.

---

[3]Cf. Council of Trent, Session 5, June 17, 1546, *Decree on Original Sin* (DS 1510-1516).
[4]Pope Paul VI, *Professio Fidei* ("The Credo of the People of God," June 30, 1968).

Divine Justice

God is just. Those who die in original sin, but without having committed any personal grave sins, will not suffer the pain of damnation for that.[5]

The losses that mankind has incurred as a result of original sin are not losses of anything due to man by right. Freedom from death and from the sufferings that seem to flow from our creaturely state is no clear right of ours. That we have been created at all, and have been given hope, is God's great mercy, the Creator's own free gifts to men.

170
343

Man's Freedom and Responsibility

The many sorrows of human life are by no means the fruit of original sin alone. In fact, the most severe and unbearable of human evils are the fruit of the continued deliberate sins of men.

The history of the world is a record of sorrows, of sorrows arising from evils that need not have been. The sins of man are not predetermined and inevitable. God gives man freedom, and it is man who chooses to abuse that gift by sinning. God offers the help that makes resistance to temptation possible (cf. 1 Cor. 10.13). Trials may be too great for our strength, but they are not too great for His; and we can draw upon His strength if we invoke Him. He remains present to us, a Father who cares, ready to fortify us, if we wish to respond to Him, against the terrible tragedy of doing evil, which is far worse than suffering it.

The meaning of responsibility, the gravity of sin, and something of the ways of God are revealed to us in man's fallen state. The result of Adam's sin makes clear how sinful failure to accept responsibility is a matter of far greater importance than we might otherwise have imagined. It reveals how God is a strong and just God, a God who is serious about the freedom and responsibility He gives to man.

Yet the whole account of original sin reveals even more the immensity of God's mercy. Though God allowed sorrows to come to man because of his sin, His permission of evil involved a plan in which the latter state of man would be better than the first. Christ's redemptive love on the cross was to be a gift of such overflowing richness that it would lighten the whole burden of sin.

85

---

[5]Cf. Pope Innocent III, *Letter* to Ymbertus (1201) (DS 780); Pope Pius VI, Constitution, *Auctorem Fidei* (August 28, 1794) (DS 2626).

Man sins only by his own free choice. God did not make man in such a way that man would have to sin. Man chooses to do or not to do, and by his choosing determines his own ultimate fate. "If you will, you can keep the commandments. . . . Before a man are life and death, and whichever he chooses will be given to him" (Sir. 15.15, 17).

THE DEVIL

That fallen spirits, like fallen men, really exist and behave maliciously in this world is a teaching drawn from Scripture (cf., e.g., Luke 8.29-30; John 8.44; Rev. 12.7-9) and faithfully taught by the Church.

The Church does not teach terror of Satan. It commends only a fear of God, and a fear of deliberately doing evil. For the influence of Satan is decisively subordinated to the power of God. As the Second Vatican Council recalled time and again, Christ "has freed us from the power of Satan" (SC 6; cf. GS 2, 22; AG 3, 9). Because of Christ's redemptive work, the devil can genuinely harm only those who freely permit him to do so.

Anyone sensitive to the profound and bitter depths of the mystery of evil can hardly be inclined to a superficial optimism, that is, to a belief that evil in the world is merely an incidental flaw in a world ever evolving toward better days. There are traces of deep malice that puzzle us. The dark mystery of Satan is that there are personal agents in the universe, poorly known to us, malicious and always ready to do evil, irrevocably alienated from God and hostile to Him (cf. Matt. 25.41). That human history is often marked by sad and irrational currents is partly due to such influences.

God remains the Lord of all. Satan and the other fallen spirits are themselves mere creatures. God made them, though He did not make them to be evil or to be sources of evil. "For the devil and the other demons were created by God good by nature, but they of themselves became bad."[6]

THE FAITHFULNESS OF GOD

The first man sinned, and his descendants have followed him in sin, but God remains merciful. "If we are faithless, He remains faithful — for He cannot deny Himself" (2 Tim. 2.13).

---

[6]Fourth Lateran Council, November 1215, *The Catholic Faith* (DS 800).

Through the ages of salvation history preceding Christ, God repeatedly called men to repentance, to renewed greatness, and to salvation. 243 He never forgets that it was He who had made man, and He made man not only to be His creature but also to share in His own divine life and friendship. Repeatedly He speaks of His love for His chosen people as that of a faithful husband for his wife, a love that endures even if the wife is unfaithful; His is an unfathomable and eternal love that will at length lead her to faithfulness.

Promises of the Covenant

"In carefully planning and preparing the salvation of the whole human race, the God of supreme love, by a special dispensation, chose for Himself a people to whom He might entrust His promises. First He entered into a covenant with Abraham (cf. Gen. 15.18) and, through 156 Moses, with the people of Israel (cf. Exod. 24.8)" (DV 14). In this covenant God pledged Himself to care for them and to save them; He required them in return to pledge themselves to faithfulness to Him.

God's covenants with men are a sign of the freedom and the richness of His love. By these covenants the Lord of all creation freely 87 binds Himself to men. He enters into covenants with those whom He freely chooses to bless with special mercies. At the same time, however, His love remains universal: it is directed toward all. Even to those most specially chosen He makes it clear that they are chosen to be the ones by whom He wills to bring salvation to all. Thus He said to Abraham: "I will indeed bless you . . . and by your descendants shall all the nations of the earth bless themselves . . ." (Gen. 22.17-18).

Teaching of the Prophets

Through the prophets He sent, God taught His people how to live as they awaited His redeeming mercy. These prophets were God's spokesmen. God had called them, and He was able to make others recognize them as His prophets. The words of the prophets were not always accepted, however, for they demanded personal faith and inner conversion, and they insisted on faithfulness to all of God's law.

The prophets taught men to hope for the salvation the Messiah would bring. Indeed, the Gospel Christ was to commission the apostles to preach was "promised in former times through the prophets" (DV 7). Thus the prophets of old spoke of the saving mercy to come, the good 97 tidings of Christ, who already was the salvation of those who faithfully awaited their Savior.

There is, to be sure, a certain obscurity in prophecy, for prophecy speaks of a mystery and addresses faith. Moreover, the language of the prophets is often the language of symbols and poetic imagery. Even so, in the centuries before Christ's coming the prophetic promises of that event confirmed God's people in hope, and at the time of that coming bore witness to Christ (cf. John 5.46). The Church teaches that the Old Testament prophecies of Christ, like Jesus' own prophecies in the Gospels, are "most certain signs of divine revelation."[7]

Preparation of the Nations

Among the pagan nations as well God kept alive the hope for salvation, and Christ brought salvation to many who did not even know His
28 name. Through the natural gifts of the various cultures, God was preparing the world for the advent of His Son and for the spreading of His Gospel.

This divine work of preparation continues even today, for there are still many who do not know Christ and His message, and some who have not yet arrived at an explicit knowledge of God. Thanks to His
130 grace, these too can attain salvation if they strive in their lives to do what is right according to the dictates of their conscience. "Whatever of goodness and truth is found among them is looked upon by the Church as preparation for the Gospel, and as given by Him who enlightens all men so that they may finally have life" (LG 16).

Old Testament and New

Catholics are encouraged to read and meditate on the books of the Old Testament, for these books "give expression to a lively sense of God, contain a store of sublime teachings about God, sound wisdom about human life, and wonderful treasuries of prayers, and in them the mystery of our salvation is present in a hidden way" (DV 15). These books, however, are always to be read in the light of Christ, who is their fulfillment.

"God, the Inspirer and Author of Testaments, wisely arranged that

---

[7]First Vatican Council, Session 3, April 24, 1870, *Dogmatic Constitution on the Catholic Faith*, ch. 3 (DS 3009).

the New Testament be hidden in the Old and the Old be made manifest in the New. . . . The books of the Old Testament . . . acquire and show forth their full meaning in the New Testament (cf. Matt. 5.17; Luke 24.27; Rom. 16.15-16; 2 Cor. 3.14-16) and in turn shed light on it and explain it" (DV 16).

PROVIDENCE IN A FALLEN WORLD

The Church believes that God cares for all men, wishes all to be saved, invites all to holiness, and would have His kingdom and His peace present even now on earth. The world, however, is deeply flawed. There has been no failure on the part of God. Though men have sinned, time and again, God in His mercy still calls them to inherit a blessing, and indeed He makes the occurrence of sin the occasion for even greater gifts.

The world, then, has a double aspect. In its sin and sorrow it mirrors the frailty and malice of creatures who resist their Creator God. In its grandeur and in the grace that yet penetrates it, however, the world continues to show the boundless bounty of God. This goodness we often see too dimly. To grasp reality in truth, we need most of all to see in the light of Christ.

.　　.　　.

Questions related to the material in this chapter:

1. In what sense do we speak of evil as a mystery?

2. What was Job's reply to the problem of evil?

3. Is there any completely human answer to the problem of evil in this world?

4. How did Jesus react to the evil in the world that He found all around Him?

5. What do we mean when we say that all human beings are born in the state of "original sin"?

6. After reading Romans 5.12-15, how can we define original sin?

7. What does the Church mean when it says that persons are not predetermined to good or to evil, but that each enjoys personal responsibility?

8. What does Scripture indicate about the reality and significance of the devil?

9. In a world in which so many people seem embarrassed to talk about Satan, why does the Church insist on teaching the reality of his existence?

10. Why do we say that God remained faithful even though man sinned?

11. What do the prophets have to say about God's promise to save all men?

12. In what sense can we say that God continues to care for us even after we sin?

6

The Son of God
Becomes Our Brother

"You know the grace of our Lord Jesus Christ, that though He was rich, yet for your sake He became poor, so that by His poverty you might become rich" (2 Cor. 8.9). When God's gift of a Savior came, it was a far richer fulfillment of the promises than any man could have hoped for.

In this chapter we speak of the good news of Jesus, of how He who was born on earth as our Savior is clearly a man like us, our Brother, but is also our God; and of how He is nonetheless but one Person, the eternal Son of God. He suffered the humiliations and limitations of humanity; but in His humanity He also bore the saving gifts needed to heal our infirmities.

THE BIRTH OF JESUS

The Gospels speak with a sublime simplicity of the events surrounding the conception and birth of Jesus (cf. Matt. 1-2; Luke 1-2). The 70 coming of Christ was quiet and gentle.

He who came to all came among the poor and the little. In view of the greatness of the divine promise, the circumstances of His coming seemed most unlikely. His mother was, in earthly estimation, an unimportant figure, as was also her husband Joseph, a carpenter.

Mary had been told: "And behold, you will conceive in your womb and bear a Son, and you shall call His name Jesus. He will be great and will be called the Son of the Most High; and the Lord God will give to Him the throne of His father David, and He will reign over the house of Jacob for ever; and of His kingdom there will be no end" (Luke 1.31-33).

Only great faith could have accepted such a promise in calm confidence. Only in faith was hope sustained in the utter poverty of Jesus' birth. Away from her home at Nazareth, at the royal city of Bethlehem, Mary "gave birth to her first-born Son and wrapped Him in swaddling clothes and laid Him in a manger, because there was no place for them in the inn" (Luke 2.6). But in all its poverty, this first Christmas was an event of supreme joy. On that day the Lord of glory appeared as our Brother.

JESUS IS TRULY MAN

Because He was to be our Savior, Jesus "had to be made like His brethren in every respect" (Heb. 2.17). "He who is 'the image of the invisible God' (Col. 1.15) is Himself the perfect man. . . . He worked with human hands, He thought with a human mind, acted by human choice, and loved with a human heart. Born of the Virgin Mary, He has truly been made one of us, like us in everything except sin" (GS 22).

69   The solemn teaching of the Church[1] has always confirmed the clear teaching of Scripture that Jesus is truly a man. He truly became one of us. He had not only a human body, but also a human soul, a human mind, a human will, human emotions. He was fully and perfectly a man.

In His passion the reality of His humanity was clearly evident. He suffered excruciating pain of mind and body. He suffered the sharp physical pains of scourging and crucifixion; and He truly died.

He never abandoned the humanity which for our sake He took on and made His own.

The humanity of Jesus is overwhelmingly important: because in Him human nature is most ennobled, and He is the perfect pattern for
89 human living (cf. Matt. 11.29); because through His humanity He redeemed us; and because He is far more than man.

JESUS IS TRULY GOD

The Catholic faith steadfastly professes that Jesus is literally and truly God, the eternal Son of the eternal Father.

This is the good news of Christian faith: that He who is almighty, the eternal Lord of all, whose unseen might and mercy sustain all
192 things, "stepped into the tide of the years"[2] and "dwelt among us" (John 1.14) in the visible humanity He had made His own.

The books of the New Testament record a gradual development in the disciples' recognition of who Jesus was and is. They reflect the

---

[1]Cf., e.g., Fourth Lateran Council, November 1215, *The Catholic Faith* (DS 801).
[2]St. Augustine, *Sermo* 191.1 (ML 38.1010).

Church's development in Christological insight, its continuing growth in understanding the mystery of His person. Already in the New Testament, however, Jesus is explicitly called God.

In the prologue to the Gospel of St. John, for example, Jesus is identified as the Word of God, a Person who was "in the beginning" and was with the Father in the beginning. "The Word was God" (John 1.1).

In the joy of his Easter faith, St. Thomas cried out to Jesus: "My Lord and my God!" (John 20.28).[3] God the Father is portrayed as addressing Christ as God: "But of the Son He says, 'Your throne, O God, is for ever and ever'" (Heb. 1.8). Christian life is lived in expectation, "awaiting our blessed hope, the appearing of the glory of our great God and Savior Jesus Christ" (Titus 2.13; cf. also 2 Peter 1.1; Rom. 9.5).

Far more often the title "Lord" is given to Jesus. The risen Savior is called Lord in recognition of His divine glory. "At the name of Jesus every knee should bow, in heaven and on the earth and under the earth, and every tongue confess that Jesus Christ is Lord, to the glory of God the Father" (Phil. 2.10-11).

But the New Testament does more than name Jesus God. Throughout, it portrays Him as doing the deeds of God, acting as One with the dignity, status, and power of God; and it presents Him as believed, trusted, prayed to, and regularly reverenced as God by those who come to faith in Him.

Thus faith proclaims that God alone created all things and sustains all things in being. But Jesus too is proclaimed the Lord of creation. "All things were made through Him" (John 1.2; cf. Col. 1.16-17). 34

In God alone is salvation; only God can forgive sins, and give back life to soul and to body. But Jesus is the Savior of all. He personally forgives sin, out of His own compassion and on His own authority (cf., e.g., Luke 5.20-25). "I am the Resurrection and the Life; he who believes in Me, though he die, yet shall he live" (John 11.25-26).

The power of God is seen in Jesus, power to heal the sick and to raise the dead to life.

It is God who is Judge of all (cf. Heb. 12.23). But Jesus has the divine role of judging. All the nations of the earth will assemble before the Son of Man, and He will pass judgment (cf. Matt. 25.31, 46). 359

To God is the final glory and honor to be given; only God can be

---

[3]The Second Council of Constantinople authoritatively declares that Christ is being called God in this passage. Cf. Second Council of Constantinople, Session 8, June 2, 553, Canon 12 (DS 434).

given the total assent of faith, be the foundation of hope, the object of love that truly rules our life. But because Jesus is God all this is due to Him. Christ Jesus is "our hope" (1 Tim. 1.1), and we are to love Him above all, just as we are to love the Father above all (cf. Matt. 10.37; John 14.21, 23).

One with the Father

110 The mystery of Jesus could only begin to be grasped as the mystery of His union with the Father began to be understood. Jesus is not the Father; He was sent by the Father, and He honors the Father. Though they are different Persons, they are forever together. "Believe Me that I am in the Father and the Father in Me" (John 14.11). Indeed, Jesus and the Father are one: "I and the Father are one" (John 10:30). They are one in sharing the same nature, the same one eternal love and wisdom and power that created and sustains the world.

True Son of God

In the eternal love that is the Blessed Trinity the Father is eternally the Generator of the Son, and the Son is always the Only-begotten of the Father (cf. John 1.14). Many are called "sons of God" because God gives His grace and friendship to many and adopts them as His own. But there is only One who is Son by nature, God's own Son (cf. Heb. 1.1).

The Church teaches that Jesus is Son of God not by adoption but by nature. He is not "a man bearing God in him," but "the one natural Son of God."[4] He alone is the true natural Son, possessing fully and properly with His eternal Father the full nature of God.

JESUS IS ONE PERSON

Jesus is man and Jesus is God; but Jesus is one Person. "One and the same Christ, Son, Lord, Only-begotten, must be acknowledged in two natures unconfused, unchangeable, undivided, inseparable."[5] Jesus

---

[4]St. Cyril of Alexandria, Anathemas against Nestorius, n. 5 (DS 256).
[5]Council of Chalcedon, Session 5, October 22, 451 (DS 302).

remains always the Son of God, which He is from all eternity; He took to Himself a human nature in time, and He remains a man forever. But it is one Person, Jesus Christ, who is both God and man.

This the faith has always proclaimed. The same Christ who was born of Mary and who suffered for us is also God. The Jesus whom the apostles saw, who walked this earth, is the Lord who created all things. He who in His divine nature cannot be seen by bodily eyes or comprehended by human minds, lived and suffered in our humanity so that He might be with us, save us, and draw us to share in His divine nature and life.

Such was the strategy of divine mercy. God in His own nature dwells in eternal blessedness. That He might be with us in our trials, that He might redeem us by suffering to atone for our sins, He created in the womb of Mary a human nature in which in a very real way He could share our life. To bring creation to perfect unity and peace, God formed in the womb of the Virgin Mary a human nature that He united 72 to the Person of the Son of God. When this human nature began to be, a new person did not begin to be; rather, the eternal Son of God then began to live in a new nature, in a humanity in which He was to unite all things to Himself.

Our Lord Jesus Christ is one Person. He is truly God, and in His divine nature He dwells eternally with the Father, with whom He is "one in Being."[6] He is man as well: "He has truly been made one of us, like us in all things except sin (cf. Heb. 4.15)" (GS 22). His humanity is united with His divinity not merely by grace and friendship; there is a union in "hypostasis" or person. He who is the Son of God is this man.[7] This man, Jesus, is God.[8]

Because Jesus is one Person who lives in two distinct natures, one can truthfully say of the Son of God whatever is true of Him in either of His natures. He suffered and died in His human nature, and He is God, and so we may say that God suffered and died.[9] This is literally true, although in His divine nature Jesus could not and did not suffer. The sublime truth that Jesus is one Person, though He is both God and man, reveals much of the greatness of God's generosity in the incarnation.

---

[6]That is, "consubstantial," *homoousios.* Cf. Creed of the Council of Nicaea, 325 (DS 125), and Creed of the First Council of Constantinople, 381 (DS 150).
[7]Cf. Second Council of Constantinople, Session 8, June 2, 553, canon 4 (DS 424).
[8]Council of Chalcedon, Session 5, October 22, 451 (DS 301-302).
[9]Cf. St. Cyril of Alexandria, Anathemas against Nestorius, n. 12 (DS 263).

Catholic teaching states that Jesus is one Person, and that a divine Person, "one of the Holy Trinity."[10] Thus, Jesus is "not a human person."

When we say that Jesus is not a human person, we are using the word "person" in a precise sense, important to the faith. In some senses it might be true to call Him a human person. This person, Jesus, *is* human. But when we say He is not a human person, we are using the word "person" in its technical meaning of "distinct intelligent being." 60 Jesus is not a being distinct from the Person who is the Son of God.

The point here is this: Jesus is not divided. There is no human person "Jesus" who would be other than the Person who is the eternal Son of God.

Devotion to the Sacred Heart of Jesus grows out of this sound faith. For He who is truly our Brother, because He is Himself our Lord, has loved us with an undivided love. To this man Jesus we are personally known and related, because He is no mere human person, but a true man who is the Son of God.[11]

One Adoration

It is because this man Jesus is not a separate created person that He is rightly adored as God. The apostle Thomas saw the risen Jesus and greeted Him in adoration: "My Lord and my God!" (John 20.28). In the same way Catholic devotion worships the one Jesus in the Eucharist. With a single adoration and faith and love, Christian devotion salutes the one, undivided Lord Jesus.

THE SON OF GOD HUMBLED HIMSELF

The Son of God is God, of one substance with the Father, sharing forever with Him the divine nature and glory. But at the moment of His incarnation the Son of God began to exist also in our human nature. He, "though He was in the form of God, did not deem equality with God a 237 thing to be grasped, but emptied Himself, taking the form of a servant,

---

[10]Second Council of Constantinople, Session 8, June 2, 553, canon 10 (DS 432). Cf. also DS 485, 561.
[11]Cf. Pope Pius XII, Encyclical, *Haurietis Aquas* (May 15, 1956) (DS 3922-3926).

being born in the likeness of men" (Phil. 2.6-7). He came among us as truly one of us, appearing "in the likeness of sinful flesh" (Rom. 8.3). He "humbled Himself and became obedient unto death, even death on a cross" (Phil. 2.8).

Daily in the Eucharistic liturgy the Church cries out in hope that we may "come to share in the divinity of Christ, who humbled himself to share in our humanity."[12]

Nothing mythical is said here, nothing unworthy of God. The Son of God remains forever infinitely perfect, unchangeable in His divine glory when in His infinite mercy He begins to exist also in a human nature. By no means does the Son of God cease to be the eternal Son of God when He begins to be the Son of Mary. Had Christ ceased to have the glory of God, it would not have been the Son of God who shared our sorrows and came to our poverty.

THE GLORY OF HIS MANHOOD

Jesus, the Son of God, is in His human nature perfect man. He is 102 fully God and fully man. Thus He has divine intelligence and human intelligence, a divine will and a human will. Faith teaches that His human knowledge has a wealth appropriate to His role as Savior of all, and that His human soul, heart, mind, and will are enriched with all virtues and holiness.

Knowledge of Christ

Christ's human knowledge was surpassingly rich. In His risen glory His wisdom is indescribably great. In Him "are hid all the treasures of wisdom and knowledge" (Col. 2.3). Even in His earthly days His wisdom did nothing to make Him less human and less near us; it is a compassionate wisdom, warm with understanding and love, binding us to Him and to His Father, whom He reveals to us.

Christ had immediate and intimate knowledge of the Father. He *saw* the Father, and made Him known (cf. John 1.18, 8.54-55).   28

Christ also knew Himself, the mystery of his own Person, of His Messianic dignity, and the task the Father had given Him.

His human knowledge, even in His days on earth, extended to all

---

[12]Roman Missal, Liturgy of the Eucharist, prayer at the pouring of wine and water into the chalice.

He should appropriately be concerned with as Savior and Shepherd of all. The Gospels proclaim that He knew the hearts of men (cf. Matt. 9.4, 12.15, 16.8) and even future contingent things (cf., e.g., Matt. 20.18-19, 24.5 ff., 26. 21-24).

The Gospels also speak of Jesus as growing in knowledge (cf. Luke 2.52), as knowing wonder about the things He came to experience humanly, and even as professing Himself unaware of the time of the last things (cf. Matt. 24.36; Mark 13.2). Of such matters theologians and Scripture scholars speak in discussing various forms of Christ's human knowledge: of beatific vision, infused knowledge, and experiential knowledge. Faith has room for various interpretations in these matters, as long as they are in accord with revealed teaching on the Person of Christ and on the explicit teaching of the Church in matters that affect an understanding of His wisdom.

Sinlessness of Jesus

Christ was entirely without sin all the days of His life on earth. "He committed no sin; no guile was found on His lips" (1 Peter 2.22). Indeed, to know who Christ is, that He is God and the Son of God, is to realize that He is entirely incapable of sin because of the divine dignity of His Person.

The Gospels indeed portray Christ as undergoing temptation, but never as feeling any inner inclination toward evil such as we in our concupiscence experience. Rather, He was assailed from without by Satanic malice. His human heart was steadfastly fixed on His Father's will. "Nevertheless, not My will, but Yours, be done" (Luke 22.42).

Holiness of Jesus

Jesus in His human nature was from the beginning uniquely holy. Clearly He had a human soul and a human will; but they were the soul and the will of a Person who is God.

Jesus was holy not only because He is the Son of God, but also because He is the crown of creation, and the source of holiness for all who are called to life.

In the human soul, heart, will, and affections of Jesus there dwelled most sublime virtue and all the gifts of the Holy Spirit. Neither Scripture nor Church teaching ever declares Jesus to have had strictly faith or hope; for Jesus did not merely believe the Father, but He knew His Father (cf. John 8.55) as "the only Son, who is in the bosom of the Father" (John 1.18).

Freedom of Jesus

The gracious and saving deeds of Jesus were done in full freedom. His human will was not overwhelmed and cancelled by the divine will; in His humanity were retained all the traits essential to man,[13] and precious among these is freedom. Only in freedom can meritorious deeds be done,[14] and in His humanity Jesus "merited for us justification 174 by His most holy passion."[15] In His humanity He always did the will of 89 His Father (cf. John 8.29), but He did so freely.

Power of Jesus

Jesus was "mighty in deed and word before God and all the people" (Luke 24.19).

In addition to the created powers that graced His humanity, Jesus, because of the personal union of His humanity with His divinity, exercised also divine power through His humanity. For His human reality served instrumentally the mercy and strength of His own divine nature (cf. LG 8). Hence Jesus, in His visible humanity, performed personally and authoritatively works that are proper to God (cf. Matt. 11.5-6; John 80 11.43).

Such deeds of Jesus are sometimes called His "theandric" (Godman) works, deeds in which He acted through both His natures in perfect harmony. "For each nature performs the functions proper to itself, yet in conjunction with the other nature. The Word does what is proper to the Word, and the humanity what is proper to the humanity."[16]

THE MYSTERY OF JESUS

"God so loved the world that He gave His only Son, that whoever believes in Him should not perish but have eternal life" (John 3.16). It is this love that underlies the whole mystery of the incarnation, the mystery that lies at the center of Christianity.

---

[13]Cf. Third Council of Constantinople, Session 18, September 16, 681 (DS 556-557).
[14]Cf. Pope Innocent X, Constitution, *Cum Occasione* (May 31, 1653) (DS 2003).
[15]Council of Trent, Session 6, January 13, 1547, *Decree on Justification,* ch. 7 (DS 1529).
[16]Pope St. Leo I, *Letter* to Flavian ("Tome of Leo," June 13, 449) (DS 294).

God so loved the world that He sent His Son to be with us and to save us. The whole purpose of creation was to bring created persons into friendship with the Persons of the Blessed Trinity.

169   Creation is the glory of God; but nothing created so glorifies God as the humanity of Christ. The human love in Jesus' heart is the greatest of all created glories of God. He makes perfect faith possible, for He is the perfect witness of God, perfect in what He proclaims and in what He is, God and man.

•   •   •

Questions related to the material in this chapter:

1. What is the real significance of the holiday we celebrate as Christmas, the birth of Jesus Christ?

2. When we say that Jesus is truly man, how is that different from saying that Jesus *appeared* to be a man?

3. Is there any Scriptural indication that the Church at the time of the New Testament considered Jesus to be truly God?

4. Is the Son of God different from or less than truly God?

5. In Catholic theology about Christ the word "person" has a precise meaning. What is this?

6. When we say that Jesus Christ is one Person with a divine and a human nature, what do we mean?

7. Did Jesus know that He was God?

8. When we say that Jesus is truly man, does that mean that He was also guilty of sin?

9. How could Jesus work miracles?

10. Why did God send His Son to us in the first place?

11. Why is the fact that Jesus Christ is born "good news" to all men and women?

7

The Mother of Jesus

Everything faith teaches us about Mary is intended to draw us nearer to Jesus. She is His mother; no created person is closer to Him.

In a later chapter we shall speak of Mary's association with Jesus in the Ch. 15 mystery of our redemption, and of her maternal relationship to the Church and the faithful. Here we treat the first gifts of God that bound her so closely to Jesus: the gift by which she was made the mother of God; the grace of her faithful and fruitful virginity; and the holiness that God gave her for the glory of her Son.

THE MOTHER OF GOD

Faith is rooted most deeply in that central saving event by which the Son of God entered history, "born of woman" (Gal. 4.4). Mary is not contemplated for her own sake; she is the mother whose Child changes everything.

The historical events which provide a setting for this mystery of Mary, the mother of God, are recounted in the New Testament. The inspired word of God not only records the basic facts surrounding Mary's unique role in the birth and life of Jesus of Nazareth, but it also provides the prophetic framework that gives us insight into their deeper meaning.

MARY IN SCRIPTURE

The New Testament does not speak at length about Mary, but the essential truths concerning her place in the mystery of Christ and His Church are rooted there.

The Second Vatican Council introduces its discussion of Mary (LG 52-69) with a reference to one of the earliest New Testament testimonies concerning her: "Wishing in His supreme goodness and wisdom to effect the redemption of the world, 'when the fullness of time came, God sent His Son, born of a woman, . . . that we might receive the adoption of sons' (Gal. 4.4-5)" (LG 52). This very early expression of

69

Christian faith immediately identifies Mary as the human way by which the Son of God entered history. In the text Mary is implicitly associated with our salvation, since by her motherhood God's Son has become one of us in order to liberate us from the bondage of sin and bestow on us adoption as free children of the Father through the Spirit.

The fullest treatment of Mary in the New Testament is found in St. Luke's Gospel and in his Acts of the Apostles. Mary appears as a central figure at the outset of his Gospel in the infancy narrative; we also behold her persevering in prayer with the disciples in the upper room at the beginning of his Acts of the Apostles (cf. Acts 1.14). St. John opens and closes his account of the public life of Jesus with two scenes in which Mary figures very prominently, Cana and Calvary (cf. John 2.1-12; 19.25-27).

Mary in the Infancy Narratives

59   The so-called infancy narratives appear in the opening chapters of the Gospels of St. Matthew and St. Luke (cf. Matt. 1-2; Luke 1-2). Although both accounts exhibit Old Testament and Jewish influences, each is distinctive.

St. Matthew, writing the history of Jesus' origins, reflects on them in the light of the Mosaic tradition and promises. His account is largely a collation of quotations from the Old Testament whose promises are fulfilled in Jesus. He takes care to connect Jesus with Mary His mother,
154 because he wished to make clear that Jesus was not Joseph's natural son, but was virginally conceived through the power of the Holy Spirit. The substance of St. Matthew's message to his audience of Jewish origin is that Jesus, born of a human mother, is the promised Messiah who brings His people a new presence of the saving God.

St. Luke's account provides further insight into the theological meaning of Mary's motherhood of Jesus. His infancy narrative may be divided into two parts, that covering the period before the births of John the Baptist and Jesus (Luke 1.5-56) and that recounting their births (Luke 1.7-2.40). He intends both to parallel and to contrast Jesus and John, as well as Mary and Zechariah. His theological purpose is to portray Jesus as divine Messiah and Lord.

The Annunciation

St. Luke's account of the angel Gabriel's message to Mary is the central revelation concerning our Lady in the New Testament.

The heavenly messenger greets Mary: "Hail, full of grace, the Lord 41
is with you!" (Luke 1.28). She is called "full of grace" or "highly favored" because of her unique role in God's saving plan as mother of the
Redeemer. She is "blessed among women" (cf. Luke 1.28) because she is
so highly favored by the Lord's presence in her.

It is obvious from the ensuing dialogue that Mary's Son will live up
to all Jewish expectations of the Messiah as "Son of the Most High" (cf.
Isa. 9.6; Dan. 7.14). Mary's words, "How can this be, since I have no
husband?" (Luke 1.34), recall her commitment to serve the Lord with
the undivided love of a virginal heart. Once God's plan was made clear
to her, Mary freely gave her consent in an act of humble faith and loving obedience: "Behold, I am the handmaid of the Lord; let it be to me according to your word" (Luke 1.38).

Visitation, Nativity, Presentation

St. Luke's infancy narrative praises Mary's great faith through the
lips of Elizabeth, mother of John the Baptist: "And blessed is she who
believed that there would be a fulfillment of what was spoken to her
from the Lord" (Luke 1.45). Mary's reply to her cousin's greeting comes
to us in the form of her magnificent canticle, the *Magnificat* (Luke 1.46-
55).

The nativity of the divine Messiah occurs in a setting of poverty
which, by divine design, seems to call attention to the reality of the
Child's humanity. And at the presentation in the temple, His parents 60
observe the law of the Lord; they offer the least expensive of sacrifices,
the offering of the poor (cf. Luke 2.24; Lev. 12.8).

Mary in the Gospel of St. John

Although the fourth Gospel speaks of Mary only twice, once at the
beginning of the Lord's public life and again at the foot of the cross, the
inspired author reveals much to us about this woman of faith, by implication and through his symbolic interpretation of historical events.

At Cana, Christ chose to anticipate the "hour" in which His glory
would be manifested by working a miracle (or "sign") at her bidding.
"This, the first of His signs, Jesus did at Cana in Galilee, and manifested
His glory; and His disciples believed in Him" (John 2.11). The structure
of this Gospel, in which Mary's request came before Christ had ever
worked a miracle, indicates that her faith was unparalleled among His

71

associates. Furthermore, it was as a result of her intercession that the others "believed in Him."

The same idea is suggested by the scene on Calvary, where the words of Jesus to His mother, "Woman, behold, your Son!" (John 19.26), point symbolically to Mary's spiritual motherhood of all the faithful. Now that the "hour" of His saving death and glorification in the Spirit by the Father has been accomplished, Mary is definitively designated as the "Woman," the "New Eve" associated with the "New Adam" in bringing forth the adopted children of God, the brothers and sisters of her divine Son.

MARY'S MOTHERHOOD OF GOD IN TRADITION

153 "The understanding of Mary in Christian history unfolded along the lines of the Scriptures. The Church saw herself symbolized in the Virgin Mary. The story of Mary, as the Church has come to see her, is at the same time the record of the Church's own self-discovery."[1]

Theotokos, God-bearer

60 In accord with the biblical portrait of Mary, the basic affirmation of the faithful during postapostolic times concerned her motherhood. During the early patristic period, the Church's primary need was to safeguard the reality of the Lord's humanity against the heresies of docetism and gnosticism, heresies which denied that Christ was really a man or that He truly had a human birth from Mary. But when the truth of Christ's divinity was denied by Arius in the fourth century, the response of the Church opened the way for a more explicit understanding of Mary's role. Efforts to minimize Mary's role seemed to flow from lack of faith in Jesus. Thus the Nestorian denial of the traditional teaching about Mary's motherhood of God seemed to flow from the Arian denial that Jesus, her Son, was the eternal Son of God.

In 431 the Council of Ephesus made its own the doctrine of St. Cyril of Alexandria, who had written to Nestorius: "For it was not that He was first born of the holy Virgin as an ordinary man and then the Word descended on this man; on the contrary, united from the womb itself He is said to have undergone birth according to the flesh, thus appropri-

---

[1]United States National Conference of Catholic Bishops, Pastoral Letter, *Behold Your Mother: Woman of Faith* (November 21, 1973) n. 38.

72

ating for Himself the birth of His own flesh. . . . And so (the holy Fathers) have not hesitated to call the Holy Virgin 'mother of God' (Theotokos). . . ."[2]

There is no doubt that *Theotokos* represented a Christological dogma, centered on the mystery of the Incarnation. At the same time, 60 the dogma asserts that Mary enjoys a unique relationship with Christ, that she is truly mother of the eternal Word who took His human flesh from her. This doctrine was clarified further at the Council of Chalcedon in 451 and at the Second Council of Constantinople in 553. Meanwhile, devotion to Mary as mother of God spread more and more, especially in the liturgy.

Theological Elaboration

In the thirteenth century St. Thomas Aquinas contributed in a special way to making the mystery of Mary's motherhood of God more intelligible and meaningful. As the Church had traditionally done, he interpreted the dogma as fundamentally Christological: "The humanity of Christ and the motherhood of the Virgin are so interconnected that he who has erred about the one must also be mistaken about the other."[3]

St. Thomas provides an extended discussion of Mary in the section on Christology in his *Summa Theologica*. He asks whether the Blessed Virgin should be called the mother of God.[4] Obviously his purpose in raising the question is not to "prove" a mystery which we accept as true by faith. Rather, he wishes to penetrate to the meaning of the mystery by showing theologically that the language about her divine maternity is not merely metaphorical or symbolic, but is literally true. He bases his reflections on the more fundamental mystery of the hypostatic union, that is, the mystery that in Christ the divine and human natures are united in the Person of the Word.

The traditional teaching about Christ is that the Word, the second Person of the Trinity, became incarnate from the first moment of His conception in Mary's womb. Although the divine nature of Christ is eternally begotten by the heavenly Father, by the incarnation He was conceived and born of Mary. She is, therefore, truly the mother of God.

---

[2]Council of Ephesus, 431, Letter of Bishop Cyril of Alexandria to Nestorius (DS 251).
[3]St. Thomas Aquinas, *Commentary on the Sentences of Peter Lombard* III dist. 4, 2, 2.
[4]Cf. St. Thomas Aquinas, *Summa Theologica* III, 35, 4.

Closely connected with the Bible's portrait of Mary as the mother of Jesus is its treatment of her virginity. The infancy narratives in the Gospels clearly communicate the belief that Christ was conceived by the power of the Holy Spirit which "overshadowed" Mary without the 62 intervention of any human father (cf. Matt. 1.20-25; Luke 1.34).

Virginal Conception

102   That Mary conceived Christ solely through the power of the Spirit is a dogma of Catholic faith. True, it has never been solemnly defined as such by the extraordinary magisterium of a pope or ecumenical council. But it is a dogma, founded on the words of Scripture, as understood and constantly taught by the universal and ordinary teaching authority of the Church.

The patristic witness to this truth is ancient and constant. The doctrine was incorporated into the universal conciliar creed promulgated by the First Council of Constantinople in 381. It was presupposed at the Council of Ephesus in the definition of the *Theotokos,* and Pope St. Leo the Great taught it clearly in his authoritative letter to Chalcedon.[5]

Virginity in Childbirth

The Church also proclaims that Mary gave birth to Jesus in a virginal way. "She brought Him forth without the loss of virginity, even as she conceived Him without the loss of virginity . . . it was a miraculous birth."[6]

Perpetual Virginity

The truth that Mary remained a virgin throughout her entire life is also a dogma of faith taught in the Church from very early times.

The perpetual virginity of Mary is not a revealed truth which can 138 be clearly demonstrated from the New Testament without the light of tradition. But what is implicit in the Scriptures concerning this dogma gradually came to light in the Church's faith-consciousness. Thus, in

---

[5]Cf. DS 150, 252, 291-292.
[6]Pope St. Leo I, *Letter* to Flavian ("Tome of Leo," June 13, 449) (DS 291, 294).

the fourth century "ever-virgin" became a popular title for Mary. The Church has steadfastly believed that Mary remained true to God in the intense fervor of her virginal love.

Belief in the perpetual virginity of Mary was clearly expressed by the time of the Council of Ephesus in 431 and was accepted by all Christians until the time of the Protestant Reformation in the sixteenth century. In 1555, Pope Paul IV reaffirmed the Church's traditional faith in the dogma of Mary's virginity "before birth, during birth, and forever after birth."[7]

The Second Vatican Council referred to Mary as "perpetual Virgin" (LG 52), and taught that "the union of the Mother with the Son in the work of salvation was manifested from the time of Christ's virginal conception up to His death" (LG 57) and that "this association was shown also at the birth of Our Lord, who did not diminish His mother's virginal integrity but sanctified it" (LG 57).

Significance of Mary's Virginity

Accepting by faith Mary's perpetual virginity as a fact, one should humbly seek out the meaning that makes it a fruitful mystery, and much more than a physical fact.

The Fathers and saints have often spoken of the reasons why God wished the mother of Jesus to be a virgin forever. Mary's virginal conception is a fitting witness to the divine transcendence of her Child who has no human father. At the same time, the virginal Theotokos gives testimony to His real immanence in the Incarnation: He truly assumed His human flesh from her. Mary's virginity also has an ecclesial and eschatological significance. For, metaphorically speaking, the Church is a virgin mother who brings forth the adopted brothers and sisters of Christ through her ministry of the Word and the sacraments. Moreover, Mary is the model for those who choose chastity as priests or religious; she inspires them to bear witness to the ultimate meaning and final goal, or eschaton, of salvation history, the heavenly city where there will be no marriage (cf. Mark 12.25).

MARY'S HOLINESS

The account of the annunciation in the Gospel of St. Luke expresses both the fact and the divine source of Mary's holiness. She is

---

[7]Pope Paul IV, Constitution, Cum Quorumdam (August 7, 1555) (DS 1880).

greeted by Gabriel with words which imply she has fullness of grace precisely because of her intimacy with God. Because she was predestined to be the virginal *Theotokos,* God readies her to be a fitting bearer of the Word incarnate. Her free and generous response (cf. Luke 1.38) gives the key to the secret of her sanctity.

The Immaculate Conception

Mary is "the most excellent fruit of the redemption" (SC 103). This teaching climaxes a long tradition about her perfect sinlessness. The question of whether or not God's saving grace in her divine Son preserved Mary from original sin as well as from personal fault perplexed such outstanding saints of the Middle Ages as Bernard of Clairvaux and Thomas Aquinas. The crux of the difficulty was this: How could she be 90 said to be redeemed by Christ, the Redeemer of all, if she was never touched by sin, even original sin?

William of Ware and John Duns Scotus developed the concept of "anticipatory redemption." Although as a descendant of Adam in a sin- 52 ful human race Mary would naturally have incurred the guilt of original sin, a special divine decree kept her free from it in light of the foreseen or anticipated merits of Jesus Christ. Pope Pius IX solemnly defined the Immaculate Conception as a truth of revelation in 1854: "The Blessed Virgin Mary in the first instant of her conception, by a singular grace and privilege of almighty God, in view of the foreseen merits of Jesus Christ the Savior of the human race, was preserved free from all stain of original sin."[8]

ATTRACTIVENESS OF MARY FOR ALL MANKIND

Mary's Immaculate Conception and virginal motherhood of God are the greatest revelation of what God's redeeming love can accomplish in a human personality. Her attractiveness is almost without limit because she shares so intimately in God's own infinite goodness. After the humanity of God in Jesus Christ and through its merits, Mary is the greatest outward sign of what each of us in his own limited way is called to become as a Christian.

Some of these thoughts will be developed further in Chapter 15, when we reflect on Mary in the perfect holiness of her glorious Assump-

---

[8]Pope Pius IX, Bull, *Ineffabilis Deus* (December 8, 1854) (DS 2803).

tion which makes her spiritual motherhood of mankind complete. Enjoying the fullness of glory with her divine Son, she intercedes for us so that we may grow in the Christian life of faith, hope, and love. For us the grace of baptism is our "immaculate conception," our entry into the new life of Jesus Christ. We, too, can share in her "virginal motherhood" of Jesus by helping to bring forth new adopted brothers and sisters in the Lord until all the redeemed are gathered together in glory with Jesus and His mother, Mary.

305

. . .

Questions related to the material in this chapter:

1. Why does the Church place such a special emphasis on Mary?

2. Is devotion to Mary a late development in Catholic practice or is there a scriptural tradition that points out her special place in the Church?

3. Both St. Matthew and St. Luke record the story of Christ's birth. What do these accounts teach us of Mary and her Son?

4. What is the central point at issue in the scriptural account of the Annunciation?

5. What events recalled in the Joyful Mysteries of the rosary are found in Scripture?

6. Does the Gospel of St. John make any reference to Mary distinct from those found in the other Gospels?

7. What does the Greek word *Theotokos* mean? Why is it a proper title for Mary?

8. What do we mean when we speak of the virginal conception of Jesus?

9. Does the perpetual virginity of Mary have any meaning in God's plan for our salvation or is it just a special gift to Mary?

10. In what way is Mary a model for all Christians?

11. How is Mary the mother of God also our mother?

8

The Public Life of Jesus

The Church's love for Jesus, flowing from faith in Him as the divine Savior, has always led it to have a special appreciation of eyewitness testimony about the Messiah. The most esteemed material is found in the inspired texts of the New Testament.

Here, then, we speak of the words and deeds of Jesus in His public life. This chapter treats of the truth of the Gospels, Jesus' public life, His miracles, His preaching, His self-revelation, and His first planting of the seeds of His Church.

THE GOSPEL TRUTH

The earliest recorded Christian preaching stressed our Lord's death and resurrection. Clear examples of this teaching appear in St. Luke's history of the Church's early years, the Acts of the Apostles (cf., e.g., Acts 2.14-36, 3.12-26, 13.16-41), and in the pastoral letters of the apostles preserved in the Bible as Epistles (cf., e.g., 1 Cor. 15.1-11). But the faithful longed to have and preserve more details of Jesus' saving message.

To satisfy this desire the four Gospels were composed (cf. Luke 1.1-4). Ever since, the new People of God has treasured these four Gospels
365 as historical (cf. DV 19) and divinely coauthored (cf. DV 11) narratives of Jesus' life.

Christian scholars rightly study the structure of the Gospels, their literary origins and forms.[1] But Catholics also affirm that the evangelists "told us the honest truth about Jesus" (DV 19). For, as St. Luke tells us, care was taken to search out the testimony of "those who from the beginning were eyewitnesses and ministers of the word," so that the reader or hearer of the Gospel might know "the truth concerning the things of which you have been informed" (Luke 1.2, 4).

---

[1]Cf. Pontifical Commission for Promotion of Bible Studies, Instruction, *Sancta Mater Ecclesia* (approved by Pope Paul VI, April 21, 1964) (DS 3999-3999e).

BEGINNINGS

The beginning of the public life and work of Jesus of Nazareth is closely connected with the preaching of His cousin, John the Baptist. John worked to prepare his fellow countrymen for the imminent manifestation of God in their history. "Repent," he urged, "for the kingdom of heaven is at hand" (Matt. 3.2; cf. Mark 1.1-8; Luke 3.3-17). Great crowds flocked to hear his call to repentance, to seek his advice, and to submit to his baptism as an outward sign of their turning back to God.

Jesus also went out to the arid Judean countryside along the Jordan to present Himself for John's baptism (cf. John 1.1-34). John recognized and greeted Jesus with the title of the classical sacrificial figure from the Old Testament, "Lamb of God" (John 1.29; cf. Isa. 53.7). Later, as Jesus rose up out of the water after being baptized, the Spirit of God was seen in the form of a dove over His head and a voice was heard from the heavens declaring: "This is My beloved Son, with whom I am well pleased" (Matt. 3.17).

After His baptism, Jesus was led by the spirit into a desert where He fasted for forty days and nights (cf. Matt. 4.1-11; Mark 1.12-13; Luke 4.1-13). At the end of this period the devil tried repeatedly to entice Jesus into a warped and materialistic understanding of the identity revealed at His baptism. Jesus showed Himself utterly unmoved by 66 these temptations. At this time Jesus was about thirty years old (cf. Luke 3.23).

It was after hearing about John's arrest that Jesus actually began to appear publicly. He also gathered around Himself a small band of close followers who accepted Him as their teacher and who traveled with Him 125 wherever He preached (cf. Matt. 4.18-22, 10.1-4; Mark 1.6-20, 3.13-19; Luke 5.1-11, 6.12-16).

Working with this select group and accompanied by a number of women who provided them with material assistance (cf. Luke 8.2-3), Jesus began His own proclamation of the kingdom of God. Like John before Him, Jesus encountered many who were eager to hear His good news, that is, Gospel. He became well-known. At times the crowds that walked with Him were so large that it became impossible for some individuals, even people of political prominence or His own relatives, to get physically near to Jesus (cf. Matt. 12.46-50; Mark 3.31-35; Luke 8.19-21).

It was clear that people were drawn to Him. Even when Jesus attempted to withdraw for periods of prayer, the multitudes often came and sought Him out (cf. Mark 1.35, 45; Luke 4.42).

The reaction of the religious leaders of the Jews to this popularity was not long in turning from curiosity to hostility; there may have been some suspicion that the new teaching of Jesus was not faithful to the word of God long handed down, but jealousy was also evident (cf. Luke 20.1-47).

What was there about Jesus which drew all this attention, both favorable and unfavorable?

One reason certainly lay in the fact that Jesus combined His preaching activity with signs of power which seemed indeed to be seals of God's approval. As Jesus said when the disciples of His imprisoned cousin came to ask Him about Himself: "Go and tell John what you hear and see: the blind receive their sight and the lame walk, lepers are cleansed and the deaf hear, and the dead are raised up, and the poor have the good news preached to them" (Matt. 11.4-5).

JESUS' MIRACLES

71 The first of Jesus' miracles was worked at Cana. While He was attending a wedding reception with His disciples and His mother, the wine ran out. At Mary's request, and in order to build faith, Jesus changed ordinary water, six large stone jars of it, into wine (cf. John 2.1-11).

It was the first of many signs. Jesus continued to exert divine power over physical nature throughout His ministry. Once when He was out on the Sea of Galilee with His disciples a big storm came up. Jesus had fallen asleep. In a panic the disciples awakened Him. Jesus brought the wind and the waves under control immediately by commanding them to be calm (cf. Matt. 8.23-27; Mark 4.35-41; Luke 8.22-25).

324 Jesus' fame spread with the reports of such incidents. But an even more urgent desire to come to Jesus was created by His many healing miracles. One Sabbath morning, Jesus was told that the mother-in-law of His disciple Peter was ill with a high fever. Jesus went to her, ordered the fever to cease, and helped her up. She was cured instantly (cf. Matt. 8.14-15; Mark 1.29-31; Luke 4.38-39).

Once word got abroad of such healing power, Jesus became a symbol of hope for the afflicted.

11 Jesus did not want men to develop a taste for "signs and wonders" (John 4.48). Rather, He wished the signs to lead men to faith in a divine presence and mercy more important than any sign.

One of Jesus' more frequent signs was a demonstration of His superiority over the powers of darkness by driving out devils from the possessed. The reaction of those who made themselves His rivals was not to celebrate the triumph of good over evil, but to accuse Jesus of collaboration with the very demons He was exorcising: "He casts out demons by the prince of demons" (Matt. 9.34; cf. Matt. 8.28-34, 9.32-34, 12.22-28). Jesus exposed the fallacy of their position by drawing the hearers' attention to those among their own people who also cast out evil spirits, and, especially, to His own consistent goodness.

JESUS' PREACHING

The miracles, impressive as they were, were only one reason why people not only came to Jesus but stayed with Him. A major attraction was His preaching itself. Jesus' manner of speaking was both simple and profound. Even the illiterate crowds could grasp His message; even the most sophisticated were astounded at its wisdom and depth. Even those who went to spy on Him in a hostile spirit reported: "No man ever spoke like this man!" (John 7.46). One of the keys to this happy combination was His skillful use of comparisons and parables.

The parables reflect the agricultural background of most of the Palestinians and speak of the most ordinary activities and things of their everyday lives: the sowing and harvesting of crops, the baking of bread, the lending and losing of money, the patching of clothes, and so on. Yet He used these simple examples to teach important lessons or to show the paradoxical nature of commonplace events in a way that captures the interest of readers down to our own day.

The value of these stories, however, lies not simply in their style, but in the fact that Jesus uses them to communicate the nuances of a religious message. Jesus' preaching presents the kingdom of heaven, the reign that God intends to exercise among men; the parables illustrate, in an analogous way, various aspects of that kingdom.

Many parables center on the theme of the Father's great kindness and generosity in His dealings with us.

Jesus' parables also teach that the Father's concern for sinners requires an appropriate response and that the opportunities for this are conditioned with a deadline (cf. Luke 16.19-31).

Another major theme is that of love of neighbor. When asked to identify the greatest of the commandments, Jesus ranked concern for one's neighbor second only to the obligation to love God. It is this moral

316 which is incorporated into the story of the good Samaritan (cf. Luke 10.29-37).

As Jesus presented all these teachings, the crowds were impressed not only with their content, but also with the fact that Jesus taught as one having authority, not in the manner of their professional teachers, the scribes, who could do little more than debate theological opinions (cf. Matt. 7.28-29; Mark 1.22; Luke 4.32, 7.1; John 7.15).

But just as the signs of Jesus had occasioned opposition from religious sects within Judaism, notably from the fanatically traditionalistic Pharisees, so did His teaching. His opponents tried persistently to catch Him doing or saying something against the normative parts of the Old Testament, the "Law and the Prophets." He went out of His way to fulfill obligations such as the payment of the temple tax and the observance of the pilgrimage feasts. In fact, though grace would make their
183 burden light, Jesus made even greater demands on His own followers (cf. Matt. 5.20-48).

In these and similar cases Jesus showed that an important distinction was to be made between observance of the true spirit of the law and an insensitive literalism. On the strength of this He corrected the customary interpretations of the law concerning certain Sabbath practices (cf. John 5.8-11). This He did not only because as God's true Son He was Lord of the Sabbath (cf. Matt. 12.8; Mark 2.28; Luke 6.5), but because "the sabbath was made for man, not man for the sabbath" (Mark 2.27).

JESUS HIMSELF

People were attracted to Jesus for a third reason, one even stronger than that of His miracles and His preaching. The external activity of
65 this Galilean Preacher pointed to Him Himself as the strongest attraction of all.

In all His signs, Jesus never did anything merely for His own personal advantage. He showed a consistent and deep concern for others. He cared about people and their problems: the embarrassed wedding couple at Cana (cf. John 2.1-11), the sick and the possessed (cf. Luke 4.40-41), the parents of ailing children (cf. Luke 8.40-56). He had time for women with marriage problems (cf. John 4.15-30) and for mothers who wanted Him to bless their children (Mark 10.13-16). He talked about loving those around Him and He accepted dinner invitations from both sinners and those who harassed Him in His work (cf. Matt. 9.11).

When those who followed Him a long time to hear Him speak did not have enough to eat, He multiplied food for them (cf. John 6.1-15).

Nevertheless, as His contemporaries slowly became aware, Jesus was far more than just an exemplary human being. At first, this fact was not taken by many as a serious possibility. But eventually, the mounting evidence demanded a decision one way or the other, and independently of anything else Jesus said or did, His identity became the key issue (cf. John 6.42; Matt. 16.13-16).

This was at least as apparent to His enemies as it was to His friends. "We stone You for no good work but for blasphemy; because You, being a man, make Yourself God" (John 10.32-33).

Here was the enigma. God's living Word has taken on flesh and dwelt among and beside us. To those who could accept this fact, He of- 60 fered Himself as the Way (cf. John 14.6). Acceptance of Jesus for what He is with all its consequences is what the arrival of the kingdom of God means.

JESUS' CHURCH

As Jesus continued to teach and defend His doctrine, it became increasingly obvious that He was inviting people to a relationship with God that could not be contained within the religious institutions of Judaism.

In effect, Jesus was offering the possibility of a new covenant with God, the opportunity to belong to a new people, to be the subjects of God's kingdom. There were very demanding requirements for entrance into this kingdom: faith in the signs of Jesus and the realities they pointed to, faith in the teachings of Jesus about the Father and the kind of response the Father wants from men, and personal faith in Jesus as the Cornerstone of the whole arrangement (cf. LG 5, 7, 8).

Jesus looked for this faith among the band of disciples. When He found this faith among them, He strengthened and prepared it for the 125 future.

First, the disciples underwent careful and extensive education. They were not only present when Jesus spoke to larger audiences, but they had ample opportunity to ask questions about things they had not understood in the public discourses. They were tutored in the attitudes necessary for prayer through instruction, example, and sharing Jesus' own prayer life.

Secondly, they were directed to missionary work and their fledg-

164 ling efforts in this were carefully supervised by Jesus so that they would learn what to preach and how to conduct themselves, especially in the face of opposition and adversity (cf. Luke 10.1-16).

Thirdly, they were given a share in Jesus' power and authority. Those who were sent out on mission participated in His ability to cure and to exorcise evil spirits (cf. Matt. 10.1). Moreover, they were promised: "He who hears you hears Me, and he who rejects you rejects Me, and he who rejects Me rejects Him who sent Me" (Luke 10.16; cf. LG 18-29).

At first, the disciples had difficulty in deciding just who Jesus was. 125 Eventually they came to firm faith. The leader among them, Simon Peter, expressed it for all who believed when he confessed to Jesus: "You are the Christ, the Son of the living God" (Matt. 16.16).

His disciples had found faith in Him. Now Christ was able to turn their eyes toward the cross, and to help them see His mission as Savior. "From that time Jesus began to show His disciples that He must go to Jerusalem and suffer many things . . . and be killed, and on the third day be raised" (Matt. 16.21).

•   •   •

Questions related to the material in this chapter:

1. Does any firsthand reliable historical account of Christ exist today?

2. With what events do we connect the beginning of the public life and work of Jesus?

3. What was the first of Jesus' signs or miracles?

4. Why did Jesus work miracles?

5. Why did Jesus use parables in His teaching?

6. What are some of the major themes of Jesus' preaching and teaching?

7. Jesus is described as a strong personality. In what way can we describe this strong personality?

8. When Jesus taught and worked miracles people came to love and follow Him. What were some of the reasons for this attraction and attachment?

9. Is there any reason to believe that Jesus intended to organize His disciples and form them into a Church?

9

By Dying
He Destroyed Our Death

"We believe that our Lord Jesus Christ by the sacrifice of the cross redeemed us from original sin and all the personal sins committed by each one of us, so that, in accordance with the word of the apostle, 'where sin abounded, grace did more abound' (Rom. 5.20)."[1]

In this chapter we speak of Jesus Christ the Redeemer, of His passion and death for us, and of the meaning of our redemption.

JESUS CAME TO SAVE US

The Son of God became man to save us. Christ is shown in the New Testament as one fully aware that His mission was to suffer and die for us, and to bring us to life. He Himself foretold His passion, death, and resurrection (cf. Luke 18.31-33). But His disciples could not begin to understand this mystery of redemption (cf. Luke 18.34) until it had been accomplished (cf. Luke 24.25).

The "Necessity" of the Passion

The passion of our Lord was not something which absolutely had to be. Certainly God did not have to save man when man fell into sin. And certainly God could have saved man in any of many other ways. He could simply have forgiven the sin.

It was God's will, however, that redemption be achieved in the 169 most perfect and fitting way. For this, it was necessary that the Son of God should become man and suffer. It is in this sense, then, that we speak of the necessity of Jesus' passion and death.

Jesus Himself declared that He had to suffer to bring us eternal life (cf. John 3.14-15). He had to suffer, for His eternal Father willed that His human nature, the crown and unifying bond of all creation, should 269 receive its glory as a fruit of the cross (cf. Luke 24.26). Prophetic words

---

[1] Pope Paul VI, *Professio Fidei* ("The Credo of the People of God," June 30, 1968).

had foretold Christ's sufferings; the Gospels allude to these often (esp. Isa. 53 and Ps. 22). These prophecies were expressions of God's will, and they had to be fulfilled (cf. Luke 24.44).

Perfect Redeemer

Jesus was sent into this world as a perfect Redeemer. Though He is God, He is also truly man, our brother.

62   Because His humanity is the humanity of One who is the Son of God, His saving acts are the acts of a Person who is God. They have, then, superabundant value (cf. Rom. 5.15-21). The man Christ Jesus, who is God's true Son, is the only One who could offer the Father a fitting atonement for sin.

Mediator

Jesus is our "Mediator." He who is Himself God and man rescued man from his alienation and misery and restored him to peace with the Father.

The mediation Jesus achieved through His passion is unique. Only He who is God and man could in such a way restore men to their God.[2]

151   Others may play a role in His saving work, but only in a secondary way, and in total dependence upon Jesus, for He is the necessary and indispensable Mediator of peace. "For there is one God, and there is one mediator between God and men, the man Christ Jesus" (1 Tim. 2.5).

Perfect Act of Redemption

That Christ should redeem us by the cross was willed by God as a 193 most fitting way to save us. The cross of Christ teaches us the gross malice of sin.

In the heroism of the passion Christ gave us a pattern for the obedience, humility, and steadfastness we need to serve God faithfully, and He showed us the need to do works of justice and mercy even if we ourselves are being treated unjustly.

Most of all, the passion was the perfect form of redemption because it best reveals the greatness of God's love (cf. John 3.16). Man needed to

---

[2]Cf. St. Thomas Aquinas, *Summa Theologica* III, 26, 1-2.

see how much he is loved by his God, so that he would learn to love God in return.

THE PASSION OF JESUS

Jesus was rejected by those to whom He came. His passion, however, was a sign of such great love (cf. John 15.13) that men would ever after be drawn to Him (cf. John 12.32).

When the early Church preached the good news of salvation, it preached, as the Church still preaches, the infinite love that shines from the cross of Christ. "We preach Christ crucified" (1 Cor. 1.23). "But far be it from me to glory except in the cross of our Lord Jesus Christ" (Gal. 6.14).

Last Supper

In each of the Gospels the passion narrative begins with an account of the Last Supper. Christ there clarified the meaning of His sufferings and revealed the greatness of His saving love. He instituted the sacrament of the Eucharist, and the priesthood which serves the Eucharist. He made it clear that His death would inaugurate a new and eternal cov- 55 enant between men and their God and that He, in His cross and His saving mercy, would always be present to His disciples in His sacrifice of the Mass (cf. Matt. 26.26-28; Mark 14.22-24; Luke 22.19-20; 1 Cor. 277 11.23-25).[3]

Christ also spoke with clarity of the Father and of the Holy Spirit, for by the cross He was to bring us to be children of God in whom the Blessed Trinity would dwell (cf. John 14.9-26). Then in words addressed to the Father He showed what the cross would accomplish: the human unity in the love of God that it would make possible (cf. John 17.1-26). There too He promulgated a new commandment: "A new command I give to you, that you love one another; even as I have loved you, that you also love one another" (John 13.34).

Agony in the Garden

After the Last Supper, Jesus went with His disciples to the Mount of Olives, and there in a garden He prayed to His Father. He began to

---

[3]Cf. Council of Trent, Session 22, September 17, 1562, *Doctrine on the Most Holy Sacrifice of the Mass,* ch. 1 (DS 1739-1742).

feel dread of the sufferings He was about to experience (cf. Matt. 26.39). So great was His anguish that "His sweat became like great drops of blood falling down upon the ground" (Luke 22.44). His human heart and will yet remained steadfastly loyal to the Father: "Nevertheless, not as I will, but as You will" (Matt. 26.39).

237

Trials and Sentencing

With great patience Jesus underwent unjust trials before the priests, Herod, and Pilate. He was the target of insults and mockery; He was denied, as He Himself had foretold, three times by Peter; He was scourged, spat upon, and crowned with thorns. Finally Pilate, after halfhearted attempts to spare Jesus, in the face of a crowd grown hostile, sentenced Him to die on the cross.

The Crucifixion

Upon the cross Jesus suffered extreme physical pain. But even in the terrible torment of those hours, Jesus, the Son of God and High Priest of our salvation, retained patience and greatness of soul. Some insight into His mind and heart may be gained from His "seven last words" as recorded in the Gospels:

- "Father, forgive them; for they know not what they do" (Luke 23.34).

- To a thief who had been crucified with Him and who asked for mercy: "Truly, I say to you, today you will be with Me in Paradise" (Luke 23.43).

150

- To His mother and to the apostle John: "Woman, behold, your son! . . . Behold, your mother!" (John 19.26-27).

- In prayerful words drawn from a prophetic Psalm: "My God, My God, why have You forsaken Me?" (Matt. 27.46; cf. Ps. 22.1).

- "I thirst" (John 19.28).

- "It is finished" (John 19.30).

- Again in words drawn from a prophetic Psalm: "Father, into Your hands I commit My spirit" (Luke 23.46; cf. Ps. 31.5).

Jesus then "bowed His head and gave up His spirit" (John 19.30). Thus the Son of God died for us sinners.

The passion of Jesus has eternal effects. Through His suffering we were saved from sin and all its consequences, and have received every 171 grace and gift leading to eternal life.

This liberation won for us by Jesus in His passion has effects even in this world. Men freed from sin can transform this world also into a kingdom of greater freedom, justice, and peace, into an image and even a beginning of God's kingdom.

God Triumphs in Christ

"God was in Christ reconciling the world to Himself" (2 Cor. 5.19). It is God Himself who is always the Savior. The eternal love and power of the Father, Son, and Holy Spirit effected man's redemption. God triumphed in Christ, winning victory over sin and Satan, over the bondage of the old law and of death. 344

Jesus Redeemed Us

The Catholic faith firmly teaches that Jesus truly saved us (cf. Matt. 1.21) by deeds performed in His human nature, by His obedient love and patient endurance (cf. Heb. 5.8) and by offering "His own life as a ransom for the many" (Matt. 20.28). Jesus as man freed us from sin.

Jesus the Priest

Jesus is the "great high priest" (Heb. 4.14) of the new and everlasting covenant (cf. Heb. 3-10). From the moment Jesus entered this world He was a priest (cf. Heb. 5-7). In His public life He performed the priestly work of teaching, forgiving sins, sanctifying. As a priest of a new order, superior to every former priesthood (cf. Heb. 7.1-28), He an- 287 nounced the new covenant with God at the sacrificial banquet of the Last Supper, revealing there also the sacrificial nature of His then-impending death. By offering the one perfect sacrifice of Himself, He achieved eternal salvation for us, and abrogated the previous covenant and priesthood (cf. Heb. 9.1-10.18).

His sacrificial death established a new covenant. He as priest generously offered Himself "by His death on the altar of the cross to God the Father, so that He might there accomplish an eternal redemption."[4]

---

[4]Council of Trent, Session 22, September 17, 1562, *Doctrine on the Most Holy Sacrifice of the Mass,* ch. 1 (DS 1739).

Reconciliation

Christ's passion was a work of reconciliation. Because Christ's saving love atoned for man's sin, it made possible a healing for all the
194 divisions and hostility that had been created by sin.

Christ "is our peace . . . and has broken down the dividing wall of hostility" (Eph. 2.15). Through Christ the Father willed "to reconcile to Himself all things, whether on earth or in heaven, making peace through the blood of His cross" (Col. 1.20).

The Cross and Resurrection

The sufferings of Jesus and the glory of His resurrection are inseparably joined in the paschal mystery. "By dying he destroyed our death; by rising he restored our life."[5] Christ merited all blessings for us and glory for Himself by the cross; in the resurrection God confers the graces and gifts won by Jesus through His sufferings and obedient love.

Christ Died for All

God "desires all men to be saved" (1 Tim. 2.4), and so Christ "died for all" (2 Cor. 2.15).
241 Although Christ did indeed die for all men, He does not force anyone to accept eternal life. Only those to whom the merit of His passion is communicated are saved, but through His Holy Spirit He saves all who are willing. The invitation is to all, even the unwilling.

Redemption Completed and Continuing

Christ has redeemed us. This is a fact. St. Paul writes to the early Christians in Corinth: "Therefore, if anyone is in Christ, he is a new creation; the old has passed away, behold, the new has come. All this is from God, who through Christ reconciled us to Himself" (2 Cor. 5.17-18). But the saving work of Jesus is yet to be received in the lives of many, and the full flowering of its richness is yet to be seen. There is apostolic work yet to be done, and, as St. Paul goes on to say, God "gave us the ministry of reconciliation" (2 Cor. 5.18).

---

[5]Roman Missal, Preface I for Easter.

THE CROSS IN CHRISTIAN LIFE

The cross is part of every Christian life. By Christ's cross and resurrection men are saved. The sacraments are sacred signs and instruments through which Jesus communicates the fruits of redemption 270
from the tree of the cross. Nothing of Christian life can be understood
apart from the cross.

Jesus taught His disciples ever to carry the cross: "If any man
would come after Me, let him deny himself and take up his cross daily
and follow Me" (Luke 9.23). The crosses in our daily lives, the difficul- 245
ties and sufferings, and the self-denials and sacrifices willingly offered,
are made saving and sacred by His holy cross.

"By suffering for us He not only provided us with an example, for
us to follow in His steps (cf. 1 Peter 2.21; Matt. 15.24; Luke 14.27), but
He also opened the way, and if we follow that way, life and death are
made holy and take on a new meaning" (GS 22).

*   *   *

Questions related to the material in this chapter:

1. What was the purpose of the Incarnation? Why did the Son of
God become man?

2. Did Jesus "will" to die for us or did He "have" to?

3. We say that Jesus is our Mediator. In the context of Sacred
Scripture, what does the word "mediator" mean here?

4. Why does the account of the passion and death of Christ form so
important a part of the Church's retelling of Jesus' life and mission?

5. When did the Last Supper take place and under what circumstances?

6. In what sense did Jesus undergo an "agony" in the garden the
night before He died?

7. What are the biblical sources for the five decades of the rosary
called the Sorrowful Mysteries?

8. Why do you think the early Church bothered to record the
words of Jesus on the cross?

9. What was accomplished by Christ's death on the cross?

10. When we say Jesus is the Eternal High Priest, what do we mean?

11. How was Christ's passion a work of reconciliation?

12. If Jesus died once and for all, how can we speak of redemption both as completed and as continuing?

13. What do we mean when we say that every Christian must carry the cross?

10

By Rising
He Restored Our Life

The Church celebrates the resurrection of Jesus with surpassing joy. For the rising of Jesus not only confirms the Church's faith, but is the central mystery through which God calls us to life.

In this chapter we speak of the mystery of the resurrection, of what it means to believe in the resurrection, and of the reality of the Lord's rising in the flesh, in the very body which was crucified. We also speak of the ascension of Jesus, in which His enduring presence among men acquired a new form.

THE MYSTERY OF THE RESURRECTION

"The Lord has risen indeed . . . !" (Luke 24.34). The Easter announcement is about a singular event of universal significance. It was at a particular time, "on the third day,"[1] that is, on the second day after the day of the death on the cross. It was in a particular place, in a stone sepulchre near the site of the crucifixion on Golgotha (cf. John 19.41). Then and there God raised from the dead and elevated to Himself a particular man, Jesus of Nazareth.

From the first day that the apostles preached the Gospel (cf. Acts 2.14-36) the resurrection of Jesus has been the core of the good news. 269 The Catholic faith has ever taught, and ever teaches against all denials, that Christ's rising from the dead was an historical event for which there is convincing evidence.

By His Own Power

Faithful to the message of Scripture, the Church teaches both that the Father raised Jesus from the dead and that Jesus rose by His own power. "God raised Him up" (Acts 2.24). "I lay down My life, that I may take it again. . . . I have power to take it again" (John 10.17-18).

---

[1]Apostles' Creed.

93

The explanation is this: It was by the power of God that the human- ity of Jesus was raised from the dead. This power of the one God belongs to the Father and the Son equally. When the resurrection is seen as the seal of the Father's approval, the glorification of Jesus' humanity is viewed as the work of the Father; when it is seen as a manifestation of Jesus' divine power and personality, it is viewed as the act of the Son Himself.

THE RESURRECTION AND FAITH

Sincere belief in the resurrection does not spring up casually. To believe in the resurrection is to believe firmly that a Man who died a cruel death on the cross returned to life. It is to believe that He rose to a new kind of life, that He returned to His friends in the same flesh which was crucified and as the same person, but now glorified, no longer sub- ject to the limiting conditions of ordinary life (cf. John 20.19; 1 Cor. 15- 42-49).

Christ's death had been a devastating blow to His apostles. They had truly had hope in Him (cf. Luke 24.21), but after the tragedy of the cross they were not prepared to believe again. The Gospels make no secret of these early doubts (cf. Matt. 28.17; Mark 16.11-24). When the risen Jesus appeared to His followers, almost always additional proofs were required to identify Him.

By His presence, words, and gestures, Christ led His apostles to- ward faith. By His tangible presence He made them realize that His res- urrection was indeed real, not a dream or illusion. He enabled them to see the meaning of His rising, to see that it was an event that illumines all history and heals all sorrows.

But the outer signs and words were confirmed also by the inner gift of the Spirit. By valid signs they were led to faith, but by God's inner gift faith was made immovably strong.

Belief and Unbelief

The risen Christ was not seen by all, but by "us who were chosen by God as witnesses" (Acts 10.41). Still, to all to whom His word is addressed, He gives sufficient evidence of His resurrection in forms ap- propriate to their circumstances.

For those in Jerusalem at the time, there was the witness of the empty tomb. But there was also much more: the transformation of the

94

apostles and the confident testimony they gave to the risen Christ, the miraculous cures they worked in His name (cf. Acts 4.9-10; 5.12-16), and the new energy of their lives that gave evidence of the inner presence of the Spirit. Many saw these signs and believed, and they too received the gift of the Spirit and began to share in the life of the resurrection.

Through all the ages of Christian history there have been persons who have tried to explain away the Easter events. Often such persons seem to forget or ignore completely the nature of the facts and experiences to be explained. Some declare that Christ did not actually die on the cross, but in fact survived to serve as a sort of underground leader. Others say that purely subjective experiences led the apostles to a sincere but false belief that Christ had risen. Some others suggest that the apostles may indeed have had real visions, and that in some spiritual way Jesus may yet continue to be, and even manifest Himself, but that all of this is to be understood without the "scandal" of a risen body. And there are still others who more subtly insist that the proclamation of the resurrection is not to be taken as a claim that Jesus literally rose from the dead, but rather as an assertion that Jesus still lives in the sense that His cause lives on in the continuing struggle against hatred and oppression.

Clearly none of these positions explains the reality of what did in fact occur. Doubts there were, but the resurrection was a fact. The persistent mercy of Christ, His own showing of Himself (cf. Matt. 28.17), and the reasonableness of trustworthy testimony conquered the doubts. 135

The Test of Gamaliel

Believers today do not see all the same evidences that men of apostolic times saw. Nevertheless, many signs of His resurrection still shine in the Church that is built upon Christ. There is clearly the sign that the Pharisee Gamaliel said would be decisive.

Gamaliel it was who urged caution on the Sanhedrin when that body wanted to kill the apostles (cf. Acts 5.33). Gamaliel reminded the council of earlier movements which had died out quickly once their leaders were dead. The apostles were in fact making broad and startling claims. But Gamaliel gave the council this advice: "If this plan or this undertaking is of men, it will fail; but if it is of God, you will not be able to overthrow them. You might even be found opposing God!" (Acts 5.38-39). If Christianity had died out long ago, if its ability to win con-

verts had not continued through the centuries, then Christianity would
122 have shown itself to be a human enterprise. But Christianity did not die
out. For Christianity comes from God.

THE BODILY RESURRECTION

The records of the New Testament tell what actually happened and
make sense of what followed in history. Faith in Christ's rising changed
the world. This faith sprang up after Jesus had died in disgrace. His followers proclaimed and announced Him with confidence and persis-
tence, and they showed they were prepared even to suffer pain and
disgrace gladly in His name (cf. Acts 5.41).

Faith in the resurrection survived because Christ truly rose. His
witnesses were truthful, and His living power remained in them and in
their words.

359 St. Paul speaks of the many who saw the risen Christ appear. "For I
delivered to you as of first importance what I also received, that Christ
died for our sins in accordance with the scriptures, that He was buried,
that He was raised on the third day in accordance with the scriptures,
and that He appeared to Cephas, then to the twelve. Then He appeared
to more than five hundred brethren at one time, most of whom are still
alive, though some have fallen asleep. Then He appeared to James, then
to all the apostles. Last of all, as to one untimely born, He appeared also
to me" (1 Cor. 15.3-8).

It was only about thirty years after the death of Jesus when St. Paul
wrote these words, and he here refers to his earlier instruction of the
Corinthians in what he himself had "received," that is, at a time earlier
still. Most of the men he mentions were alive when he wrote, and thus
they were available to confirm or deny the accuracy of his statements
about them. This passage of St. Paul shows clearly that belief in the resurrection of Jesus formed part of the earliest confessions of faith of the
Christian community.

The appearances of the risen Christ are recorded in varying ways
by the evangelists. But in spite of the variations in the formulations, the
Easter message ever exhibits the same essential aspects and is based on
the same facts.

The Very One Who Died

All the scriptural accounts insist that the risen Jesus is truly the
same Jesus who had died. The disciples not only see the risen Christ

with their eyes, but they are urged to touch His solid flesh and know that He is bodily among them (cf. Luke 24.39). When doubts arise, the risen Jesus asks for food, so that by the act of eating He might convince them of the tangible reality of the resurrection (Luke 24.41-43). Thomas is invited to examine the wounds (cf. John 20.27), to see that it is the very body that was crucified that is now present to give life.

Easter faith is newness of life, and it is firmly rooted in the personal 301 and concrete Christ. Belief in the bodily rising of Jesus is not in itself acceptance of the fullness of the Easter mystery, but it is an indispensable grounding for the new life. The Jesus who is alive now is the same Jesus who was dead before. The witnesses of Christ understood the resurrection in the factual terms of a Man who died, was buried, and then came to life again.

The fact of the resurrection is of fundamental importance. "If Christ has not been raised, then our preaching is in vain and your faith is in vain. . . . If Christ has not been raised, your faith is futile and you are still in your sins. Then those also who have fallen asleep in Christ have perished" (1 Cor. 15.14, 17-18).

FULFILLMENT OF DIVINE PROMISES

Jesus rose on the third day "in fulfillment of the Scriptures."[2] The rising of Jesus was not merely a happy incident, nor was it simply a dramatic way of signifying Christ's divine authority. Rather, it was an event predestined from the beginning of creation. The New Testament 55 recalls prophetic statements concerning the resurrection not only to fortify faith in the truth of Christ's rising, but also to show the centrality of this work in God's plan of salvation.

Though the Old Testament references are not always clear, the apostolic Church, aided by the Holy Spirit, saw the resurrection of Jesus as the fulfillment of prophecies such as this in Isaiah: "He shall see the fruit of the travail of His soul and be satisfied; by His knowledge shall the righteous one, My Servant, make many to be accounted righteous; and He shall bear their iniquities. Therefore I will divide Him a portion with the great, and He shall divide the spoil with the strong" (Isa. 53.11-12). That is, in the mind of the apostolic Church the resurrection is the response of the Father to the submission of Christ on the cross, the reward given to the Servant who has been obedient unto death (cf. Phil. 2.7-8).

---

[2]Roman Missal, The Order of Mass, Profession of Faith.

The Church also sees in the resurrection of Jesus the deepest meaning of those passages of deliverance in the Psalms such as this: "Therefore my heart is glad, and my soul rejoices; my body also dwells secure. For You do not give me up to Sheol, or let Your godly one see the Pit" (Ps. 16.9-10; cf. Acts 2.31; 13.36).

The Father's Seal of Approval

Thus the glorified Jesus appears as vindicated in His Messianic prerogatives. His resurrection evidences the Father's approval and ratification of Christ and His work (cf. Acts 3.13-15).

The resurrection of Jesus assures us that the death of Jesus was pleasing to the Father, that His miracles were performed with the power and approval of God, and that His teachings and commandments were teachings and commandments intended by God for us. Because of the resurrection we are sure we are right when we take Christ as our way to the Father.

The resurrection points also to the transcendence of Christ. The title *Kyrios*, "Lord," is always attributed to the risen Christ. With this title the New Testament writers proclaim His sovereignty. Christ acknowledged by the Father, shining in Easter glory, is recognized as Lord just as the Father is Lord.

THE POWER OF THE RESURRECTION

The resurrection does far more than confirm the eternal value of Jesus' life and work.

It is the risen Jesus Himself who gives persons of faith the ability to experience His presence. He does this by allowing them to share in His own life, by bringing them even now, in their lives here on earth, into a real participation in His new way of existence. This He does by bringing the faithful to a true mystical death, burial, resurrection, and ascension with Him in order that they might receive, as members of His mystical body, a share in His spirit.

Jesus came in order to lead humanity into a "spiritual incorruption" by a radical transformation. He Himself, as the new Adam, as the Head of the new generation, is both the model and the means of this transformation. The rising of Him who is the "first fruits of those who have fallen asleep" (1 Cor. 15.20) is the prototype and the beginning of the transformation of man.

356

98

The resurrection of Jesus, then, is the foundation of the Christian life of faith, prayer, and spiritual growth. Jesus' resurrection and glorification provide the basis for our hope and faith in the immortal life of our bodies after the final resurrection at the end of time.

THE ASCENSION INTO HEAVEN

The Easter mystery approaches its culmination in the ascension of Jesus. After His appearances here on earth in His risen body, and "after He had given commandment through the Holy Spirit to the apostles whom He had chosen" (Acts 1.2), Jesus "was lifted up, and a cloud took Him out of their sight" (Acts 1.9). He ascended "with the flesh in which He had risen and with His soul."[3]

The mystery of the ascension has two distinct aspects. First, it is the glorification of Jesus. Secondly, the ascension indicates the time when Christ brought His visible ministry on earth to completion.

St. Luke notes that forty days elapsed between the resurrection and the ascension (cf. Acts 1.3). But the time is not the essential point. Nor does belief in the ascension involve any special cosmological theories, or any doctrinal positions on spatial relationships between heaven and our planet earth. When Scripture says Christ "ascended far above all the heavens" (Eph. 4.10) it is not teaching astronomy, but telling the status of the glorified Redeemer sitting at the right hand of the Father (cf. Eph. 1.20).

The ascension is not an event which changes the relationship of Jesus to heaven, but it does affect His relationship to the world. Jesus in His ascension is not turning away from the earth, but His relationship to earth is no longer limited to specific times and places. In His glorified life He makes all times and places present to Himself.

He has ascended, but He has not abandoned us. He comes to the Father as the eternal High Priest, "able for all time to save those who draw near to God through Him, since He always lives to make intercession for them" (Heb. 7.25). Scriptural accounts of the ascension relate the event to the sending of the Holy Spirit and to the mission of the Church. Through His Holy Spirit and the life the Spirit nourishes in the Church, the risen Christ will be present to those who belong to Him. He will be with the Church always (cf. Matt. 28.20). He is present in the 251

---

[3]Second Council of Lyons, Session 4, July 6, 1274, *Profession of Faith of Emperor Michael Paleologus* (DS 852).

268 Church's life of faith and prayer, and especially in the sacramental meetings with His glorified body. He is present also in our life of chari₋ ty.

Christ Himself will remain with us through the gift of the Holy Spirit. "When the Spirit of truth comes, He will guide you into all the truth. . . . He will glorify Me, for He will take what is Mine and declare it to you" (John 16.13-14).

·   ·   ·

Questions related to the material in this chapter:

1. How would you describe the central fact of Christian faith?

2. Did Jesus return from the dead by His own power?

3. Even though the resurrection is a fact, faith is required to accept it. Is there any evidence in Scripture that the apostles and disciples had doubts before coming to faith in the resurrection?

4. Why have so many tried so hard to explain away the resurrection of Christ?

5. What was the so-called "test of Gamaliel"?

6. Why does the Church teach that Christ rose bodily from the dead?

7. Is Jesus risen from the dead the same Jesus who died on the cross at Calvary?

8. Does the resurrection of Christ have any effect on the whole of creation according to God's plan?

9. The mystery of the ascension has two distinct aspects. What are they?

10. How is the event of the ascension related to the sending of the Holy Spirit and to the mission of the Church?

11

The Holy Spirit

"We believe in the Holy Spirit, the Lord, the giver of life, who proceeds from the Father and the Son."[1] The Holy Spirit is a Person of the Blessed Trinity, truly and eternally God.

In this chapter we speak of the Holy Spirit, of His work in the Church, of His presence in each member of the faithful, and of the gifts He gives, distributing them to each one as He wills (cf. 1 Cor. 12.11).

THE SPIRIT OF GOD

Catholic faith believes that God dwells with us most intimately by 241 the gift of the Holy Spirit. The Spirit is sent by the eternal Father and by Jesus to give light, comfort, and strength, and to stir up within us a newness of life. The Holy Spirit seals our friendship with God (cf. 2 Cor. 1.22), and He unites us with one another by the divine love He pours forth in our hearts (cf. Rom. 5.5).

The centuries of salvation history saw a gradual revelation of the 110 Holy Spirit. The Old Testament shows a developing awareness and understanding of the working of God's Spirit in this world. But the mystery of the Trinity, one God in three divine Persons, was not yet revealed. Not until the era of the New Testament, in the paschal mystery and in the joys of Pentecost, was the Holy Spirit revealed as a distinct divine Person.

In the Old Testament

The presence of God through His Spirit is suggested through several analogies in the Old Testament. The prophets used the word *Shekinah* to describe God's presence among His people, a presence sometimes manifested visibly by a light, a cloud, or a wind. The Hebrew word for Spirit, *Ruah,* has many closely interrelated meanings: it is 31

---

[1] Roman Missal, The Order of Mass, Profession of Faith.

spirit, and breath; it is the source of life breathed forth by God; through it God is present and active in this world.

Breath and spirit signified also the dynamic force under which a person acts, whether for good or for evil.

The Spirit of the Lord descended upon the prophets (cf. Isa. 61.1; Jer. 1.4); under His impetus they could proclaim the word of the Lord with courage and absolute faithfulness.

The Old Testament belief in the Spirit looked forward to a future fulfillment. The days would come when God would pour out His Spirit on all mankind (cf. Isa. 44.3; Ezek. 36.26-27; Joel 2.28-29). Most of all, 309 the Messiah who was awaited would be entirely filled with the Holy Spirit (cf. Isa. 9.6, 11.2-3, 42.1).

Thus the Old Testament speaks of the coming of the Spirit of God as a presence of God, acting with living energy from within. But the Old Testament does not speak of the Holy Spirit as a divine Person distinct from the Father.

In the Gospels

It is through Jesus that the mystery of the inner life of God is revealed to us. He it is who made men know more fully the Father. It is also through Jesus that the Spirit of God is revealed most richly, as a Person distinct from the Father and the Son, as the personal Love within the Trinity that is the source and pattern of all created love (cf. GS 24).

74 The Gospels speak often of the Spirit in. describing the events surrounding the conception and birth of Jesus. The Gospel of St. Matthew tells us that Mary "was found to be with child of the Holy Spirit" (Matt. 1.18), and that Joseph was told by an angel: "That which is conceived in her is of the Holy Spirit" (Matt. 1.20). In the Gospel of St. Luke we read of the earlier Annunciation to Mary. When Mary had asked how she, a virgin, could conceive, the angel had replied: "The Holy Spirit will come upon you, and the power of the Most High will overshadow you" (Luke 1.35). When Elizabeth was visited by Mary, Elizabeth was "filled with the Holy Spirit" (Luke 1.41). Zechariah too was "filled with the Holy Spirit" (Luke 1.67) when he uttered his prophecy at the time of John's circumcision. When Simeon held the infant Jesus in his arms, he was able to speak of Jesus' saving work, for he had received a special revelation from the Holy Spirit (cf. Luke 2.25-35).

While the Gospels speak often of the Holy Spirit, the words that speak of Him most clearly as a Person distinct from the Father and the Son are those of Christ at the Last Supper and after His resurrection. Jesus refers to Him as a "paraclete," or "counselor," that is, an ad- 313 vocate, comforter, or helper.

In these passages the Holy Spirit is clearly presented as One who is a Person as the Father and Son are Persons, and yet One who is distinct from the Father and the Son, and sent to us by the Father and the Son.

In Faith and Doctrine

Jesus and the Holy Spirit together were always believed, loved, and adored in the Christian community. Absolute confidence was 113 always placed in Jesus and in His Holy Spirit. Although Scripture nowhere uses the word "Trinity" to express the mystery of the Triune God, the Trinity Itself was certainly known and adored before that word was adapted into special Christian usage.

As the early councils of the Church faithfully expressed the true and eternal relationship between the Father and the Son, so also they expressed the truth about the Holy Spirit. The ancient profession of faith still recited or sung each Sunday at Mass summarizes the Church's belief in the Holy Spirit.[2] The Church proclaims belief in the Holy Spirit in precisely the same way in which it proclaims belief in the Father and in the Son.

The Son is the Word of the Father, eternally begotten; all that the Father is, is perfectly expressed in the eternal Word who is His Son, so that the Son is forever equal to the Father. The Father and the Son love each other with an eternal Love that fully expresses everything that each of Them is, and is eternally equal to each; this Love which proceeds from the Father and the Son is a Person, the eternal Holy Spirit.

Devotion to the Holy Spirit

The warm prayers of the Church to the Holy Spirit, especially on the feast of Pentecost and in administering the sacrament of confirmation, reflect the adoration and devotion to Him that have lived in the Church since earliest times. The witness of the ancient writers of both East and West to this devotion is supported by the evidence of Christian art and archaeology, hymnology, and liturgy. Surges of devotion to

---

[2]Roman Missal, The Order of Mass, Profession of Faith.

the Holy Spirit have marked many periods of Church history, as in the Middle Ages, in the seventeenth century, and in modern times. Papal encyclicals of the past century have done much to encourage this devotion.[3]

THE HOLY SPIRIT AND THE CHURCH

312 Jesus told the apostles that the richest outpouring of the Holy Spirit would come only after His own mission had come to its perfection and He had returned in His glorified humanity to the Father (cf. Acts 1.4-9). The decisive coming of the Spirit on Pentecost is described in the second chapter of the Acts of the Apostles. It is in the scriptural books that record the experiences of the early Church that the meaning and mission of the Holy Spirit are most clearly portrayed.

365 The Church recognizes all the books of the Bible as sacred because, "having been written under the inspiration of the Holy Spirit (cf. John 20.31; 2 Tim. 3.16; 2 Peter 1.19-21; 3.15-16), they have God as their Author" (DV 11).

141
118 The early Fathers of the Church insisted that the Church and the Holy Spirit are inseparable. "Where the Church is, there also is the Spirit of God; and where the Spirit of God is, there is the Church."[4] Today as well the Church proclaims that it is the Holy Spirit who gives life and being to the Church.

The Holy Spirit is the "soul" of the Church,[5] that is, of the Body of Christ. It is the Holy Spirit "who, with His heavenly breath of life, is to be considered the Principle of every vital and truly saving action in all parts of the Body. It is He who, though He is personally present in all the members and is divinely active in them, yet also works in the lower members through the ministry of the higher ones."[6]

The gifts of Christ are poured out upon the Church by the Holy Spirit. All the charisms, free gifts, are intended to increase faith, hope, and love, "for building up the body of Christ, until we all attain to the unity of the faith and of the knowledge of the Son of God" (Eph. 4.12-13).

---

[3]Cf. Pope Leo XIII, Encyclical, *Divinum Illud Munus* (May 9, 1897); Pope Pius XII, Encyclical, *Mystici Corporis* (June 29, 1943).

[4]St. Irenaeus of Lyons, *Adversus Haereses* 3.24.1 (MG 7.966).

[5]Cf. Pope Leo XIII, Encyclical, *Divinum Illud Munus* (May 9, 1897) (DS 3328), with quotation there from St. Augustine, *Sermo* 264.4 (ML 38.1231).

[6]Pope Pius XII, Encyclical, *Mystici Corporis* (June 29, 1943) (DS 3808).

Of primary importance, therefore, are those gifts that minister to the faith, love, and unity of the whole Church, that is, the hierarchical and sacramental gifts of Christ and His Spirit to His people. "The whole 140 flock of Christ is preserved and grows in the unity of faith through the action of the same Holy Spirit" who gives the "charism of the Church's infallibility" (LG 25) to the successor of Peter and the "sure charism of truth" (DV 8) to the successors of all the apostles. It is the Holy Spirit who "calls all men to Christ by the seeds of the word and by the preaching of the Gospel, and stirs up in hearts the obedience of faith" (AG 15).

But the ministry of the word is aimed ultimately at love. We are to recognize and believe God's word, that we might begin to share His love. As we share in His love we participate in His life. To share in the divine life won for us by Jesus Christ is a gift imparted through His sacraments, in which the Holy Spirit also exercises His sanctifying influence.

THE HOLY SPIRIT IN THE FAITHFUL

The Holy Spirit works in the People of God corporately as the Church, but His warmth and love are directed also to each individual Christian.

The essential task of the Holy Spirit within the souls of the faithful 258 is this: to make them holy. To become holy, the Christian must be enlivened and guided by the Spirit. The process of becoming holy begins at baptism, when the Holy Spirit begins to dwell in the soul, to endow it with sanctifying grace, to implant in it faith and love and other rich gifts.

Gifts of the Holy Spirit

All the generous gifts by which God calls us to holiness are attributed to the Holy Spirit, the "Sanctifier." The expression "gifts of the Holy Spirit" is used also in a particular sense, however, to refer to a special set of endowments which are most conducive to growth in the life of grace. These gifts of the Spirit are traditionally enumerated as wisdom, understanding, counsel, fortitude, knowledge, piety, and fear of the Lord (cf. Isa. 11.2-3).

Charismatic Gifts

In addition to the hierarchical and sacramental gifts given to the whole Church to make unity and holiness possible, and in addition to the inner gifts that make individuals holy, there are also many charismatic gifts, or "charisms." These charisms are not given for the sake of their individual recipients alone, but for the benefit of others, "for building up the body of Christ" (Eph. 4.12).

Charisms have an appropriate place in the life of the Church. A mature faith must evaluate them carefully (cf. 1 Cor. 14). Authentic spiritual gifts are the work of the Holy Spirit (cf. 1 Cor. 12.4), and God's favor is received "according to the measure of Christ's gift" (Eph. 4.7). St. Paul always insists that the charisms are intended to unite the Church, not to divide it; though each member may have a special gift, he is to use it for the benefit of all in the unity of faith and love (cf. 1 Cor. 12.22-26).

262 One may rightly desire to have a charism, for authentic charisms serve the good of the Church. All the charisms are of their nature ordered toward "a still more excellent way" (1 Cor. 12.31), that is, the way of Christian love.

By the end of the second century, extraordinary and miraculous charisms had largely disappeared from the Christian communities. St. Gregory the Great, who lived in the sixth century, noted this fact and explained it by pointing out that such charismatic signs were necessary in the first days of faith, but not in later years.[7] When a visible family of faith had become rooted in the world, then the Church itself with its marks of unity, faith, and love became the principal sign of God's presence.[8]

Prophecy

One of the most important charisms is that of prophecy. Prophets are moved by the Holy Spirit to speak His words and His will rather 55 than their own. Often "prophecy" is used for "foretelling the future." Under God's inspiration men can do this, and have done so. But the charism of prophecy is more frequently concerned with proclaiming God's will for the present. Prophecy calls men earnestly to faithfulness to God and to performance of deeds of justice and mercy.

---

[7]Cf. St. Gregory the Great, *Homiliae in Evangelia,* hom. 29.4 (MG 76.1215-1216).
[8]Cf. First Vatican Council, Session 3, April 24, 1870, *Dogmatic Constitution on the Catholic Faith,* ch. 3 (DS 3013-3014).

Prophecy serves the "upbuilding and encouragement and consolation" (1 Cor. 14.3) of the Church, and it will not be absent from a community that is strong in faith.

Discernment of Spirits

Among the gifts listed by St. Paul is "the ability to distinguish between spirits" (1 Cor. 12.10). This charism is also called "discernment of spirits." Such a gift is necessary in the Church. For it is possible for us to be deceived, and to believe that the Holy Spirit is urging us when really we are being moved merely by some deep desire of our own, or even by hidden and unworthy motives, or by a spirit of the world or an evil spirit.

Jesus Himself gave the basic criterion for the discernment of spirits: "You will know them by their fruits" (Matt. 7.16). Charisms are not to be used in disorder, but in peace and obedience.

Charismatic gifts are to be evaluated and their use governed by those to whom God has entrusted the care of the community of faith. 137 "These charismatic gifts, whether they be the most outstanding or the more simple and more widely diffused, are to be received with thanksgiving and consolation, for they are exceedingly suitable and useful for the needs of the Church. Still, extraordinary gifts are not to be rashly sought after, nor are the fruits of apostolic labor to be presumptuously expected from them. In any case, judgment as to their genuineness and proper use belongs to those who preside over the Church, and to whose special competence it belongs, not indeed to extinguish the Spirit, but to test all things and hold fast to that which is good (cf. 1 Thess. 5.12; 19.21)" (LG 12).

THE MISSION OF THE SPIRIT

The mission of the Holy Spirit in salvation history is summarized in the following words of the Second Vatican Council:

"When the work which the Father had given the Son to do on earth (cf. John 17.4) was accomplished, the Holy Spirit was sent on the day of Pentecost in order that He might forever sanctify the Church, and thus believers would have access to the Father through Christ in the one Spirit (cf. Eph. 2.18). He is the Spirit of life, a fountain of water springing up to life eternal (cf. John 4.14, 7.38-39). Through Him the Father gives life to men who are dead from sin, till at last He revives in Christ even their mortal bodies (cf. Rom. 8.10-11). The Spirit dwells in the Church and in the hearts of the faithful as in a temple (cf. 1 Cor. 3.16, 6.19). In them He prays and bears witness to the fact that they are adopted sons (cf. Gal. 4.16; Rom. 8.15-16, 26). The Spirit guides the Church into the fullness of truth (cf. John 16.13) and gives her a unity of fellowship and service. He furnishes and directs her with hierarchical and charismatic gifts, and adorns her with His fruits (cf. Eph. 4.11-12; 1 Cor. 12.4; Gal. 5.22). By the power of the Gospel He makes the Church keep the freshness of youth, perpetually renews her, and leads her to perfect union with her Spouse. The Spirit and the Bride say to the Lord Jesus, 'Come!' (cf. Rev. 22.17)'' (LG 4).

• • •

Questions related to the material in this chapter:

1. Is the Holy Spirit truly God or are references to the Spirit just a way of speaking about some kind of presence of God?

2. Is there any hint in the Old Testament of the existence of the Holy Spirit?

3. What are some New Testament references to the Holy Spirit?

4. We say that all books of the Bible were written under the inspiration of the Holy Spirit. What does this mean for us?

5. In what sense is the Holy Spirit the "soul" of the Church?

6. Why does the Holy Spirit dwell in each member of the faithful? What is His purpose?

7. The Church has always recognized certain gifts or graces as "gifts" of the Holy Spirit. What are they?

8. What is a "charism" or "charismatic gift"? Give some examples.

9. Are charismatic gifts signs or tokens of personal holiness or are they gifts given for the benefit of the whole Church?

10. How might we explain the fact that extraordinary or clearly miraculous charisms have largely disappeared since the early years of the Church?

11. What is the charism of prophecy?

12. Whose role is it in the Church to make judgment as to the genuineness and proper use of charismatic gifts?

13. What is the mission of the Holy Spirit in the Church today?

12

The Holy Trinity

The central mystery of Christian faith is the mystery of the Holy Trinity.

In this chapter we speak of the mystery of the Trinity, and of what it means to believe in the Trinity. We discuss how the mystery of the Trinity transcends human reason but is not contrary to it; how the works of the Trinity in salvation history reveal to us something of the inner life of the Triune God; and how in Its saving deeds for men the Trinity works in unity.

THE MYSTERY OF THE TRINITY

The mystery of the Blessed Trinity is the mystery of God in Himself. Because it illumines so many other teachings of the faith, and because belief in it is presupposed by so many other revealed truths, it stands clearly as the most basic and essential of teachings in the "hierarchy of the truths of faith."[1]

The key importance of the Trinity in Christian doctrine is evident from the beginning. When Christ commissioned the apostles to go forth and "make disciples of all the nations" (Matt. 28.19), He instructed them to baptize in the name of the Trinity (cf. Matt. 28.19). From the earliest centuries the Church's professions of faith have proclaimed belief in the Trinity of the Father, the Son, and the Holy Spirit. "Now the Catholic faith is this: that we worship one God in the Trinity, and the Trinity in unity. . . . The Father is a distinct Person, the Son is a distinct Person, and the Holy Spirit is a distinct Person; but the Father and the Son and the Holy Spirit have one divinity, equal glory, and co-eternal majesty."[2]

To believe in the Trinity is to believe that there is only one God, and that there are three distinct Persons who possess eternally the same divine nature.

---

[1]Sacred Congregation for the Clergy, *General Catechetical Directory* (April 11, 1971) n. 43. Cf. UR 11-12.
[2]Creed "Quicumque," often called "Athanasian Creed" (DS 75).

Mystery of Faith

The Trinity is one of those "mysteries hidden in God which, unless divinely revealed, could not come to be known."[3] Mysteries like that of the Trinity can be grasped only by believing God, and only by those who have recognized His testimony in the message of faith.

The fact that mysteries such as that of the Trinity can be grasped only by faith is in no way an affront to human reason. The things God tells us of His intimate life are above reason, although reason, enlightened by faith, can come to some understanding of them.

But the human mind can never fully grasp the divine mysteries in the way it can comprehend finite and created things. "For the divine mysteries by their very nature so surpass the created intellect that even when delivered by revelation and accepted by faith, they yet remain covered by the veil of faith itself and shrouded as it were in a sort of obscurity so long as in this mortal life 'we are away from the Lord, for we walk by faith and not by sight' (2 Cor. 5.6-7)."[4]

At Center of Faith

The dogma of the Trinity is the central dogma of Catholic faith. Only with belief in it can one grasp and explicitly believe other central Christian teachings.

62 Clearly one could not believe that Jesus is the Son of God, and true God, sent by the Father, if one did not believe in the plurality of Persons 360 in one God. Nor could one grasp the meaning of eternal life, or of the grace that leads to it, without believing in the Trinity, for grace and eternal life are a sharing in the Trinitarian life.

The basic importance of the doctrine of the Trinity is that it communicates to us light on the inner life of God. God reveals to us primarily Himself (cf. DV 2), and all of God's merciful deeds in salvation history are aimed at uniting our lives with the life of the Trinity.

THE TRINITY IN REVELATION

101 The doctrine of the Trinity was not revealed with full clarity at the start of salvation history. In the Old Testament there were foreshad-

---

[3]First Vatican Council, Session 3, April 24, 1870, *Dogmatic Constitution on the Catholic Faith,* ch. 4 (DS 3015).
[4]First Vatican Council, Session 3, April 24, 1870, *Dogmatic Constitution on the Catholic Faith,* ch. 4 (DS 3015).

owings, but the mystery of the Trinity was not formally revealed. In the New Testament the mystery is revealed: the Son and the Holy Spirit are made known, and are recognized as God and as Persons distinct from the Father.

The word "Trinity" does not appear in the New Testament and the meanings of the words "person" and "nature," in the precise senses in which these words are used to bear the message of God, had to be carefully refined to bear that message rightly. But what the New Testament teaches is in truth captured with care and reverence in the exact statements of the early councils of the Church.[5]

Old Testament

The Old Testament proclaims clearly part of the mystery of the Trinity, for it proclaims clearly that there is only one God. But it does not speak of a plurality of Persons in God or reveal the inner life of God. 101

Yet there are some passages in the Old Testament which seem to be veiled references to, or in a way preparations for the revelation of, distinct Persons in God. Many of the Fathers saw such suggestions in the frequent use of the plural noun (Elohim) and plural personal pronoun for the one God (cf. Gen. 1.26, 3.22, 11.7) and in the triple repetitions of the divine name or attributes (cf. Deut. 6.4; Ps. 67.7-8; Isa. 6.3). More significant are the special names and titles that suggest some distinction in divinity (cf. the uses of "Wisdom" and "Spirit" in reference to God in Wisd. 7; Prov. 8.22 f.; Isa. 32.15, 42.1).

New Testament

Jesus Christ, by His presence, by His promise of the Holy Spirit, and by His teaching, made known to men the mystery of the Trinity.

Christ instructs the apostles to baptize "in the name of the Father and of the Son and of the Holy Spirit" (Matt. 28.19). In His discourse at the Last Supper Jesus talks with warmth of the Persons of the Trinity. He, the Son, has been sent by the Father; in turn He will ask the Father, and the Father "will give you another Counselor, to be with you for ever, even the Spirit of Truth" (John 14.16-17). The divine mission that has been Christ's will be completed by the divine gift of the Holy Spirit (cf. John 12.49, 15.26, 14.9-21).

---

[5]Cf. Sacred Congregation for the Doctrine of the Faith, *Declaration for Protection of Faith in the Mysteries of the Incarnation and the Trinity* (February 21, 1972).

In the Gospel of St. John there are several passages that imply the Father, Son, and Holy Spirit are distinct Persons (cf. John 1.29-35, 14.16, 14.26, 16.15). St. Paul often refers to the three Persons of the Trinity in a single passage: "The grace of our Lord Jesus Christ and the love of God and the fellowship of the Holy Spirit be with you all" (2 Cor. 13.14); "Now there are varieties of gifts, but the same Spirit; and there are varieties of service, but the same Lord; and there are varieties of working, but it is the same God who inspires them all in every one" (1 Cor. 12.4-6; cf. also 2 Thess. 2.13-14; Gal. 4.6; Rom. 15.30). In this text, as often in the New Testament, "God" is used to name the Father, the first Person of the Trinity.

The revelation of the Blessed Trinity is reflected also in many other passages of the New Testament, as, for example, in these phrases from the First Epistle of Peter: "chosen and destined by God the Father and sanctified by the Spirit for obedience to Jesus Christ" (1 Peter 1.2; cf. also Titus 3.4-6; Heb. 10.29; Jude 20-21).

THE ETERNAL TRINITY AND HISTORY

Jesus did not reveal the mystery of the Trinity in abstract language but in the context of God's saving deeds for mankind. Through His saving deeds among us, God reveals His inner life to us.

The Eternal Trinity

25   By His saving deeds and words God reveals to us first of all Himself (cf. DV 2). When the Father sent His Son into the world, and when the Holy Spirit was sent by the Father and the Son (cf. John 14.16-17, 15.26), something of the inner life of God was revealed to us. Within the Trinity the Son proceeds eternally from the Father, and the Holy Spirit proceeds eternally from the Father and the Son.

Scripture speaks in two ways of the relationship between the first 62 two Persons of the Blessed Trinity. The second Person is Son to the first, the Father. He is also the Word of the Father, who dwells with the Fa- 45 ther eternally, with Him "in the beginning" as the Word through whom all c eated things come to be (cf. John 1.1-3). The Son is the perfect image of the Father (cf. 2 Cor. 4.4), perfectly mirroring and expressing all that the Father is.

The Father is absolutely without origin. The Son is uncreated, eternal, equally God; but without beginning and eternally He proceeds from

112

the Father. He is the eternal, unchanging, infinite Son who is God equally with His Father.

The Holy Spirit, a Person distinct from the Father and the Son, is equally truly God. The Father and the Son love one another with a 103 boundless love, a love that fully expresses all Their reality, a love which is personal and living as are the Father and the Son, and this personal Love proceeding from the Father and the Son is the Holy Spirit. The Spirit is not created; He is a Person co-equal and co-eternal with the Father and the Son.

Intimately present to one another, bound together in inexpressible love, distinct Persons dwelling in perfect unity, the Blessed Trinity is the model and goal of every personal society. "The Lord Jesus, when He 360 prayed to the Father, 'that all may be one . . . as We are One' (John 17.21-22), opened up vistas closed to human reason. For He implied a certain likeness between the union of the divine Persons and the union of God's sons in truth and charity" (GS 24).

Here we see one of the basic reasons why the doctrine of the Trinity is central for Christian faith. While there is but one God, and He is the Source of all else that is, God is not an utterly solitary God, nor is He an impersonal sea of being. The Trinity, the one true God, is a community of Persons eternally bound together in perfect understanding and love. In knowing the mystery of the Trinity, we realize that divine life can be shared, and shared even by us created persons, who as adopted 169 sons and daughters can be brought into the joy of the perfect community.

Inadequacy of Analogies

Many have tried to find ways of expressing at least something of the mystery of the Trinity by analogy with created things. However helpful these various analogies may be to some, they are all inadequate. The mystery of the Triune God so far transcends creation that no analogies from created things can express it adequately.

Yet those ways of speaking of the Trinity that are commended by the Fathers, and especially those rooted in Scripture, are to be profoundly respected. We can certainly say that the two divine processions (of the Son from the Father, and of the Spirit from the Father and the Son), whose existence is guaranteed by Scripture, are related to the two basic acts which we know belong to persons: knowledge and love. This is firmly rooted in God's word. Even there, of course, there is less than full and perfect expression of that Reality which is greater than all else.

113

371   The first councils of the Church sought to express more clearly and precisely as well as faithfully the message God has given of Himself.

Thus the heresies of Arianism and Macedonianism were rejected, for they failed to admit the co-equality and co-eternity of the Persons who are God. Sabellianism and other kinds of Modalism were rejected, for they held that there are not really three distinct Persons, but only One. Also rejected were rationalistic theories that were really tritheisms.

All these heresies the Church steadfastly denies, because there is a literal truth which God has revealed to us. The Church steadfastly professes faith in three Persons who are distinct, but are the one God. "We believe in one God, the Father almighty. . . . And in one Lord Jesus Christ, the only-begotten Son of God, born of the Father before all ages. Light from Light, true God from true God, begotten, not made, consubstantial with the Father; through Him all things were made. . . . And in the Holy Spirit, the Lord and giver of life, who proceeds from the Father, and who together with the Father and the Son is adored and glorified, who spoke through the prophets. . . ."[6]

The Saving Works of God

Since the Father, Son, and Holy Spirit subsist in the one divine nature, the creative and conserving and saving acts of God are acts of all the Persons of the Blessed Trinity.

The three Persons have "one substance, one essence, one nature, one divinity, one immeasurableness, one eternity, and all things are one where there is no distinction by opposition of relation."[7] The last words here refer to what are called "the divine relations," that is, the relationships of the three Persons to one another in the life of the Trinity. The Father, Son, and Holy Spirit are indeed distinct Persons, and in God's inner life They are present to each other with intimate personal presence. Thus, what is done by the Father in works outside the Trinity,
94   in creating and conserving the universe and in deeds of salvation, is done by all three Persons together. It is not the Father alone who

---

[6]Creed of the First Council of Constantinople, 381 (DS 150). In later forms of this creed, and in the liturgical use of it, "and the Son" is added after the words "proceeds from the Father."

[7]Council of Florence, Bull, *Cantate Domino* (February 4, 1442) (DS 1330).

creates, but the Father with the Son and the Holy Spirit. So also it is God the Blessed Trinity who guards and saves us in all things. What is done by one Person through the divine nature is shared by the three Persons who subsist in one nature, one wisdom, one love.

Still, certain works done by the Trinity, and thus literally by all the Persons, are fittingly attributed to one of the Persons when the work or action in question reflects that which is, in God's inner life, most proper to one Person. The technical word for such attribution is "appropriation." To the Father are appropriated especially the works of power, like creation; to the Son, the works of wisdom; to the Holy Spirit, the works of love.[8]

Some truths are spoken literally of one Person and not of the other Persons. It is the Son, "one of the Holy Trinity,"[9] who became man and suffered for us, not the Father or the Holy Spirit. Hence it would be incorrect to say that the Father or the Holy Spirit suffered for us on the cross. For what Jesus did and suffered for us in His human nature was done by the Son of God rather than by the Father or the Holy Spirit. But 64 the eternal divine love of the Son for us is shared equally by the Father and the Spirit.

THE TRINITY AND CHRISTIAN LIFE

The Father sent His only Son that we might have supernatural life. It is only in and through the Son, Jesus Christ, that we receive this life and become adopted children of God our Father. The Spirit sent by the 242 Father and the Son is to complete the work of the soul's sanctification, even to the point of transformation in Christ.

Through the gift of sanctifying grace the soul is admitted to the fellowship of the three divine Persons, who dwell in the soul of the just. The soul then becomes a mirror of the Trinity — the Father generating the Word in the soul and the Father and the Word together infusing the Spirit of love.

This "indwelling" of the Trinity is in Scripture attributed in a special way to the Holy Spirit. When the Holy Spirit enters the soul, He comes with all His gifts, so that if the soul responds it can be led to the perfection of the life of grace and charity.

---

[8]Cf. Pope Leo XIII, Encyclical, *Divinum Illud Munus* (May 9, 1897) (DS 3326).
[9]Second Council of Constantinople, Session 8, June 2, 553, *Anathematisms concerning the Three Chapters,* canon 10 (DS 432).

The goal of all Christian life is to know the Blessed Trinity, to know the Father, the Son, and the Holy Spirit even as They know us, and so to share in God's inner life of wisdom and love (cf. 1 John 3.2). This the just will do in the eternal life to come, and they will be eternally happy "with a joy very similar to that with which the most holy and undivided Trinity is happy."[10]

* * *

Questions related to the material in this chapter:

1. What do we mean when we say we "believe in the Trinity"?

2. Why do we say that the Trinity is a "mystery" of faith?

3. Why is doctrine on the Trinity of fundamental importance?

4. Is there any hint in the Old Testament of the existence of a plurality of Persons in God?

5. What are some New Testament passages that tell us of three Persons in God?

6. What do we know of the inner life of God, and what does this mean for us?

7. Has the Church ever solemnly defined its teaching and faith on the Holy Trinity?

8. What do we mean when we say that certain works of God are "appropriated" to one or another of the Persons of the Trinity?

9. What works of God are usually attributed to the individual Persons of the Trinity?

10. What is meant by the divine "indwelling"?

11. Will we ever come to know God as He is?

---

[10]Pope Pius XII, Encyclical, *Mystici Corporis* (June 29, 1943) (DS 3815).

13

The Catholic Church

The Catholic Church belongs entirely to Christ. He is the Head of the Church, its Founder, its Spouse and Savior. He continues to do His saving work in and through the Church.

In this chapter we speak of the Church as the continuation of Christ in the world and as the sacrament of His presence; as a reality illumined in Scripture by many titles and images; as a visible family of faith sealed with many marks to show that it is Christ's; and as a community having a design and structure fashioned by Christ Himself.

CHRIST IN THE CHURCH

Christ is the Light of the world. The Church receives its being and 21 mission from Him.

The Catholic professes his belief in "the holy Catholic Church," but precisely because he sees the Church as a presence of Christ and of His Spirit. The Catholic believes what the Church teaches, but precisely because he recognizes Christ's authority in the Church. The Catholic recognizes a duty to further the work of the Church, but precisely because he sees the mission of the Church as a continuation of Christ's work in the world.

Our faith and our hope, including our hope in the Church, are in Christ. He organized the Church to carry on His work in the world, bringing His ministry and truth to all men and all ages. It is Christ who accomplishes all that is done in the Church for men's salvation. The institution which is the Church survives because it comes from Christ, and He promises to be with it to the end of time (cf. Matt. 28.20).

The Church Is a Sacrament of Christ

"By her relationship with Christ, the Church is a kind of sacrament or sign and instrument of intimate union with God, and of the unity of the whole human race" (LG 1).

A sacrament is a sacred sign. In Catholic usage the word "sacra-

117

ment" has been used especially for baptism, or the Eucharist, or any of 270 the seven sacraments in which visible realities are, by the will of Christ, made effective signs of His saving gifts. The Church is as it were a more universal and comprehensive sacrament; it is a visible reality that Christ has formed in this world as a sacred sign of His presence, a sign and also the means He uses to give the unity and holiness He actually confers through it.

The very purpose of a "sign" is to lead beyond itself. Because the Church is a sign, it must lead us to what it signifies, that is, to Christ, to God. And when we come finally to God, with Christ, in eternity, the Church in this aspect of a sign will have no further reason to exist.

The sacrament which is the visible Church is now, in time, a precious and indispensable gift of Christ. It is the work of Christ, and will 360 last, as He promises, until the end of the world when it reaches its fulfillment in glorious union in Christ.

The Mystery of Christ in the Church

The Church is a living continuation on earth of its divine Founder. Jesus is indeed the Son of God, but He is truly an individual Man, too, the Son of Mary. Similarly, the Church is the presence of Christ and His 104 Holy Spirit, a bearer of heavenly gifts, yet is also very human, very much of the earth. Its sublime mission is carried out by human agents. In doing their work these human agents perform sacred ceremonies (entrusted to them by Christ) that are linked, in what we commonly call the sacraments, with ordinary realities of human life: bread, water, wine, oil.

But many come to faith in Jesus because the signs He gave, most of all His resurrection, made them able to recognize Him as Lord and Maker of all. So also those who love Him can come to recognize His visible Church. The signs with which He has marked the Church, and the inner graces by which He makes men able to understand these signs, enable men to see the saving presence of Jesus in the works He does in the Church.

To come to the Catholic faith is to see that the Church acts for Christ. It is to understand that when a priest gives us a sacrament, it is Christ who gives us the sacrament through him. It is to know that when the Church speaks His word to us, it is He who speaks and calls to faith. It is to recognize in the teaching and ruling authority of the Church the shepherding of Christ.

The essential activity of the Church is its spiritual life: its believing, hoping, and loving, and its services of teaching and shepherding that nourish such life in Christ. All the external structures and activities of the Church exist to serve the spiritual purposes.

There are not two churches, one visible and external, the other invisible and spiritual. There is one Church of Christ. It is the visible 131 Church in which and through which Christ acts.

THE MYSTERY IS TAUGHT BY IMAGES

We can learn best about the Church from the images and titles our Lord and His apostles used to illumine its nature.

The People of God

The Second Vatican Council chose especially to speak of the Church as the "People of God" (cf. LG 9-17). The Church is made up of all the members of the family of faith.

Pope, laymen, bishops, religious, priests, and members of every degree and vocation, all gathered together in Christ, are the Church. We are Christ's people, the "People of God." All receive the same Spirit in baptism, all are nourished with the one Eucharist, all share the same hope of our calling. A fundamental equality in the new dignity of children of God is a basic note of the people of God.

Old Testament Origins

The phrase "People of God" was first applied to Israel, and it has to 156 be understood in the light of our dependence on the Old Testament. In effect it characterizes the Church as the fulfillment of the Old Testament prophecies. Christ is the fulfillment of the prophecies and promises given to the world through the Jewish people. Because we possess Him, and His new gifts, and the enduring heritage of the Old Testament, we can speak of ourselves as "the People of God."

A People Called Together by Christ

The very phrase, with its Old Testament origins, serves to keep us aware that we are all alike in being members of the "assembling" of God's people.

The Old Testament doctrine of the calling of God's people made it abundantly clear that they were a *"qāhāl"* (the Hebrew word which lies behind our word "church"), a "congregation called together," only because God had made them that. The same is true of the Church; it had to be "called together" by Christ. "The people" can be a Church only because they are united by the grace of Christ.

The Kingdom of God

God rules in the midst of His people. The Church and the kingdom of God are not precisely synonymous. But the Church is a realization on earth of God's kingdom, the final fulfillment of which is in eternity (cf. LG 5).

The Gospels tell us that Jesus "went about all Galilee . . . preaching the gospel of the kingdom" (Matt. 4.23). When Christ spoke of the kingdom of God, or the kingdom of heaven, He was using language familiar to His Jewish hearers. In His teaching Christ was careful to free the idea of the "kingdom" from the nationalistic hopes of the people among whom He lived. To do this He often emphasized the heavenly aspect of the kingdom, and its interior, religious character.

The Church and the Kingdom

Aware of the intimate bond between the kingdom of God on earth and the Church, we can consider some of what Jesus taught about His kingdom. Like the reign of God, it is spiritual and it will be perfected in the last days. It is not a political kingdom: "My kingship is not of this world" (John 18.36). Yet His kingdom is planted in this world. Christ shows it to us as something visible, a community called together by Him and of which He is the Good Shepherd (cf. John 10.11-16).

The Church Is Visible

The Church was made in reality a visible Church when Christ sent the apostles to preach the kingdom in His name. He made it evident that their work was His: "And they went forth and preached everywhere, while the Lord worked with them and confirmed the message by the signs that attended it" (Mark 16.20). The early growth of the visible Church is traced in the Acts of the Apostles and in the Epistles. Its established reality is celebrated in the work of the earliest Fathers, like St.

120

Ignatius of Antioch, who writes so forcefully of the duty of a Christian to be united visibly with the visible Church.[1]

The Bride of Christ

One of the most beautiful images used by St. Paul to portray the nature of the Church and its relation to Christ is that of a bride whom Christ deeply loves. So much does He love the Church that He "gave Himself up for her" (Eph. 5.25).

The Church is a faithful bride of Christ. It is necessary always to distinguish what the Church is because of Christ's loving presence to her, and what her frail and sinful members are. By virtue of Christ's never-failing love, she is a faithful spouse, ever teaching the truth, ever 123 calling to holiness, the fruitful source of all His saving gifts.

The Church Is Our Mother

The Church is called a mother because, in virtue of Christ's love, she gives birth to many children (cf. LG 12). All the faithful are born of 153 her: "By her preaching and by baptism she brings forth to a new and immortal life children who are conceived of the Holy Spirit and born of God" (LG 64). Moreover, Christ is to "be born and grow in the hearts of the faithful through the Church" (LG 65).

St. Cyprian has expressed this forcefully: "You cannot have God for your Father if you have not the Church for your mother."[2]

The Mystical Body of Christ

The Church is not only dear to Christ and the bearer of all His saving gifts. In a real way, the Church is Christ. She is made one with Him as His Mystical Body (cf. LG 7).[3]

Christ often identified Himself with His followers, with His Church. At the Last Supper He spoke of the intense unity that makes Him one with those who are united by faith and love to Him. "I am the vine, you are the branches" (John 15.5). The vine and branches are one living reality. So is it also with Christ and His Church, Christ and those who love Him.

---

[1]Cf. St. Ignatius of Antioch, Epistula ad Philadelphenses proem. (MG 5.699); Epistula ad Ephesios 4 (MG 5.648).
[2]St. Cyprian, De Ecclesiae Catholicae Unitate 6 (ML 4.502 = ACW 25.48-49).
[3]See Pope Pius XII, Encyclical, Mystici Corporis (June 29, 1943).

St. Paul develops the teaching on the Mystical Body in a number of his Epistles. "Now you are the body of Christ and individually members of it" (1 Cor. 12.27). "For by one Spirit we were all baptized into one body — Jews or Greeks, slaves or free . . ." (1 Cor. 12.13).

It is true that we have diverse roles to play in the Church, just as in the natural body eyes and ears and feet have diverse functions. So in the body of Christ some are apostles, some are teachers, some are administrators, and some have more humble roles (cf. 1 Cor. 12.28-31). All, however, are called to the greatest gifts and duties, to the glory of believing, hoping, loving (cf. 1 Cor. 13).

283   The Eucharist in a special way brings about the unity of Christ's body. "The bread which we break, is it not a participation in the body of Christ? Because there is one bread, we who are many are one body, for we all partake of the one bread" (1 Cor. 10.16-17). Thus it is precisely through our union with Christ that we become members of one another in the Church (cf. Rom. 12.5). So united, the members are to love one another as themselves, even to love one another as Christ.

Christ "is the head of the body, the church" (Col. 1.18). To live as a Christian is to grow up in Christ, to be more and more identified with Him, more and more to have His rich life penetrate and be our life.

THE MARKS OF THE CHURCH

In many ancient creeds the Catholic Church identifies itself as "one, holy, catholic, and apostolic."[4] These words refer to what are traditionally known as the "marks" of the Church, that is, traits that make it possible for one to recognize it for what it truly is.

Many Catholics who write about the Church today refer to "signs of the Church" rather than to its "marks." This flows from a growing re-
96 alization of how important it is to see the Church as a "sacrament" of the presence of Christ (cf. LG 1). These qualities, "one, holy, catholic and apostolic," are seen as being of the essence of the Church as a sacrament, that is, a "sign" of Christ and His presence.

The Signs Are Paradoxes

The signs of the Church strengthen the faith of the believer and can attract the attention of the unbeliever and lead him to investigate the

---

[4]Creed of the First Council of Constantinople (381) (DS 150).

Church. But they also have a puzzling aspect. Their effectiveness as signs is sometimes lessened by the scandals which arise from the imperfection of the human members who are the Church.

That the Church is made up of sinners is amply evident from history. The Church ever remains one, holy, catholic, and apostolic in spite of its sinner membership. The presence of sinners in the Church is enough to explain its flaws; but men alone could not account for the qualities to which the marks refer.

The marks are more than signs. They are rich gifts Christ promised to give His Church. Catholic creeds profess firm faith in His word, that the Church will never cease to be one, holy, catholic, and apostolic. The Church is confident, for it has Christ's promise: "I am with you always" (Matt. 28.20).

The Church Is One

Christ's Church is one in the faith its members believe and profess. It has an essential unity of worship. All are united to one saving sacrifice of Christ in the Eucharist, and eat of the one Bread that unites all in Christ. They receive the same sacraments. There is also a unity in our community with other parts of the Church throughout the world. The "local churches" (or dioceses), each under its own bishop, are united in a common allegiance to the Pope, who is a sign and servant of unity. It is a living unity, springing spontaneously from the gifts of Christ's grace.

The Church Is Holy

The Creed proclaims that the Church is holy. This holiness is to be 121 found first of all in its Founder, Jesus Christ. From Him, and from His Holy Spirit, comes all holiness. Because of Him the doctrine the Church teaches is holy; it remains unchangeably His doctrine. The Church's worship is holy, and the sacraments it ministers to the members of the 171 Church make it possible for them to live Christian lives.

The Church invites all to a holy life (cf. LG 39-42). Without ignoring the scandals and sins of some of the Church's members, we can say in all confidence that there is holiness in the Church because so many of its members have shown eminent holiness, even to the point of martyrdom. There is such holiness in the Church in the present age as in ages past.

The Church Is Catholic

Christ's Church must be "catholic." The word "catholic" means "universal." The Catholic Church is a Church for all peoples in all places and in all times.

Moreover, the Church is universal, or catholic, in that it continues to teach all of what Christ taught. And it regards itself as obliged by Christ to teach that doctrine to all men.

The Church Is Apostolic

Finally, the Church is apostolic. It is the same community as the Church of the apostolic age.

Christ founded His Church on the apostles. They in turn had successors, and the Church is apostolic because it continues to be governed by such successors. It is apostolic also because it teaches the same doctrine and way of life as the apostles taught.

292

The Church in History

The Church in its heart remains ever unchanged, always sealed with the marks that identify it as Christ's. But it is also a Church immersed in history. It is called always to speak and live in a way that serves each succeeding age and culture.

It is a duty of the Church in each passing age to be the instrument through which Christ brings His truth and His gifts to men of that age. It must speak the language of each age; it must live in the circumstances of very diverse times.

The world's great cultures all pass away in time. But when a culture perishes and its great cultural institutions die, the Church continues. The Church survives every transition, for the Lord of history has promised the Church that it will endure until the end of time.

125

THE HIERARCHY IN THE CHURCH

The Church is a hierarchical community by the will of Christ (cf. LG 18-29). A hierarchy is a "sacred leadership." To say that Christ willed the Church to have a hierarchy is to say that Christ Himself chose to rule His people through the bishops and pastors He has appointed to care for it.

Christ by His divine authority appointed men to teach, sanctify, and rule the Church in His name. The Church teaches that those who succeed in the office of the men chosen directly by Christ are equally rulers and guardians of the Church by the will of God Himself (cf. Acts 20.28). For Christ promised that He would be with those teaching and shepherding His flock, not for a single generation but until the end of time (cf. Matt. 28.20).

The Scriptural Foundation

We find in the New Testament many remembrances of the words and works of Jesus that had shaped the reality of the young Church. While our Lord yet lived, before the Paschal mysteries and the coming of the Holy Spirit, much of His message concerning the Church might well have escaped the clear understanding of His hearers. But the Gospels and Epistles, written under the inspiration of the Holy Spirit, bear strong witness to the truth that the Church is of Jesus' own making, and carries on His work.

Early in His public life Jesus called together a special group of privileged associates who would be the foundation of the new household of 83 God (cf. Luke 6.13-16; Eph. 2.20). During His public life Jesus prepared the apostles for leadership roles. To them He committed the tasks of teaching, baptizing, forgiving sin, celebrating the Eucharist. At the Last Supper He promised that He would send them the Spirit of Truth to guide and guard their work (cf. John 16.13).

The New Testament's witness concerning the hierarchy in the 216 Church is not a matter of isolated passages, but rather a rich vision of the Church itself in which the members of the hierarchy (the apostles, their associates, and those they appointed to roles of leadership) have special functions to perform. Anticipations of this are seen throughout the Gospels; the early exercise of leadership is traced in the Acts of the Apostles and in the New Testament Epistles.

The Promises to Peter

Some of the central passages deserve special notice. At a climactic moment in St. Matthew's Gospel, Simon makes a stirring profession of faith in Jesus as the Messiah. Because Simon had recognized His iden- 84 tity, Jesus conferred on him a sacred new role and identity, giving him a new name, Peter. The name Peter means "Rock," and Jesus promised

Peter that he would be the rock or foundation on which He would build His Church. And to Peter, the Rock, He would give the keys of government and the power to bind and to loose with authority (cf. Matt. 16.17-20).

The fulfillment of these promises is recorded as well. During the passion of Jesus, Peter proved frail. Three times he denied his Master. After the Resurrection Jesus recalled Peter to a threefold profession of atoning love, and in so doing confirmed Peter in the role of shepherd and leader of all the flock (cf. John 21.15-17).

In many ways the New Testament suggests the entirely exceptional role of Peter in the Church. Through Peter all the faithful were to be fortified in faith in the hours of difficulty.

To the apostles as a group, in association with Peter, Christ gave a similar commission to exercise authority in His Church (cf. Matt. 18.18; LG 22). The mission of the apostles as a group was compared by Christ
291 to the mission Christ Himself received from the Father (cf. John 17.18). The apostles were sent forth as a group to convert the world (cf. Mark 16.15).

Successors of the Apostles

St. Peter and the other apostles were mortal, but the mission given them was to be carried out until the end of time (cf. Matt. 28.20). "For this reason the apostles took care to appoint successors in this hierarchically structured society" (LG 20; cf. Acts 20.25-27; 2 Tim. 4.6). This is noted by the earliest Fathers of the Church, who lived at the end of or immediately after the apostolic age. Thus Pope St. Clement of Rome, writing around the year 96, says that the apostles themselves "laid down a rule once for all to this effect: when these men die, other approved men shall succeed to their sacred ministry."[5]

From these first days of the Church, bishops appointed by or succeeding to the apostles were recognized as shepherds who rightly ruled and guarded the Church in the name of Christ. Loyalty to Christ was visibly expressed by loyalty to the bishop.

A Hierarchy of Service

The Second Vatican Council presents the hierarchy as a "diako-
297 nia," a ministry of service.

---

[5]St. Clement of Rome, *Epistula ad Corinthios* 44 (MG 1.296 = ACW 1.36).

Christ insisted that those who had authority in His Church were to exercise it with a humility patterned on His own (cf. Matt. 20-28). But He taught all to recognize legitimate authority, and to profit by the divine gifts conferred through it, even if those who in fact have the authority should personally live lives unworthy of it (cf. Matt. 23.3). The leaders of the Church are to be active in their service. A pope or bishop who failed to serve his people by protecting them in their faith and guiding them in moral matters would be derelict in his duty (cf. 2 Tim. 4.1-5; 1 Cor. 9.16).

THE HIERARCHY TODAY

The roles of St. Peter and the other apostles were in many ways unique. They were privileged personal associates of Jesus. Many of their duties, however, were to persist in the Church. Their enduring responsibilities, the tasks of teaching, ruling, and sanctifying the flock, are borne in the Church today by the pope, who succeeds to St. Peter's office as the first shepherd and bishop, and by the whole body or "college" of bishops, who inherit the tasks of the "apostolic college."

The Pope

The First Vatican Council explained the enduring nature of the primacy in Peter's successors.

"Now, what Christ the Lord, the Prince of Shepherds and Great Shepherd of the Sheep, established in the person of the blessed apostle 125 Peter for the perpetual welfare and everlasting good of the Church must, by the will of the Same, endure without interruption in the Church, which, founded on the Rock, will stand firm to the end of the world. Indeed, 'no one doubts, in fact it is known to all ages, that the holy and most blessed Peter, prince and head of the apostles, the pillar of faith and foundation of the Catholic Church, received the keys of the kingdom from our Lord Jesus Christ, the Savior and Redeemer of the human race; and even to this time and forever he lives' and governs 'and exercises judgment in his successors,'[6] the bishops of the Holy Roman See, which was founded by him and consecrated by his blood. Therefore, 142 whoever succeeds Peter in this Chair holds Peter's primacy over the

---

[6]These are the words of Philip, papal legate to the Council of Ephesus (431), in an address to the council fathers.

127

whole Church according to the plan of Christ Himself. 'Therefore, the disposition made by Truth endures, and blessed Peter, persevering in the rocklike strength he received, has not given up the government of the Church undertaken by him.'[7] Hence, 'because of its greater sovereignty' it has always been 'necessary for every church, that is, the faithful who are everywhere, to be in agreement'[8] with the Roman Church, that, in the See from which 'the rights of sacred communion'[9] flow to all, they might, as members joined in the head, coalesce into one compact body.''[10]

The council then solemnly defined the doctrine that by the will of Christ there has been a continuous line of successors to the office of St. Peter, and that the Roman Pontiff does succeed in Peter's primacy over the universal Church.[11]

The council then described the nature and extent of the pope's jurisdiction, that is, his right and duty to rule or shepherd the Church.[12] The pope has jurisdiction over the entire Church. He is bishop not only of Rome, but of the universal Church. His authority as bishop is "immediate," that is to say, each member of the flock, of whatever rank, is required to accept the pastoral direction of the first shepherd. He is bishop of all the Church, of his fellow bishops and all the faithful, individually and collectively. The pope's authority and duty extend not only to the teaching of faith and moral doctrine, but also to whatever pertains to the discipline and government of the Church throughout the world.

The College of Bishops

"By the Lord's will, St. Peter and the other apostles constitute one apostolic college" (LG 22). Though Christ gave a true primacy to Peter, he was to shepherd the Church not in isolation, but in fraternal, collegial unity with his fellow apostles. In a similar way, the Pope, as successor to St. Peter, governs the Church in collegial unity with his fellow bishops, successors of the apostolic college. Fully respecting the special

[7]Pope St. Leo I, *Sermo 3 de Natali Ipsius* 3 (ML 54.146B).
[8]St. Irenaeus, *Adversus Haereses* 3.3.2 (MG 7.849A).
[9]St. Ambrose of Milan, *Epistula* 11.4 (ML 16.986B).
[10]First Vatican Council, Session 4, July 18, 1870, *First Dogmatic Constitution on the Church of Christ,* ch. 2 (DS 3056-3057).
[11]First Vatican Council, Session 4, July 18, 1870, *First Dogmatic Constitution on the Church of Christ* (DS 3058).
[12]First Vatican Council, Session 4, July 18, 1870, *First Dogmatic Constitution on the Church of Christ,* ch. 3 (DS 3059-3064).

role Christ wishes the Holy Father to undertake in His name, the bishops over the whole world cooperate with him in the care for all the Church.

This "collegiality" has always been recognized in the living practice of the Church. Even in the earliest years of the Church, when dangers threatened the purity and unity of faith, the bishops gathered together in councils to make, with the assistance of the Holy Spirit (cf. Acts 15.28), decisions for the direction of the whole Church.

Another expression of collegiality in antiquity was the great concern for "communion" among the various local churches and between each of them and the Roman See.

Collegiality at Work

The collegial nature of the bishops taken as a whole is seen in a vivid way when they come together for an ecumenical council. Such 371 councils, of which there have been twenty-one, bring together bishops from every part of the Church to discuss some part of the Church's doctrine or discipline.

In 1965, during the final session of the Second Vatican Council, Pope Paul VI instituted a new form of collegial cooperation in the Church: the Synod of Bishops.[13] Consisting of a group of bishops representing bishops from all over the world, the Synod of Bishops is called together by the Holy Father to discuss certain matters and pastoral questions facing the Church. The first session of the Synod of Bishops was convened in 1967; others have been held at regular intervals since then.

The Bishop in His Diocese

In the Catholic Church there are many local churches or dioceses. Each of these is entrusted to an individual bishop, who has the responsibility to care for the Church in that particular place. The bishop in charge of a diocese is called the Ordinary, a title which refers to his authority in the diocese. Sometimes the Ordinary of a diocese is assisted by one or more auxiliary or coadjutor bishops in the care of his flock.

The bishop is the authentic teacher of the faith in his own diocese; he is a sign and center of unity; he is the "administrator of the mysteries

---

[13]Cf. Pope Paul VI, Apostolic Letter, *Apostolica Sollicitudo* (September 15, 1965).

of God" (cf. 1 Cor. 4.1) for the people committed to his care. To be a true teacher of his flock, the bishop must, of course, be in harmony with the pope and the other members of the college of bishops. Within his diocese, the bishop works together with and through his priests and deacons. Their mission in the Church depends upon the bishop; they have been made "co-workers" with him by ordination (cf. LG 28).

The bishop shepherds his flock as a true ambassador and vicar of Christ. When he is consecrated into the order of bishops by others who have preceded him in that office, and is assigned by proper authority to care for a particular diocese, he governs his flock as a true successor of the apostles, with an authority given by Christ Himself.

SALVATION THROUGH THE CHURCH

156   The Catholic Church steadfastly believes that it is the one and only Church of Jesus Christ. To say this is certainly not to say that other Christian communities are without value, or insincere, or that their members are not deeply devoted to Christ. It is to profess that Jesus indeed willed to remain present among men in the Church that grew up, through the grace of the Holy Spirit, from the preaching of the apostles He sent. It is to say that the one community of faith He planted through His apostles continues to live, as He said it would, through all the ages, sealed with sacred marks: "one, holy, catholic, apostolic." It is to say that Christ, dwelling in the Catholic Church, invites all men to complete unity of faith and the close communion of love in this visible, living Church; and that in saving mercy Christ requires all who come by grace to recognize this Church as the sacrament of His presence to join it, and rejoice in the life He gives through it.

"This Church, constituted and organized in this world as a society, subsists in the Catholic Church, governed by the successor of Peter and the bishops in communion with him" (LG 8). To say that Christ's Church "subsists" in the Catholic Church is to say that Christ's Church 118 is a concrete historical reality, and that that concrete reality is found in the living, visible Catholic Church.

Separated Brethren

Many who are not members in the full sense of the Catholic Church Ch. 16 are surely Christ's own, and linked to the saving sacrament of His Church by many bonds. Even though they are not bound to it by a full sharing in the joy of Catholic faith, nor by a full communion with those in whom Christ shepherds His flock, they do share many true gifts of Christ, as faith in Him and baptism, gifts that "possess an inner dynamism toward Catholic unity" (LG 8). The Catholic should honor God's gifts in them, and so live his own Catholic life as to make more apparent its real nature, that others may come to know the blessings of full unity with Christ in His Church.

Salvation in the Church Alone

"Outside the Church there is no salvation," St. Cyprian taught in the third century.[14] The Church has always taught this doctrine. But this is no fierce proclamation that those who, through no fault of their own, have not come to recognize Christ's presence in the Church and His command to come to this life (cf. Mark 16.16) will be excluded from salvation. Certainly those who earnestly intend in their hearts to do all that God requires of them are not excluded from the hope of eternal life, as they are not excluded from a certain membership by desire in the Church.[15]

There is, however, a note of urgency in the classic expression of St. Cyprian. If one were to recognize the reality of the Catholic faith and the personal will of Christ that we live in it, and yet deliberately disobey so important a call, he would be turning himself away from the Savior 164 and from salvation. "For this reason, those who, aware of the fact that the Catholic Church was made necessary by God through Jesus Christ, would yet refuse to enter her or persevere in her, could not be saved" (LG 14).

This is not a matter of loyalty to men, but of faithfulness to Jesus Christ. It is He who invites all to life, and there "is no other name under heaven given among men by which we must be saved" (Acts 4.12).

* * *

Questions related to the material in this chapter:

1. Does our faith in Christ include faith in the Church He founded?
2. In what sense is the Church a sacrament?
3. How is Christ present in His Church?

---

[14]St. Cyprian, *Epistula* 73.21 (ML 3.1169A).
[15]Cf. Letter of the Holy Office to the Archbishop of Boston (August 8, 1949) (DS 3870).

4. Why does the Church call itself "the People of God"?

5. To what extent do we equate the Church and the kingdom of God?

6. What do we mean when we call the Church the Bride of Christ?

7. Why do we call the Church the Mystical Body of Christ?

8. What are the four "marks" or "signs" of the Church and what do they tell us about the Church?

9. What does the word "hierarchy" mean?

10. What is the scriptural foundation for the leadership structure we find in the Church today?

11. Are bishops properly called successors of the apostles?

12. Does the pope have authority over the universal Church, including other bishops?

13. What do we mean by "college of bishops" and "collegiality"?

14. What is the role of a bishop as head of a local church or diocese?

15. Why does the Catholic Church proclaim itself as the one and only Church of Christ?

16. Does the teaching that "outside the Church there is no salvation" mean that no non-Catholics are saved?

14

Christ Shepherds His People

The Church traditionally has spoken of three offices of Christ the Savior. He is Prophet or Teacher of truth; He is King or Ruler who 289 shows the way; and He is above all the Sanctifier who gives His people abundant life (cf. John 14.6).

In this chapter we speak of how Christ teaches, rules, and sanctifies in His Church. The chapter treats especially the teaching mission of the Church: why sacred teaching is needed, to whom this teaching is committed, and the various ways in which the teaching office of the Church guides the life of the faith.

CHRIST TEACHES HIS PEOPLE

Christ is the Teacher of His people. A major part of His saving mis- 17 sion was to free men from the despair of ignorance and doubt, from the frightening fear that perhaps nothing makes sense at all. "For this I was born, and for this I have come into the world, to bear witness to the 81 truth" (John 18.37).

Jesus was concerned so much with truth because He is Himself the Truth, as He is the Way and the Life (cf. John 14.6). Much of His public life on earth was spent in teaching. The common title He received was "Teacher."

Jesus teaches also through those He sends. Anyone who did not accept the word of those He sent would be rejecting not mere men, but 159 Him, whereas acceptance of their word would be acceptance of Christ (cf. Luke 10.16).

HUMAN NEED FOR DIVINE TEACHING

"No one knows the Father except the Son and any one to whom the Son chooses to reveal Him" (Matt. 11.27). Men have heard of God, but none has known Him with the saving, loving understanding of faith 81 except through the gift of Jesus. "No one has ever seen God; the only Son, who is in the bosom of the Father, He has made Him known" (John 1.18). Christ came to give us personal and saving knowledge of God.

Even the knowledge revealed to us by Christ is not immediate acquaintance with God or direct vision of Him. Though Jesus speaks the truth about God, and in His own person and reality reveals the goodness of God, we see His divinity only in seeing Him as a man, and we hear the divine, infinite truth spoken in human and finite language. Faith gives life, certainty, and joy, but we will not see God clearly until the day of eternal life dawns and we see "face to face" (1 Cor. 13.12).

But the wisdom of faith is itself a splendid reality. It does not give us that vision of God we hope to enjoy in heaven, but it does give us truth. It provides us, on the authority of Jesus the perfect Witness, with sure and liberating access to the Father.

Human Language and Faith

We see only created, finite things. All our language and ideas are conditioned by them. Our words, therefore, cannot worthily and fully express the reality of the infinite God as He is in Himself. Yet it is possible in a number of ways to speak of God truthfully.

We may say of God truly that He is immortal, all-knowing, eternal — that is, that He lives without the flaws we know too well in human life. True statements can be made of God also in expressing awareness that all flows from Him, and that all good has its origin and roots in Him. Truth, goodness, life, wisdom — it is true to say that God has all these perfections.

When Jesus and the prophets before Him spoke to us of God, they claimed to speak the truth about the infinite Lord of all. They used human language. But Scripture has also insisted that such language did not bear the fullness of that truth. "No eye has seen, nor ear heard, nor the heart of man conceived" (1 Cor. 2.9; cf. Isa. 64.3) what is the splendor of that God who shall be our eternal beatitude.

42, 67   Still human language is able to bear the message God wishes it to bear.

The word of God, the expression in language of divine truth, is not the creation of man working alone. The Father is Himself the source of revealed knowledge. Christ, who is the Lord, receives all truth from the Father; at the same time He is a man who uses human language, and speaks truly in human language the message He came to give.

134

How the Divine Message Is Grasped

The teaching of faith, which is a "witnessing," has a pattern dif- 28
ferent from that of ordinary human teaching. It is a gift of God. It is a
personal revelation He makes, and the truth of the word He gives can be
known only on His word. Only by divine faith can we grasp this message with certainty. Until one enters the blessed vision of God, it is only
testimony, or witnessing, that makes possible a knowledge of the word
of faith.

But witnessing is sufficient here. God's witnessing is altogether different from man's: "the testimony of God is greater; for this is the testimony of God that He has borne witness to His Son. He who believes in
the Son of God has the testimony in himself" (1 John 5.9-10). God is
able so to place His message in history, surrounded by signs that He 95
chooses, and so to move the apprehension of man from within, that one
can with full certainty come to recognize that the spokesman God sends
is indeed His spokesman.

If it were only a long argument that led us to believe that someone
was God's spokesman, we might continue to have doubts. But God is
able to lead those whom He calls to know with great certainty that it is
He who speaks in the spokesmen He sends. Through grace He gives us
an obscure but certain sharing in His own wisdom, so that men acquire
in faith a certainty that is in many ways puzzling but nonetheless more
sure than all else they know.

THE WORK OF THE CHURCH IS TO TEACH

Only God can make known to men the truths they most need, the
mysteries hidden in God, the purposes and plans of Him who is the
source and final goal of all that is real. God stirred up men to speak in
His name (cf. Rom. 10.14-15), and in His providence He made it possible
for hearers to recognize that these men, called prophets, did speak for
Him. But most of all it is Christ who reveals God to the world. God's Son
continues to speak to us through those He chooses to send in His name
(cf. John 15.16). Spokesmen for God must not be self-appointed; they
must be called in His name (cf. Jer. 23.13-28).

God's Word and the Apostles

Christ committed to the apostles the task of preaching His word in
His name, that is, authentically. He assured them of the assistance of
the Spirit who would guard them in all truth in speaking (cf. John 14.16, 104

135

125 26). He commanded them to teach His word to all nations, binding men to the duty of believing their words as the words of God, and He promised to be with them in their preaching until the end of time (cf. Matt. 28.20).

Preserving the Deposit of Faith

With the end of the apostolic age the time of new public revelation came to an end (cf. DV 4). The task of the Church thereafter was to hand on the word which had been entrusted to the apostles, the deposit of faith, to grow in it, to nourish its development, and to make it living and effective, a leaven to renew the earth. We say that revelation continues in the sense that the living God remains present to His people, and by His continuing care and His gifts of grace enables them to recognize and love Him and the good news of the Gospel. But Jesus proclaimed the full saving message and gave it to His people, "and now no new public revelation is to be expected before the glorious manifestation of our Lord Jesus Christ (cf. 1 Tim. 6.14 and Titus 2.13)" (DV 4).

234 Christ is the one Savior; there will never be a Gospel other than that which He has given us (cf. Gal. 1.6-8), the message the Church has always preached. His word is to be guarded by those who, as successors to the apostles, are authentic teachers and witnesses of the faith. The bishops who are to guard the truth will be assisted by the Spirit of God. They will not have special revelations, but by God's mercy, for the sake of His people, they will be enabled to preach the word with unfailing truth (cf. DV 8).

Bishops must be vigilant and active to fulfill their tasks. In the inspired words of St. Paul's message to his disciple Timothy the task of teachers in the Church for all centuries to come is made clear: "I charge you in the presence of God and of Christ Jesus who is to judge the living and the dead, and by His appearing and His kingdom: preach the word, be urgent in season and out of season, convince, rebuke, and exhort, be unfailing in patience and in teaching" (2 Tim. 4.1-2).

Though the task of bishops is demanding, and to be a faithful bishop is to suffer much for the faith (cf. 2 Cor. 11.28-29), yet the charisms with which God surrounds their preaching give it an effectiveness and make it a joy. "We also thank God constantly for this, that when you received the word of God which you heard from us, you accepted it not as the word of men but as what it really is, the word of God, which is at work in you believers" (1 Thess. 2.13).

136

Development of Doctrine

The Church does not hand on doctrine in a static way; it teaches and believes a living faith. As centuries pass, the prayer and study of the Church, and the guidance of the Holy Spirit, lead the Church into an ever-greater understanding of the divine word.

Development of doctrine never means abandonment of doctrine, or the substitution of new doctrine for old; it never means that what the Church once firmly assents to it will ever deny. "Hence also that meaning of the sacred dogmas which has once been declared by holy Mother Church must always be retained."[1]

Genuine development of doctrine always proceeds along consistent lines: it is growth from partial to fuller vision, so that what has been 111 believed continues to be believed, though its depths and consequences are more and more fully realized. Moreover, what is implicit in the faith, and not fully realized because of temporary obstacles, may become re-splendently clear as truly present in the Gospel message. This is not by 344 virtue of a new revelation, but because of a clearer insight into the message that has been handed on. This growth of "understanding, knowledge, and wisdom" is always to be "in the same doctrine, in the same meaning, and in the same sense."[2]

Authentic Teachers in the Church

The Catholic Church teaches that just as the Holy Father and the other bishops are the successors of the apostles in ruling His flock, so also are they the apostles' successors as the authentic teachers and wit- 107 nesses of the faith. They are the witnesses that Christ has established to teach the Church; and to the word of the Holy Father and of the college of bishops as teachers God has given the charism of truth that does not fail (cf. LG 25; DV 8). Clearly the Catholic bishop has a duty to teach collegially, in unity of faith with the Holy Father and his brother bishops.

Other teachers assist the bishops in their work. Priests preach the

---

[1]First Vatican Council, Session 3, April 24, 1870, *Dogmatic Constitution on the Catholic Faith,* ch. 4 (DS 3020). Cf. Pope Benedict XV, Encyclical, *Ad Beatissimi Apostolorum* (November 1, 1914) (DS 3626); Pope Pius XII, Encyclical, *Humani Generis* (August 12, 1950) (DS 3886).

[2]Vincent of Lerins, *Commonitorium primum* 23 (ML 50.668), quoted in First Vatican Council, Session 3, April 24, 1870, *Dogmatic Constitution on the Catholic Faith,* ch. 4 (DS 3020).

Gospel, as officially sent by their bishops to the task. They are committed to speak faithfully the word that Christ preserves pure and untainted in the successors of the apostles.

Theologians and scholars teach the word, and help the Church to grow in penetrating its depths. To be sure, they are not official teachers; as bishops, the successors of the apostles, are; and theologians do not as such receive with the bishops that "sure gift of truth" (DV 8) which the apostolic witnesses of faith receive. But they are important helpers of the bishops; for bishops are not exempt from the responsibility of seeking appropriate assistance for the understanding of divine revelation.

Other teachers are parents, "the first and foremost educators of their children" (GE 3). Very important teachers also are those who teach the faith in schools and in centers of catechetical learning. All these too draw their certainty and sureness not from mere scholarship, from human philosophies and sciences, but from the word Christ causes to be proclaimed by those He has sent.

THE MESSAGE TO BE TAUGHT

The Holy Father and the other bishops are servants of the word of God. They have a duty to believe the Scriptures and the word that has been handed down to them in the Church, by the bishops and apostles who preceded them. There is a continual "handing on" of faith. But to enable men to guard divine faith purely, to have unshaken faith in it, and to remain unified in their understanding and love of it is not the
107 work of men, but of God. It is the Spirit of God who gives the charism of truth to authentic teachers and the charism of faith to these teachers and to those who hear them.

Tradition, Scripture, and the Magisterium

Bishops and those who assist them in teaching the word of God are to hand on all the saving word of Christ, the message in its entirety. "Tradition" means "handing on," and the Church is responsible for handing on faithfully all that it has received from the Lord. "Tradition" also means "that which is handed on." "Now that which was handed on by the apostles includes everything which contributes to holiness of life, and the increase in faith in the people of God; and so the Church, in her teaching, life, and worship, perpetuates and hands on to all generations all that she herself is, all that she believes" (DV 8).

There can also be in the Church human traditions, which may be of only temporary value. It is only by Christ's gift of the Spirit, guarding the living teachers He sets over the Church, that the Church is able rightly to distinguish that which is the enduring word of God, and unfailingly to be handed on, from that which is only of passing worth.

Sacred tradition is inseparably united with the Sacred Scriptures, which were written under the inspiration of the same Holy Spirit who guides the Church in handing on sacred tradition (cf. DV 8).

The writings of the New Testament had their origin in the Church. They were written to confirm and enrich faith (cf. Luke 1.1-4; John 20.31) and meet the questions and problems that the apostles met in the life of the Church. They were written, by divine inspiration (cf. 2 Tim. 3.16; cf. DV 11), to preserve for coming generations rich insights into the Gospel message, which had been preached and was being preached by the apostles, and lived in the whole Church. From the beginning, then, they have been proclaimed by the Church's own teachers, and have been believed and understood in the light of the whole living tradition and faith of the Church.

Thus it is "not from Sacred Scripture alone that the Church draws its certainty about everything which has been revealed" (DV 9). Sacred tradition and Sacred Scripture form "one sacred deposit of the word of God, which is committed to the Church" (DV 10), and both "are to be accepted and venerated with the same sense of devotion and reverence" (DV 9).

Interpreting this word of God is a task of the magisterium or teach- 369 ing office in the Church. "The task of authentically interpreting the word of God, whether written or handed on, has been entrusted exclusively to the living magisterium of the Church, whose authority is exercised in the name of Jesus Christ" (DV 10).

The gifts of tradition, of Scripture, and of the living magisterium, with the presence of the Spirit guiding the faithful to be open to the truth, are all gifts of God. The close union of these gifts cannot be forgotten. "It is clear, therefore, that sacred tradition, Sacred Scripture, and the magisterium of the Church, in accord with God's most wise design, are so linked and that all together, each in its own way under the action of the one Holy Spirit, contribute effectively to the salvation of souls" (DV 10).

INFALLIBILITY AND FAITH

Christ promised to send His Holy Spirit to those who believed in Him to guide them in all truth (cf. John 16.13). An important gift to the whole believing Church, and to the teaching Church, is the gift of infallibility, that is, a certain inability to err in believing or teaching revealed truth.

Infallibility in Believing

God alone is completely infallible. Men are by nature capable of falling into error. But faith does give them light and certainty in some matters that are of essential importance for their salvation. The God who gives the Church a share in the light of His own knowledge by the gift of faith grants to the Church also a certain participation in His own infallibility. "The body of the faithful as a whole, anointed as they are by the Holy Spirit (cf. 1 John 2.20, 27), cannot err in matters of belief. Thanks to a supernatural sense of the faith which characterizes the People of God as a whole, it manifests this special quality when 'from the bishops to the last members of the laity' it shows universal agreement in matters of faith and morals" (LG 12).[3]

Infallibility in Teaching

The teaching office Christ gave St. Peter and the other apostles has by His will been handed on to their successors, the pope and the other bishops. This teaching office is exercised in two ways in the Church, through the "ordinary magisterium" and through the "extraordinary magisterium."

Ordinary Magisterium

The bishops normally teach the Church in simple pastoral ways. They preach the Gospel; they see to the catechetical instruction of the faithful in their care; they watch over the forms of prayer and worship in which the faith is lived and exercised; in their instructions and pastoral letters they guide the faithful in what they are to believe and do to attain salvation, in accord with the revelation that has been entrusted to them in their pastoral office. This is their "ordinary magisterium."

Infallibility does not extend to all the teaching of each individual bishop. But the bishops, as authentic teachers of Christ's people, can

---

[3]The interior quotation is from St. Augustine, *De Praedestinatione Sanctorum* 14.27 (ML 44.980).

proclaim His teaching infallibly. "This is so, even when they are dispersed around the world, provided that while maintaining the bond of unity among themselves and with Peter's successor, and while teaching authentically on a matter of faith and morals, they concur in a single viewpoint as the one which must be held conclusively" (LG 25).[4]

When the bishops throughout the world teach that any matter of faith or morals is revealed by God, their unified witness is a certain sign of the authenticity of their message. What they proclaim is a part of Catholic faith, and part of the Church's infallible teaching (cf. LG 25).

Extraordinary Magisterium

The "extraordinary magisterium" of the Church, which is also infallible, has two forms. The first of these is found in the ecumenical councils. The second form is the *ex cathedra* ("from the chair") definition of doctrine by the Holy Father.

Ecumenical Councils   371

The authority of ecumenical councils was foreshown in the Acts of the Apostles by what is said there of a council of apostles and apostolic co-workers not many years after the resurrection of Jesus (cf. Acts 15.1-28).

After Peter and others had spoken, there was agreement on the decision to be made: the Gentiles would not be bound to observe the whole Mosaic code. The announcement of this decision was made with great confidence: "It has seemed good to the Holy Spirit and to us to lay upon you no greater burden than these necessary things" (Acts 15.28). That is, they taught confidently that the Spirit's guidance, which had 104 been promised to the leaders of the Church, was in fact being given. When these leaders solemnly and publicly proclaimed that something was an element of the true faith, it certainly was so.

Since that apostolic period, when major heresies and discords have arisen the Church's bishops have gathered in ecumenical councils. There have been twenty-one such councils in the course of the Church's history. The first was the Council of Nicaea in 325; the most recent was the Second Vatican Council, from 1962 to 1965.

---

[4]Cf. also First Vatican Council, Session 3, April 24, 1870, *Dogmatic Constitution on the Catholic Faith*, ch. 3 (DS 3011).

Anyone who wishes to be a true Christian has always been held required to accept what the ecumenical councils teach as matters of faith. As the Second Vatican Council declared, the infallible teaching office of the bishops "is even more clearly verified when, gathered together in an ecumenical council, they are teachers and judges of faith and morals for the universal Church. Their definitions must then be adhered to with the submission of faith" (LG 25).

Not everything said by ecumenical councils is meant to be infallible teaching.[5] Some conciliar statements are directed rather at offering pastoral considerations or disciplinary legislation.

But ecumenical councils have often made exact formulations of doctrine, and taught these solemnly to the whole Church as infallibly true. These solemn "definitions" state the revealed truth in a way that is "irreformable" and "unalterable." This means that the dogmatic formulations of the Church's magisterium express revealed truth aptly, and in such a way that "as they are they remain forever suitable for communicating this truth to those who interpret them correctly,"[6] that is, in the sense in which they were solemnly made.

Papal Magisterium

The Holy Father has a special teaching office among the bishops. Succeeding to St. Peter's role as shepherd of the whole flock, he has a duty to care for the faith of the entire Church.

127   The pope does not derive his authority and power from other bishops, or by delegation from the Church, but from Christ. Because it is a personal duty of his office to teach the whole Church, his words have authority from his own sacred office, and do not need approval or acceptance by others to deserve reverent hearing and acceptance from each member of the Church (cf. LG 25).

Christ, having committed the chief pastoral care of the Church to Peter and his successors, Himself teaches the Church through the pope. He does not remove freedom from the pope, nor does He assure us that all popes will be holy men.

---

[5]Cf. *Declaration* of March 6, 1964, by the Second Vatican Council's Doctrinal Commission (text included in "Announcements" document printed in AAS as an appendix to LG); cf. also the Council's note appended to the title of GS.

[6]Sacred Congregation for the Doctrine of the Faith, *Mysterium Ecclesiae* ("Declaration in Defense of the Catholic Doctrine on the Church against Certain Errors of the Present Day," June 24, 1973) n. 5. Cf. Pope Paul VI, Encyclical, *Mysterium Fidei* (September 3, 1965).

Even when a pope is unworthy of his office, the Lord guards the Church from false teaching at his hands. Through the Holy See, Christ 104 has wonderfully guarded the purity and consistency of faith over the centuries. Christ's prayer for Peter at the Last Supper was efficacious: "But I have prayed for you that your faith may not fail; and when you have turned again, strengthen your brethren" (Luke 22.32). In his successors as in his life (cf. Acts 15.7-11), St. Peter has, by the support of Christ, ever confirmed the faith of his brothers.

Papal Infallibility

The Holy Father is infallible in certain of his pronouncements. That the Church itself may be a secure witness, and men may have access to faith with confidence, Christ gives to the chief shepherd the ability to witness with recognizable validity in His name. Christ guards the chief shepherd whom He places in charge of His flock from leading His own 125 astray.

The First Vatican Council, after showing how securely this teaching of faith is rooted in the Gospel, how through the centuries God had guarded the faith and unity of the Church through the successors of St. Peter, and how the Church had constantly acknowledged that the supreme teaching authority for the faith rests with the Bishop of Rome as St. Peter's successor, gave its solemn definition of papal infallibility: "Therefore, faithfully adhering to the tradition received from the beginning of the Christian faith . . . we teach and define that it is a dogma divinely revealed: that the Roman Pontiff, when he speaks *ex cathedra,* that is, when acting in the office of shepherd and teacher of all Christians by virtue of his supreme apostolic authority he defines doctrine concerning faith or morals to be held by the whole Church, by the divine assistance promised him in Blessed Peter, is possessed of that infallibility with which the divine Redeemer willed His Church to be endowed in defining doctrine concerning faith or morals; and that therefore such definitions of the Roman Pontiff are of themselves, and not from consent of the Church, irreformable."[7]

The infallibility of the pope, like that of the believing Church and that of the whole body of bishops, is not the same thing as revelation or 25 inspiration. It does not imply any special supernatural insight or wisdom. 365

---

[7]First Vatican Council, Session 4, July 18, 1870, *First Dogmatic Constitution on the Church of Christ,* ch. 4 (DS 3074). Cf. also LG 25.

Papal infallibility applies to the same matters as the infallibility of the whole Church, that is, to "doctrine concerning faith or morals to be held by the whole Church."

The pope teaches infallibly with the other bishops when he and they exercise the infallible ordinary or extraordinary magisterium of the college of bishops. His individual infallible magisterium is exercised only in his *ex cathedra* statements.

AUTHENTIC TEACHING

Catholic teaching is far more than the proclamation of a limited number of infallibly defined dogmas or articles of faith. The Catholic 225 knows that Christ is present in His Church, and is teaching there, making known a rich mystery that needs always to be more richly learned.

Faith in the dogmas of the Church themselves means more than acceptance of the formulas in which the dogmas are expressed. To believe an article of faith rightly one must hold it in the very sense in which the Church means it, as expressing a truth the Church has believed and does believe.[8]

181 The Catholic is expected to assent to all the authoritative teachings of the Church, even when the Church is not using its full infallible authority. "Bishops teaching in communion with the Roman Pontiff are to be respected by all as witnesses to divine and Catholic truth. When their bishop speaks in the name of Christ in matters of faith and morals, the faithful are to accept his teaching and adhere to it with a religious assent of soul. This religious submission of will and of mind must be 128 shown in a special way to the authentic magisterium of the Roman Pontiff even when he is not speaking *ex cathedra*. That is, it must be shown in such a way that his supreme magisterium is acknowledged with reverence, and the judgments made by him are sincerely adhered to, according to his manifest mind and will. His mind and will here may be known chiefly either from the character of the documents, from his frequent repetition of the same doctrine, or from his manner of speaking" (LG 25).

The encyclical letters of the Holy Father, in which he addresses the Church in an especially solemn and serious manner, have a special claim to reverent assent, even when they are not intended to announce

---

[8]Cf. First Vatican Council, Session 3, April 24, 1870, *Dogmatic Constitution on the Catholic Faith*, ch. 4 (DS 3020).

any solemn definitions of faith. "Such teachings belong to the ordinary magisterium, of which it is true to say: 'He who hears you, hears Me' (Luke 10.16). For the most part, what is expounded and stressed in encyclical letters already belongs to Catholic doctrine for other reasons. But if the supreme pontiffs in their acts give attention to and pass judgment on a matter up to that point controverted, it is obvious to all that the matter, according to the mind and will of the same pontiffs, can no longer be considered a question for free debate among theologians."[9]

The proper interpretation of an encyclical or other Church document is not always easy to determine. Careful study of the text is required, in the context of other papal pronouncements and of relevant theological writings.

The assent to authentic teachings which are not clearly infallible teachings is called a "religious assent." Because a Catholic believes that God gives the successors of the apostles authority to guide the faith and religious life of the Church, he "abides not only by the extraordinary decision of the Church, but by its ordinary life as well where faith and discipline are concerned."[10]

Such religious assent is required of all who profess faith in the Catholic Church. It is required of the Holy Father and bishops, of priests and theologians, as well as of the laity.

Those who instruct others in the faith must be careful to teach the authentic message of the Church. For the Catholic there should never be any doubt about what the Church teaches. The Catholic deserves as teacher a priest who is in accord with his bishop, and a bishop who is in unity of faith with the college of bishops and with the pope.

CHRIST RULES IN HIS CHURCH

It is in Christ that all authority of the Church natively dwells (cf. Matt. 28.18). On earth Christ rules through people whom He selects, whom He makes visible as His own spokesmen and shepherds, and to whom He gives the duty to give His commands and directives to His people. "Go therefore and make disciples of all nations, baptizing them . . . , teaching them to observe all that I have commanded you . . ." (Matt. 28.19-20).

Those to whom this commission was spoken had earlier been given

---

[9]Pope Pius XII, Encyclical, *Humani Generis* (August 12, 1950) (DS 3885).
[10]United States Bishops, Pastoral Letter, *The Church in Our Day* (November 1967).

promises that they would have authority in His name. It was to be an authority used in love with the strength of love, but also with humility and personal concern (cf. Matt. 20.25-28; John 13.12-17).

125   The authority was given in a special way to one of the apostles. To Peter, the Rock, there was specially assigned the role of bearer of the keys, of the symbols of the ruler in the house. To him the shepherding care for all the flock was entrusted.

This ruling office in the Church which is exercised by the pope and the other bishops has been discussed in the preceding chapter. Often called the power of jurisdiction, the office of ruling exists to serve the growth of faith and holiness in the Church. The laws of the Church (especially the Code of Canon Law) and the legitimate commands of the pope and bishops are issued with the authority Christ gave to the Church (cf. Matt. 16.19, 18.18) for the good of the People of God. Hence the faithful owe obedience to them. The bishops of each country generally list the most notable of special duties of Catholics as "precepts of the Church."[11] They cover such obligations as those to attend Mass on Sundays and holy days of obligation, and to avoid unnecessary and inappropriate work on such days; to lead a regular sacramental life; to observe the marriage laws of the Church; to strengthen and support the Church; to do penance at the appointed times.

CHRIST SANCTIFIES IN HIS CHURCH

Teaching and ruling in the Church are each ordered to the more important task of sanctifying. Sacred teaching is aimed at giving the saving truth, love of which is both a part of holiness and guide to doing the will of God in love. All ruling in the Church is directed toward holiness, to be used for edification, and not for any personal gratification or glory of those called to serve by allowing Christ to rule in them (cf. LG 39-42).

But there are certain most precious specifically sanctifying powers Christ gave to the Church. For example, He instructed His apostles to baptize, to celebrate the Eucharist, to forgive sins.

Some of the sanctifying forces Christ gave to the Church He gave to all. The whole Church is to be "a royal priesthood, a holy nation" (1 Peter 2.9; cf. LG 9). In baptism and confirmation His people is to be

---

[11]Cf., e.g., United States National Conference of Catholic Bishops, *Basic Teachings for Catholic Religious Education* (January 11, 1973) Appendix B.

made suitable to share in His perfect worship, the one sacrifice that is the healing of the world (cf. Heb. 10).

Some of the sanctifying works of Christ are to be done through the shepherds of His flock, the bishops and priests. Not to every Christian is there given the call or the ability to make present the Eucharistic sacrifice of Christ, and His bodily presence, by speaking His sacred words. Not to everyone is given the task and the power to forgive sins in Christ's name (cf. John 20.22-23). Only those called, sealed with the sacrament of orders as priests or bishops, can be instruments by which Christ confers many of His gifts on His people. The powers of orders do not, of themselves, make those who are ordained better men. It is the intensity of one's Christian love that is the measure of one's greatness before God and in reality; and everyone in the Church is called equally to be holy, to become perfect. But as servants of the holiness of others, some are called to special posts that minister the greater gifts.

* * *

Questions related to the material in this chapter:

1. Christ is the Teacher of His people. What do we mean when we say He teaches also through those He sends?

2. Why do people have a need to be taught by God?

3. Can the message of God be expressed in human language?

4. Why do we speak of faith as a gift of God?

5. The time of new public revelation came to an end with the end of the apostolic age. In what sense, then, do we say that revelation continues?

6. What is the "deposit of faith"?

7. Does "development of doctrine" ever mean that what was once valid is no longer valid?

8. Why are the pope and the other bishops the authentic teachers in the Church? What is the role of other teachers?

9. What do we mean when we say that Sacred Tradition is inseparably united with Sacred Scripture, and that it is "not from Sacred Scripture alone that the Church draws its certainty about everything which has been revealed"?

10. We speak of the "infallibility" of the Church, of "infallibility in believing" and "infallibility in teaching." What do these terms mean?

147

11. What is the "ordinary magisterium" of the Church? What is the "extraordinary magisterium"?

12. What is an ecumenical council?

13. What is the special teaching office of the pope and how does he exercise it?

14. What is the obligation of Catholics with regard to authentic teaching of the Church?

15. Do the rules and laws of the Church have any binding force?

16. We say that teaching and ruling in the Church are each ordered to the task of sanctifying. How is that so?

15

Mary, Mother
and Model of the Church

Mary, the mother of Jesus, was with Him in the hour of His passion (cf. John 19.25). In many ways she was associated with His redemptive work.

The first part of this chapter treats Mary's role as Mother of the Church and of each of the faithful. The chapter then treats Mary's position as model of the Church. The final part of the chapter speaks of the role of St. Joseph, Mary's husband, in Christian life.

MOTHER OF THE CHURCH

Catholic devotion salutes Mary as "Mother of the Church."[1] Mary deserves this title because she is the mother of Jesus, and because of her special association with His saving work, which is continued in the Church. The title aptly expresses the spiritual maternity she exercises in the life of the faithful. It suggests her role as model of the Church in the way she shows forth the Christian virtues.

Mary Redeemed by Christ

Christ alone is the Redeemer of all. Mary, then, was redeemed by 86 Him. Her redemption, however, was unique. Christ did not take away His mother's sins, for she had none; rather, by His redemptive mercy He kept her from incurring sin, so that she was conceived without origi- 76 nal sin and was guarded by His grace against falling into sin.

We received the fruits of redemption as God's pure gift in our baptism. Mary received this gift at the moment of her immaculate conception. Those who receive baptism in infancy must offer their free response later. So Mary, too, as her personality developed, gave her free consent to this gift.

Mary belonged to the sinful human race. She therefore stood in need of redemption. The fact that she did not actually incur original sin is not due to her action but Christ's. He truly suffered and died for her;

---

[1]Cf., e.g., Pope Paul VI, *Address* at the close of the third session of the Second Vatican Council (November 21, 1964).

in fact, in a certain sense He suffered and died more for His mother than for the rest of mankind, for He redeemed her so thoroughly as to preserve her from all sin and to give her the fullness of grace. Because she shared in a unique way in His redemptive grace, she led a life free from any personal sin or evil inclination. The totality of her cooperation with grace corresponded with the abundance of Christ's gifts to her, so that she is the first fruits of redemption.

Mary's Share in Our Redemption

Mary's consent to be the mother of Yahweh's suffering Servant was an implicit acceptance of His Crucifixion. Certainly she did not under-
71 stand this fully from the beginning; but the "let it be to me" she uttered at the Annunciation was never retracted, and her words reached their fullest meaning at the foot of the cross. With compassionate and sacrificial love she accepted in freedom and pain her Son's passion and death for the redemption of the world.

After her Son's ascension, the Acts of the Apostles tells us, Mary was among those gathered together with the apostles in prayer (cf. Acts 1.14). Scripture thus portrays her in the midst of the infant Church, awaiting in faith the first Pentecost. Mary's unique grace among the redeemed made her most responsive to the inspirations of her divine Spouse, the Holy Spirit, and her motherly presence influenced the infant Church to grasp more fully its apostolic mission of preaching the Gospel to the ends of the earth.

Mary's unique role in our redemption follows from her complete cooperation in her own personal redemption. Though Christ alone is our Redeemer reconciling us with the Father, she, by virtue of her faith and divine maternity, is both the spiritual and bodily mother of our redemption in her divine Son. Her free act of identification with His objective redemption of mankind has a redemptive meaning and value for all of us. This is the basis for Mary's "spiritual motherhood" of all men and women, insofar as all are called to be members of her Son's Mystical Body, the Church.

Mary's Spiritual Motherhood

72 "Our Blessed Mother" is a title especially dear to Catholics. Mary is our spiritual mother because of her special role in communicating to us our life in Christ. Mary is spiritual mother of all men because Christ suffered, died, and rose for the redemption of all. In a special way, however, she is the mother of all the faithful who are actually members of His

150

Body the Church. For this reason she is called "Mother of the Church."

The Second Vatican Council borrowed the words of St. Augustine to speak of Mary's spiritual maternity. She is "clearly the mother of the members of Christ . . . since she cooperated out of love so that there might be born in the Church the faithful, who are members of Christ their Head."[2] Spiritual kinship with Christ belongs to all who do the Father's will. Thus Mary's outstanding faith gives her physical motherhood of Christ a deep meaning in salvation history, a meaning which justifies speaking of her "spiritual motherhood" of all mankind.

Mary's Mediation and Intercession

Mary's spiritual motherhood must be considered not only in the light of the Church's traditional and growing understanding of the biblical message about her association with Christ on earth, but also in the light of the Church's teaching about her special relationship to the risen Lord and to us in the communion of saints. "This maternity will last without interruption until the eternal fulfillment of all the elect. For, taken up to heaven, she did not lay aside this saving role, but by her manifold acts of intercession continues to procure for us gifts of eternal salvation" (LG 62).

One of the titles under which Mary is invoked in the Church is "Mediatrix" (cf. LG 62). This title, as the Second Vatican Council explained, is understood in such a way that it "neither takes away from nor adds anything to the dignity and efficacy of Christ the one Media- 86 tor" (LG 62).

Mary's role in the distribution of graces does not compete with the centrality of Christ as the one Mediator between God and men (cf. 1 Tim. 2.5-6). "The maternal duty of Mary toward men in no wise obscures or diminishes this unique mediation of Christ, but rather shows His power. For every saving influence of the Blessed Virgin on men originates, not from some inner necessity, but from the divine pleasure. It flows forth from the superabundance of the merits of Christ, rests on His mediation, depends entirely upon it, and draws all its powers from it. It in no way impedes, but rather fosters the immediate union of the faithful with Christ" (LG 60).

Jesus, having entered glory as the eternal High Priest, continues to 99 pray for us (cf. Heb. 7.24-25). Mary, ever associated with her Son, prays for us with Him. She is not alone in this. The whole community of the

---

[2]St. Augustine, *De Sancta Virginitate* 6 (ML 40.399), quoted in LG 53.

352 blessed in heaven imitate Christ in continuing their concern for us. But, among those redeemed by her Son, Mary's intercessory power is by far the most extensive and effective.

Mary's love, inspired by her close union with her Son, embraces all men and all their needs. She cares with intense personal love for the entire fulfillment of His work of salvation. That is why, under Jesus, she is said to be the mediatrix of graces.[3]

Special Devotion to Mary

While it would be wrong to say that it is absolutely necessary to be devoted to Mary in order to be saved, one who does not invoke her special intercession misses a valuable opportunity for grace to grow in Christ. Without her maternal guidance, received through some form of devotion to her, one will not mature as fully in Christian worship and mission as Christ wishes.

Honor has always been shown to Mary in the Church, and the faithful have persistently had a devoted love for her. Devotion to Mary,
253 of course, "differs essentially from the cult of adoration" (LG 66) which is given to God alone. Though Mary has sublime dignity as the Mother of God, she is a fellow creature. In devotion to her one should avoid both exaggeration and minimalization.

At times devotion to Mary has been stimulated by word of her appearance to devout suppliants, as at Lourdes, Fatima, and Guadalupe. The Church does not give any definitive teaching on the authenticity or nature of such apparitions. But the Church does study them carefully, and if the fruits of an event breathe of the presence of God's providential designs, it approves the consequent devotions. "These providential happenings serve as reminders to us of basic Christian themes: prayer, penance, and the necessity of the sacraments."[4]

Personal devotion to Mary ought to imitate the patterns found in the Church's liturgy, in its joyful worship of God and praise of her in the feasts in which the honoring of Mary leads us to a warmer love of her Son, and in the daily recognition that the liturgy gives to her closeness to Jesus. Liturgical worship is always rooted securely in the doctrines of

---

[3]Cf. Pope Pius X, Encyclical, *Ad Diem Illum* (February 2, 1904) (DS 3370); Pope Pius XII, Encyclical, *Ad Caeli Reginam* (October 11, 1954) (DS 3914-3917).
[4]United States National Conference of Catholic Bishops, Pastoral Letter, *Behold Your Mother: Woman of Faith* (November 21, 1973) n. 100.

faith, as are the traditional private Marian prayers most honored and most warmly encouraged in the Church, such as the Angelus and the rosary.[5]   376

MARY, MODEL OF THE CHURCH

Mary is truly a member of the Church founded by her divine Son Jesus Christ. But she occupies a special place in that community. Not only is she "mother" of the Church, communicating the life of Christ the Head, but she is also "model" of the Church in the unique example 121 she gives of Christian virtue.

Motherhood of Mary and of the Church

There is a close relationship between Mary's spiritual motherhood 72 and the motherhood of the Church. The Church, too, is both mother and virgin, holy and sanctifying. Mary is the model of the Church as the great sacrament, the efficacious sign of the saving presence of Jesus Christ. She is also a pattern for all whose task in the Church is to assist in Jesus' saving work. Her maternal concern for all that leads fallen humanity to redemption in her divine Son gives the greatest example of the fidelity to continuing Christ's mission to which the Church is called. Every pope, bishop, priest, deacon, religious, and lay person can look to Mary as the exemplar of fidelity to his or her special vocation of mediating salvation.

Holiness of Mary and of the Church

The most basic truth about the mystery of the Church is that it is a community of brothers and sisters in the Lord. In this community Mary also is our sister, just as every member, whether pope or lay person, whether scholar or simple unlettered believer, is our brother or sister in the Lord.

Mary's example of complete openness to God's will is a constant source of edification for our growth in Christian holiness. A unique lay person in the Church, she did not possess the ministerial powers of the 293 priesthood. Yet her life of deep faith, humble obedience, persevering hope, fruitful purity, poverty of spirit, and courageous love provides a model for every member of the Church.

---

[5]Cf. Pope Paul VI, Apostolic Exhortation, *Marialis Cultus* (February 2, 1974) nn. 40-55.

After her life on earth had ended, Mary was reunited with her Son. She was taken up to heaven in body as well as in soul. There is no explicit reference in Scripture to the Assumption of Mary. But the doctrine has deep roots in the Scripture's teaching on the holiness and dignity of Mary, and on the meaning of man, sin, death, and the resurrection of the body.[6]

356

Devotion to Mary in the glory of her Assumption is ancient in the Church. Toward the middle of the eighth century St. John Damascene, in three magnificent homilies on Mary's Dormition, summed up the traditional faith and teaching of the Eastern and Western Church concerning her glorious Assumption and mediation of graces in heaven.[7]

Thus many centuries of belief and devotion were crowned when the doctrine of the Assumption was formally defined by Pope Pius XII on November 1, 1950: ". . . we proclaim, declare, and define it to be a dogma revealed by God that the immaculate Mother of God, Mary ever Virgin, when the course of her earthly life was finished, was taken up body and soul into the glory of heaven."[8]

Like all the special graces and privileges bestowed on Mary through the merits of Christ's redeeming love, the Assumption does not separate Mary from the rest of the redeemed People of God, but unites her more intimately with each one of us. As Jesus did not abandon us by ascending to heaven but continually sends His Holy Spirit to sustain His Church, so Mary, in the Assumption, has not been separated from us but instead remains a sign of sure hope that each one of us is called to share as she has in the fullness of Christ's glory. As the most faithful spouse of the Holy Spirit, she is the model of all that the Church and mankind hope to become in heaven.

ST. JOSEPH IN OUR CHRISTIAN LIFE

One cannot adequately consider Mary's place in Christian life without reference to St. Joseph's special role in our salvation. As guardian of the Holy Family, most chaste spouse of our Lady, and foster fa-

---

[6]Cf. Pope Pius XII, Apostolic Constitution, *Munificentissimus Deus* (November 1, 1950).
[7]Cf. St. John Damascene, *Homiliae in Dormitionem Beatae Virginis Mariae* (MG 96.699-762).
[8]Pope Pius XII, Apostolic Constitution, *Munificentissimus Deus* (November 1, 1950) (DS 3903). Cf. also LG 59.

ther of our Savior, he received from God one of the highest vocations in the plan of redemption.

Joseph was truly married to Mary, in a virginal marriage, but a marriage of devoted personal love. Jesus was not merely Joseph's adopted Son; He was born of Joseph's wife. God chose to make the deep personal love of the Virgin Mary and of the chaste Joseph provide the human context for the birth of the Savior of all. It is true that Joseph was not naturally or physically the father of Jesus, "yet to the piety and love of Joseph a Son was born of the Virgin Mary — He who was also the Son of God."[9] Like Mary, Joseph must have had a profound influence upon the Child who was "obedient to them" (Luke 2.51).

On December 8, 1870, Pope Pius IX proclaimed St. Joseph Patron of the Universal Church, a title which aptly described his special place in Christian life. His special virtues of justice and fidelity are particularly appropriate for imitation by fathers of families and working men. But for every person devotion to St. Joseph can lead to a deeper faith in the new life of Christ communicated through Mary.

* * *

Questions related to the material in this chapter:

1. Why is "Mother of the Church" an appropriate title for Mary?
2. In what way was Mary's redemption by Jesus unique?
3. How did Mary play a part in our redemption?
4. "Our Blessed Mother" is a term we frequently use in referring to Mary. How is Mary our spiritual mother?
5. Since Christ is the one Mediator, how can Mary be a mediatrix of grace?
6. Does proper devotion to Mary detract in any way from devotion due to Christ?
7. Why do we speak of Mary as "model of the Church"?
8. How does Mary's openness to the will of God make her a guide to Christian living for all the Church?
9. What is the doctrine of the Assumption?
10. What do the Gospels tell us of Mary's spouse, St. Joseph?

---

[9]St. Augustine, *Sermo* 51.30 (ML 38.351 = ACW 15.64).

16

Faith Lived
in a Divided World

130   The Catholic Church, "God's only flock" (UR 2), carries on Christ's work in a world in which men profess many different religions and indeed many men profess no religion at all.

In this chapter we discuss the Catholic response to the multiplicity of religions in the world today. The chapter also discusses the responsibility of the Church to the world, and the meaning and importance of true religious freedom.

JUDAISM

Of the non-Christian religions, Judaism holds a unique place in the history of salvation. The Old Testament records the history of the Jews and it shows how God chose them in a special way and revealed Himself to them. This was part of the divine plan and preparation for the salvation of man.

God Himself entered into a covenant, a pact or agreement, with 55 Abraham (cf. Gen. 15.16) and, through Moses, with the people of Israel (cf. Exod. 24.8). When the Son of God became man, He came among men as a Jew. Those He chose as apostles were Jews. Most of the early disciples were Jews.

Christians should always remember that the beginnings of their faith are found already among the patriarchs, Moses, and the prophets. It was through God's chosen people of old that the Church received the revelation of the Old Testament. All who believe in Christ are included in the call of Abraham, and are "sons of Abraham" (Gal. 3.7). "Indeed, the Church believes that by His cross Christ, our Peace, reconciled Jew and Gentile, making them both one in Himself (cf. Eph. 2.14-16)" (NA 4).

Thus there is a spiritual bond linking the people of the New Cove-119 nant, the new People of God, with the people of the Old Covenant. "The history of Judaism did not end with the destruction of Jerusalem, but rather went on to develop a religious tradition. And, although we believe that the importance and meaning of that tradition were deeply af-

156

fected by the coming of Christ, it is still nonetheless rich in religious values."[1] Certainly the Jews "still remain most dear to God because of their fathers, for God does not repent of the gifts He makes nor of the calls He issues (cf. Rom. 11.28-29)," and, together with the prophets and St. Paul, the Church "awaits that day, known to God alone, on which all people will address the Lord in a single voice and 'serve Him with one accord' (Zeph. 3.9; cf. Isa. 66.23; Ps. 65.4; Rom. 11.11-32)" (NA 4).

Christian-Jewish Relations

In addressing the question of relations between Christians and Jews, the Second Vatican Council recalled the great heritage common to both and encouraged "that mutual understanding and respect which is the fruit above all of biblical and theological studies, and of brotherly dialogues" (NA 4).

The urgings of the Council in no way deny or alter the Church's mission to the whole world; nor indeed do they in any way call for a rewriting of history. It remains true that authorities of the Jews and those who followed their lead did press for the death of Jesus (cf. John 19.6). But what happened in Christ's passion and death cannot be blamed without distinction on all the Jews who were then living, and even less can the events of that time be blamed on the Jews of today. 164

There have been Christians who with sincere but misguided zeal have used various scriptural passages (e.g., Matt. 23.27-39, 27.25; 1 Thess. 2.14-16) to "justify" a view that the Jews, because they do not accept Jesus as the Messiah, are truly an accursed race, rightly and permanently punished because of their treatment of Christ. Indeed, the Church firmly warns against such use of God's word: "Although the Church is the new People of God, the Jews should not be presented as repudiated or cursed by God, as if such views followed from the Holy Scriptures. All should take pains, then, lest in catechetical instruction and in the preaching of God's word they teach anything out of harmony with the truth of the Gospel and the spirit of Christ" (NA 4). 90

All sinners share in the guilt for Christ's passion and death. As the Church holds and has always held, Christ "in His boundless love freely underwent His passion and death because of the sins of all men, so that all might attain salvation" (NA 4).

---

[1]Commission for Religious Relations with the Jews, *Guidelines and Suggestions for Implementing the Conciliar Declaration 'Nostra Aetate' (n. 4)* (December 1, 1974) III.

It is clear, then, that anti-Semitism, that is, hostility toward Jews or discrimination against them, is unchristian.

The harsh facts of history should of course never be allowed to mute the facts of joy and salvation in the saving actions of Christ. But they can serve as a constant reminder to us to repent for any injustice 322 we have done to the Jews and to purge ourselves of any anti-Semitic attitudes we may have. The Church, "mindful of her common patrimony with the Jews, and motivated by the Gospel's spiritual love and by no political considerations, deplores the hatred, persecutions, and displays of anti-Semitism directed against the Jews at any time and from any source" (NA 4).

SEPARATED CHRISTIANS

123   Although unity, or oneness, is an essential mark of the one true Church, there are in fact many Christian communions today which present themselves to the world as the true heritage of Jesus Christ.

The divisions among Christians are in truth a scandal to the world. There have been many efforts in the past to heal these divisions. Recent decades have seen new efforts, with new vigor, and the growth of what is known as the Ecumenical Movement. The Second Vatican Council took account of these various efforts and desires, and called on all Catholics to work for what it said was one of the chief concerns of the council: promoting the restoration of unity among all Christians (cf. UR 1, 4).

Separations: Schism and Heresy

To separate oneself deliberately and culpably from the Church is to fall into "schism" or "heresy." Although neither of these words is in great use today, what they are and stand for is relevant for understanding the present situation and how it came about.

The sin of schism is formal and willful separation from the unity of 114 the Church. The sin of heresy is formal denial or doubt about one or more elements of the Catholic faith. Schism does in fact always involve some heresy, at least in regard to Catholic teaching on the unity and authority of the Church.

Because the sins of schism and heresy are both willful acts, it is not really appropriate to use the words "schismatic" and "heretic" in refer-

ence to Christians who through no fault of their own do not have the 193
fullness of Catholic faith. They may in a sense be said to be "in schism"
or "in heresy," but the sin of willful separation is not theirs.

The Early Centuries

From the very beginning of the Church there appeared certain rifts
(cf. 1 Cor. 11.18-19; Gal. 1.6-9; John 2.18-19). These were censured
strongly by St. Paul (cf. 1 Cor. 1.11-13, 11.22), and throughout the history of the Church the seriousness of separation from the Church and its
teachings has been recognized.   133

The early Christian writers speak of heresy and schism in various
ways and in various figures. Separation from the Church is as it were a
rent in the seamless robe of Christ (cf. John 19.23), this robe itself being
seen as a symbol of unity. Very common among the early Fathers is the
concept that contaminated faith, or heresy, debauches the faith and attacks the Church's virginity.

The number of heresies and schisms which arose during the course
of the first centuries of the Church was large. St. Augustine, in a work
written in 428 or 429, listed eighty-eight heresies, from that of Simon
Magus to that of Pelagius.[2] The life-spans of these early separations
varied greatly. Some died out quickly. Others developed and spread,
then seemingly disappeared, only to flare up again under different
names. Some indeed have continued, in one form or another, under one
name or another, from the early days of the Church to the present. Certainly there are few if any doctrinal errors current in modern times
which cannot be found in some form in the heresies resisted by the
Church in the days of the Fathers.

Divisions Today

The principal divisions in Christendom today are the result of separations which took place hundreds of years ago. We are speaking here
primarily of the break between the Holy See and the Eastern Patriar-
chates in the eleventh century and, in the West, of the separation of
various communions, both national and denominational, in what is
commonly called the Reformation, largely in the sixteenth century.
Neither in the case of the Orthodox Churches in the East nor in the case

---

[2]Cf. St. Augustine, De Haeresibus ad Quodvultdeum (ML 42.21-50).

of Protestantism in the West was the separation a single historical event; the separations we know today in fact evolved over long periods of time, from different causes, resulting in divisions different in nature.

The Eastern Orthodox Churches, although they are not in ecclesiastical communion with the Holy See, and thus are separated from the Catholic Church, nonetheless "possess true sacraments, above all — by 292 apostolic succession — the priesthood and the Eucharist, whereby they are still joined to us in a very close relationship" (UR 15).

The Second Vatican Council reminds us that the Eastern churches have had from their beginnings "a treasury from which the Church of the West has amply drawn for its liturgy, spiritual tradition, and jurisprudence" (UR 14). A number of basic dogmas of the faith were defined at Ecumenical Councils held in the East, and "to preserve this faith, these churches have suffered much, and still do so"(UR 14). Variety in 38 liturgy, customs, and traditions is by no means a bar to Church unity; nor indeed is variety in theological expressions of doctrinal truth.

There are of course many Catholics who, in the Eastern Catholic churches, or rites, are preserving the rich heritage of the East while living in full communion with the Holy See and with all who follow the tradition of the West. The Eastern Catholic churches "have a special role to play in promoting the unity of all Christians, particularly Easterners . . ., first of all by prayer, then by the example of their lives, by religious fidelity to ancient Eastern traditions, by greater mutual knowledge, by collaboration, and by a brotherly regard for objects and attitudes" (OE 24).

The divisions which developed in the West in the Reformation and in the post-Reformation period are of a different type. Here the non-Catholic Christian communions "differ not only from us but also among themselves to a considerable degree" (UR 19), and it is difficult to speak of them in a collective way. But the separations in the West were, and are, more than a rupture of Church unity. For there are genuine differences in doctrine (not merely differences in expressions of doctrine), in the interpretation of revelation and in the ways of considering Holy 305 Scripture (cf. UR 21). Although baptism provides a sacramental bond of unity linking all who are reborn by means of it (cf. UR 22), these separated Christians "lack that fullness of unity with us which should flow from baptism, and we believe that especially because of the lack of the sacrament of orders they have not preserved the genuine and total reality of the Eucharistic mystery" (UR 22).

Nonetheless, these separated churches and ecclesial communities

160

remain close to us. Their Christian way of life is nourished by faith in 130
the one Christ and is strengthened by the grace of baptism and the hearing of God's word; and the faith by which they believe in Christ does
bear fruit in a number of ways (cf. UR 23).

Promoting Christian Unity

All Catholics are called to share in the task of ecumenism, the fos- 233
tering of unity among Christians. Few are equipped or in positions to
participate in all phases of ecumenical work, but all can contribute to
the effort.

Catholics have an obligation to bear witness to their Catholic faith, 234
and they assist the cause of unity to the extent they do this well. Certainly Catholics must be concerned for their separated brethren, praying for them, communicating with them about Church matters, and
making the first approaches to them. But there is a primary duty to see
that the Catholic family of faith bears witness more faithfully and more
clearly in its life to those things which have been handed down from
Christ through the apostles (cf. UR 4).

At the same time, Catholics "must joyfully acknowledge and es-
teem the truly Christian endowments derived from our common heritage which are to be found among our separated brethren" (UR 4). We
should be willing to be edified by God's grace in them, for "whatever is
wrought by the grace of the Holy Spirit in the hearts of our separated
brethren can contribute to our own edification" (UR 4).

Ecumenical dialogue, especially by competent representatives, can
contribute much to the mutual understanding and clarification of points
of agreement and points of difference. Discussions of this sort, entered
into a spirit of charity and humility and conducted with honesty and
frankness and mutual respect, have in some important matters shown
that actual areas of differences are often smaller than had been believed.
This assists the search for unity and encourages prayerful hope that by
the grace of God the distance of separation may be narrowed to the
point of nonexistence.

There is wide room for cooperation between Catholics and non- 216
Catholic Christians (cf. UR 12), and this too promotes understanding
and the cause of unity.

In no way, however, does the practice of ecumenism call for any
submergence of Catholic identity or any suppression of Catholic truth.
In ecumenical dialogue, doctrine is to be presented clearly in its en-

282 tirety. "Nothing is so foreign to the spirit of ecumenism as a false concil-iatory approach which harms the purity of Catholic doctrine and ob-scures its assured genuine meaning" (UR 11). Catholics believe that "it is through Christ's Catholic Church alone, which is the all-embracing means of salvation, that all fullness of the means of salvation can be ob-tained" (UR 3), and "are bound to profess that through the gift of God's mercy they belong to that Church which Christ founded and which is governed by the successors of Peter and the other apostles, who are the depositaries of the original apostolic tradition, living and intact, which is the permanent heritage of doctrine and holiness of that same Church."[3] Catholic ecumenical activity should be devoid of all "superficiality or imprudent zeal" and be always "fully and sincerely Catholic" (UR 24).

Still, the Church realizes "that the holy task of reconciling all Christians in the unity of the one and only Church of Christ transcends human energies and abilities. It therefore places its hope entirely in the prayer of Christ for the Church, in the love of the Father for us, and in the power of the Holy Spirit. 'And hope does not disappoint, because the charity of God is poured forth in our hearts by the Holy Spirit who has been given to us' (Rom. 5.5)" (UR 24).

OTHER RELIGIONS AND CULTURES

A large part of the world's population does not know or has had minimal exposure to the Gospel of Christ and His Church, and looks to 27 various religions for answers to the profound questions of men about good and evil, about the origins of man and his ultimate fate.

Islam

The Second Vatican Council spoke in a special way about the Mos-lems. They, "professing to hold the faith of Abraham, along with us adore the one and merciful God, who on the last day will judge man-kind" (LG 16). Though the Islamic faith does not acknowledge Jesus as God, it does revere Him as a prophet, and also honors His virgin mother. Moslems "prize the moral life, and give worship to God espe-cially through prayer, almsgiving, and fasting" (NA 3). Noting that

---

[3]Sacred Congregation for the Doctrine of the Faith, *Mysterium Ecclesiae* ("Declaration in Defense of the Catholic Doctrine on the Church against Certain Errors of the Present Day," June 24, 1973) n. 1.

there have been many quarrels and hostilities between Christians and Moslems, the council urged that all "forget the past and strive sincerely for mutual understanding, and, on behalf of all mankind, make common cause of safeguarding and fostering social justice, moral values, peace, and freedom" (NA 3).

Other Non-Christian Religions

The non-Christian religions, including Hinduism, Buddhism, and many others besides Islam, differ in many ways from the Catholic Church. This, however, does not put their followers in good conscience outside the plan of salvation. For "the divine design of salvation embraces all men; and those who without fault on their part do not know the Gospel of Christ and His Church, but seek God sincerely, and under the influence of grace endeavor to do His will as recognized through the promptings of their conscience, they, in a number known only to God, can obtain salvation."[4]

The Catholic Church rejects nothing which is true and holy in these non-Christian religions. The Church exhorts Catholics that they "prudently and lovingly, through dialogue and collaboration with the followers of other religions, and in witness of Christian faith and life, acknowledge, preserve, and promote the spiritual and moral goods found among these men, as well as the values in their society and culture" (NA 2).

Atheism

In this world of many religions there are also many people who have no religious belief and profess atheism.

Some contemporary forms of atheism, as Marxism, have some of the characteristics of Christian heresy. They promise confidently a kingdom of justice and peace, and their promise seems in a way to mirror the confident Christian hope; but they seek for such a kingdom only on this earth, and as effected by blind historical laws. They clearly reject large and essential areas of Christian teaching.

The Church rejects atheism completely. Here also, however, some dialogue is useful. For the Church strives to detect in the atheist's mind

---

[4]Pope Paul VI, *Professio Fidei* ("The Credo of the People of God," June 30, 1968). Cf. LG 16; NA 2.

the reasons for the denial of God, and it invites the atheist to examine the Gospel with an open mind. Moreover, the Church believes that all men, believers and unbelievers alike, ought to work for the rightful betterment of this world in which all alike live, and this cannot be brought about without "sincere and prudent dialogue" (GS 21).

MISSIONARY TASK OF THE CHURCH

In the pluralistic world in which it works, and in which it seeks good relations with all, the Church is ever mindful of the charge given it by Christ: "Go into all the world and preach the gospel to the whole creation" (Mark 16.15; cf. Matt. 28.19).

84   The Church is "missionary by her very nature" (AG 2). The Gospel message has not yet been heard, or scarcely so, by many in this world, and there is still a "gigantic missionary task" (AG 10) to be accomplished. Every follower of Christ has an obligation to do his part in spreading the faith (cf. LG 17; AG 23, 35); indeed, "by its very nature the Christian vocation is also a vocation to the apostolate" (AA 2). But some are called specifically by Christ to work in mission fields, and they dedicate themselves to this task (cf. AG 23).

The Church has an obligation ever to proclaim the message of Christ, and those who come to awareness that that Catholic Church was
131 made necessary by God through Jesus Christ have an obligation to enter the Church and persevere in it (cf. LG 14). Although God "in ways known to Himself can lead those inculpably ignorant of the Gospel to that faith without which it is impossible to please Him (cf. Heb. 11.6), yet a necessity lies upon the Church (cf. 1 Cor. 9.16), and at the same time a sacred duty, to preach the Gospel. Hence missionary activity today as always retains its power and necessity" (AG 7).

RELIGIOUS FREEDOM

213   Among the basic human rights flowing from the dignity of the human person is the right to religious freedom. This right to immunity from external coercion in matters religious is a right which governments as well as individuals must respect.

The Second Vatican Council declared that the right to religious freedom "has its foundation in the very dignity of the human person"
188 (DH 2), for man is a being endowed with reason and free will and therefore privileged to bear personal responsibility. This right in civil

164

life does not in any way negate or alter the moral obligation men have to seek the truth, especially religious truth, and to adhere to that truth when it is known, and to order their lives in accord with the demands of truth. But the right to religious freedom is so basic that it is had even by those who do not live up to their obligation to seek and to follow truth.

Although revelation does not affirm in so many words the right of man to immunity from external coercion in matters religious, it does disclose the dignity of the human person in its full dimensions, and it gives evidence of the respect which Christ showed toward the freedom with which man is to fulfill his duty of belief in the word of God (cf. DH 9).

God calls men to serve Him, but He does not force them. "It is one of the major tenets of Catholic doctrine that man's response to God in faith must be free. Therefore no one is to be forced to embrace the Chris- 170 tian faith against his own will. . . . The act of faith is of its very nature a free act. Man, redeemed by Christ the Savior and through Christ Jesus called to be God's adopted son (cf. Eph. 1.5), cannot give his adherence to God revealing Himself unless the Father draw him (cf. John 6.44) to offer to God the reasonable and free submission of faith" (DH 10).

Thus it is completely in accord with the nature of the faith that in matters religious every manner of coercion on the part of man should be excluded. Indeed, the principle of religious freedom "makes no small contribution to the creation of an environment in which men can without hindrance be invited to Christian faith, and embrace it of their own free will, and profess it effectively in their whole manner of life" (DH 10).

*   *   *

Questions related to the material in this chapter:

1. What is the special place of Judaism in the history of salvation?

2. Does the heritage common to Christians and Jews have any significance for Christian-Jewish relations today?

3. What is the attitude of the Church with regard to anti-Semitism?

4. What are the principal divisions in Christendom today, and how do they differ in character?

5. What is ecumenism? What are some Catholic principles for ecumenical activities?

6. Does the practice of ecumenism involve any submergence of Catholic identity or any suppression of Catholic doctrine?

7. Does the Church have anything in common with Islam, Hinduism, Buddhism, and other non-Christian religions?

8. What is the Church's attitude toward atheism?

9. Some people today seem to think that in this era of ecumenism and interfaith dialogues missionary activity is no longer necessary or even meaningful. What truths does that view fail to take into account?

10. The right to religious freedom, to immunity from external coercion in matters religious, is a basic human right. Does this right in any way change the moral obligation people have to seek the truth, especially religious truth, and to live in accord with it?

Part Three

WITH CHRIST: SHARING THE LIFE OF GOD

17

Christ Comes to Give Life

Jesus came to give us life. He offers a life richer than any we could ever otherwise have, a life so radically new that we must be born again to have it (cf. John 3.3-8).

This chapter first discusses how this new life is an entirely free gift of God in Christ. It notes some of the basic elements of the new life, and outlines the major ways in which one obtains this new life and grows in it.

THE NEW LIFE GIVEN US BY GOD

The good news of Jesus is proclaimed to the world by those who have already tasted the new life He has given us through the Holy Spirit. Just as the sins and sorrows from which He has called men are very real, so the life Christ has given is very real. Loneliness and despair, inability to believe and to love, the utter frustration of human efforts — all these are terribly real in the world. But even more real and present are the life, faith, freedom, and healing that Christ brings.

Because they have already lived the new life, the disciples of Jesus can bear witness to its reality and accessibility. They have themselves experienced that faith which "throws a new light on everything" (GS 11) and have learned in some measure to live in His love.

Christ in God's Eternal Plan

The Apostle Paul was always grateful that he had been called to make known to the nations God's merciful plan. "To me, though I am the least of all the saints, this grace was given, to preach to the Gentiles the unsearchable riches of Christ, and to make all men see what is the plan of the mystery hidden for ages in God who created all things" (Eph. 3.8-9).

Christ is the reason why there is a world. The love He freely gave 68 to His Father on the cross and the generous love He makes possible in the hearts of men, binding them to Himself and to the Father in friendship, freedom, and life, explain the why of the world. God made the world so that the love which is the inner life of the Trinity might

169

be shared by other persons, whom He would call to Himself in Christ.

The world was made, then, so that created persons might, in Christ, come to share the life of the Trinity. But they were to come to God only freely. The freedom God gave man also made it possible for man to reject His call and to sin. But "we know that in everything God works for good with those who love Him, who are called according to His purpose" (Rom. 8.28). He is able to overcome in Christ all the evil that sin creates, and to make even suffering and pain instruments of His healing love.

The story of creation is told anew at the beginning of the fourth Gospel, now in the light of Christ's revelation. In the very beginning, we are told, the Word was creatively present with the Father. This was the Word, the Son of God, who was to become our brother. Everything that was created was made through Him, so that through Him men might also become children of God.

God's Free Gift

St. Paul often reminded the early Christians that this new life is a free gift of God (cf. Eph. 2.8-10).

Those who come to faith should not imagine that God's blessings are due to their merits. Absolutely everything is due to God's generous, free love. Sensitive to our helplessness to do anything by ourselves alone to acquire the new life of the Spirit, Jesus said: "Apart from Me you can do nothing" (John 15.5). "No one can come to Me unless the Father who sent Me draws him" (John 6.44).

He predestines us; He gives without our prior deserving (cf. Eph. 1.5). But God's predestination of us does not mean that He treats us as controlled puppets or robots. He calls us as free persons, and He desires
165 from us a free response of love and friendship. He does not call any to life in such a way that they are forced to come; neither does He exclude any from His favor arbitrarily, simply willing that they be lost forever. Those who in fact accept His grace do so not because they are good;
360 their ability to respond freely to Him is itself a gift of grace. Those who refuse His grace do not do so because He has abandoned them, but because they themselves choose to reject His gifts.

Life in Christ

Ch. 23   Christ is the life of the world in many ways. First, God has graced
178 the humanity of Jesus with the fullness of all divine gifts. Jesus is

always attractive, an invitation to life, for all who come to know Him. In Him the "goodness and loving kindness of God" (Titus 3.4) were made visible to men.

He is also the Teacher of life, and the Exemplar of life. In His words and in His actions men can find the best guide and model for the way they themselves most wish to live. Even more, He is the Fountain and Source of life. We are not merely to imitate Him, but to live in Him and from Him. For "we are members of His body" (Eph. 5.30).

We are made one with Him by the gift of His Spirit. "Any one who 105 does not have the Spirit of Christ does not belong to Him" (Rom. 8.9). But to have this Spirit is to be a new person. For it is to have faith, hope, and at least some measure of true love of God; and these are transforming gifts.

ELEMENTS OF THIS NEW LIFE

Human integrity has been wounded by sin, and so it is in his very humanity that man is healed by the new life Jesus brings.

But the gift of Christ's life does far more than restore man's full hu- 89 manity. Through Christ men are called to a true friendship with the Trinity, with the God who chooses to dwell within the one who loves Christ (cf. John 14.23); they are called to share in the very nature of God (2 Peter 1.4). They are called to be "God's children now" (cf. 1 John 3.2), to live already on earth in a divine way, sharing God's knowledge in unshakable faith, and sharing in God's inmost life by the gift of His love (cf. Rom. 5.5).

Healing and Freedom

In his Epistle to the Romans, St. Paul speaks of the dehumanizing 18 consequences of sin in human life. St. Paul had himself tasted bitter helplessness before he received Christ's mercy and the gift of the Spirit. The grace of realizing how one should live does not of itself give power to live that way. "I am carnal, sold under sin. I do not understand my own actions. For I do not do what I want, but I do the very thing I hate. . . . For I know that nothing good dwells within me, that is, in my flesh. I can will what is right, but I cannot do it. For I do not do the good I want, but the evil I do not want is what I do" (Rom. 7.14-15, 18-19).

Here St. Paul is describing a situation that has been experienced by many. When men seek within themselves, from mere human strength and wisdom, resources to overcome evil consistently, they find they are helpless.

18   This precisely is the gift of Christ: power to do the good. "But to all who received Him, who believed in His name, He gave power to become children of God" (John 1.12).

God's grace liberates; it gives a man freedom. Grace supposes freedom of choice, for grace is not forced on a man, but offered to him.[1] But there is a kind of freedom which grace itself gives: an ability to do the good and saving acts that one could not do before, to share in the strength of Christ, to be fortified by the gift of the Spirit.

This liberation is precious. Without the grace of Christ, men are hard pressed in every way. But the freedom grace offers is rich and real, if one chooses to accept and grow in it. "For sin will have no dominion over you, since you are not under law but under grace" (Rom. 6.14).

When, by the gift of a new life in Christ, God heals a man and gives
240 him freedom, He effects a profound transformation within him. This change is sometimes slow to come to completion; though conversion may at times be instantaneous, growth in grace is generally gradual over time. St. Paul speaks of this change in a variety of ways: It is a transition from bondage to freedom (cf. Rom. 6.12-20), from condemnation to acquittal (cf. Rom. 5.18), from death to life (cf. Rom. 6.6-7), from the old man to the new man (cf. Eph. 4.21 f.), from darkness to light (cf. Col. 1.12-13), from slavery to salvation (cf. Titus 3.3-5). Indeed, the justifying act by which God so brings us to life is one in which He makes us sharers in His own life, children of God, heirs of heaven.

ACQUIRING AND LIVING THE NEW LIFE

In the chapters which follow we shall speak chiefly of three main ways of coming to, growing in, and expressing the new life of Christ. Here we note them only briefly. These three ways, all closely related, are: by sharing in the sacramental acts of Christ, by prayer, and by works of love.

Chs. 26-30   *By the Sacraments*

By baptism we are born to newness of life. Though men serve as
272 agents for Christ, Christ Himself is the principal minister of baptism and

---

[1]Cf. Council of Trent, Session 6, January 13, 1547, *Decree on Justification,* ch. 6 (DS 1526).

of every sacrament. For this reason the Church declares that the sacred signs we call sacraments are deeds of Christ in His Church. Sacraments 271 are outward signs instituted by Christ to give grace.[2]

Sacramental participation underscores both aspects of the mystery of grace. The initiative is entirely the Lord's. The sacraments implant and nourish faith and love. Christ causes this faith and love to grow; but the acts of faith and love are also the free acts of the Christian.

This is one of the mysteries of grace. Divine mercy enables us to do freely acts that are far above our human power. The saving actions by which we cling to Christ and express our sharing of His life are both the work of God and the free, joyful deeds of man.

By Prayer Chs. 24-25

Prayer is a vital part of the Christian life. Prayer is itself a gift of God, the work of the Spirit within us (cf. Rom. 8.26); only because God's mercy arouses us to prayer can we fruitfully cry out to Him to save us.

But prayer is far more than a plea for life. It is an essential way of living the Christian life and seeking perfection in it.

By Works of Love Chs. 18-21

Christ tells us that "he who does the will of My Father who is in heaven" will enter the kingdom of God (cf. Matt. 7.21). It is by leading a life pleasing to God, obeying His commandments, all rooted in the demanding commandments of love, that we live in the world the life we have received.

Growing up in Christ

The Christian is not called merely to conversion, and to a static preservation of a gift once received. Life has been given to him, a life that must grow. "Rather, speaking the truth in love, we are to grow up 246 in every way into Him who is the head, into Christ" (Eph. 4.15).

Merit

By ever becoming more intensely alive in Christ, and by exercising this life in union with Jesus in personal prayer and in liturgy and in

---

[2]Cf. Council of Trent, Session 7, March 3, 1547, *Decree on the Sacraments,* canons on the sacraments in general (DS 1601-1608).

353 deeds of love, we also prepare for and truly merit the heavenly life to which all earthly sharing in Christ's life is ordered as its final crown and final perfection.

All our prayer, worship, and works of love in this world are imperfect. We live in a state of faith and obscurity, in a world still suffering, awaiting final redemption (cf. Rom. 8.22-23). While the works of a Christian may bring this world ever closer to conformity with the plan of God's kingdom, that kingdom cannot be perfected here. What we strive after in living now the life of Christ will be fully realized only when we have come to see God face to face, and in His light learn to love Him and one another perfectly, and to rejoice in the utter victory of Christ over all sin, death, and imperfection (cf. 1 Cor. 15.24-28).

240 Our good deeds, moved by the grace of Christ, build up the Body of Christ and merit eternal life for us. It is not, however, our own power which makes our good deeds so effective, so fruitful. It is Christ who merited for us all the good we hope for.

47 But it is also His gift that He treats us as persons, and calls us to serve Him freely. When He has given us the power to do freely such sublime deeds, then, in virtue of God's promises and of the genuine abilities He has given us by His graces, those deeds genuinely merit eternal life.

God is truly just to reward those who were freely faithful to grace when they might have failed Him, though they also know that the glory is rightly His. It is His gift that we have seen and cared and served.
361 "When God crowns our merits, is He not crowning precisely His own gifts?"[3]

*   *   *

Questions related to the material in this chapter:

1. St. Paul speaks of God's plan for us. In what does this plan consist?

2. We say that the new life Christ offers is a free gift of God. What does this mean?

3. Does God's "predestination" of us destroy our freedom?

4. What do we mean when we say that Christ is the life of the world?

---

[3]St. Augustine, *Epistula* 194.5.19 (ML 33.880).

5. What are some elements of the new life offered by Christ?

6. When St. Paul speaks of our liberation, he means liberation from what and for what?

7. How is the new life to be acquired and lived?

8. "When God crowns our merits, is He not crowning precisely His own gifts?" What do these words of St. Augustine mean?

18

God's Plan for Human Living

Called to a new life, the Christian must live his life on this earth and in the midst of his fellowmen.

In this chapter we discuss first the problems involved in the shaping of a good human life. Then we speak of Christ's place in solving these problems. The chapter treats of what conscience is and how it is to be guided; how God makes known the natural law and the commandments; and how the grace-rooted virtues we have as His gifts enable us to grow in freedom in doing His will.

THE SHAPING OF HUMAN LIFE

43   To be a man is to be free. Man can make choices, and because he can, he must. Thus this freedom of man presents him with a problem: How should one live? And with this freedom there can come deep doubts: Is my freedom genuine? Are my moral efforts really worthwhile?

These are disturbing questions. But not every factor in man's free life is so puzzling. Although specific ways of responding to basic human values vary greatly from place to place, anyone can appreciate that life and health and safety, considered simply in themselves, are good. Death, disease, injury, and pain, on the other hand, are bad. The play of the senses, the exercise of human capacities and skills, the appreciation of beauty, and the knowledge of truth are good. Stupor, insensitivity, ignorance, and error are bad. The sharing of goods with others, peace and harmony within oneself and with others, freedom to pursue goods in ways which seem reasonable — these, too, are basic forms of goodness.

These basic forms of human goodness mark out the whole field of
217 human action, the broad range of human possibilities. All personal growth and all enrichment of community life are realizations of one or more of these basic forms of goodness. It is the attractiveness of these values, of life and friendship and truth and the rest, in one form or another, that stimulates all human efforts, all historical movements.

176

But as soon as one begins to think about what to do oneself, many questions arise.

Am I my neighbor's keeper? And who is my neighbor? What forms of good should I now be realizing? How much? For whom? With whom? Of all the choices I could make, which are the ones I really ought to make? What are the proper standards to use in choosing?

The variety of moral systems and approaches to morality suggests the complexity of the moral problem. Straightforward human reasonableness and simple human friendship can carry one far toward a solution.

Reasonableness demands that like cases be treated alike and that different cases be treated differently. Since the same goods can be realized as much in one person as in another, reasonableness urges one to avoid preferring one person to another without some real reason. The Golden Rule,. "As you wish that men would do to you, do so to them" (Luke 6.31; cf. Matt. 7.12), emerged in human conscience long before Christ revealed its full weight (cf. Tobit 4.16).

In carrying one beyond mere self-interest, the call of reason reinforces the call of friendship. Friendship carries a man outside himself, 334 and establishes for him a new practical perspective. But his friendships would be neither true nor really valuable if he entered into them solely for the sake of his own well-being. Friendship establishes a kind of im- 231 partiality, of shared unselfishness, in the pursuit of goods.

One's perspective can be shifted still further from immediate self-interest by reflection on one's life as a whole, not merely as a set of separate moments. Looking back on this life at the moment of one's death, one presumably would see many choices one made which now seem irrational, a waste of opportunities, a stunting of one's own free development, a failure, a shame.

"In all you do, remember the end of your life" (Sir. 7.36). These 343 words are a reminder not so much of the life hereafter as of the proper perspective for living this life. Wise men in every age have realized that the right measure of the pursuit of values is established by finding the proper viewpoint.

Thus, even without God's revelation men have found and can always find in reason an inward guide for the exercise of freedom. Pagan philosophers, reflecting on the inwardness and force of this guidance, called it the "law of nature" or the "law of reason." 181

Anyone can make the shift from concentrating exclusively on his own pain and pleasure to thinking in terms of what is really worthwhile in itself. Judgments about what is worthy, just, and right, we call judgments of conscience.

But new questions arise. Why should I do what is worthy? Why should I respond to the voice of conscience? Why should anyone take seriously his spontaneous inclination to seek truth, to be reasonable, to be a friend? How can one be sure that the moral good is really good?

43 And with these questions comes doubt about the authenticity of one's freedom. If there is nothing really good, truly worthy, for one to know, is not one simply the creature of one's psychology, one's upbringing, one's society? Or else is not one the prisoner of one's passions? How real is a "freedom" which can "choose" only by following an illusion or a compulsion?

God has given us an answer to these doubts about human life and actions. It is in Christ.

SHAPING ONE'S LIFE IN CHRIST

212 Christ's call to each of us is an appeal to our desire for truth. Then
46 He calls upon our capacity for gratitude and love; these, if we allow them, will spur us to follow His way and imitate Him. Thus His call is a call to *faith*.

Christ's call is an appeal to our intelligent sense that nothing could be more desirable and worthwhile than to attain what would be ours if we could contemplate the depths of God's creative purpose and of His own being. Thus it is a call to *hope*, a hope that through friendship with
547 God we may overcome all difficulties, see Him face to face, and know even as we are known (cf. 1 Cor. 13.12).

Christ's call is a call to apply our intelligence and all of our talents to discovering and furthering the loving purpose of His Father, the pur-
192 pose for which He became man. Thus it is a call to *love*.

In these chapters on the moral life we consider Christ's call only insofar as it is an appeal and guide to choice and action, an answer to the question, "What shall I do?" We take for granted all that has been and
Ch. 23 will be said in other parts of this book about the direct action of God's grace in us. We take for granted that in the last analysis the message of

Christ is "written not with ink but with the Spirit of the living God, not on tablets of stone but on tablets of human hearts" (2 Cor. 3.3).

Conforming to the Mind of Christ

The value of Christ's life and teaching consists in their conformity to the intention of God the Father. "My judgment is just, because I seek not My own will but the will of Him who sent Me" (John 5.30). Christ's own prayer in the face of the terror of death was: "Father . . ., not My will, but Yours, be done" (Luke 22.42). Christ lived and died in the spirit of the prayer He taught us: "Our Father . . ., Thy will be done, on earth as it is in heaven" (Matt. 6.9-10). He makes this the very meaning of His Sonship, through which we become sons of God: "For whoever does 66 the will of My Father in heaven is My brother, and sister, and mother" (Matt. 12.50).

To conform to the mind of Christ is to conform to the mind of the Father. If we ask what we must do to "be doing the works of God," Jesus replies: "This is the work of God, that you believe in Him whom He has sent" (John 6.28-29).

Judging by God's Standards

We see correctly when we see with the eye of God. On this princi- 250 ple every part of Christian moral teaching depends. When what we choose to be or to do conforms to God's plan, then and only then is that choice good.

In the search for the worthwhile, the right, the morally good, the only way to satisfy the demands of reasonableness is to see as God sees, to judge as God judges, to love as God loves. "Do not be conformed to this world but be transformed by the renewal of your mind, that you may prove what is the will of God, what is good and acceptable and perfect" (Rom. 12.2; cf. Col. 1.9-10).

The struggle to attain this standard of judgment, to put it into prac- 197 tice in one's life, and to return to it when one has fallen away from it, is simply the struggle to judge and act conscientiously.

Conscience as the Voice of God

Conscience is one's practical judgment about the rightness or 27 wrongness of one's acts. Judgments of conscience are the outcome of a

179

person's effort to avoid being arbitrary and unresponsive in pursuing the values which attract human love. When this effort succeeds, then 43 the answers are right. Then the conscience is true and upright, and a person attains what he was implicitly or explicitly seeking: the knowledge of God's design and will.

"The Creator of the world has stamped man's inmost being with an order which his conscience reveals to him and strongly enjoins him to obey."[1] The Church has constantly taught that to say that a conscience is correct is to say that its judgments are right and correspond to God's judgments.

"In the depths of his conscience, man detects a law which he does not impose upon himself, but which holds him to obedience. Always summoning him to love good and do it and to avoid evil, the voice of conscience can when necessary speak to his heart more specifically: do this, shun that. For man has in his heart a law written by God. To obey it is the very dignity of man; according to it he will be judged" (GS 16).

Conscience, then, is not a device for making exceptions to objective requirements of morality. On the contrary, "through the mediation of conscience man perceives and acknowledges the imperatives of the divine law" (DH 3; cf. GS 16).

This "divine law" is "eternal, objective, and universal," and is the "highest norm of human life" (DH 3). Fidelity to conscience is fidelity in 214 the search for truth, and insofar as his search is successful a man turns aside from blind choice and wishful thinking; he is guided by "objective norms of morality" (GS 16).

Conscience and Error

Even when one's quest for the truly good is sincerely motivated and intelligently pursued, it is possible for the judgments of conscience to be mistaken. For when we work from the grasp of basic principles of good toward particular decisions, we are working in the midst of our passions and inclinations even as we seek to make a reasonable judgment about them.

"Conscience frequently errs from invincible ignorance without losing its dignity" (GS 16).

Ignorance or error is not excusable, however, when it results from 212 negligence in the pursuit of truth and goodness. When the Second Vati-

---

[1] Pope John XXIII, Encyclical, *Pacem in Terris* (April 11, 1963) (DS 3956).

can Council said that an erring but sincere conscience need not lose its dignity, it immediately added: "But the same cannot be said of a man who cares but little for truth and goodness" (GS 16). If, therefore, one's conscience errs because of one's complacency, prejudice, rashness, or self-centeredness, one will be in the wrong whether one rejects or follows its dictates.

Conscience and Authority

Conscience is not a matter of "seeing" what is right by a special personal intuition. Judgments of conscience have the authority of objectivity only if they are the judgments that would be made by a man who is as reasonable as anyone can be and who has reached the impartiality that comes with full friendship with God and man.

It is Christ above all who makes known to us the will of God. A Christian conscience cannot be individualistic. We must conform our consciences to the teaching of Christ. Most of all, the Christian heeds Christ by conforming his conscience to the teaching of those who teach 144 all nations all that He commanded (cf. Matt. 23.20).

The Second Vatican Council stated: "In the formation of their consciences, the Christian faithful ought carefully to attend to the sacred and certain doctrine of the Church. The Catholic Church is, by the will of Christ, the teacher of the truth. It is her duty to give utterance to, and authoritatively to teach, that Truth which is Christ Himself and also to declare and confirm by her authority those principles of the moral order which have their origin in human nature itself" (DH 14). Thus a Christian has the right and duty to follow his conscience, but also the responsibility to form his conscience in accord with truth and in the light of faith.

THE NATURAL LAW

The Second Vatican Council, in a section on international hostili- 224 ties, says: "Contemplating this melancholy state of humanity, the Council wishes to recall first of all the permanent binding force of universal natural law and its all-embracing principles" (GS 79).

The Church uses "natural law" in a classical Christian sense. In this sense, "natural law" signifies the plan of God in relation to human life and action, insofar as the human mind in this life can grasp that plan

181

and share with God the role of directing human life according to it (cf. DH 3).[2]

Why does the Church speak of "natural law" as well as of "the will of God" and "God's plan," and of the conscience which discerns that plan? First of all, the expression "natural law" emphasizes that the fundamental moral principles are not extrinsic commands, arbitrarily imposed on man by God. Fundamental moral principles follow from our being what we are.

51 Moreover, by speaking of "natural" law the Church recalls that in this life we do not in fact share God's full understanding of all the details of His divine plan. In particular, we do not understand how it is that God will bring greater good out of every evil and failure.

But we do know for certain that the basic forms of human self-realization are good. We can grasp the certainty and constant relevance of the principles which express that goodness, such as, for example, the principle that human life is a good to be realized, preserved, and favored, and that whatever threatens life is to be feared, avoided, defended against. We also recognize the principle of reasonableness, which provides all the goods and principles with their moral force, and which illumines the path from basic principles to particular decisions.

Principles for All Men

The expression "natural law" is also used by the Church to emphasize that the moral principles taught by Christ and by the Church are principles for all men, for all times and places, for all cultures and situations.

180 The principles of natural law are recognizable by all. Man's intellect is naturally inclined toward this understanding of human well-being. But man's response in applying these principles is variable and varied.

The Church always has considered that men normally come to an adequate knowledge of natural law only through revelation, above all through the example and teaching of Christ. This is why it is a function of the magisterium of the Church to interpret the moral natural law. "It is in fact indisputable, as our predecessors have many times declared,

---

[2]Cf. also Pope Leo XIII, Encyclical, *Libertas Praestantissimum* (June 20, 1888) (DS 3247); Pope John XXIII, Encyclical, *Pacem in Terris* (April 11, 1963) (DS 3956, 3973). See also St. Thomas Aquinas, *Summa Theologica* I-II, 91, 2.

that Jesus Christ, when He communicated His divine authority to Peter and the other apostles and sent them to teach all nations His precepts, constituted them authentic guardians and interpreters of the whole moral law, that is, not only of the law of the Gospel but also of the natural law, which is also an expression of the will of God, the faithful fulfillment of which is equally necessary for salvation."[3]

THE COMMANDMENTS

What is right can be known by the natural light of reason. But it is crystallized in the Decalogue, the Ten Commandments of the old covenant with Israel, and is brought to full clarity in the new law of Christ.   82

The Decalogue

The moral commands or laws given by God to Israel through Moses are listed in two places of the Old Testament, in Exodus (20.2-17) and in Deuteronomy (5.6-22). In summary form the Ten Commandments are:
1. I, the Lord, am your God. You shall not have other gods besides me.
2. You shall not take the name of the Lord, your God, in vain.
3. Remember to keep holy the Sabbath day.
4. Honor your father and your mother.
5. You shall not kill.
6. You shall not commit adultery.
7. You shall not steal.
8. You shall not bear false witness against your neighbor.
9. You shall not covet your neighbor's wife.
10. You shall not covet anything that belongs to your neighbor.

What does God teach us in these commandments? First, He teaches the absolute priority of loving service of God.

Second, God teaches that serving Him requires unconditional respect, in deeds and thoughts and words, for one's neighbor.

Third, the Decalogue teaches that certain types of acts, and even, as the last two commandments show, the inner disposition to such types of acts, are incompatible with love of God and respect for neighbor. Acts of such types are thus always and everywhere wrong; they may not be 203 done in any situation.

---

[3]Pope Paul VI, Encyclical, *Humanae Vitae* (July 25, 1968) n. 4. Similarly, GS 89, DH 14.

The Decalogue does not identify these types of acts with complete precision. This identification is in many respects left to the consciences of the people of God as they move through history, guided by the saints and doctors who strive to see as God sees and to love as He loves, and by "the Church's teaching office, which authentically interprets the divine law in the light of the Gospel" (GS 50), and thus by Christ Himself.

The Law of Christ

231   Christ ratified the Decalogue, both as a whole and in its parts (cf. Matt. 19.17-19; Mark 10.17-19; Luke 18.18-20).[4] He also ratified the Deuteronomist's summary on love of God (cf. Matt. 22.37-38), and He added a summary of the last seven commandments: "You shall love your neighbor as yourself" (Matt. 22.39).

This command of love of neighbor was not new (cf. Lev. 19.18), and Christ did not say it was new. But Christ did give a new commandment of love: "A new commandment I give to you, that you love one another; even as I have loved you, that you also love one another" (John 13.34).

What is new in Christ's commandment of love is the standard which He sets, the standard which He Himself is. Christ's love for us is not only the maximum of human love. Jesus loves us in the way the Father loves Him. "As the Father has loved Me, so have I loved you . . ." (John 15.9). The Father's love for the Son is divine; Jesus' love for us is divine; our love for one another is to be divine.

The standard is that of children of God. We are summoned to "be imitators of God, as beloved children. And walk in love, as Christ loved us . . ." (Eph. 5.1-2). By following this way we are given title to become sons and daughters of God (cf. John 1.12). And as adopted children of God we are called to share Christ's entire lot, both His suffering as man and His glorification as Son of God (cf. Rom. 8.16-17). St. Paul summed up "the law of Christ" as the demand that we not merely respect our neighbor but actually "bear one another's burden" (Gal. 6.2).

VIRTUES AND GRACES IN THE MORAL LIFE

We can live the law of Christ only because, by God's utterly free grace, we can live in Christ. He is not only our Teacher, Master, Leader,

---

[4]Cf. also Council of Trent, Session 6, January 13, 1547, *Decree on Justification,* canon 19 (DS 1569).

and Model; He is God's Son who sends us the Spirit, the Spirit who pours God's love into our hearts (cf. Rom. 5.5), the Spirit by whom we are adopted children of God (cf. Rom. 14.16).

The life of grace will be the theme of a later chapter. What concerns Ch. 23 us here is the new man generated within by the grace of the Spirit. This new man is a second self, a second nature. This new nature is to express itself in new ways of living; Christian theologians, following the language of pagan philosophers but the thought of the New Testament, call these new ways of living "virtues."

A virtue is a settled disposition characteristic of the good person, a tendency toward the altogether good, truly loving, and therefore morally right action in any relevant situation. A virtue is an aspect of the identity which a good person establishes for himself by his love and responsible pursuit of what is good.

The virtues natural to man, good as they are, are insufficient for the life of full friendship with God and with other men. They are perfect- 243 ed and given a new orientation by God "working in us without us."[5] When transformed in this way, the virtues are called by theologians "infused virtues," the "infused" here meaning that they are poured into our hearts with the love of God by the Spirit (cf. Rom. 5.5).

Primary among the virtues of the new man are those which dispose us in a special way toward God. All virtues, insofar as they are dispositions toward human goods, are dispositions toward that sharing in divine goodness which is naturally open to men. But faith, hope, and love dispose human persons to a life destined to be lived in everlasting friendship with God. These virtues are called "theological virtues," not because they pertain to the study of theology, but because they orient us toward God directly.

FREEDOM AND THE CHRISTIAN MORAL LIFE

A person's response to God's call is not really a personal response if it is not free. Moreover, God's call is a call to completely authentic freedom, a freedom to do with joy and spontaneity what one's heart 240 most desires. Morality is the pattern of a growth from freedom to freedom.

St. Paul sums up the whole matter: "For you were called to free-

---

[5]On this classic phrase and the thought here, cf. St. Thomas Aquinas, *Summa Theologica* I-II, 55, 4; 63, 2.

171 dom, brethren; only do not use your freedom as an opportunity for the flesh, but through love be servants of one another. . . . But I say, walk by the Spirit. . . . But if you are led by the Spirit you are not under the law" (Gal. 5.13, 16.18).

In this and all the New Testament writings we find an awareness of moral obligation which could scarcely be more intense, yet with it an awareness that in the final analysis obligation is not what morality is all about.

That is why St. Augustine put forward his summary of Christian morality — "Love, and do what you will"[6] — in his commentary on the equivalent summary in the First Epistle of John (cf. 1 John 5.2-3). Since the will of God is the rule of goodness, those who are united with God also have freedom to do as they please, for what pleases them is to please God.

THE CHRISTIAN NATURE OF MORALITY

Christ came to set us free, by the truth of His call to us and the spirit of His life within us: free not only from our own failure, inertia, compulsiveness, misdirection of effort, and waste of opportunity, but also from enslavement to public opinion, to the standards and taboos of a merely human culture, to the image and upbringing of perhaps all-too-human parents.

Christian morality is not a morality for Christians only. It is for all 131 men, for all men are called to follow Christ. Christian morality is the authentic, central, and integral form of morality. Apart from faith in Christ, the great questions about the reality of freedom, the rationality of conscience, and the value of pursuing human goods unselfishly cannot be fully answered.

In Christ we find the questions answered, answered with a divine Word who tells us more than we asked, who surpasses our expectations. In Christ we see that questioning itself is part of the movement of His grace within us. If we respond to this movement, we will question and reject every form of arbitrariness and inertia in the pursuit of good as unworthy — unworthy of the dignity of the human person created in the image of God and re-created as a new man in the image of His Son, unworthy in the sight of God who through His Word summons us out of nothing and makes us all that we can freely choose to be.

* * *

---

[6]St. Augustine *In Epistulam Ioannis ad Parthos* 6.4.8 (ML 35.2033).

Questions related to the material in this chapter:

1. When we speak of human "good," what do we mean?

2. When we speak of reasonableness and of fairness or justice in moral behavior, what do we mean?

3. How does friendship help to establish a perspective on living well?

4. In what way is acceptance of Christ's call an acceptance of a call to faith, hope, and love?

5. We speak of "conforming to the mind of Christ" and "judging by God's standards." What do these phrases mean?

6. What is conscience and what is its role?

7. Can my conscience be wrong? How is the Christian to form his or her conscience?

8. What do we mean by "natural law"?

9. Why are the Ten Commandments still in force today?

10. The law of Christ is a law of love. How are the commandments an expression of this law of love?

11. How do the Holy Spirit and gifts of grace affect the way the law of Christ operates within us?

12. Why is Christian morality not a morality for Christians only, but a morality for all persons?

19

Living Faith, Hope, and Love

"So faith, hope, love abide, these three" (1 Cor. 13.13).

The preceding chapters have said much of faith, hope, and love. Here all that needs to be added is further clarification of the place of these theological virtues in the moral life, and of the special obligations that they imply.

THE LIFE OF FAITH

The first duty of one to whom God addresses His word is faith. When the Lord who has created us invites us to faith and makes it possible for us to know that it is He who calls, the "obedience of faith" (Rom. 16.26) is required of us. Only if we believe Him can we trust and love Him. Faith "is the beginning of human salvation."[1] Without faith it is impossible for fallen man in the course of his life not to fail morally, not to become arbitrary, or selfish, or unresponsive (cf. AA 4). "Without faith it is impossible to please Him" (Heb. 11.6).

Because man is free, it is possible for one who received faith as a gift of God not to respond in hope and love to the call which faith recognizes. In such a case, the faith is real, but it is dormant and fruitless.

The Church teaches that it is possible for a sinner to have faith. The Church has flatly denied that "with the loss of grace through sin faith is also always lost."[2] When a Christian commits a serious sin, one which is not itself a sin of denial or rejection of faith, he does not lose the gift of faith.

But "faith without hope and charity neither unites a man perfectly with Christ nor makes him a living member of His body. Therefore it is

---

[1]St. Fulgentius, *De Fide, ad Petrum prolog.* 1 (ML 65.671), quoted by the Council of Trent, Session 6, January 13, 1547, *Decree on Justification,* ch. 8 (DS 1532), and by the First Vatican Council, Session 3, April 24, 1870, *Dogmatic Constitution on the Catholic Faith,* ch. 3 (DS 3008).
[2]Council of Trent, Session 6, January 13, 1547, *Decree on Justification,* canon 28 (DS 1578).

most rightly said that 'faith without works is dead' (cf. James 2.17 ff.) and unprofitable, and that 'in Christ Jesus neither circumcision nor uncircumcision is of any avail, but faith working through love' (Gal. 5.6, 6.15)."[3]

The personal, grace-moved act of believing God is at the very roots of the moral life. Faith provides the plan of Christian living. The man whom God calls to know and serve Him must first of all be a hearer and believer of the word.

Duty to Believe

Faith is a virtue infused by the Holy Spirit. It is the enduring gift of a faithful God. One who has been brought by God to the gift of an explicit Christian and Catholic faith has the duty never to abandon it (cf. Heb. 10.26-31). Those who have never received the gift of explicit faith may indeed believe God and serve Him generously outside the visible Church; but those who have received the gift of a full Catholic faith 164 must not reject it.

"Therefore, the condition of those who by the heavenly gift of faith have embraced the Catholic truth is by no means the same as that of those who, led by human opinions, follow a false religion. For those who have received the faith under the teaching authority of the Church can never have a just reason to change this same faith or to call it into doubt."[4]

Of course, a believer always has questions. In what faith teaches us, it gives full assurance, but this is not the clear vision proper to eternal life. One who loves the saving truth may well ask further questions, but he will ask in the light of faith, thereby straining toward that perfect knowledge which we are to enjoy in heaven.

Faith and Fidelity

As the Second Vatican Council teaches, "the disciple is bound by a grave obligation toward Christ his Master ever more adequately to understand the truth received from Him, faithfully to proclaim it, and vigorously to defend it" (DH 14). Our Lord demands of us that we shape

---

[3]Council of Trent, Session 6, January 13, 1547, *Decree on Justification*, ch. 7 (DS 1531).
[4]First Vatican Council, Session 3, April 24, 1870, *Dogmatic Constitution on the Catholic Faith*, ch. 3 (DS 3014).

our life by our faith. But He also demands that we be prepared to profess and acknowledge our faith when it is called into question seriously, or whenever silence on our part would give bad example to others (cf. Matt. 10.32-33; Luke 10.8-12).

"All must be prepared to confess Christ before men, and to follow Him along the way of the cross through the persecutions which the Church will never fail to suffer" (LG 42).

CONFIDENT HOPE

In faith we believe not only what God tells us about Himself, but also what He promises for us. By hope we look forward with confidence Ch. 32 to the fulfillment of those promises.

Hope and Self

It might seem to some more Christian, at least as an ideal, to think 198 not at all of oneself. This "ideal," however, is not Christian. Christ teaches us to hope for our own salvation. Each person seeks eternal life as one of many brothers and sisters who will inherit the kingdom together (cf. Rom. 8.29, 8.18; 1 Peter 1.4-5).

It is right to hope for the reward which Christ promises. The fulfillment of oneself in the community of the divine family is the glory of God and the fulfillment of His will (cf. GS 32). To hope for the one and for the other is to hope for the same reality, described from different points of view.

Hope and This World

Just as there is no real conflict between hoping for one's salvation and hoping for God's glory, so there is no real conflict between hoping for heaven and hoping for the redemption of human life in this world. "Human fulfillment constitutes, as it were, a summary of our duties," and this fulfillment is not merely individual self-fulfillment, but the development and progress of all mankind.[5]

227 But this Christian hope for a better world is quite different from mere optimism. Our duty to our neighbor is a duty in love, and it is equally insistent whether his life, or our life, or the life of all men, seems to be waxing or waning.

Christians of course hope that the future of this world will be one of

---

[5]Cf. Pope Paul VI, Encyclical, *Populorum Progressio* (March 26, 1967) nn. 16-17.

development, not ruin. Christians are free to speculate about the course of the world and man in it in the years ahead. But the Christian message does not itself sponsor such speculations or depend upon them. It teaches that "the People of God has no lasting city here below, but looks forward to one which is to come" (LG 44), for "the structure of this world is passing away" (LG 42; cf. 1 Cor. 7.31).

That Which Endures

Yet not everything passes away. The words of Christ remain. Love remains. And, in some way, the good works of mankind in this world 354 remain. "For after we have, in obedience to the Lord and in His Spirit, nurtured on earth the values of human dignity, brotherhood, and freedom, and indeed all the good fruits of our nature and enterprise, we will find them again, but freed of stain, burnished and transfigured . . ." (GS 39).

Thus, the solution to the tension between this-worldly and other-worldly hope is that the Christian should not regard life on this earth as isolated from the eternal life to come. Rather, eternal life somehow be- 228 gins here. The world which passes away is the world in which evil abounds, the world misshapen by the sins of creatures.

Not Doing Evil to Achieve Good

The distinctions between mere optimism and hope, and between progress of this world and progress in building eternal life in this world, help us to understand why we may not do evil that good may come of it (cf. Rom. 3.8). Some kinds of "new morality" hold that a very important end or goal justifies the use of any means necessary, even acts otherwise deemed evil. But Christ's Church remembers that the future is hidden with God and that "we do not know the day or the hour" (LG 48; cf. 278 Matt. 25.13). The truly new morality, the morality of Christ, counts the good which cannot be seen, the good which is hidden but is known to us by faith. This good, the kingdom already present, demands that all of its aspects — truth, life, holiness, grace, justice, love, and peace — be respected in every human action.

One who lives in Christian hope will not do even a "small evil" for 204 the purpose of achieving a great good or avoiding a great hardship. For even a small sin is, in the eyes of faith, more grievous than any amount 196 of physical evil. Never is one in a situation in which, whatever he does, he must commit sin.

We hope in God when we confidently expect from Him all that we
54 need to attain eternal life: grace, mercy, forgiveness, and the overcoming of obstacles and temptations.

The confidence of Christians in their own salvation is not based on any supposition that no one can lose his soul. One who has turned to God is still free to turn away from Him. We, too, must be faithful. No one can be absolutely certain that he will persevere; all must firmly trust in God.

A right fear of God is essential to Christian living, a reverent fear that knows His justice and almighty power. But this fear is not to be a slavish fear, or a childish fear.

Sorrow for sin is necessary, but sin should not be the central focus
39 of a Christian's life. Instead, the central focus should be what God already has done and what we can confidently expect He will do.

LASTING LOVE

The first teaching of one of the earliest Christian writings after the
230 New Testament is: "Now, the way of life is this: 'First, love the God who made you; secondly, your neighbor as yourself.' "[6] The order of priority is that underlined by the Second Vatican Council: "The first and most necessary gift is that charity by which we love God above all things and our neighbor because of God" (LG 42).

The Love of God

Love of God is the heart of Christian life. When God revealed Himself in Christ, men came to know more confidently the perfect Goal of
60 all striving, the Goodness all human goods can only dimly reflect.

God's love for us is prior to our love for Him. He created us. He redeemed us. He pours His love into our hearts. God's love is the supreme model for us. We could never have known this model by reason alone. But the limitations of our wisdom and the extent of God's love are made clear in the folly of the cross.

---

[6]The *Didache* 1.2.

The life of the Trinity is for mankind the model of love. The Father, Son, and Holy Spirit eternally love one another with that boundless love which is Their Being and the creative force that made and sustains the universe. We were created for the very purpose of sharing in the 113 personal life and love of the divine family.

If one loves God, one keeps His commandments, just as one who loves another person seeks to do what is pleasing to that person. One 184 who loves his neighbor tries to do good to and for him. The highest act of Christian love is the effort to help others attain eternal life.

The Church does not regard unloving obedience to God's law, or the doing of what is right toward one's neighbor for merely humanistic reasons, as something worthless.[7] Still, without love one cannot effectively serve Christ's kingdom or do anything to merit eternal life. "If I give away all I have, and if I deliver my body to be burned, but have not love, I gain nothing" (1 Cor. 13.3). The Christian must base his life upon an explicit commitment to God, and must renew this act of love from time to time.[8]

Sin

The central focus of our new life is Christian love. Sin is the opposite of this love.

Just as we can strive freely to see things from God's point of view and to act in accord with His will, so we can freely choose to ignore God's plan and the role He invites us to play in it. In short, just as we can accept the invitation God has made to adopt us as members of His own family, so we can refuse this offer in favor of a selfish and isolated life. Such a refusal of God's gift to us of Himself is sin.

Sin is basically a personal offense against God, a turning from God. For this reason it is important to distinguish between actions which are 52 done with knowledge and freedom and those which are not. Some actions which are in themselves wrong are done without personal guilt because the doer acts in ignorance or without freedom. The actions in these cases are to be distinguished from sin in the strict sense, sometimes called formal sin, in which one freely and knowingly does what he judges to be wrong. A formal sin is a deliberate violation of the known will of God.

---

[7]Cf. Pope St. Pius V, Bull, *Ex Omnibus Afflictionibus* (October 1, 1567) (DS 1916).
[8]Cf. Decree of the Holy Office (August 24, 1690) (DS 2290).

Mortal Sin

Formal sin may be either mortal or venial. A mortal sin is a sin that separates one from friendship with God, or deepens one's alienation from God. Sin can be a particular action, or it can be a state of alienation from God. As an act, a mortal sin in the formal sense is an action which is in itself seriously wrong, or is judged by the doer to be so, and which nonetheless is performed knowingly and deliberately.

There are actions that are in themselves seriously wrong, of such a kind that they can exclude a person from the kingdom of heaven (cf. 1 Cor. 6.9-10; Gal. 5.19-21; Eph. 5.5; 1 Tim. 1.9-11; Rev. 21.8, 22; 22.15). The Church does not teach that such passages of Scripture provide complete "lists" of mortal sins, or that the precise meaning and range of mortal sins can be determined from isolated scriptural texts. But in each age the Church performs its duty of clarifying God's law; and it persistently teaches that there are kinds of gravely evil acts which are strictly forbidden by God, and that one who knowingly and deliberately does such acts is deliberately turning himself from God.

43   The degree of knowledge and deliberateness required to constitute a mortal sin cannot be stated with precision. To commit mortal sin one must be substantially aware that what one is doing is gravely wrong, and one must be substantially free in one's conduct. Catholic teaching readily recognizes that emotional problems and the influence of external conditions can reduce and even take away one's freedom and
54   responsibility. But the Church does not teach that people are rarely free to choose, that only seldom are they really able to do good or to do evil.[9]

Mortal sin is sometimes spoken of as a disposition, an orientation of life, rather than as a single action. There is a sense in which that is clearly true. One can be in the "state of mortal sin," that is, living a life in which one is not committed to love of God and faithfulness to Him. One can fall from the friendship of God to this sad state only by free and deliberate action. Such an action is an actual mortal sin. The action by which one who is a child of God places himself in hostility to God will not be a casual or slight one. Normally the gravely sinful act by one who has really loved God will be preceded by many failings in loyalty. One certainly does not pass thoughtlessly from love of God to mortal sin and back to love. Only serious and deliberate sin turns one from God; only a

---

[9]Cf. Pope Pius XII, *Address* to psychotherapists, AAS 45 (1953) 278-286, esp. 280.

genuine conversion returns divine life and love to one who has sinned gravely.

If one deliberately and knowingly offends God in a serious matter, he thereby loses his share in divine life and gives up his title to a place in heaven. To die having forfeited the friendship of God is to face the terrifying prospect of God's judgment and the eternal separation from God of which He has warned us (cf. Matt. 25.41).

The sinner can do nothing to begin to bring himself back to life without God's first moving him to repent. God's merciful acceptance of the sinner's consequent repentance, God's gracious forgiveness of one who promises to act once more as His friend — only these acts of God 243 can heal the breach caused by mortal sin.

Fundamental Option

In recent years many Christian thinkers have adopted the expression "fundamental option" as the name for the persistent will or attitude that shapes a person's life: the basic intent to live as one who believes God's word and accepts His call to a new life, or to decline to do so. The expression is an apt one to the extent that it highlights those basic stances which in fact determine many choices men must make.

The expression underlines another important point also. The act of faith and love by which one turns to God is not an isolated act. It has roots in prior responses to grace, and it establishes a friendship with 245-246 God that is the fundamental orientation of one's life. Similarly, a mortal sin ordinarily has roots in prior acts of unfaithfulness, and it endures in a deliberately chosen life without God.

Human lives tend to have a basic orientation, that is, to become established in a rooted loyalty to God or to become more set in the selfishness that turns one from God. But this does not mean that those who would wish to serve God simply cannot commit mortal sins. We have many frailties. If we deliberately choose to be unfaithful in small things, we can drift toward an act of disloyalty and disobedience so radical that it brings about and reveals a very different orientation. It would be presumptuous to claim that one's life has been so steadfastly turned toward God that it would not be possible for a single act of lust or abortion or blasphemy to change the direction of one's life. For if one is prepared to do, and does, an action that is gravely evil and known to be opposed to the demanding will of God, and does this with sufficient awareness and freedom, one reveals that one is not firmly devoted to

God, and expresses the spirit of one who does not love Him (cf. John 14.15).

Venial Sin

We use the word "sin" in another sense when we speak of venial sin. For venial sin does not deprive one wholly of the life of grace and of friendship with God; it is not a conscious and free decision to do what is gravely wrong. Venial sin is a less serious offense against the law of God.

191 Although venial sin is an offense less serious than mortal sin, it disposes one toward mortal sin, and is the greatest of all evils except for mortal sin.

Care is needed in distinguishing venial from mortal sin. Sometimes a sin is venial because the wrong done is not so base or serious a disorder that it involves turning from the love of God. Sometimes a sin is venial because it violates a serious responsibility in only a slight degree. An example is the theft of a quite trivial item. Sometimes a sin is venial because, although the violation is of something central and is significant, still one is not acting with full awareness and willingness. No human action, however evil it might appear to be, can be a mortal sin in the strict formal sense, with all the grave consequences that that implies, unless the action is done with an awareness that it is evil and a willingness to do it despite that.

The First Three Commandments

The first commandment obliges us to recognize only the one true God as God, and to worship Him alone. We worship Him first by faith, hope, and love. An act of these virtues can be expressed in many ways, especially by participation in Christ's perfect sacrifice, renewed in the Mass. We worship Him also by praying to Him in our needs, thereby acknowledging His power and providence. By seeking to keep all His commandments we acknowledge His divine authority.

377 By sincere prayers of faith, hope, and love, we elicit acts of such worship. The act of love is by far the most important. At the hour of death, as often in life, we should if possible express explicitly our love for our heavenly Father.

Sins against faith, hope, and love are violations of the first commandment. Sins against faith include apostasy, or the abandoning of

196

faith entirely, and heresy, the deliberate denial of some revealed truth or truths that He has given us grace enough to be able to recognize.

One would sin against hope by presumption, that is, by supposing one could find salvation without God's help and without prayerfully seeking this help, or by pretending that salvation can be had without personal cooperation with His grace. Despair is a sin more directly opposed to hope.

The most bitter sin against love is hatred. Envy, or sadness at another's good fortune, and sloth, or distaste for things that lead to growth of charity because of the efforts required, also are enemies of love. Of special social importance are scandal and cooperation in the sin of others.

Sins of superstition and sacrilege also are directly opposed to faithful worship of God. Especially serious is sacrilegious reception of sacraments, approaching those sacraments which signify and demand love of God in one's heart, as the Eucharist, confirmation, orders, or matrimony, when one has committed grave sin and not repented.

The second commandment requires reverence for God's name. God's name is dishonored in especially grave ways in false oaths, or perjury, that is, when one lies after calling upon the name of God as a pledge that one will speak the truth. God's name is dishonored if one is false to one's vows, that is, if one does not fulfill promises made to God and sealed with His name. One dishonors God by cursing, that is, by calling on Him who is Savior of all to do harm to others; and especially by blasphemy, that is, by any words or behavior intended to insult or express contempt for almighty God.

The third commandment requires an expression of one's worship of God: keeping the Lord's day holy. Church law specifies for the Catholic certain fundamental duties in this matter. Attendance at Mass ought to be counted a joy and a privilege; but the Catholic has also the serious duty to attend Mass on Sundays and on certain holy days. Such days are to be kept holy also by avoiding needless labor and unnecessary commercial dealings, that is, activity of a kind that hinders the spirit of celebration and joy in the Lord that should mark such days. At times, of course, one is dispensed from these precepts on worship and rest, if some real necessity requires this. The necessity might be an urgent demand of charity. Worship is a great duty, but charity a greater one.

Sin and Self-Love

There is a proper order of love. After love of God comes love of self. Christ commanded: "You shall love your neighbor as yourself" (Mark

197

12.31; cf. Luke 10.27; Rom. 13.9; Gal. 5.14; James 2.8). But the love of self that is set as the standard for love of one's neighbor is a right love of self, a love that is governed and guided by love of God. A man who does not have a right love of self, a love that flows from a grateful love of God, is not able to love his neighbor rightly. Every individual should think of his own salvation, his own pursuit of the truly good, as his first responsibility.

On the other hand, disordered self-love is the root of all sin. There can be only one center of a person's life. Everything else will revolve about that center. That center can be God, or it can be oneself. The second choice is pride, the root of sin.

Love and the Moral Virtues

Christian self-love, which grows out of a grateful love of God and blossoms into unselfish love of neighbor, is supported by certain indispensable virtues. The first of these is humility, one of the most distinctive of Christian virtues. Paradoxically it exalts a person by leading him to acknowledge his true status: he is a creature, and every good in him is God's gift and should glorify God, not his own small ego (cf. Luke 14.11).

Patience, or endurance, is equally needed. To love oneself rightly in an existence in which the entire fulfillment of one's hopes is not immediately possible, in which the cross precedes the resurrection, in which one must await the time of God's appointing, requires patience. It has obvious links with humility, poverty in spirit, temperance, self-control, fortitude, and perseverance.

A man cannot truly love himself or others if he does not have temperance or self-control. By a false love of self catering to immediate cravings, intemperance destroys the better self one should love. Sins against temperance include such self-destructive ones as gluttony, drunkenness, drug abuse, lust. Such sins can destroy one's freedom. Sometimes the circumstances that lead human frailty toward such sins reduce personal responsibility for them very much.

But even weak men, sustained by God's grace (cf. Rom. 7.24), can acquire the virtues we have mentioned. Out of motives of faith and love, they freely do acts which are not strictly required and forgo goals not strictly forbidden. Gradually a new nature, a new life, a new spontaneous and free ease is acquired in so acting. Thus it is possible to "put on the new nature, created after the likeness of God" (Eph. 4.24).

Unless these virtues are fostered in one's character, one will hardly be able to live a life worthy of the calling we have received, "with all lowliness and meekness, with patience, forbearing one another in love" (Eph. 4.2; cf. GS 8), a life in "purity, knowledge, forbearance, kindness, the Holy Spirit, genuine love" (2 Cor. 6.6), perhaps seeming to have nothing and yet "possessing everything" (2 Cor. 6.10).

Love of Neighbor

We approach the end of this chapter without seeming to have said much about love of neighbor.

Love of neighbor certainly is important, and indeed is treated in the last seven commandments of the Decalogue. Love of neighbor is in one sense the whole of Christian morality. "For he who loves his neighbor has fulfilled the law" (Rom. 13.8; cf. Rom. 13.10; Gal. 5.4). One cannot read the New Testament without being struck by its emphasis on love of others. "And this commandment we have from Him, that he who loves God should love his brother also" (1 John 4.21).

But the discussions here and in the preceding chapter have not omitted love of neighbor. These chapters have laid the groundwork for treating it, and the next two chapters will discuss the moral significance of the basic forms of human good for self and neighbor alike.

Moreover in dealing with Christian love, and with the life based on it, the sharp distinctions sometimes made between love of God, love of self, and love of neighbor begin at a certain point to break down. In 184 Christ, God has become our neighbor. Through Christ we become more than neighbors to God; we become His children, brothers of one another and of Christ. In this family of God, love of neighbor becomes love of a brother in Christ, love of one who shares or is called to share in divine life. Therefore, love of neighbor, proper love of oneself, and love of God in Christ become one.

Charity and the Body of Christ

St. Paul's most thorough and most beautiful word on charity is in his letter responding to problems or order in the church at Corinth. Members of that church with diverse gifts and duties were contending with one another instead of cooperating. For example, some claimed that their particular gift of speaking in tongues was superior, others that their particular gift of prophecy was better.

Paul explained that just as each part of the human body has its own 121-122 function, so each member of the Church has his own role to play. No

199

part of the body is independent. Each part needs the rest; even the noblest needs the least noble. The members of the Church must not contend for themselves as if each were living by and for himself.

Therefore, the gifts over which members of the church at Corinth were contending, gifts which will pass away, are far less important than the gifts which unify them, gifts which will last. "So faith, hope, love abide, these three; but the greatest of these is love" (1 Cor. 13.13).

Love vivifies the unity of the Body of Christ: "If I speak in the tongues of men and of angels, but have not love, I am a noisy gong or a clanging cymbal. And if I have prophetic powers, and understand all mysteries and all knowledge, and if I have all faith, so as to remove mountains, but have not love, I am nothing" (1 Cor. 13.1-2).

Today, as then, charity, the love which should bind the Church together, is far more important than any lesser considerations which
169 would divide us. For this love, as we have seen, is participation in divine life.

•   •   •

Questions related to the material in this chapter:

1. What is "faith"? Why is faith called the beginning of human salvation?

2. Can someone who has fallen into sin still have the gift of faith?

3. What are the primary duties of faith?

4. How do faith and hope differ?

5. Is there any real conflict between hoping for heaven and hoping for a better world?

6. Can it ever be right for one to do an evil deed in order that good may come of it? Can a good end justify evil means?

7. Why do we say that love of God is the heart of Christian life?

8. What is sin? What is the difference between mortal and venial sin?

9. How is the expression "fundamental option" used? To what extent is it an apt expression?

10. What do the first three commandments of the Decalogue require of us?

11. Why are the virtues of humility, patience, and temperance so important?

12. Why does the Church place so much emphasis on love?

20

A Life Worthy of Our Calling

Only by cultivating "natural goods and values" can a person come to "an authentic and full humanity" (GS 53).

In this chapter we consider how, in the light of faith, Christian hope and love should heal and perfect our attitudes toward three basic human values: life, procreation (the transmission of life), and truth.

HUMAN LIFE

The Church has always proclaimed the dignity of each human person. Because man is the image of his Maker and is called through Christ Ch. 4 to share in the personal life of the Trinity, each human being has a transcendent worth.

"Through his bodily composition man gathers to himself the elements of the material world. Thus they reach their crown through him, and through him raise their voice in free praise of the Creator (cf. Dan. 3.57-90 V). For this reason man is not allowed to despise his bodily life" (GS 14).

There is a "growing awareness of the exalted dignity proper to the human person, since he stands above all things, and his rights and duties are universal and inviolable," and therefore there should be made available to him "everything necessary for leading a life truly human, such as food, clothing, and shelter . . ." (GS 26). "Coming down to practical and particularly urgent consequences, this Council lays stress on reverence for man . . . taking into account first of all his life and the means necessary to living it with dignity" (GS 27).

"Furthermore, whatever is opposed to life itself, such as any type of murder, genocide, abortion, euthanasia, and willful self-destruction 205 . . . all these things and others of their like are infamies indeed. They poison human society, but they do more harm to those who do them than to those who suffer the injury. Moreover, they are a supreme dishonor to the Creator" (GS 27).

"For God, the Lord of life, has conferred on man the surpassing ministry of safeguarding life — a ministry which must be fulfilled in a manner which is worthy of man. Therefore, from the moment of its conception life must be guarded with the greatest care; abortion and infanticide are unspeakable crimes" (GS 51).

Among the actions which "deliberately conflict" with the universal principles of natural law "must first of all be counted those actions designed for the methodical extermination of an entire people, nation, or ethnic minority" (GS 79).

Finally, the Second Vatican Council, "making its own the condemnations of total war already pronounced by recent Popes," declared: "Every act of war which tends indiscriminately to the destruction of entire cities or of extensive areas along with their populations is a crime against God and man himself, and is to be condemned firmly and without hesitation" (GS 80).

Respect for Human Goods

A human value is realized and fostered only in concrete acts of love and justice. In the case of life, for example, it is not "human life" in the abstract we are speaking about, but the life and flourishing of people, of individual persons.

Thus each of us is to realize the value of life both in his own person and in the person of others. The individual must not despise his own bodily life, and he must not despise bodily life in others. He has a solemn duty to preserve his own life by his own labor, and he has a solemn duty to feed the hungry and to help a neighbor in distress (cf. Matt. 25.41-46; Luke 10.30-37). He is not to commit suicide, and he is not to murder; both types of acts are "opposed to life itself" (GS 27). The flourishing life of each and every person manifests God's glory.

The call of the basic values for realization in one's action is, then, fundamentally positive. To be a mature Christian requires more than not doing certain things. It is not enough simply to restrict one's activity, to do no murders, to tell no lies, and so on.

There is, of course, more than one basic value. It is not possible for each of us to be always and everywhere actively engaged in realizing each one of them, and certainly we are not bound to try to do so. But all of us are obliged to reverence life through care for the safety of others and through works of mercy. Moreover, each of us is strictly bound never to choose directly against life.

45   The teaching of the Second Vatican Council on actions "opposed to life itself" (GS 27) is in the unwavering Christian tradition. The Chris-

tian must never do evil that good may come of it (cf. Rom. 3.8); particularly he must not do the direct evil of attacking directly a basic human value, such as human life, for any motive whatever, or in any circumstances.

Acts "Opposed to Life Itself"

The Church does not consider that every act which causes or might cause death is opposed to life itself. "You shall not kill": the language and context of the fifth commandment (Exod. 20.13; Matt. 5.21, 19.18; Mark 10.19; Luke 18.20; Rom. 13.9), and its interpretation by Israel and the Church, show that the general formulation can be made more precise: "Do not slay the innocent and righteous" (Exod. 23.7; cf. Jer. 7.6, 22.3).

Thus, though war is undoubtedly a great human tragedy, the Church does not condemn every act of war as evil. Since war "has not been rooted out of human affairs" and there is at this time no "competent and sufficiently powerful authority at the international level," when "every means of peaceful settlement has been exhausted" governments "cannot be denied the right to legitimate defense" through "military action for the just defense of the people" (GS 79; cf. Heb. 11.33-34).

Those who are attacked unjustly have a right to resist. Those responsible for defending justice in a community may have a duty to defend the helpless when they are assailed; under certain conditions they might even be called upon to perform defensive actions that result in the death of the assailants. Indeed, in times when there has seemed to be no other way of preventing the unjust violence of a criminal, the Church has not condemned the execution of a criminal according to law by properly constituted authority.[1]

But this does not mean that public authorities, or anyone else, can rightly do anything and everything, without exception, to prevent the triumph of an unjust attack. Indiscriminate destruction of whole populations is always wrong, wrong even if a nation could defend its freedom in no other way. If an unjust attack could be prevented only by killing innocent hostages, one would still be obliged to refrain from such killing. While making every morally permissible effort to prevent the evils

---

[1]Cf. Pope Innocent III, *Profession of Faith Prescribed for the Waldensians* (December 18, 1208) (DS 795); Pope Pius XI, Encyclical, *Casti Connubii* (December 31, 1930) (DS 3720, 3722).

which flow from the triumph of the unjust, we must leave the outcome to God's providence rather than directly attack innocent life to attain our ends.

Providence and Human Choices

The foreseeable consequences of a morally upright decision may at times seem harsh. The results of a decision not to kill the innocent will often seem to many to be worse, sometimes much worse, than the death of the innocent. Many more persons may seem certain to die, or perhaps to suffer spiritual harm.

Here the Christian faith helps our understanding. It reminds us that certain kinds of acts "do more harm to those who do them than to those who suffer the injury" (GS 27). For ultimately nothing matters so much as remaining in friendship with God. All the perceptible evils and suffering in a situation are outweighed by the moral evil of dishonoring God's goodness by choosing against the basic values of His creation. It is basic in Christian morality that the deliberate doing of an immoral act, 196 even a single venial sin, is a worse evil, because it is a far graver kind of evil, than the occurrence of any physical evils whatever.

Our faith also reminds us of the limits of our vision. We are unable to see all the good or evil which may result from our choices. We know 39 that God in His providence brings good out of evil, but we do not know how.

Faith further reminds us that we are not morally responsible for harm and suffering which we could have averted only by doing evil. If a person suffers a martyrdom which he could have avoided only by apostatizing from the truth, he is not to blame either for his own death or for the harm which might come to his family or others as a result, even if these consequences were foreseeable by him.

Nevertheless, moral problems can often be extremely complex. What Christian faith demands is steadfast faithfulness to certain basic principles. We must care about doing good; we must do no evil whatever, not even to achieve noble objectives or to avoid terrible losses.

Refusing to Do Evil

Men of great goodness instinctively, not without the light of the Holy Spirit, find the solution to deep moral problems in ways that do not 191 involve the doing of evil. The Church in its pastoral teaching expresses the principle for such solutions in terms of the distinction to be made between the direct and the indirect consequences of an act.

The case of a martyr can be illuminating here. There is something the martyr directly does, what he directly achieves or intends to achieve. What he chooses to do is to proclaim the truth and to remain loyal to his God. On the other hand, there is his death, and there may be other quite foreseeable effects, perhaps death or ruin for others, as a result of his choice. But it is not the martyr's own deed that directly causes these results.

Thus, the martyr knows that he will die; but he is not a suicide. He knows perhaps that others will die whom he could save by denying the faith; but he is not a murderer. His decision to remain steadfast has for him and perhaps for others a death-dealing effect; but his choice is clearly not a choice "opposed to life itself."

The distinction between direct and indirect consequences makes it clear that, while there are difficult situations in which any choice a person makes will have painful consequences, there are no situations of ultimate moral dilemmas, in which every possible choice a person can 54 make is immoral. Christ does not command the impossible.

Abortion

Christ's law concerning attacks on human life has been proclaimed most fully by the Church on the subject of abortion.[2] The victims of 201 abortion are clearly innocent and are particularly helpless.

Though the reasons that prompt people to kill the unborn are not always negligible, the insufficiency of the reasons is usually clear. A desire to escape burdens, for example, or to maintain a higher standard of living, is understandable, but it clearly is not reasonable to kill for that. No one who wishes to act according to the mind of God could fail to discern the contempt for a basic human value, the lack of love of neigh- 179 bor, and the glaring lack of justice that are involved here.

It sometimes happens that two lives seem to be at stake, the life of a mother and the life of her unborn child. How is one to act in such situations? Pope Pius XII treated this question in some detail:

"Any direct attempt on an innocent human life as a means to an end — in this case to the end of saving another human life — is unlaw-

---

[2]Cf., e.g., Sacred Congregation for the Doctrine of the Faith, *Declaration on Abortion* (November 18, 1974). The tradition of the Church is summarized in nn. 6 and 7.

ful. Any direct deliberate attack on innocent human life, in whatsoever condition it is found from the very first moment of its existence, is wrong. This principle holds good both for the life of the child and for that of the mother. Never and in no case has the Church taught that the life of the child must be preferred to that of the mother. . . . No, neither the life of the mother nor that of the child can be subjected to an act of direct suppression. In the one case as in the other, there can be but one obligation: to make every effort to save the lives of both. . . .

"Deliberately, we have always used the expression 'direct attempt on the life of the innocent person,' 'direct killing'; because if, for example, the saving of the life of the mother-to-be, independently of her pregnant condition, should have as an accessory consequence, in no way desired or intended, but inevitable, the death of the fetus, such an could no longer be called a direct attempt on an innocent life. Under these conditions the operation can be lawful, like other similar medical interventions, granted always that another good of high worth is concerned, such as life, and that it is not possible to postpone the operation until after the birth of the child, nor to have recourse to other efficacious remedies."[3] Such an operation, then, can be a morally good act. It is aimed entirely at saving life, and is in no way directed against innocent life. The death of the unborn is neither desired nor intended.

203   Here the lines are finely drawn. But they are drawn precisely where the Christian conscience has always drawn them, and in a way that rings true for all who have reverence for every kind of basic value. They are not determined by a weighing and calculating of expected consequences; such weighing and calculating in an effort to "justify" a

191 direct attack on human life for a "sufficient" reason can only be a cloak for arbitrariness.

Even though the moral judgments which must be made are not always easy, it is possible to reach correct conclusions by keeping in mind the fundamental perspective of our hope in Christ: "And do not fear those who kill the body but cannot kill the soul; rather fear him who can destroy both soul and body in hell" (Matt. 10.28). Help in these difficult areas can be found in various guidelines presented by authentic teachers in the Church.[4]

---

[3]Pope Pius XII, *Address* to the Family Associations (November 26, 1951).
[4]Cf., e.g., *Ethical and Religious Directives for Catholic Health Facilities,* approved November 16, 1971, by the United States National Conference of Catholic Bishops as the national code, subject to the approval of the bishop for use in the diocese.

Parents rightly rejoice when a child is born as a fruit of their love. 334
To have children and help them grow to a rich maturity is one of the
strongest motivating forces. From end to end the Bible celebrates full realization of this good in positive images of courtship, betrothal, wed-
dings, conjugal love, sexual intercourse, procreation, childbirth, and the
family life in which children grow to full maturity.

The Importance of Sex

The Church has always considered sex a precious and sacred reality. For that very reason it has condemned the abuse and degradation of 209
sex. Faithful to Scripture,[5] the Church insists that love of God is incompatible with every form of fornication, sexual promiscuity and un-
cleanness, sensuality and licentiousness, lustful desires, incest, homosexual acts, and other sexual perversions. Christ warns solemnly that
fidelity to God can be broken even by a lustful look (cf. Matt. 5.28).

Sex in Marriage

"Have you not read that He who made them from the beginning 44
made them male and female, and said, 'For this reason a man shall leave
his father and mother and be joined to his wife, and the two shall become one'? So they are no longer two but one. What therefore God has
joined together, let no man put asunder" (Matt. 19.4-6; cf. Mark 10.7-9).

In this perspective, marriage calls for a total giving of oneself to 333
one's partner, in body as in other ways. Sexual intercourse represents
and expresses the mutual gift of self. Thus sexual activity is deformed if
separated from this mutual self-giving.

Sexual intercourse is important, then, because through it conjugal
love "is uniquely expressed and perfected" (GS 49). Through this "mutual gift of themselves, which is properly theirs and exclusive to them
alone," husband and wife "develop that union of two persons in which
they perfect one another. . . ."[6]

---

[5]See Matt. 15.19; Mark 7.21; Rom. 1.24, 26-27, 13.13; 1 Cor. 5.1, 6.13, 16, 18; 7.2, 10.8; 2
Cor. 12.21; Gal. 5.19; Eph. 5.3, 5; Col. 3.5; 1 Thess. 4.3-4; 1 Tim. 1.10; Heb. 13.4; 1 Peter
4.3; Jude 4.
[6]Pope Paul VI, Encyclical, *Humanae Vitae* (July 25, 1968) n. 8.

Hence, a person's capacity for sexual intercourse fits him or her in a quite special way for that form of companionship which "produces the primary form of interpersonal communion" (GS 12). This potentially great significance provides a first answer to the question why virtuous sexual conduct is so important in the way of Christ.

Sex and Procreation

Why, however, is sexual intercourse so special as an expression of mutual self-giving and communion between man and wife? Why must it be engaged in only within marriage?

The answer to these questions — and the fundamental reason for the human and moral significance of sex — is based on the fact that sexual intercourse naturally tends to transmit human life. Those who engage in sexual intercourse thereby bring themselves, whether it occurs to them or not, within the range of a basic human good, the procreative good.

Knowing the biological fact, a couple can choose to foster the value, by trying or hoping to have a child. Or they can simply proceed without regard for the possible outcome, neither acting against nor deliberately seeking the procreative good. Another possibility is that they can choose against the procreative good as it is at stake in their action, and so engage in sexual intercourse in such a way that it is not, as a human action, open to the transmission of life. Sexual activity thus cannot fail to be morally significant, because for anyone who knows its biological potential it cannot fail to express, either immediately or mediately, an attitude of respect or disrespect toward a basic human good.

Procreation in Marriage

To join fully with another person in passing on to children both life and fullness of life is a basic form of human self-realization. Indeed, this is the value which primarily makes sense of that exclusive and lifelong form of association which we call marriage.

"By their very nature, both the institution of matrimony itself and conjugal love are ordained for the procreation and education of children, and find in them their ultimate crown" (GS 48).

334   "Marriage and conjugal love are by their nature ordained toward the begetting and educating of children. Children are really the supreme gift of marriage and contribute very substantially to the well-being of

their parents. . . . Spouses should regard as their proper mission the task of transmitting human life and educating those to whom it has been transmitted" (GS 50).

The double aspect of marriage, and of sexual intercourse within marriage, is expressed in a sentence of Pope Paul VI which sums up the whole Christian tradition and above all the teaching of the Second Vatican Council: "Husband and wife, through that mutual gift of themselves which is properly theirs and exclusive to them alone, develop that union of two persons in which they perfect one another, in order to cooperate with God in the generation and education of new lives."[7]

Sins against Marital Values

The ties between sex and the values of friendship and procreation are so close that any sexual act will be objectively wrong if it is performed outside that friendship adapted to procreation, that is to say, if it is performed outside marriage. Similarly wrong will be any sexual act performed in such a way that one is equivalently separating it from the good of procreation or the good of friendship between man and wife.

The Church has constantly taught that specific kinds of sexual activity which obviously involve a departure from either or both of these values at stake in human sexuality are forbidden by God. Such acts as masturbation, fornication, and adultery, homosexual acts, and other like sexual vices, have throughout the centuries been condemned by the ordinary teaching of the Church and by formal judgments of the magisterium.[8]

Clearly, human frailty is such that man can fall into these sins without clear realization of their malice and without full freedom. For these reasons it is extremely difficult to assess the personal guilt involved in some disordered sexual acts.[9] Nonetheless, these acts are such evident departures from respect for basic human values that the

---

[7]Encyclical, *Humanae Vitae* (July 25, 1968) n. 8.

[8]Cf., e.g., Pope St. Leo IX, *Letter* to Peter Damian (1054) (DS 687-688); Pope Innocent IV, *Letter* to the Bishop of Tusculum (March 6, 1254) (DS 835); Council of Vienna, Session 3, May 6, 1312, Constitution *Ad Nostrum Qui* (DS 897); Pope Pius II, *Letter* (November 14, 1459) (DS 1367); Decrees of the Holy Office (September 24, 1665; March 2, 1679; July 24, 1929) (DS 2044-2045; 2148-2150; 3684).

[9]Cf. *Principles to Guide Confessors in Questions of Homosexuality* (1973) approved by the Bishops' Committee on Pastoral Research and Practices, United States National Conference of Catholic Bishops.

Church has clearly and persistently taught that the performance of such
194 an act deliberately and freely is a mortal sin, a sin which excludes one
from the kingdom of God

The deliberate intention to commit sexual sins, or a deliberate will to delight in them in the imagination, is sinful, just as a serious intent to perform or approve of any gravely wrong act would be. Other sexual fantasizing, when it is deliberate, may be sinful for another reason: to the extent that it tends to stir up the passions unreasonably and becomes an occasion of sin.

Modesty

Modesty is an important safeguard to chastity. Forms of dress, dancing, conversation, entertainment, and other external things can have a strong influence in shaping one's attitude and behavior in sexual matters. Christian modesty inclines one to govern his conduct in all these areas in an intelligent way, properly responsive to one's Christian vocation.

Christian chastity and modesty are by no means impossible to achieve even in an age and atmosphere of great sexual laxity. Growth in these virtues, which will be assisted by a spirit of prayer, faithful reception of the sacraments, and devotion to the Blessed Virgin Mary, leads not to prudery and narrowness, but to joy and peace. Chastity and
198 modesty establish conditions that make possible enduring and unselfish love.[10]

Contraceptive Birth Control

334 Marriage is to be a fully human and thus Christian response to the call to foster a special kind of friendship, one open to the responsible transmission of life. Since friendship and life come into question in every sexual act, there should be a fully human response to them, not only in marriage as an institution and in each marriage as a whole, but also in each marital act of sexual intercourse.

As we have already seen, the way of Christ always and every-
203 where demands respect for the basic forms of goodness in each and every one of our actions. At all times, then, implicitly in Scripture and

---

[10]Cf. Pope Pius XII, Encyclical, *Sacra Virginitas* (March 25, 1954); Pope Paul VI, *Address* during General Audience (September 13, 1972).

explicitly since the early patristic age, it has been Christian doctrine that "preserving the full sense of mutual self-giving and of human procreation" (GS 51) is demanded in each and every act of sexual intercourse within marriage.

As Pope Pius XI put it: "Each and every marriage act which in its exercise is deprived by human interference of its natural power to procreate life is an offense against the law of God and of nature."[11] As Pope Pius XII put it: "Any attempt on the part of the husband and wife to deprive their marital act of its inherent force or to impede the procreation of a new life, either in the performance of the act itself or in the course of the development of its natural consequences, is immoral."[12] And Pope Paul VI: "Every act that intends to impede procreation must be repudiated, whether that act is intended as an end to be attained or as a means to be used, and whether it is done in anticipation of marital intercourse, or during it, or while it is having its natural consequence."[13]

The Second Vatican Council, following in this all Christian tradition, instructed: "Sons and daughters of the Church . . . may not undertake methods of regulating procreation which are found blameworthy by the teaching authority of the Church in its unfolding of the divine law" (GS 51).

Excluded from Christian behavior, then, will be all acts that are performed with the purpose of directly preventing conception. Similarly excluded will be all forms of direct sterilization for this purpose.[14]

Responsible Family Limitation

The good of procreation clearly does not demand of a married couple that they have as many children as possible. In considering how many children to have, and when to have them, husband and wife "will thoughtfully take into account both their own welfare and that of their children, those already born and those which may be foreseen. For this accounting they will reckon with both the material and the spiritual conditions of the times as well as of their state in life. Finally, they will consult the interests of the family group, of temporal society, and of the

---

[11]Encyclical, *Casti Connubii* (December 31, 1930) (DS 3717).
[12]*Address* to a meeting of the Italian Society of Midwives (October 29, 1951).
[13]Encyclical, *Humanae Vitae* (July 25, 1968) n. 14.
[14]Cf., e.g., Pope Pius XI, Encyclical, *Casti Connubii* (December 31, 1930) (DS 3722-3723); Pope Paul VI, Encyclical, *Humanae Vitae* (July 25, 1968) n. 14.

Church herself. The married partners themselves should make this judgment, in the sight of God" (GS 50).

But in putting this judgment into effect, the couple is not to act arbitrarily, but must follow right principles (cf. GS 50). When a husband and wife have good reason not to procreate, they may adopt a policy which has two elements. First, they may abstain from sexual intercourse at times when conception is more likely or possible; by this abstention they do not act against the good of procreation. Second, they may engage in intercourse at other times of their choice, to express the faithfulness and experience the joy of their married love.

Provided it is not the expression of a wrong attitude toward the good of procreation, the practice of periodic abstinence to regulate human birth not only is completely right and reasonable, but also can have a real value of its own. Such natural family planning can avoid procreation which would be irresponsible.

Providentially, more effective ways have been learned in recent years, at a time when social and economic pressures have become greater, to make possible family planning that is genuinely responsible, that is, that faithfully refuses to assail any basic human value. Even 198 those who must share more intimately in the cross to remain faithful to God's requirements in this matter may know with certainty that God always gives sufficient grace and strength to keep His precepts.

TRUTH

Jesus Christ came into this world "to bear witness to the truth" (John 18.37). His revelation of "the deepest truth about God and the salvation of man" (DV 2) is an aspect of God's invitation to man to enter into a fellowship so complete that it amounts to sharing in the divine nature.

Understanding the truth and living in contact with reality are basic 179 aspects of the full human freedom which Christ came to restore to man. Indeed, understanding is possible at all only because man "shares in the light of the divine mind" (GS 15).

Precisely because this search for truth is central to human dignity, and because an authentic grasp and personal acceptance of truth, especially 164 the truth about God, are so precious, human persons have a right to religious freedom.

The Second Vatican Council declared that the right to religious freedom has its foundation in the very dignity of the human person. "It is in accordance with their dignity as persons — that is, beings endowed with reason and free will and therefore privileged to bear personal responsibility — that all men should be at once impelled by nature and also bound by a moral obligation to seek the truth, especially religious truth" (DH 2).

Rights and Duties Connected

Throughout the moral teaching of the Church, "natural rights are 223 joined together, in the very person who is their subject, with an equal number of duties. . . . Therefore, to cite some examples, with the right to life there is the duty to preserve one's life; with the right to a decent standard of living there is the duty to live in a becoming fashion; with the right to be free to seek out the truth there is the duty to devote one- 164 self to an ever deeper and wider pursuit of it."[15] And this does not exhaust the demands of a basic natural good, such as attaining truth.

For instance, besides the right to immunity from unreasonable interference in pursuing, expressing, and propagating what one considers to be true (cf. DH 2; GS 59, 60, 62), one enjoys the right to be given appropriate information (cf. IM 5, 12; GS 26, 59).[16] And since information is useless unless one is ready to receive it, there is a right to education (cf. GE 1; GS 26, 60).

Christians "need that undeviating honesty which can attract all men to the love of truth and goodness, and finally to the Church and to Christ" (AA 13). The Catholic scholar or student, young or old, must put away any self-centered pride, any immoderate desire to dominate, detestation of those who disagree with him. He will need to cultivate all his self-discipline, diligence, patience, perseverance, his gratitude for abilities he did not give himself, his humility before the truth to be learned about creation, his appreciation of the reflection of God in this creation.

Lying

We have a duty to seek the truth and to speak the truth. We must be honest with ourselves and with others.

Truth is attained primarily in an interior judgment of the mind.

---

[15]Pope John XXIII, Encyclical, *Pacem in Terris* (April 11, 1963) (DS 3970).
[16]Cf. Pope John XXIII, Encyclical, *Pacem in Terris* (April 11, 1963) (DS 3959, 3970).

Hence, one way of dishonoring truth is by an inward obscurantism, a
180 willful blindness, a determination to think only what is convenient, a
willingness to rest in and rationalize one's prejudices and, perhaps,
one's lusts.

Communication is the heart of life in community with others, and
truth is, of course, dishonored by the lie. A lie is an assertion, in a context in which genuine communication is reasonably expected, of something which one considers to be false.

Lying is wrong. It is forbidden by the eighth commandment: "You
shall not bear false witness against your neighbor" (Exod. 20.16; cf.
Deut. 5.20).

203   As in the case of the other human goods, Christian doctrine rejects
210 the notion that a choice directly against truth can be justified by an appeal to expected good consequences. The direct lie is forbidden even if
one could thereby avert an injury or loss, or even save a life.

Lying under oath is a particularly serious wrong. In accord with the
injunctions of Scripture (cf. Lev. 19.12), the Church has faithfully taught
197 that deliberate perjury is always a grave sin, whatever the reason or occasion.[17]

As was indicated in the preceding chapter, the Christian tradition
has always insisted that when one is questioned about one's faith by
public authorities, it is wrong to keep silent. "All must be prepared to
confess Christ before men . . ." (LG 42).

But there are circumstances in which one must show concern for
the proper keeping of secrets (which itself can be a serious obligation),
for allowing reasonable privacy, and for maintaining authentic interpersonal harmony. Hence there can be situations in which one may remain
silent, or may rightly allow others to be deceived, or fail to point out the
way in which one's reply is restricted or otherwise affected by the context.[18] No simple rule can provide the right answer for all such cases. In
each instance one must carefully consider what kinds of silence, or
forthrightness, or evasive or partial response, would fairly serve all the
interests rightly involved, and at the same time avoid any direct contradiction of what one judges to be the truth.

In all situations the Christian must not only be sincere and authen-

---

[17]Cf. Pope Martin V, Bull, *Inter Cunctas* (February 22, 1418) n. 14 (DS 1254); Decree of
the Holy Office (March 2, 1679) n. 44 (DS 2144); Pope Pius IX, *Syllabus* (December 8,
1864) n. 64 (DS 2964).
[18]Against laxity in assessing appropriate occasions for evasive or ambiguous answers,
cf. Decree of the Holy Office (March 2, 1679) nn. 26-28 (DS 2126-2128).

tic in himself, but also be trustworthy and honest in his representation of reality to others.

* * *

Questions related to the material in this chapter:

1. Why does the Church put so much emphasis on the dignity and value of each human life?

2. Why is it that a proper Christian attitude toward basic human values, in our own lives and in the lives of others, requires more of us than just the avoidance of evil?

3. What are acts "opposed to life itself"?

4. The foreseeable consequences of a moral decision may at times seem harsh. What does faith tell us about responsibility for such consequences?

5. Is one ever in a situation in which it is impossible to avoid doing evil?

6. What is the Church's attitude toward abortion? How does it reveal reverence for life?

7. Church teaching regarding sexual morality is strikingly at variance with many popular attitudes today on lust, fornication, adultery, masturbation, homosexual acts, and so on. What is the Church's view and the basis for it?

8. What is the relationship between sexual intercourse and marriage?

9. Is it possible to be modest today?

10. What is the Church's attitude toward contraceptive birth control? toward sterilization for the prevention of conception?

11. Does the Church's teaching support responsible and morally upright forms of family limitation?

12. What is a lie and why is lying wrong?

21

Building a Just
and Good Society

Man is a social being. Community with others not only helps him
44 secure such basic goods as knowledge and life itself, but is itself a basic
element in his well-being and fulfillment as a person.

The first part of this chapter discusses the principles that underlie
man's social life. The chapter then treats of the basic forms of this social
life: the family, economic society, the political community, and the family of nations.

THE PERSON AND HIS COMMUNITIES

19   The social teaching of the Church is an essential part of its message.[1] The Church's social teaching is a working out of certain elementary requirements of Christian faith, hope, and love. This whole social teaching rests on two fundamental principles.
45   First, a person cannot find fulfillment unless he has some community with others, community in which he serves and is served, loves and is loved. Second, a person cannot find fulfillment without making his own deep personal commitment to God. That is, man is indeed a social being, but he is much more than that. He is a social being who is also a person with a transcendent dignity, a being called to an immediate personal relationship with God.[2]

This destiny of the person is not limited to the goods a temporal society can provide. Even in relation to the fullest temporal community, the political community, the human person has a "transcendence" (GS 76).

It is precisely because of man's supra-temporal destiny that no per-

---

[1]Cf. Pope John XXIII, Encyclical, *Mater et Magistra* (May 15, 1961) Part IV, esp. nn. 218, 222. The Second Vatican Council stressed the importance of Christian social teaching; cf., e.g., GS 43, 76, and *passim;* AA 31 and *passim.*
[2]Cf. Pope Paul VI, Encyclical, *Populorum Progressio* (March 26, 1967) nn. 15, 16.

son can be simply subordinated to the good of any society and that all persons are basically equal. "True, all men are not alike from the point 333 of view of varying physical power and the diversity of intellectual and moral resources. Nevertheless, with respect to the fundamental rights of the person, every type of discrimination, whether social or cultural, whether based on sex, race, color, social condition, language, or reli- 322 gion, is to be overcome and eradicated as contrary to God's intent" (GS 29; cf. DH 6). Why? "Because all men, having a rational soul and being created in God's image, have the same nature and origin, and because all men, having been redeemed by Christ, enjoy the same divine calling and destiny" (GS 29).

The Common Good

A community is bound together by the pursuit of a "common 360 good." God's goodness can be called the common good for all men, since His goodness is the common source and goal of all creatures. God's goodness is also common in the sense that He shares it in common with all those created persons He has called to life with Himself.

Human goods reflect God's goodness, and basic human goods are common goods in the sense that they pervade all of human life. They 176 are common, too, in the sense that all men can be joined in authentic friendship, in unselfish shared pursuit of what is truly good.

In its social teaching the Church uses the term "common good" in the sense that the common good of society "consists chiefly in the protection of the rights and the performance of the duties of the human person" (DH 6). The Church also speaks of the common good as "the sum of those conditions of social life which allow not only groups but also their individual members to achieve their own fulfillment more fully and more readily" than they otherwise could (cf. GS 26, 79; DH 6).

Man and Socialization

In our own era a sensitive awareness of the need for many social ties and groups has given rise to a great variety of public and private organizations and associations: cooperatives, unions, corporations, professional, cultural, and recreational societies, international institutions, and so on. "This development, which is called socialization, while certainly not without its dangers, brings with it many advantages with respect to consolidating and increasing the qualities of the human person, and safeguarding his rights" (GS 25).[3]

The Principle of Subsidiarity

The Church's accounts of the common good often refer specifically to the fulfillment of families and other associations as well as to the self-fulfillment of individuals.

Implicit in these accounts of the common good is that principle which Pope Pius XI, Pope John XXIII, and the Second Vatican Council call the principle of subsidiarity. This principle is expressed as follows: "Just as it is wrong to withdraw from the individual and commit to the community at large what private initiative and endeavor can accomplish, so it is likewise an injustice, a serious harm, and a disturbance of proper order to turn over to a greater society, of higher rank, functions and services which can be performed by smaller communities on a lower plane. For any social undertaking, of its very nature, ought to give aid to the members of the body social, and ought never to destroy and absorb them."[4]

In accord with the principle of subsidiarity, decisions should be made at the lowest reasonable level in order to enlarge freedom and to broaden participation in responsible action. Only when an individual or small social unit cannot properly fulfill a task should that task be taken over by a wider society.

THE FAMILY

The principle of subsidiarity may be illustrated first in relation to
Ch. 30 the family. The marital companionship between a man and woman is "the primary form of interpersonal communion" (GS 12). Moreover, it is "the beginning and basis of human society," and its mission is to be "the first and vital cell of society" (AA 11; cf. GS 52). Although each marriage is contracted by the free decision of the two persons involved, it is

---

[3]Cf. Pope John XXIII, Encyclical, *Mater et Magistra* (May 15, 1961) Part II, esp. nn. 59-67.
[4]Pope Pius XI, Encyclical, *Quadragesimo Anno* (May 15, 1931) n. 79 (DS 3738); quoted in Pope John XXIII, Encyclical, *Mater et Magistra* (May 15, 1961) Part II, n. 53 (DS 3943); cf. Pope John XXIII, Encyclical, *Pacem in Terris* (April 11, 1963) Part IV (DS 3995); GS 86; GE 3, 6.

neither they nor the laws and customs of their community that determine what marriage is.

The family "is a society in its own original right" (DH 5). The family is not the product of artificial convention; it is not established by, nor is it subject to essential change by, any higher human authority.

It follows that "public authority should regard it as a sacred duty to recognize, protect, and promote the authentic nature" of marriage and the family, "to shield public morality, and to favor the prosperity of domestic life" (GS 52). In particular, "attention is to be paid to the needs of the family in government policies regarding housing, the education of children, working conditions, social security, and taxation" (AA 11).

Needs of Families

The needs of many families are urgent and great. Families that are victims of economic change and of long-standing social injustices often must struggle for existence in intolerable living conditions in crowded urban centers. Those that belong to racial minorities or to migrant groups find it especially difficult to claim their legitimate social rights. Christians should cooperate with others of good will to ensure that the policies of their governments give attention to these ills (cf. AA 11).

Those in public authority also "have rights and duties with regard to the population problems of their own nation," but only "within the limits of their own competence" (GS 87).[5] It is not the function of governments and public authorities to supplant the essentially personal roles of husband and wife.

Thus, for example, "in view of the inalienable human right to marry and beget children, the question of how many children to have belongs to the right judgment of parents and can in no way be commit- 211 ted to the decision of public authority" (GS 87).

Education of Children

The education of children is also a basic parental concern. Civil so- 266 ciety has rights and duties in relation to the education of children, but this is because the family needs help in its educative task (cf. GE 3).

Here civil society plays its part "by guarding the duties and rights of parents and of others who have a role in education, and by providing

---

[5]Cf. Pope Paul VI, Encyclical, *Populorum Progressio* (March 26, 1967) n. 37.

219

225 them with assistance; by implementing the principle of subsidiarity and by completing the task of education, with attention to parental wishes, whenever the efforts of parents and of other groups are insufficient; and, moreover, by building its own schools and institutes, as the common good may demand" (GE 3). The principle of subsidiarity requires that "no kind of school monopoly arise" (GE 6). Governments "must acknowledge the right of parents to make a genuinely free choice of schools and of other means of education" (DH 5).

Relationships within the Family

45   The sexes are equal in human dignity and fundamental rights (cf. GS 29; DH 6).[6] This fact is particularly significant for a husband and 333 wife, for theirs is a union in marital love and friendship. Each has an equal claim on the other's respect, affection, sexual attentions, and assistance of every kind.

Marriage usually requires a specialization of function. Ordinarily one partner works in the wider community for the support of the family while the other devotes time more directly to the upbringing of the children.

In distinguishing between the permanent reality and the changing expressions of the family, the Church teaches that the mother has a "domestic role which must be safely preserved" (GS 52). Young children in particular normally need their mother at home (cf. GS 52). In the family, the mother ordinarily has a certain priority of responsibility in caring for the children, while the father has the prior responsibility in deciding the basic fortunes of the family. If the husband is the head of the family, the wife is its heart.[7] Ideally, decisions will be made in mutual understanding and with joint deliberation (cf. GS 52).

All Christians ought to be "subject to one another out of reverence for Christ" (Eph. 5.21), honoring the various forms of priority and dig-332 nity that each has in his or her own role. Thus when St. Paul speaks of the way in which a wife should be subject to her husband, he does not compromise her dignity. She is not related to her husband as a child is to parents, but as the Church is related to Christ, who Himself lived in our midst as the servant of all (cf. Luke 22.27).

---

[6]Cf. also Pope Pius XI, Encyclical, *Casti Connubii* (December 31, 1930) n. 76.
[7]Cf. Pope Pius XI, Encyclical, *Casti Connubii* (December 31, 1930) nn. 27-29 (DS 3709), 74.

Sincere personal love should be the basic form of relationship between husbands and wives. For the Christian family the love between Christ and the Church forms the ideal pattern for the relationship between husband and wife.

Obedience in the Christian Family

"Children, obey your parents in the Lord, for this is right. 'Honor your father and mother' (this is the first commandment with a promise), 'that it may be well with you . . .' " (Eph. 6.1-3; cf. Exod. 20.12; Deut. 5.16). The commandment to honor one's parents is included in the reply Jesus gave to the man who asked what he must do to share in everlasting life (cf. Mark 10.17-19).

A child's responsibility with regard to his parents is not limited to mere compliance with expressed parental directions. Children have a duty to honor their parents and to have concern for them all their lives (cf. GS 48; Sir. 3.12-13).

The obedience of children should be motivated not by fear but by 198 love, gratitude, and humility (cf. Sir. 7.27-28). Such attitudes equip one for free and responsible cooperation with other men and with Christ Himself. When young children have grown into young men and young women, they must make decisions which their parents have no right to make for them. They alone can rightly decide the path of their mature life.

ECONOMIC LIFE

The main elements of the Church's teaching on socioeconomic matters are rooted in the sublime dignity of the person and his destiny. Ch. 4 They are rooted in the principles of freedom, personal development, equality, subsidiarity, and participation.

Freedom and Personal Development

Ownership and other forms of private control over material goods are to serve the development of personality. Their purpose is to provide 47 everyone with a necessary area of independence; private ownership should be regarded as "an extension of human freedom" (GS 71).

Indeed, the principal original source of private property lies in the exercise of human freedom. Thus, for example, there is that exercise of freedom whereby "the person stamps the things of nature with his seal and subdues them to his will" (GS 67), as when a man on his own initiative cultivates what was barren waste, or shapes what was without humanly relevant form. Then there is the free decision of a person to accumulate savings out of the payment for his work, payment which in justice "must be such as to furnish a man with the means to cultivate his own and his dependents' material, social, cultural, and spiritual life worthily . . ." (GS 67).

Fundamental Equality of Economic Rights

"God intended the earth and all that it contains for the use of all human beings and all peoples. Therefore, created goods ought equitably to flow to all, with justice as the guide, accompanied by charity" (GS 69).

Prior to man's natural right to own private property, then, whatever the forms of ownership may be in particular times and places, is the right of every person to have a share of material goods for his subsistence (cf. GS 60).[8]

"In using his lawful possessions, therefore, a man ought to regard them not merely as his own, but also as common property in the sense that they can be of benefit not only to himself but also to others" (GS 69). This is what the Fathers and Doctors of the Church meant when they taught that men are obliged to come to the relief of the poor, "and to do so not merely out of their superfluous goods" (GS 69).

Moreover, "if a person is in extreme necessity, he has the right to take care of his needs for himself from the riches of others" (GS 69).

Subsidiarity and Participation

19   Economic activity and production, like private property, should serve the common good. Their fundamental purpose is "the service of man, and indeed of the whole man, viewed in terms of his material needs and the demands of his intellectual, moral, spiritual, and religious life; and when we say man, we mean every man whatsoever . . ." (GS 64).

Corporations, banks, and other powerful economic forces have a duty to serve the common good, not merely the narrow interests of

---

[8]Cf. Pope John XXIII, Encyclical, *Mater et Magistra* (May 15, 1961) n. 43 (DS 3942), citing there Pope Pius XII, Broadcast (June 1, 1941), AAS 33 (1941) 199.

management or owners. Theories which in the name of a false liberty deny the need for any social planning are to be rejected (cf. GS 65).

Economic activity "must not be entrusted solely to the authority of government" (GS 65).[9] Theories which "subordinate the basic rights of individual persons and groups to the collective organization of production" are to be rejected (cf. GS 65). Among the basic rights relevant here is the right (and duty) of individual persons under normal circumstances to provide for the support of themselves and of their families.[10]

Hence, "at every level the largest possible number of people should . . . have an active role in the directing" of economic development (GS 65). The Church recognizes the right of private ownership of productive goods, as it acknowledges the right to form corporations, to establish trade unions, and to set up ways of assisting the participation of workers in the economy as a whole.[11] The principle of participation applies not only to the economic system as a whole, but also within each economic enterprise. It also applies within the institutions which, at a higher level, make decisions affecting those enterprises and their employees, and in the unions which represent the workers of one company or of one industry (GS 68).

POLITICAL COMMUNITY

Each person's active participation in community affairs is a good as 213 relevant in political life as in other forms of community. The particular ways in which a given state will structure itself and regulate public authority may, of course, vary "according to the particular character of a people and its historical development" (GS 74; cf. GS 31).

Again, the common good is the criterion of good and bad in the public order. "Individuals, families and various groups which compose civil society are aware of their own insufficiency in the matter of establishing a fully human condition of life. They see the need for a wider community in which each would daily contribute his energies toward an ever better attainment of the common good. And so they constitute political community, in a variety of forms. It is for the common good that political community exists" (GS 74).

---

[9]Pope John XXIII, Encyclical, *Mater et Magistra* (May 15, 1961) n. 51 (DS 3943).
[10]Cf. Pope John XXIII, Encyclical, *Mater et Magistra* (May 15, 1961) n. 55.
[11]Cf. Pope John XXIII, Encyclical, *Mater et Magistra* (May 15, 1961) nn. 82-103, 108-121.

181 From the very nature of things it is essential that there be real authority in the political community.

Governments have a certain right to command. When legitimate public authority is exercised within the limits of the moral order and on behalf of the common good, citizens "are conscience-bound to obey" (GS 74; cf. Rom. 13.5). This moral obligation can extend even to laws which might reasonably have been different (such as speed limits and tax rates) but which nonetheless are intelligibly related to the needs of the common good and established in good faith (cf. GS 30; Rom. 13.5-7). Indeed, even where public authority oversteps its bounds, the people should in some circumstances obey. Unjust authorities as such do not deserve obedience, and unjust laws do not oblige; obedience is due only to the extent that the common good in particular cases requires it (cf. GS 74).

"Obedience to just laws and reverence for legitimately constituted authorities" is part of the Christian faith (cf. CD 19; DH 8). Obedience to civil authorities is not obedience paid to them as men; rather, as Pope John XXIII said, by their obedience men "pay homage to God, the provident Creator of the universe, who decreed that men's dealings with one another be regulated in accordance with that order which He Himself established."[12]

But God, of course, does not command immoral actions. If civil authorities issue laws or decrees which are in contravention of the moral order, "and therefore against the will of God," these "cannot be binding on the consciences of the citizens, since 'one ought to obey God rather than men' (Acts 5.29)."[13] Moreover, "if any government does not acknowledge human rights, or violates them, not only does it fail in its duty, but its orders are wholly lacking in binding force."[14]

Human Rights and Public Order

213 Since the Church has expressed so much of its social teaching in terms of human rights, it must be noted that these rights are of two kinds. First, there are those rights which are inalienable and which must be supported in every situation whatsoever. An example is the right of

---

[12]Pope John XXIII, Encyclical, *Pacem in Terris* (April 11, 1963) n. 50 (DS 3981).
[13]Pope John XXIII, Encyclical, *Pacem in Terris* (April 11, 1963) n. 51 (DS 3981).
[14]Pope John XXIII, Encyclical, *Pacem in Terris* (April 11, 1963) n. 61 (DS 3985).

an innocent person to life. To such rights correspond unqualified duties. One must never take the life of an innocent person directly, not for any reason whatsoever. 203

There are also many rights which are inalienable and inviolable in a somewhat different sense. An example here is the right to a good education (cf. GE 1). These rights belong to all persons as such, and may never be discounted or treated as irrelevant by other persons or by public authority (cf. DH 6). But the positive fulfillment of these rights is subject to other moral considerations, for it is not always possible to provide for the full realization of all such rights. The government has a duty to assist citizens in the exercise of these rights in ways compatible 220 with the common good and with what is possible in all the circumstances of time and place.

It is also a duty of government to provide protection against the abuse of rights, whether the abuse is of the rights of property or economic initiative (cf. GS 64), or of the right to communicate with others in speech and art (cf. IM 12), or of the right to express religious beliefs (cf. DH 7).

Civil authority has no right to direct consciences or to control actions which are truly private. The political community is a "complete society" in that it has all the means necessary for advancing the temporal good of man. But it is the Church which has all the means necessary for advancing the life of the spirit. Because Christ rules in the Church, the Church can rightly speak directly to conscience, and can 144 exercise jurisdiction over even the interior life of a man.

Concern for Justice

Catholics, then, "should feel themselves obliged to promote the 233 true common good, and thus should make the weight of their opinion felt, so that civil authority may act with justice, and laws may conform to moral precepts and the common good" (AA 14; cf. LG 36).

Education for justice is an integral part of Christian education. This education for justice "demands a renewal of heart, a renewal based on the recognition of sin in its individual and social manifestations. It will also inculcate a truly and entirely human way of life in justice, love and simplicity. It will likewise awaken a critical sense, which will lead us to reflect on the society in which we live and on its values; it will make men ready to renounce these values when they cease to promote justice for all men."[15] It is a continuing education. "It is also a practical education: it comes through action, participation and vital contact with the reality of injustice."[16]

51 Catholics will also remember, however, that even God in His providence does not seek at the cost of freedom to extirpate all the evils which flow from abuse of man's freedom. Subject to the requirements of public order (to the extent that these can with reasonable effectiveness be satisfied by lawful means), "the usages of society are to be the usages of freedom in their full range," and this means that "the freedom of man is to be respected as far as possible, and curtailed only when and insofar as necessary" (DH 7; cf. LG 37).

233 While the Church thus asserts the value of freedom, it also asserts that it is generally the function of the well-formed Christian conscience of the laity to see "that the divine law is inscribed in the life of the earthly city" (GS 43; cf. AA 14).

INTERNATIONAL COMMUNITY

Instantaneous communication, rapid transportation, and a host of economic and cultural ties today bind ever more closely all the citizens and people of the world (cf. GS 84). The common good of the state "cannot be divorced from the common good of the entire human family."[17] There is a "universal common good" which "needs to be intelligently pursued and more effectively achieved" (GS 84).

The problems and the opportunities that face man on the international level require an international organization with real authority to care for them. "Today the universal common good poses problems which are worldwide in their dimensions. Problems of this sort cannot be solved except by a public authority with power, structure, and means which are in scope equal to the problems, and with a worldwide sphere of activity. Consequently, the moral order itself demands the establishment of some general public authority . . . set up with the consent of all nations."[18]

181 Nations and their leaders are not above the demands of morality and the natural law.[19] The nation state is today in many respects tend-

---

[15]Second General Assembly of the Synod of Bishops, 1971, Justice in the World, Part III.
[16]See note 15.
[17]Pope John XXIII, Encyclical, *Pacem in Terris* (April 11, 1963) n. 98 (DS 3989).
[18]Pope John XXIII, Encyclical, *Pacem in Terris* (April 11, 1963) nn. 137-138 (DS 3993). Cf. GS 82.
[19]Cf. Pope John XXIII, Encyclical, *Pacem in Terris* (April 11, 1963) n. 81.

ing to become a subordinate group; it would be a form of injustice for it to cling to prerogatives and functions it can no longer properly exercise.

Thus, the principle of subsidiarity is to be respected on the interna- 218 tional level. Some world problems are so large and complex that only an international organization with real authority will be able to deal effectively with them. Such an organization, however, must not be allowed to destroy the proper independence, diversity, and separate functioning of smaller groups.

True Nature of Our Hope

Every man must be concerned with the pursuit of world peace, and of the justice without which peace cannot endure. Peace cannot be secured simply by acquiring more, bigger, and more sophisticated weapons. "The arms race is an utterly treacherous trap for humanity, and one which injures the poor to an intolerable degree" (GS 81).

Mankind needs to redirect its thoughts and attitudes toward peace. 232 In the education of our young, we must emphasize ways to pursue peace. The international organizations that now exist should be used well. We have a duty "to strain every muscle as we work for the time when all war can be completely outlawed by international consent" (GS 82). This goal "undoubtedly requires the establishment of some universal public authority acknowledged as such by all, and endowed with effective power to safeguard, on the behalf of all, security, regard for justice, and respect for rights" (GS 82).

Peace can only be the fruit of justice and the fruit of love. The radical causes of dissension must be overcome if there is to be peace. Among the causes of tension are the excessive economic inequalities among nations. Other causes stem from the quest for power and the contempt for personal rights. Deeper explanations lie within the hearts of men, "in human jealousy, distrust, pride, and other egotistic passions" (GS 83).

To have peace, mankind needs most of all a profound change of heart. "Let us not be deceived by a false hope. For unless enmities and hatreds are put away and firm, honest agreements are concluded regarding universal peace in the future, humanity, which is already in the midst of a grave crisis, although endowed with marvelous knowledge, will perhaps be brought to that mournful hour in which it will experience no peace other than the dreadful peace of death. But while it says this, still the Church of Christ, standing in the midst of the anxiety of this age, does not cease to hope with the utmost confidence" (GS 82).

190 What is the Church's hope? It is a rich, complex hope. Its basic aspect is that "lively hope," the gift of the Holy Spirit, that men "will finally be caught up in peace and utter happiness in the fatherland radiant with the glory of the Lord" (GS 93).

Christian hope looks forward also to God's mercy in this world, to the gift of Christ's peace to the nations on earth. This peace, however, is not promised to us unconditionally; it certainly is not offered as a mere fruit of human progress. The future of this world is "as uncertain as it is changing."[20]

The ultimate concern of Christians is for eternal life. But eternal
191 life begins in this world. Christians, then, have a serious duty to bring the spirit of Christ to social life at every level, to bring mercy, justice, and peace.

•   •   •

Questions related to the material in this chapter:

1. Why is "community" so important in the Christian view of man?

2. People obviously differ in many ways. What do we mean when we say that all persons are basically equal? Why would it be wrong to treat any person as a mere means to the good of any society?

3. When we speak of the "common good," what do we mean?

4. What is the meaning of "socialization"?

5. What is the "principle of subsidiarity"?

6. The family is a society in its own right. What is the proper role of civil society with regard to families and family life?

7. Those in public authority may rightly concern themselves with the population problems of their country. Does a government ever have a right to tell a husband and wife how many children they may have?

8. Parents have a serious obligation for the education of their children. Does civil society have any rights or duties concerning the education of the young?

9. What does the Church teach with regard to basic relationships within the family, between husband and wife and between parents and children?

10. What are some basic elements of Church teaching on private

---

[20]Pope Paul VI, Apostolic Letter, *Octogesima Adveniens* (May 14, 1971) n. 7.

ownership of property, business activity and production, and economic growth?

11. Are we bound in conscience to obey civil laws? To what extent?

12. Do Catholics have any right or obligation to make the weight of their opinion felt so far as civil laws, institutions, and actions are concerned?

13. Why is there a need for an international organization with real authority?

14. In what way is justice related to our hope for peace?

22

Ways of Living
a Christian Life

There is basically only one Christian vocation: to serve God's saving plan by loving Him and one another, and to share God's life in holiness and joy. It is within that one call that there is a variety of forms of Christian life.

287   In other chapters we speak of the special duties and blessings in the
Ch. 30 lives of those called to holy orders or to matrimony. Here we treat of the universal call to perfection, of minimal service to God, of the vocation of the Christian in the world, and of the vocation of the religious.

UNITY AND DIVERSITY

184   In a sense, there is only one way of living the Christian life. Charity is the life and the perfection of the believer. "You shall love the Lord your God with all your heart, and with all your soul, and with all your strength, and with all your mind; and your neighbor as yourself" (Luke 10.27).

We live, however, in a world of immense complexity, a complexity which reflects the richness of the world's Creator. Each of us is a unique and distinct person. The basic human condition is the same for us all, but we live our lives in a vast number of different actual situations and circumstances.

The two great commandments of love are complementary. Love of
192 God comes first: "This is the great and first commandment" (Matt. 22.38). But "he who loves God should love his brother also" (1 John 4.21). The goods we will for our brother are chiefly the supreme blessings which the Gospel promises. But Christian love cares also for the neighbor's earthly needs. Secular labors too are to contribute "to a better ordering of human society, very much in the interest of the kingdom of God" (GS 39). The converse is also true. "No human law can provide such secure ground for man's dignity and liberty as the Gospel entrusted to Christ's Church" (GS 41).

Christian Love and Joy

Christian love, as it is lived in the pilgrim conditions of this life, must be correctly understood. This love indeed bears fruit in the joy which St. Paul lists among the fruits of the Spirit (cf. Gal. 5.22). But neither the love nor the joy here is to be understood in shallow ways. "Love" in particular might easily, though mistakenly, be identified with emotional feelings of affection. Christian love involves a firm will to give what is truly good to others. It requires generosity. One who cares 177 only for his own self-interest is false to himself, and loses everything; one who gives all out of unselfish love attains fulfillment, and bears much fruit (cf. John 12.24-25).

Christian joy as well has a paradoxical character. It can flourish along with great suffering. There is profound joy in love strong enough to bear the cross. Christian joy does not need to escape pain or the realities of this life in order to know happiness. It is a rejoicing in the midst of trials (cf. Rom. 5.3) and in unshakable hope (cf. Rom. 5.5).

MINIMAL LOVE OF GOD

We have no love of God if we are not resolved to do the will of God. There are those who would be pleased to be God's friends if that did not require turning from their evil and selfish deeds. But friendship with God does demand that; and those who refuse to accept the minimal demands do not rise to any level of genuine love at all (cf. Matt. 21.28- 184 31).

Some of us are satisfied with a minimal love of God. Because it is love, it will involve faith in God and reverence for Him. Because it is minimal, it is willing to let the relationship with God remain simply as it is, and it does not strive to cultivate intimate friendship with God. The person of minimal love understands the basic love of God (cf. Luke 19.18-20). Even one who has only minimal love resolutely tries to maintain a level of faithfulness and to shun serious wrong. He is not eager to share fully now in the divine favor and life, though he at least seeks to avoid mortal sin and somehow to reach eternal life. One who lives with such minimal love does not live the Christian life in glad generosity, but stingily.

GOD'S CALL

The real challenge of living a Christian life begins when we seem to hear the quiet voice of the Lord calling to us: "Friend, go up higher"

231

249 (Luke 14.10). This call may come to us in prayer, even in prayer less than fervent, or in our hearing of the word of Scripture. It can reach us in all manner of ways.

In one way or another the call will come. God is patient (cf. 2 Peter 3.9), but because He loves us He is hard to satisfy. Though He allows us to drift along for a while in our unsatisfactory ways, He also invites us to respond more generously and so to find joy in the generous giving of self which charity demands.

Meanwhile, we must live our daily lives in the old familiar trials,
171 weaknesses, and crosses, but now in this new spirit, seeing our lives as the medium in which we respond to God's call, our own particular vocation.

Vocation

The word "vocation" means "calling." Some people tend to think of
295 it only in terms of a call to the ministerial priesthood or the religious life. That is not correct, for we do appropriately speak of "the lay vocation." In fact, the lay vocation is the proper, the best vocation for most persons.

Some people also tend to think of "vocation" in excessively dramatic ways. Miraculous events can accompany vocation. Ordinarily they do not.

Every Christian has a vocation. That is to say, every Christian is called by God to some particular way of carrying out the one great service or ministry of love. The one God calls us to a thousand different tasks and life-styles. In some senses, one vocation may have an excellence beyond that of another, a call to greater service and sacrifice (cf. Acts 9.15).[1] But concretely for each man the calling God gives him is the best for him. No one's vocation is an inferior version of any other. Every vocation can be a road to the height of holiness.

THE LAY CHRISTIAN VOCATION

The Christian called to serve God in the world also has a vocation of surpassing importance.

---

[1] Cf. Council of Trent, Session 24, November 11, 1563, *Doctrine on the Sacrament of Matrimony,* canon 10 (DS 1810). Cf. also LG 42; OT 10.

Laity and the Temporal Order

Christ's redemptive work is of itself aimed at the eternal salvation of men; but it involves the renewal of the whole temporal order. Laity 226 are called to participate in both the spiritual and temporal aspects of the apostolate; but they "must take on the renewal of the temporal order as their own special obligation" (AA 7).

The world made by God is loved by Him. Every element of the temporal order ought to be affected by Christ's saving work. Laymen, moved by faith and love, should use their own particular skills and act on their own responsibility to assist in healing a world marred in many ways by sin, and to establish a temporal order based on justice and love.

To care for the temporal order is to care for the goods of life and of the family, for culture and business, for the arts and professions, for political and social institutions (cf. AA 7). "This order requires constant improvement. It must be founded on truth, built in justice, and animated by love" (GS 26).

Laity and the Apostolate

Baptism gives each believer an apostolic vocation. The apostolate of 225 "spreading the kingdom of Christ everywhere for the glory of God the Father" is not for the clergy alone, but is carried on by the Church "through all its members" (AA 2). Each believer must proclaim his faith 161 by the way he lives. But the lay apostolate "does not consist only in the witness of one's way of life; a true apostle looks for opportunities to announce Christ by words addressed either to non-believers with a view to leading them to faith, or to believers with a view to instructing and strengthening them, and motivating them to a more fervent faith" (AA 6).

The task of proclaiming and spreading the faith is not always easy. Living in an age of aggressive secularism, we may be tempted at times to view it as an impossible task. The Lord, however, never promised it would be easy. He warned us that not everyone would have ears to hear the good news (cf. Mark 4.9).

On the other hand, the need for God is still as widely felt in the world as ever it was. The great difference is that in our time this need for God is often not recognized for what it is. "Many people, including many of the young, have lost sight of the meaning of their lives and are anxiously searching for the contemplative dimension of their being."[2]

Distinctive Traits of Lay Witnessing

161   Each believer must be an active witness to God and the faith. His principal duties as a witness to the faith are two: to carry the words of life to those who are to believe and have no other way of coming to them (cf. Rom. 10.14), and to testify to those words by his words and acts.

The witness, having received the message with joy, remains
136 always subject to it and obedient before it. The message is not his to alter or distort. However personal the graces by which God calls men to Himself, He calls them to the publicly proclaimed Gospel which is to unite in one faith the whole family of God.

The more actively one works as apostle — perhaps as a writer or teacher, or as a parent, or in some other capacity — the more important it is that one's work be rooted in the obedience of faith, in full openness and assent to what Christ constantly teaches in His Church.

Formation for the Apostolate

Suitable preparation is necessary for the effective exercise of the lay apostolate. Spiritual formation is most important. One can advance in the kingdom effectively only if one's own life is firmly rooted in faith.

In addition to spiritual formation, one needs doctrinal instruction in the faith, and in the sciences and skills relevant to his apostolate. He should learn to "view, judge, and do all things in the light of faith" (AA 29).

The lay apostolate can be exercised by individuals, and preparation for it can be acquired in many ways. But there are valuable group forms of the apostolate also. Many are assisted in their formation for the apostolate by membership in a sodality, charitable association, apostolic guild, or third order. Especially to be noted are those associations which have received the title of "Catholic Action." In such groups, the laity cooperate more directly and immediately with the hierarchy, offering their own skills and experience to further the Church's apostolic aims, in a way that symbolizes fittingly the unity and community nature of the Church (cf. AA 20).

---

[2]Pope Paul VI, Apostolic Exhortation, *Evangelica Testificatio* (June 29, 1971) n. 45.

Some formal commitment will be involved in almost every serious response to God's call to an apostolic Christian life. Some will make the basic Christian commitment to faithfulness in Sunday Mass and devotedness to one's work and family responsibilities. Others will join an association like those we have noted above. A more solemn commitment can be in a "secular institute." In joining such an institute one consecrates the work of one's ordinary life to God through such means as profession of poverty, chastity, and obedience, and the following of a common rule.

Spontaneity is good. But true human spontaneity is aided by a rule of life and self-discipline. Human spontaneity is not merely doing what 254 impulse suggests; it flows more richly from an ordered life, in which one has rooted out what is false and selfish, so that the whole man, brought to inner peace, may gladly and from the whole heart do what he really wishes.

GOSPEL COUNSELS AND RELIGIOUS LIFE

Christ taught the rich man that everyone is obliged to love God and his neighbor in the faithful observance of the commandments (cf. Luke 18.10-20). But those in whom God's grace stirs a hunger for a more excellent life are called to share with Christ a generous will to give up 246 much that they may cling to God in a richer freedom. Those who enter religious life bind themselves, "either by vows or by other sacred bonds which are like vows in their purpose" (LG 44), to observance of the evangelical counsels of perfection, that is, the Gospel counsels of chastity, poverty, and obedience.

"The evangelical counsels of chastity dedicated to God, poverty, and obedience are based upon the words and example of the Lord. They were further commended by the apostles and the Fathers, and other teachers and shepherds of the Church. The counsels are a divine gift, which the Church has received from her Lord and which she ever preserves with the help of His grace" (LG 43).

A decision to follow Christ closely through the observance of His 304 evangelical counsels involves cutting away many perfectly laudable objectives which one might otherwise pursue: sexual and domestic fulfillment in marriage, ownership of property, legitimate self-concern. Yet the giving up of these things can be counted as nothing (cf. Phil. 3.8) by those who long to share emptying of self with Christ, so that they might cling to Him immediately with a full and freer heart (cf. 1 Cor. 7.32-35).

235

It is in the context of our long, slow stumbling march to another, more perfect home that religious life makes sense. Knowing we have a destination — life with our Father — the religious gladly offers himself or herself as a sign pointing the way. By a visible, dedicated life he or 89 she shows all who will look and can see that God has already begun His final work on earth and that this divine labor will culminate in glory in the life to come.

The vows of religious are to be understood positively. They are made "for the sake of the kingdom of heaven." They are a way of bearing witness to values that transcend private possessions, marital love, independent action.

Religious Poverty

By consecrated poverty, a religious renounces for himself personal possession or control of property in order to imitate Christ, who made Himself poor for our sake (cf. 2 Cor. 8.9), to draw himself far from too great a love of earthly things, and to become a consolation and support to the many poor and little ones of Christ. Religious commitment to poverty is a constant reminder to the whole Church of the Gospel demand 244 that all believers free their hearts from the treacherous charm of riches and acquire poverty of spirit.

Consecrated Chastity

Another challenge to prevailing habits of thought in the world is the virtue of dedicated chastity. The celibate offers something to God 333 that is in fact a good. More profoundly, he is bearing witness to the fact that human sexuality, although good in itself, is only one form of love. By their chastity religious "give witness to all Christ's faithful of that wondrous marriage in which the Church has Christ as her only Spouse, a marriage which has been established by God and which will be fully manifested in the world to come" (PC 12).

Not all are called to a life of consecrated chastity. But those who are called by grace and embrace this life out of the love of Christ and in the desire to serve His kingdom with greater freedom and single-heartedness (cf. 1 Cor. 7.32-35) find in chastity a means to profound self-fulfillment and growth in grace. The Church has learned by experience

236

and from the words of Christ (cf. Matt. 19.11-12) that virginity for Christ is a vocation of "surpassing excellence."[3]

Christ-like Obedience

Consecrated obedience also challenges many present-day habits of thought. Various factors, including misleading popularizations of psychology, have led many to suppose that genuine self-fulfillment is opposed to the selfless generosity required to imitate the heroic obedience 64 of Jesus (cf. Phil. 2.8). Modern demands for autonomy sometimes go far beyond all rational limits, urging a man to view any authority, even that of the saving God, as a threat to his dignity. Thus many today find it difficult to see genuine obedience as a virtue at all, and they fail to see that when obedience imitates the obedience of Christ, it enlarges the 88 human spirit.

In a sense, the obedient Christian, like Christ, both does and does not do his own will. His deep will is to do what God wishes him to do, through whatever means His will is made known. It pleases the good man to do even that which does not please him, when God calls him to generous service. By his obedience the religious bears witness to a principle the world needs ever to relearn: it is not through indulgent self-will but through self-restraint that one lays hold of freedom.

Religious Community as a Sign

Religious life normally is lived in religious community. Those living this common life can help each other in faithfulness to the Gospel generosity to which they are called. Such a common life is expected to provide a pattern of community also for the other faithful. Those freed from the burdens of secular life are expected to make the sacrifices of forgiveness and magnanimity that build community in such a way as to give heart to all the faithful.

Thus we see that within the Church, itself a sign, the consecrated 117 religious is a sign. His or her life must point out to others the love, understanding, compassion, and truth of Christ. This type of life is a sign

---

[3]Cf. Pope Paul VI, Apostolic Exhortation, *Evangelica Testificatio* (June 29, 1971) n. 13. Cf. also OT 10; Pope Pius XII, Encyclical, *Sacra Virginitas* (March 25, 1954); Council of Trent, Session 24, November 11, 1563, *Doctrine on the Sacrament of Matrimony,* canon 10 (DS 1810).

within the great sacramental sign which is the Church. By being a light, as it were, it illumines the way for others within the Church.

Personal holiness is part of the holiness of the whole Christian community. The activity of a religious, therefore, must not be directed solely toward one religious community, but toward the good of the whole Church and, through the Church, to all men.

Special Blessing of Contemplative Religious

261 The importance of the religious life, especially its contemplative aspect, can hardly be exaggerated. Every Christian knows that God is to be found and loved and served in one's neighbor. It is often forgotten, however, that one's neighbor is also to be found and loved and served in God, and that for some this will be the most practical approach to the task of even temporal charity.

Active works are essential, but their effect is particular and limited. One who realistically wishes to do something for the world and the human race on a large scale might best devote himself to a life of prayer, obedience, penance, solitude, and silence. That is how the Church has always embarked on "renewal." That is how the great efforts launched by the saints started, as witness the hermits of the Thebaid, Benedict at Subiaco, Francis at La Verna, Ignatius at Manresa, Teresa at Avila, and many more. Jesus Himself fasted in the desert. Whenever there has been in the Church what subsequent generations have recognized as a major renewal, it has started with individuals or small groups who have cared enough to go out into the desert or to the hermitage or to the cloister to wrestle alone with God and Satan, in the solitude of contemplative prayer.

249 External acts can of themselves never "save" the world; man has no ultimate hope apart from the cross and resurrection of Christ. The life of the hermit and the enclosed life of the contemplative religious are among the most "relevant" of the lives to which Christians are called.

VOCATION AND WISDOM

"Let nothing be put before the Work of God," said St. Benedict. He was referring to the ordered worship of God in the Divine Office. But whatever our vocation in life, it is in prayer and worship, especially in liturgical worship, that we are most fully human, since we are then doing the particular thing for which we were made. It may at times seem a burden, but contemplation of God is in the end the goal of our life, the whole point and purpose and joy of existence.

We must learn to care and not to care. Each of us must respond to God's particular calls, and must live accordingly. On the other hand, there is a sense in which the outward pattern or form of our lives is a matter of complete unimportance. In any situation holiness is an option available to us; in no situation will it be easy for us. Yet nothing else really matters. It is wisdom to seek first of all the kingdom of God. Everything else good flows from that pursuit (cf. Matt. 6.33).

* * *

Questions related to the material in this chapter:

1. What is the call or vocation that all Christians share, even if they respond to it in different ways?

2. Can a Christian be satisfied with a minimal love of God, with doing no more than is strictly required?

3. We say that every Christian has a vocation. What does this mean?

4. Why is renewal of the temporal order a special obligation of the laity?

5. We say that baptism gives each believer an apostolic vocation. What does this mean, and what is the importance of lay witnessing?

6. What are the particular vows or solemn commitments that each religious makes?

7. In what ways do members of religious orders give special witness in the world, and what do we mean when we say the consecrated religious is a "sign"?

8. In what way do contemplatives help the whole Church and each individual Christian?

23

To Share
in the Divinity of Christ

The Son of God became man so that men might share in the life of God. This is the great mystery of God's love in the Incarnation.

In this chapter we speak of the ways in which we share in the life of God. The chapter discusses the various kinds of grace, how God Himself dwelling in us is the uncreated grace, and how God transforms His people with the created gifts of grace. Finally, it shows why it is necessary for those who have been justified to grow in the life of grace.

THE MEANING OF GRACE

The word "grace" (or "favor") is commonly used in the New Testament to speak of the generosity by which God gives us new life. On the one hand, the word is used to suggest the pure mercy and freedom with which God so blesses us. It is also used of the gifts themselves that flow from that mercy.

Every gift of God that is related to the new life Christ came to give is called a grace. Certainly everything God enriches us with is a gift. But 174 some of His gifts are doubly gratuitous. In sublime freedom God chose to call us to be not only His creatures, but His friends. We are invited to know Him by faith and to love Him and one another with a divine love bestowed by Him. All these special gifts are aimed at our coming to full possession of God in the blessed vision of eternal life. The gifts God gives us to arouse, nourish, and fulfill this life in us are called "supernatural" gifts, or graces.[1]

Justification

We are called to this new life from a sinful state. Each person is born in original sin, and born into a world damaged by sin. But God "has

---

[1]Cf. First Vatican Council, Session 3, April 24, 1870, *Dogmatic Constitution on the Catholic Faith,* ch. 2 (DS 3004-3005).

delivered us from the dominion of darkness and transferred us to the kingdom of His beloved Son, in whom we have redemption, the forgiveness of sins" (Col. 1.13-14). St. Paul speaks of this justifying mercy of God often, especially in his Epistle to the Romans (cf. Rom. 6-8).[2]

Freedom is the keynote of justification. God does not justify us out of necessity, but because He chooses to. The grace with which He draws us to new life is utterly unmerited by us. But He treats us as free persons, not as puppets or as programmed robots. Grace is given to our freedom. In all the stages of justification of an adult, from the first invitation of grace to its full flowering, divine freedom arouses human freedom. If they do not reject His gift, God moves men in such a way that they come to have a holy and useful fear of His justice, to have hope in His mercy, and to begin to love Him, and so to hate and turn away from sin, so that they repent and come to the new birth of baptism. Then, in justification itself, they receive "not only remission of sins, but also a sanctification and renewal of the inner man through the voluntary reception of the grace and gifts whereby an unjust man becomes just and from being an enemy becomes a friend, that he may be 'an heir according to the hope of life everlasting' (Titus 3.7)."[3]

GOD'S GIFT OF HIMSELF: UNCREATED GRACE

The first of all God's gifts is the gift of Himself. He desires to give Himself to us perfectly in eternal life. Then we shall join those who already "are in glory, beholding 'clearly God triune and one, as He is' " (LG 49)[4] and share forever the richness of infinite life.

Even in this present life God gives Himself in many ways. He gives Himself to us as a friend in the gifts of revelation and charity; He gives Himself to us in Christ in whom "the whole fulness of deity dwells bodily" (Col. 2.9). At the Last Supper, however, Christ spoke of a special gift that God makes of Himself to us in time, a gift of grace known as the divine indwelling.

"If a man loves Me, he will keep My word, and My Father will love him, and We will come to him and make Our home with him" (John

---

[2]Cf. Council of Trent, Session 6, January 13, 1547, *Decree on Justification*, esp. chs. 1-8 (DS 1521-1532) for an authentic Catholic interpretation of this teaching.
[3]Council of Trent, Session 6, January 13, 1547, *Decree on Justification*, ch. 7 (DS 1528).
[4]The interior quotation is from Council of Florence, Bull, *Laetentur Caeli* (July 6, 1439) (DS 1305).

14.23). The Father and Son will dwell in those who love Christ, and They will cause the Holy Spirit to dwell there as Consoler and Advocate.

Faith teaches the true meaning of this tremendous mystery. Though we are closely joined with God and share His life as He dwells in us, He remains God and we remain creatures. While we share His life, we remain always finite and distinct from Him who is the infinite Lord of all.[5] But it is a mystery that transcends our understanding; it is truly a beginning of a heavenly life. "This marvelous union, known by the special name of indwelling, differs only by reason of our condition or state from that union in which God embraces and beautifies the citizens of heaven."[6] Such is the uncreated grace: God Himself is within us to save us.

CREATED GRACE AND GIFTS

When God dwells in those who love Him, He changes them. In justifying us He causes us to "put on the new nature, created after the likeness of God in true righteousness and holiness" (Eph. 4.24). We who had been aliens and outcasts because of sin become sons by adoption, truly sharing in His life. "See what love the Father has given us, that we should be called children of God; and so we are" (1 John 3.1).

All this reveals a profound change in our being, that "sanctification and renewal of the inner man" of which the Council of Trent spoke. God truly gives us new life when He justifies us. This change in the heart of our being, the created gift by which He binds us personally to Himself, the uncreated gift, and makes us be His sons and heirs of heaven, is called sanctifying grace.

State of Grace

Sanctifying grace is meant to be an enduring gift. For that reason, it is also called "habitual grace." Once this grace has been received by a person it remains with him, unless he separates himself from God by deliberate mortal sin. To keep sanctifying grace means to preserve one's friendship with God; to lose sanctifying grace means to separate oneself from personal friendship with the Lord.

---

[5]Cf. Pope Pius XII, Encyclical, *Mystici Corporis* (June 29, 1943) (DS 3814).
[6]Pope Leo XIII, Encyclical, *Divinum Illud Munus* (May 9, 1897) (DS 3331).

One is said to be in the "state of grace" when one possesses this sanctifying grace and the personal relationships with God that are its inner meaning. This "state" is spoken of in various ways. "Justification from sin and God's indwelling in the soul are a grace. When we say a sinner is justified by God, is given life by the Holy Spirit, possesses in himself Christ's life, or has grace, we are using expressions which in different words mean one and the same thing, namely, dying to sin, becoming partakers of the divinity of the Son through the Spirit of adoption, and entering into an intimate communion with the most Holy Trinity."[7]

The state of grace is lost by a deliberate mortal sin. But God can and does call sinners back to life; He moves them to "exert themselves to 55 obtain through the sacrament of penance the recovery, by the merits of Christ, of the grace lost."[8] This return to grace also is a serious and decisive step. An insincere confession of sins will not achieve it. There must be a change of heart, made possible by God's grace, and sincerely exercised in earnest repentance.

Virtues and Gifts

Together with sanctifying grace God gives the just man the virtues 185 of faith, hope, and love, so that, having become a child of God, he may do the works of God. These virtues orient our new life directly to God.

By the gift of faith, God enables us to share in the light of His own knowledge, so we may know Him and His saving word. By the virtue of hope, God gives an unshakable confidence in Himself (cf. Rom. 8.38-39). But the greatest of these three theological virtues is love (cf. 1 Cor. 13.13). "Poured into our hearts through the Holy Spirit" (Rom. 5.5), it enables us to cling with our whole hearts to God with an energy and life that He Himself communicates. All Christian moral life is grounded on these theological virtues.

But there are other virtues. Every good man should grow in the "cardinal virtues" of justice, fortitude, temperance, and prudence (cf. Wisd. 8.7), and in the many virtues that flow from these. To the extent that these virtues are merely human and natural, they do not of themselves minister to grace or lead men to friendship and eternal life with

---

[7]Sacred Congregation for the Clergy, *General Catechetical Directory* (April 11, 1971) n. 60.
[8]Council of Trent, Session 6, January 13, 1547, *Decree on Justification,* ch. 14 (DS 1542).

God. But grace and charity can transform natural virtues, and plant in the heart dispositions to do all humanly good deeds in a way that makes them expressions of divine love. Hence it is that supports for every kind of good action are planted in the soul with sanctifying grace.

Gifts of the Holy Spirit are also given with grace. A familiar Messianic prophecy of the Old Testament declared that the Spirit would bring to the Redeemer gifts of wisdom, understanding, counsel, fortitude, knowledge, piety, and fear of the Lord (cf. Isa. 11.2-3).[9] The Fathers and saints of the Church have persistently taught that these same gifts are conferred on Christ's members, on all the faithful who are in grace. By the gifts of the Spirit "the soul is furnished and strengthened to be able to obey God's voice and impulse more easily and promptly."[10]

"By means of these gifts the soul is excited and encouraged to seek after and attain the evangelical beatitudes."[11] These beatitudes were pronounced by our Lord at the very beginning of His public preaching (cf. Matt. 5.3-10).

236
- Blessed are the poor in spirit, for theirs is the kingdom of heaven.

- Blessed are those who mourn, for they shall be comforted.

- Blessed are the meek, for they shall inherit the earth.

- Blessed are those who hunger and thirst for righteousness, for they shall be satisfied.

- Blessed are the merciful, for they shall obtain mercy.

- Blessed are the pure in heart, for they shall see God.

- Blessed are the peacemakers, for they shall be called sons of God.

- Blessed are those who are persecuted for righteousness' sake, for theirs is the kingdom of heaven.

By the gifts of the Holy Spirit one is led toward the sublime dispositions that the beatitudes praise and the blessedness that they promise. These, together with the fruits of the Holy Spirit, "are the signs and harbingers of eternal beatitude."[12] "The fruit of the Spirit is love, joy, peace, patience, kindness, goodness, faithfulness, gentleness, self-control" (Gal. 5.22-23).

---

[9]"Piety" is not in the Hebrew text, but is in the Septuagint and Vulgate versions.
[10]Pope Leo XIII, Encyclical, *Divinum Illud Munus* (May 9, 1897), ASS 29 (1896-97) 654.
[11]Pope Leo XIII, Encyclical, *Divinum Illud Munus* (May 9, 1897), ASS 29 (1896-97) 654.
[12]Pope Leo XIII, Encyclical, *Divinum Illud Munus* (May 9, 1897), ASS 29 (1896-97) 654.

Actual Grace

God is also ever present to us with what we call "actual" graces. These are the helps which God gives us so that we may actually do deeds of love. By actual graces God enlightens our minds to see His ways and strengthens our resolve to walk in them, or to return to them if we have gone astray.

Actual graces can be internal or external. Internal actual graces are gifts by which God assists and animates us from within, so that we may 40 perform free and saving actions. External graces are infinitely varied. Every kind of gift by which God moves us toward knowing Him and sharing His life is a grace. Devoted parents, faithful friends, good books, great music — indeed anything at all may be used by God to lead toward life. Even sickness and trials may be mercies by which God is directing toward salvation those whom He loves.

DYING TO SIN

Even after justification there remains in man something of sin. It is 195 possible to be in the state of grace and at the same time to experience concupiscence, the inclination to sin. St. Paul sometimes calls this tendency toward evil that we discover in ourselves "sin" (cf. Rom. 6.12-13, 7.7; 7.14-20). But this is something very different from a deliberate rejection of God; it is not an actual mortal sin. It is called "sin" only because of its source and tendency: "it comes from sin and inclines toward sin."[13]

The Christian, grateful for God's grace, must nonetheless acknowledge he is a sinner. He was born in original sin, and he experiences tendencies toward sin. He is able to remember well his personal, deliberate sins, and he knows how much they have intensified concupiscence. Frequently he is guilty of selfish and ungrateful deeds, even if the mercy of God guards him from the tragic malice of mortal sin.

The Christian must struggle against sin. While the grace of God guarantees his final victory unless he rejects God's help, grace does not excuse him from faithful and serious effort. To be a Christian demands dying to sin, dying with Christ to something deep within oneself, so that one may rise to newness of life (cf. Rom. 6.4).

---

[13]Council of Trent, Session 5, June 17, 1546, *Decree on Original Sin,* n. 5 (DS 1515).

The Flesh

Concupiscence inclines us to every capital sin, that is, to pride, covetousness, lust, anger, gluttony, envy, and sloth,[14] and to their dismal fruits. We must persevere in penance and self-denial if we are to destroy the perverse tendencies in our hearts and make room there for the new gifts of God to take root and grow.

The World

The struggle is also against the world. God indeed is its Creator and His world is "very good" (Gen. 1.31), and "God so loved the world" (John 3.16) that He sent His Son to save it. But Scripture also speaks of the "world" in another and very different sense, of the "world" as an alignment of forces that do not believe and love God.

"If any one loves the world, love for the Father is not in him" (1 John 2.15). The Christian must guard himself from the fascinating attractions of the world, while yet retaining an unselfish love of persons in the world, for whom Christ died.

The Devil

54   Our life in Christ has cosmic dimensions as well. Although we do not understand fully what role God permits the devil and other demons to have on this earth, the reality of malign spiritual forces is only too evident in the despondent pain of the unbelieving world and in the tragic sorrows in the record of history. "For we are not contending against flesh and blood, but against the principalities, against the powers, against the world rulers of this present darkness, against the spiritual hosts of wickedness in the heavenly places" (Eph. 6.12).

GROWING IN GRACE

235   Grace is a gift of life, and we must grow in it. Even the first gifts of grace, when one first comes to justification, are sublime gifts; but with them we are really only infants in a new life (cf. 1 Peter 2.2). We are to
173 grow up in faith (cf. 2 Cor. 10.15), in doing deeds of love (cf. 1 Thess. 3.4), growing up in every way to mirror the splendid maturity of Christ our Head (cf. Eph. 4.15).

This growth which is expected of every Christian is not something

---

[14]Cf. St. Gregory the Great, *Moralia in Iob* 31.45 (ML 76.621).

to be achieved by individuals in isolation, but is a growth in love with the whole family of faith. We allow God to build us together into a dwelling place of His presence: "Like living stones be yourselves built into a spiritual house" (1 Peter 2.5).

This growth requires effort on our part, but it is God who gives the growth (cf. 1 Cor. 6.6). By accepting His call and allowing His gifts to bear fruit in us (cf. Matt. 5.8), we can become more generous in keeping 260 His commands of love, drawing near to Him in prayer, and associating ourselves with Christ's life-giving mysteries through His sacraments. In such living of faith one experiences the joy and richness of the new life which becomes more and more the eternal life of heaven anticipated already in time.

* * *

Questions related to the material in this chapter:

1. What is the main idea signified by the word "grace"?

2. What is "justification"? What are the stages of justification of an adult?

3. Is there any scriptural basis for our belief in the "divine indwelling"?

4. One is said to be in the "state of grace" when one possesses sanctifying grace. What are some other ways of expressing this?

5. We say that all Christian moral life is grounded on the theological virtues. What are these?

6. What are some other virtues and gifts given with grace?

7. Why do we need God's grace in order to practice the beatitudes?

8. God offers us daily helps to do good deeds. What do we call these helps?

9. We say that the Christian must struggle against sin, against the flesh, the world, and the devil. What does this mean? Why is this so?

10. Why is growth in grace important?

24

Christ and the Life of Prayer

"Lord, teach us to pray" (Luke 11.1). The disciples, seeing our Lord so long at prayer, asked that they might learn to pray. And Jesus taught them.

In this chapter we treat of prayer in the life of one who has accepted Jesus as Lord and Teacher. Here we discuss Christ as Model and Teacher of prayer, the necessity of prayer for the Christian life, the effects of prayer, the definition and types of prayer, and the necessity of grace for prayer.

CHRIST AS MODEL AND TEACHER OF PRAYER

The Gospels, especially St. Luke's, often describe Christ at prayer (cf. Luke 3.21, 5.16, 9.29, 10.21, 11.1, 22.32). He prayed, publicly as well as privately, before the most important acts and decisions of His ministry (cf. Luke 4.1; Matt. 14.23; Heb. 5.7). Prayer was the constant background of the Lord's life. This continuous prayer is explained by the Evangelist John as flowing from Jesus' special relationship to the Father (cf. John 1.51, 4.34, 8.29, 11.41).

In His prayer life, the Lord showed Himself an heir to the treasures and traditions of the Hebrews concerning prayer. He prayed the Psalms (cf. Matt. 27.46), especially the Hallel, the great hymn of praise formed by Psalms 113-118 (cf. Matt. 26.30). He knew well the Shema, the ritual prayer said by the Jews twice a day: "Hear, O Israel! The LORD our God is one LORD . . ." (Deut. 6.4; cf. Matt. 22.37).

The teaching of Jesus about prayer was a teaching which He was
375 already living. In many ways Jesus showed the disciples how to pray. To show them what to pray for, He gave them the Our Father, which was His prayer, the perfect prayer, as a model. Yet even the Our Father is given to us in different words in the Gospels of Luke (11.2-4) and Matthew (6.9-13). This suggests that the spirit of a prayer is more important than any exact set of words.

248

NECESSITY OF PRAYER FOR CHRISTIAN LIFE

Jesus Himself lived always in a prayerful spirit that blossomed easily into explicit prayer. Such prayerfulness He taught the apostles also. They should "watch and pray."

From the example and teaching of Jesus Christ, it is clear that a Christian should be a person of prayer. One who knows that his existence and life of grace come from God can recognize the need to remain in communion with God.

Prayer is not an attempt to inform God of our needs. Prayer can be acknowledgment of one's weakness and dependence on God. Further, prayer is not selfish, because one prays — if one prays as Christ teaches — with humble submission to God's will and in obedience to His command (cf. Luke 11.9-13). Man cannot reach salvation without graces from God — and some graces according to God's plan are granted only in answer to prayer.[1]

Prayer, therefore, is neither useless nor selfish. It flows from one's filial relationship with God. It is the loving, obedient response of a child to his Father. Any life lived in faith, hope, and love will have to express itself to God in prayer.

The Second Vatican Council repeatedly taught the necessity of prayer. Prayer is presented as an identifying mark of the Church and of the genuine Christian (cf. LG 10, 12, 40, 41).

EFFECTS OF PRAYER ON CHRISTIAN LIFE

St. Thomas Aquinas teaches that prayer brings about three effects: it merits graces from God, it obtains other benefits from God, and it brings a certain spiritual refreshment of the mind.[2]

It is certainly true that prayer, when it follows the pattern of Christ's prayer, has a transforming effect on one's life. Genuine prayer is bound into the totality of life as it is lived, affects the rest of life and is affected by the rest of life. We cannot pray well unless we are prepared to change in our lives those things which hold us back from God.

The Christian must be careful to avoid the trap of activism. The person who says, "My work is my prayer," is wrong if he does not sometimes pray explicitly. The person who truly prays by his work is

---

[1]Cf. St. Thomas Aquinas, *Summa Theologica* II-II, 83, 2.
[2]Cf. St. Thomas Aquinas, *Summa Theologica* II-II, 83, 13.

also one who enters his room and prays to the Father in secret (cf. Matt. 6.6), who takes time to be alone with the Lord.

What is the "certain spiritual refreshment of the mind" that comes from a life of prayer? As the general words used by St. Thomas Aquinas suggest, this is not something easy to describe in specific terms. Prayer does make radical demands on one. But it ultimately leads to a re-fashioning of oneself according to the plan of God. One's personality, viewed as a complex of attitudes and values, must be trimmed and cul-tivated, and trained to the mind of Christ. The end result is the peace of Christ: a harmonious order and balance within oneself; a view of this world from the perspective of God and of eternity; a strength to hold 179 oneself together despite change about and within one; a growing close-ness to God through Jesus Christ.

DEFINITION AND TYPES OF PRAYER

The traditional Catholic definition of prayer is "the raising of one's mind and heart to God." When we pray, we turn our minds and hearts to God, to adore Him and thank Him or ask favors or forgiveness of Him.

St. John of Damascus described prayer as "the ascent of the mind to God, the request for fitting things from God."[3] St. Thomas Aquinas pointed out that there is an element of petition in all prayer; indeed, ac-cording to St. Thomas, the ultimate prayer of petition is the quest of God.[4] Definitions of the word "prayer" came in time to cover also medi-tation and various degrees of contemplation.

At the present time there is a preference for the broad definition of prayer as "speaking with God." This definition has advantage. It in-cludes all types of prayer. At the same time, it indicates that prayer is not a monologue but a dialogue, a conversation. By prayer man re-28 sponds to God who first spoke to us, especially through His unique Word made flesh.

Purposes of Prayer

272   There are four general types of prayer, according to the reasons or purposes for which one prays: adoration, thanksgiving, petition, and

---

[3]St. John of Damascus, De Fide Orthodoxa 3.24 (MG 94.1089-1090).
[4]Cf. St. Thomas Aquinas, Summa Theologica II-II, 83, 17; 83, 1 ad 2.

contrition. All other kinds of prayer — love, praise, abandonment to God's will, atonement, reparation, and so on — can be included in one or the other of the four general types.

Here on earth our prayers are frequently expressions of sorrow and petition. But the Christian life requires also prayers of adoration and thanksgiving. In heaven the prayers of the blessed will be chiefly expressions of adoration and thanksgiving.

Prayers of Petition

Christ Himself told us to ask God for things (cf. John 16.23-24; Matt. 7.7). God always hears our prayers. He knows how to give good things to His children (cf. Luke 11.13). Sometimes, however, we ask for foolish or even harmful things.

For what, then, should one pray? It seems fitting to pray to God for anything one needs or might reasonably desire. Though prayer is a spiritual activity, we may ask our heavenly Father for physical and material things: our "daily bread." Everything we care about is worthy of prayer, for nothing which is important to us is insignificant to God, who loves us.

There is undoubtedly a certain order of priorities in what is worth praying for. For some things, we must pray. For other things, we are free to pray. In keeping with the Our Father, we should ask for God's glory, the coming of His kingdom, the fulfillment of His will by men, and the graces necessary and useful for salvation.

The Christian must be careful in praying for specific material goods and possessions. These can be asked for, if they are helpful toward salvation. The poverty of Christ and His warnings about riches should make us cautious about praying for superfluous material goods. No Christian would expect God to give something that might be detrimental to salvation. Consequently God does not grant every petition for improved health, employment, material possessions, and the like, for these might be spiritually harmful.

It is proper for the Christian to pray for Himself, that he accomplish 190 God's will in life and reach eternal salvation. He should also pray for his neighbor, in keeping with the requirements of Christian charity. The Church tells us to use the "Prayer of the Faithful" at Mass to pray for (a) the needs of the Church, (b) public authorities and the salvation of the world, (c) those oppressed by any need, and (d) the local community.[5]

---

[5]Cf. General Instruction of the Roman Missal, n. 46.

Our private prayer as well should have wide range. We pray for our families, for the people we work with, for our friends and neighbors. Prayers should also be offered for the Holy Father, one's bishop and all bishops, one's pastor and all priests and deacons, religious women and men, for all in the Church, for all outside the Church that there may be one flock and one shepherd, for those in authority, for relatives and benefactors, for the deceased whom one has known and for all souls in 347 purgatory (cf. LG 50), and even for enemies and persecutors (cf. Matt. 5.44).

Qualities Essential in Genuine Prayer

Christian prayer should have certain qualities. Among these are attention, devotion, confidence, and perseverance.

Attention. Christ requires that we pray with an absolute inner sincerity, not with the hypocritical externalism of the Pharisees (cf. Matt. 6.5-8). Involuntary distractions may come and go, because of human weakness. These do not destroy the value of prayer.

Devotion. Prayer is more than an exercise of the mind. It is also a genuflection of the will to God. Genuine devotion should not be confused with a feeling of satisfaction or with emotion. For devotion is properly a total dedication to God. At times devoted acts are accompanied by peace and joy. At times they are not. Yet even when prayer comes hard, the will can submit to God: "Thy will be done...." Even a sinner, though lacking in devotion, is obligated to pray.

Confidence. The Lord has told us to pray with an unshakable con-
86 fidence born of faith (cf. Matt. 11.24; Luke 17.5; James 1.5). We do this by praying "in the name of Jesus" our Mediator with full confidence in His redemptive love and in the power of His merits to obtain from the Father what is asked (cf. John 16.23-24).

Perseverance. We learn from the Gospels to pray with perseverance. "Will not God vindicate His elect, who cry to Him day and night?" (Luke 18.7; cf. also Matt. 7.7-11, 15.21; Luke 11.1-13; Eph. 6.18; 1 Thess. 5.17). The Christian should never be discouraged in prayer, should never give up, never lose heart (cf. Luke 18.1).

To Whom We Pray

The Christian prays to the one, triune God. Ordinarily in the New Testament all prayer, private as well as public, is addressed to God the

252

Father through Christ and in the Spirit. One may direct prayer to all three Persons or to one of Them. Thus occasionally in the New Testament (cf. John 14.14; Acts 7.59; 1 Cor. 1.2; 2 Cor. 12.8; 1 Tim. 1.12) and in the Mass, prayers are directed to Christ. Similarly some prayers, as the "Come, Holy Spirit," are addressed to the Holy Spirit.

The Second Vatican Council expressed clearly how our prayers are ultimately addressed to God, and how prayers to the Blessed Virgin and to the angels and saints in heaven ask them to intercede before God for us (cf. LG 50). "At the same time, let the faithful be instructed that our communion with those in heaven, provided that it is understood in the more adequate light of faith, in no way weakens, but rather on the contrary more thoroughly enriches, the supreme worship we give to God the Father, through Christ, in the Spirit" (LG 51).

So to God we give absolute worship, and to Him we pray: "Have mercy on us." To the Blessed Mother and to the saints we show a dif- 152 ferent kind of honor or devotion, and we ask them: "Pray for us" (cf. LG 67).

PRAYER AND GRACE

Christian prayer is supernatural. In prayer the mystery of God and the mystery of man meet in discourse — and the Holy Spirit works to bring this communication about.

Prayer cannot be mastered by human efforts or human techniques alone. There is no true prayer which is not the effect of grace. No matter how difficult or studied or how spontaneous one's prayer may be, it is 170 always God who raises up the heart which lifts itself to Him.   295

Ultimately, then, prayer is possible only because God makes it possible. As an expression of the supernatural virtues of faith, hope, and love, prayer itself is of the realm of grace. It is the work of the Holy Spirit within us — and yet it is we who pray.

Filial Prayer

In the New Testament, the basis for prayer is the new relationship by which Christians come to the Father through Jesus Christ. This is the relationship of adopted sonship. The Christian, joyfully aware of his 305 sonship, can pray with childlike confidence and tender intimacy to the loving Father, to "Abba" (Rom. 8.15; Gal. 4.6). This new relationship gives a special quality to the prayer of a Christian in the name of Christ. So also it gives a distinctive flavor to Christian mysticism.

Prayer a Response to God's Word

Prayer is a dialogue in which God has already spoken and has expressed the first word. The books of Sacred Scripture are in a particular way the word of God. "For in the sacred books, the Father who is in heaven meets His children with great love and speaks with them; and the force and power in the word of God is so great that it remains the support and energy of the Church, the strength of faith for her sons, the food of the soul, the pure and perennial source of spiritual life" (DV 21).

The prayer of a Christian, consequently, is a response to God's word. This is shown in the Mass: first God speaks to the assembled Church in the Liturgy of the Word; then the Church responds in the Profession of Faith and joins Christ in the Eucharistic Prayer.

The same approach is important in private prayer. Catholic tradition has strongly recommended the reading of Scripture as the basis of prayer, and has considered prayer and contemplation to be the proper response to God's word. This explains the traditional emphasis on "spiritual reading" in Catholic spirituality. In the Bible and also through other spiritual writings God's word comes to us. This word calls for our response, and the first response is prayer.

Discipline in Prayer

The hard work of persevering prayer demands faithfulness to other graces from God. Only one trying to lead a good life will have the appropriate dispositions to pray.

The state of soul that permits prayer does not come about without preparation through an entire range of circumstances. One prepares for a life of prayer by leading a good life, and prayer is an expression of that life. So every sacrifice which detaches us from the world, everything which conforms us to the image of God, every movement of love that puts us in harmony with the triune God — all this is preparation for prayer.

Every Christian who seeks to pray faithfully learns that perseverance in prayer requires self-discipline. Saints who have loved and enjoyed prayer have often reminded us that faithfulness in prayer requires effort and discipline. In *The Sayings of the Fathers,* a collection of sayings or maxims of Egyptian monks of the fourth and fifth centuries, there is the wise saying of Father Agatho: "I think there is nothing that needs so much effort as prayer to God. . . . In all the other efforts of a religious life, whether they are made vehemently or gently, there is room for a measure of rest. But we need to pray till we breathe out our dying breath."[6]

* * *

Questions related to the material in this chapter:

1. Why do we speak of Christ as Model and Teacher of prayer?
2. What is the "Lord's Prayer" and why is it called that?
3. Why is prayer necessary for Christian life?
4. What are some effects of prayer?
5. How might we define "prayer"?
6. What are the four general types of prayer?
7. For what and for whom should we pray?
8. What qualities should Christian prayer have?
9. To whom do we direct our prayers? Is it right to pray to saints?
10. Why should we pray if we do not feel like praying?

[6]*Apophthegmata Patrum* 12.2.

25

Private and Liturgical Prayer

There are various forms of prayer. Sometimes prayer is individual or private; sometimes it is shared with others; sometimes it is public or liturgical.

In this chapter we discuss each of these various forms of prayer and offer some suggestions on learning to pray.

INDIVIDUAL PRAYER

Prayer is often addressed to God by an individual in private. This form of prayer was commended by the Lord in His Sermon on the Mount: "When you pray, go into your room and shut the door and pray to your Father who is in secret; and your Father who sees in secret will reward you" (Matt. 6.6).

For prayer in private there are no particular rules. Any place is adequate, and any posture is suitable. There are no requirements on length of time, or on the use of vocal or mental prayer. There are no 378 firmly fixed hours of the day, though Christian custom strongly favors morning and evening prayers and prayers at meals, and the Christian has a duty to pray in times of danger and temptation. But the individual has complete freedom in judging the way he will pray, in being completely himself while speaking with God.

Vocal Prayer

A vocal prayer is one expressed in words, or occasionally in gestures. It may be in a fixed formula or in one's own words; it may be said aloud or silently. In any case, the words should express the thoughts of the one praying.

Vocal prayer may be a personal, spontaneous cry that springs from the heart of a person in joy or in danger. But vocal prayer is usually the recitation of a fixed formula — such as the Our Father, the Hail Mary, the Glory Be; or a Psalm or hymn; or a repetitive prayer such as a litany, the Angelus, or the rosary.[1]

That Christ made use of prayer formulas is clear from the Gospels. The Lord quoted the great prayers of the Old Testament. When asked by the disciples for instruction in prayer, Jesus gave them the Our Father as a model and as the greatest vocal prayer of Christianity (cf. Matt. 6.9-13; Luke 11.2-4).

Guided by the example and teaching of Jesus and the strong tradition of the Church, the Catholic should know and say memorized prayers. "So it is important that some of the Church's great prayers be 375 understood, memorized and said frequently. Among those are the Sign of the Cross, the Our Father, the Hail Mary, the Apostles Creed, an Act of Contrition, and the Rosary."[2]

The validity and usefulness of vocal prayer for every state of the spiritual life have been formally taught by the Catholic Church.[3]

Brief vocal prayers, according to long tradition, can be an effective way of praying. For some, this use of prayerful ejaculations has been a considerable help in learning prayer and drawing close to God. The early monks of the desert, for example, commended the practice of repeating often in the day the first verse of Psalm 70: "God, come and save me; Lord, hasten to help me." St. Francis of Assisi regularly made similar use of "My Lord and my God!"

Spontaneous Prayer

Spontaneous prayer is a type of vocal prayer which comes to one's lips because of a situation in which one finds oneself. This is the prayer that gushes forth from one at certain moments in life. Generally speaking, spontaneous prayer is possible in two kinds of situations. The first is when we become vividly aware and appreciative of God, and this awareness evokes a response of joy and worship. The other is when we are in serious difficulty. These are the times when we cry out to God in fear and anguish, from the depths of discouragement and loneliness. We

---

[1]On the Angelus and the rosary, cf., e.g., Pope Paul VI, Apostolic Exhortation, *Marialis Cultus* (February 2, 1974) nn. 40-55.
[2]United States National Conference of Catholic Bishops, *Basic Teachings for Catholic Religious Education* (January 11, 1973) Introduction.
[3]Cf., e.g., Decree of the Holy Office (August 28, 1687) and Pope Innocent XI, Constitution, *Caelistis Pastor* (November 20, 1687) (DS 2221, 2269).

sense there is no hope for us unless God rescues us: we turn to God and we pray.

We must recognize, however, that it is not sufficient to pray only when one is in danger or experiencing great happiness. We must pray regularly.

254 Most people who begin a life of prayer come sooner or later to times when all spontaneity is gone. They may think that unless they feel strongly or emotionally about the words and phrases they use, they are not sincere. But this is not true. The spiritual writers note that there can be periods of monotony, even aridity, without affecting the value of prayer. The mature Christian, then, continues to work at prayer, following a daily program in spite of any feeling of dryness.

Mental Prayer: Meditation and Contemplation

In general, mental prayer is characterized by the absence of external words or gestures. The intellect and will, however, are truly attentive to God.

Mental prayer may be either formal or informal. It is formal when one devotes a definite period of time to making these internal acts of prayer, and does nothing else at the same time. It is informal when one prays internally while also doing something else — such as cooking, sewing, or driving.

105 The process of mental prayer is a major means of developing spiritual life. The vocation of every Christian is to be a saint. Sanctity means
230 acquiring the mind of God and reaching intimacy with God. Formal mental prayer is the technique of putting off the old man and putting on the new (cf. Col. 3.9-10), of trying to become perfect as our heavenly Father is perfect (cf. Matt. 5.48).

Without earnest prayer one cannot progress far in paths of holiness. There may indeed be many simple followers of Christ who reach a high degree of spiritual perfection through a devout practice of thoughtful vocal prayer and disciplined lives of charity. Therefore, it cannot be said that formal mental prayer is necessary for all who strive for Christian perfection. Formal mental prayer is, however, a suitable means of Christian perfection for most followers of Christ.

Methods and Divisions of Mental Prayer

Many methods of mental prayer have been developed within Catholic tradition. All these methods aim at helping us gather together our human powers and concentrate our attention where it is needed. But all the spiritual guides tell us not to become preoccupied with method.

Since the seventeenth century it has been usual for spiritual writers to describe three stages of formal mental prayer. Though various terms are used, we here call them (1) meditation, (2) affective prayer, and (3) contemplation. There is a normal course of development in the spiritual life. Those who grow in a life of prayer normally advance from the more structured meditation to the more simple and direct contemplation.

Meditation

Meditation is also called "discursive prayer," because it calls for a good deal of thinking and reasoning. Meditation is strongly encouraged for beginners in the spiritual life. It is thoughtful prayer, and it involves communion with God and the saints and it leads to resolutions. During the course of the Christian centuries various methods and techniques for meditation were developed. All of them have the same general purpose of helping the individual become more Christ-like through regular mental prayer.

Structure of Meditation

In every method attention is called to three elements: the preparation, the mental prayer itself, and the conclusion.

The remote preparation for meditation is the whole pattern of one's life. The immediate preparation consists of such things as withdrawing to quiet, reading the selected text of Scripture or other religious book, placing oneself in God's presence, and asking Him to enable one to meditate well.

The body of the meditation consists chiefly in devout reflection on a chosen theme. One seeks in this prayer to give to God one's whole attention: one's memory, imagination, understanding, and all one's affections. The immediate purpose of meditation is to deepen one's faith, spiritual insight, and convictions, so that the mysteries of faith reflected on begin to be appreciated in their overwhelming richness, and so that one's commitment to God and love of Him may acquire deep and lasting roots.

A considerable amount of the time in meditation is given to think- 21 ing about Christ and His saving mysteries and message.

The conclusion of the meditation may include a more familiar discussion with God, the Blessed Mother, or some particular saint. Some firm, practical resolution should be made, so that the activity of prayer may help one direct one's life more earnestly in the way of Christ. Many spiritual guides recommend selecting a key idea from the meditation to keep gently in one's thoughts throughout the day.

Affective Prayer

A more advanced form of mental prayer is called "affective prayer." Here probing reflections play a smaller part. One's mind and heart are already rooted firmly in God, and are turned more easily and immediately to God. One has already learned much of Christ and His mysteries, but longs for a deeper kind of knowing and a closer presence of love.

Scripture often speaks of friendship with God as analogous with the friendship between human persons who love one another. When a man and woman are first attracted deeply to each other, they would like to talk with each other extensively. There are many things to learn, and each wishes to know all that concerns the other. But there comes a time when much speaking is superfluous. Quiet being together, and caring, is now more important. A glance, a gesture, a presence can be eloquence enough. This degree of friendship and love normally needs considerable preparation. So, too, is it with those advancing in friendship with God.

Affective prayer is normally found in those who have already rooted themselves in God by meditation and resolute faithfulness in Christian life. Of course, affective elements are present in all prayer, even that of beginners. But the distinctive simplicity and depth of this kind of affective prayer reveal that one has made considerable progress.

Contemplation

The highest stage of mental prayer is contemplation, which itself has many stages. Contemplation is God's most generous gift in this life to those who have loved Him with great faithfulness. In its highest forms, this prayer draws one as near to God as it is possible to come before one reaches the beatific vision.

When this contemplative prayer is authentic, it is the expression of a whole life given to God with excelling generosity. One comes to such great love through the cross, through dark nights and faithfulness in trials. Yet in contemplation one comes to the overwhelming peace of Christ. This is not a peace free of trials, but a peace born of great love. "For as we share abundantly in Christ's sufferings, so through Christ we share abundantly in comfort too" (2 Cor. 1.5).

Indeed, many religious orders seek above all to help their members to advance toward the service of God and the Church in this heroic way.

The Church speaks of religious orders of contemplatives as a "glory of the Church and an overflowing fountain of heavenly graces" (PC 7). 238 The charter for the contemplative life has often been seen in the words of Christ about one who gave Him the total gift of her mind and heart in preference even to giving Him the service of external labor. "Only one thing is required. Mary has chosen the better portion and she shall not be deprived of it" (Luke 10.41).

Growth in Prayer and Christian Living

In our approaches to mental prayer we may be surprised to realize that we are almost strangers to Christ and to spiritual values. The words of the Gospel and of spiritual writers seem to us distant and strange. The soul must do much work in meditation. But gradually one grows in knowledge and love of the Lord. Christ assists our efforts.

With persistent care the soul purifies itself of other attachments and becomes more free to concentrate on God. In time the soul knows that of itself it is nothing — but this leads only to greater confidence in God. There are slips and failures, but these need not cause discouragement. Prayer then becomes simple and easy; suffering is valued; the Holy Spirit works much. Contrition is deep and sincere; the soul shrinks from anything approaching sin. There is a remarkable tolerance of the faults and weaknesses of others, as if the person, sharing in God's forgiveness, finds it easier to forgive others. The liturgy is loved. The soul has God's viewpoint on all things, lives in a supernatural atmosphere, and is an apt instrument to accomplish God's will.

Growth in prayer essentially requires growth in all of Christian life. The life of prayer, then, is the way to reach that holiness to which every follower of Christ is called (cf. Matt. 5.18).

SHARED PRAYER

Shared prayer has become popular in some Catholic circles in the period since the Second Vatican Council. This is actually private vocal

261

prayer addressed to God but voiced aloud while gathered together with others.

106   In some of its forms shared prayer is encouraged by the charismatic movement. Pope Paul VI has noted some of the strengths such a movement can have. It can encourage "the taste for deep prayer, personal and in groups, a return to contemplation and emphasizing of the praise of God, the desire to give oneself completely to Christ, a great availability for the calls of the Holy Spirit, more assiduous reading of the Scripture, generous brotherly devotion, the will to make a contribution to the service of the Church."[4]

    Care is of course needed to guard these advantages, and to guard
107 against pride and ostentation. Discernment of spirits is necessary, as St. Paul had already noted in writing about early charismatic prayer (cf. 1 Cor. 14.26-33); there is need to maintain great love for the whole family of the Church and its ordinary, indispensable means of grace and forms of liturgical prayer, lest any separatism or elitism impair full unity with the Church.[5] Pastoral concern for such a movement "devolves upon
137 those who are in charge of the Church, 'to whose special competence it belongs, not indeed to extinguish the Spirit, but to test all things and hold fast to that which is good (cf. 1 Thess. 5.12, 19-21).' "[6]

LITURGICAL PRAYER

    Liturgical prayer is the prayer of the whole Church, of the family of God united together in Christ.

    It is important to make a clear distinction between liturgical prayer and private prayer. In private prayer, individuals or groups approach God as their own fervor and their own personalities urge them. In liturgical prayer, the individual participates not as a private individual, but as a member of the Lord's Church. The liturgy is the prayer of the Church community headed by Christ. Often called the "official" prayer of the Church, liturgical prayer is subject to regulations to which private prayer is not.

    The Mass, the other sacraments, the Divine Office, and public ritu-

---

[4]Pope Paul VI, *Address* to participants at a meeting of prayer groups, at Grottaferrata, October 10, 1973.

[5]Cf. Pope Paul VI, *Address* at General Audience, February 28, 1973, and *Address* to the Congress of Catholic Charismatic Renewal, May 19, 1975.

[6]Pope Paul VI, *Address* to participants at a meeting of prayer groups, at Grottaferrata, October 10, 1973. The internal quotation is from LG 12.

al are all part of the Church's liturgy. The Stations of the Cross, the rosary, prayer services, and so on, even when said by a group of people together, are devotions distinct from the liturgical, or public, prayer of the Church.

Private Prayer Ordered toward Liturgical

Because liturgy is the Church's prayer, community worship, it must be both exterior and interior. Liturgical acts of worship are exterior expressions of shared interior attitudes. The chief element in worship 252 must be interior, in order to guarantee the sincerity and genuineness of the exterior words and actions.

Private prayer is ordered toward this official, public prayer of the Church community. It is God's plan that Christians relate to Him not 119 merely as individuals, but as a family united in Christ. It is, then, God's plan that we relate to Him as a praying community, not only as praying individuals. As members of the Mystical Body we join especially in the prayer led by our Redeemer.[7]

Excellence of Liturgical Prayer

The excellence of liturgical prayer comes not only from the devotion of the human persons united in it, but especially from the fact that this is the prayer and action of Christ and of His Mystical Body, the Ch. 26 Church.

"In the liturgy . . . full public worship is performed by the Mystical Body of Jesus Christ, that is, by the Head and His members. From this it follows that every liturgical celebration, because it is the action of Christ the priest and of His Body the Church, is a sacred action surpassing all others. No other action of the Church can match its claim to efficacy, nor equal the degree of it" (SC 7). The liturgy is "the summit toward which the activity of the Church is directed; at the same time it is the fountain from which all her power flows" (SC 10).

The Highest Form: The Eucharistic Sacrifice

The first, highest, and central form of all Christian liturgy is the Eucharistic sacrifice, the Mass. 277

---

[7]Cf. Pope Pius XII, Encyclical, Mediator Dei (November 20, 1947) n. 20 (DS 3841).

The ceremonies of the Mass have their roots in the Old Testament liturgies that foreshadowed it. The ceremonies have developed through the ages. Even today there are somewhat different expressions of the same reality in the various rites of the Church. But the same general outline is adhered to everywhere.

There are two chief parts. In the Latin rite these are called the "Liturgy of the Word" and the "Liturgy of the Eucharist."

The Liturgy of the Word is made up of prayers, songs, and chiefly, readings from Scripture. There are also moments of quiet reflection and a homily to illumine the meaning of God's word.

The Liturgy of the Eucharist has three stages. In the offertory rite, the gifts of bread and wine are brought to the altar and offered to the Lord. In the Eucharistic Prayer, the saving mysteries of the Lord's passion and resurrection are recalled by a sacramental action which makes these mysteries present again in the midst of His people. In the Communion rite, the Body and Blood of Christ are received in a sacred meal, to gather into closest unity with Christ those who have received life through Him.

The Other Sacraments and Liturgical Prayer

Each of the seven sacraments, as instituted by Christ, is part of the liturgy of the Church. Sacraments are acts of worship and the principal actions through which Christ gives His Spirit to Christians and makes Chs. 27-30 them a holy people. In the chapters which follow we present a treatment of the sacraments.

The Divine Office

238 Another liturgical act of the entire Church is the Divine Office, or "Liturgy of the Hours." The word "office" here means duty or obligation. Prayer of praise and thanksgiving is a constant duty of the Church.

The Divine Office "is arranged so that the whole course of the day and night is made holy by the praises of God" (SC 84). It consists of (1) an Hour of Readings, (2) Morning Praises, (3) Mid-day Prayers, (4) Vespers, or Evening Prayers, and (5) a short Night Prayer, or Compline. This Office or Liturgy of the Hours is predominantly scriptural, the Psalms holding a prominent place in it. There is a separate pattern of prayer for each day, following the rhythms of the liturgical year and of the feasts of the saints.

This is the Church's prayer, and some, especially those who are in holy orders or who have made solemn religious vows, are delegated and required to pray it faithfully in the name of the whole Church. But because it belongs to the whole Church, the faithful too are invited to participate in the Divine Office, especially in Morning Praises and Vespers.

Characteristics of Liturgical Prayer

Liturgical prayer requires the following three conditions: (1) it must be prayer in a format or formula which has been approved by those responsible for Church worship; (2) it must be prayer recited in the name of the Church; (3) it must be led or presided over by a person properly assigned.

A cleric who recites the Divine Office by himself is still praying liturgical prayer because he prays it in the name of the entire Church. A priest who celebrates Mass without a congregation is joined liturgically with the entire praying community of Christ.

There are several characteristics of the Church's liturgical worship. It is always based on the priestly, redemptive work of Jesus Christ: 268 Christ is the supreme Celebrant of all liturgical worship. It is associated 272 with the Church hierarchy: those bound to Christ precisely through holy orders preside over the liturgy. It is always communal in nature: it unites the members of the Church and calls for their participation. It is sanctifying: liturgy is the sign and source of the true Christian spirit.

Pope Pius XII stated that the liturgy is the most effective way of reaching sanctity and that private devotions would be sterile if they caused a person to neglect the liturgy. At the same time, however, he strongly insisted that a life of interior dedication and prayer is necessary if the liturgy is to have its proper effect and not become an empty ritualism.[8]

Because liturgy is the worship of Christ and all His Church, respon- 273 sibility for directing this public prayer rests with those to whom Christ has entrusted the care of the Church, to the Holy Father and the bishops. Certain parts of the liturgy are rightly left open to optional forms, to permit appropriate adaptations and allow suitable elements of spontaneity. Certain elements, in reading, prayers, vestments, and sacred ges-

---

[8]Cf. Pope Pius XII, Encyclical, *Mediator Dei* (November 20, 1947) nn. 31, 32, 175.

tures are required, to express the unity in faith and worship of the whole community. It would be unfair for those without authority to do so to modify the prayer of the Mystical Body, for liturgy belongs to the whole Church, not merely to the individual ministers, cantors, or others assigned special roles in it.

LEARNING TO PRAY

Prayer is necessary for us. It is a richly rewarding gift. But faithfulness in prayer also requires patient effort. The adult who wishes to pray should recognize the need for discipline, the need to develop the habit of prayer. One way to begin is to concentrate on morning prayers, evening prayers, and daily meditation.

259   Daily meditation will present the greatest challenge. Those who would grow strong in their Christian life would do well to reserve a period of time, perhaps fifteen to thirty minutes, for mental prayer each day. For some, the devout and thoughtful recitation of vocal prayers may be a useful first step in mental prayer.

Teaching Prayer to Children

219   Parents should of course be mindful that their children should have education in prayer. This is so even for the very young, "so that the little child may learn to call upon the God who loves us and protects us, and upon Jesus, the Son of God and our brother, who leads us to the Father, and upon the Holy Spirit, who dwells within our hearts; and so that this child may also direct confident prayers to Mary, the Mother of Jesus and our mother."[9]

Children should be taught by example the habit of praying — at morning, at night, at meals. They should be instructed in the liturgy of the Mass so that they will know what the Mass is, understand its parts, participate in it well.

The teaching of prayer should take place through experiences of prayer, through the example of prayer, and through the learning of common prayers.

The long-range goal of such instruction is clear: "By instruction in prayer, through all levels of religious education, the learner is gradually

---

[9]Sacred Congregation for the Clergy, General Catechetical Directory (April 11, 1971) n. 78.

led on to a more mature prayer — to meditation, contemplation, and union with God."[10]

*   *   *

Questions related to the material in this chapter:

1. Are there any particular rules about place, time of day, or physical posture for personal private prayer?

2. What is "vocal prayer"? Is it always said aloud?

3. What is spontaneous prayer?

4. Why is it important to pray even when one does not feel like praying? Is it necessary to feel like praying for one's prayers to be sincere?

5. What is mental prayer? What is the difference between formal and informal mental prayer?

6. We speak of three basic forms or stages of formal mental prayer. What are these?

7. Does growth in prayer require growth in all of Christian life?

8. What is "shared prayer"?

9. What does the word "liturgy" mean? How does liturgical prayer differ from private prayer?

10. What is the highest form of all Christian liturgy?

11. Is the Divine Office, the "Liturgy of the Hours," for priests and religious only? What about the laity?

12. What is required for prayer to be liturgical prayer? What are some characteristics of the Church's liturgical worship?

13. Why should young children be taught to pray?

---

[10]United States National Conference of Catholic Bishops, *Basic Teachings for Catholic Religious Education* (January 11, 1973) Introduction.

26

Liturgy: The Paschal Mystery and Sacramental Life

Religion at its core is the quest for God. "One thing have I asked of the LORD, that will I seek after; that I may dwell in the house of the LORD all the days of my life" (Ps. 27.4).

In this chapter we discuss the liturgy and Christ's presence therein, the paschal mystery, the meaning of "sacrament," the seven sacraments instituted by Christ, and the use of sacramentals in the Church.

CHRIST PRESENT IN LITURGY

262   Liturgical prayer is more than community prayer. The Second Vatican Council, in its Constitution on the Sacred Liturgy, showed anew how the realities of prayer and community — and sacramentality — converge in the liturgy. The Council did not speak of only a quest, or of only an encounter, but of a presence, that is, the presence of God in Christ in the liturgy. Indeed, we seek and find God only if He first comes to us. It is we who are absent and must seek the encounter; the obstacles to be removed are in ourselves.

100   "Christ is always present in His Church, especially in her liturgical celebrations. He is present in the sacrifice of the Mass, not only in the person of His minister, 'the same one now offering, through the ministry of priests, who formerly offered Himself on the cross,'[1] but especially under the Eucharistic species. By His power He is present in the sacraments, so that when a man baptizes it is really Christ Himself who baptizes. He is present in His word, since it is He Himself who speaks when the holy Scriptures are read in the Church. He is present, finally, when the Church prays and sings, for He promised: 'Where two or three are gathered together in My name, there am I in the midst of them' (Matt. 18.20)" (SC 7).

All these presences are part of what St. Paul calls the mystery of

---

[1] Council of Trent, Session 22, September 17, 1562, *Doctrine on the Most Holy Sacrifice of the Mass,* ch. 2 (DS 1743).

God, the mystery of Christ, the paschal mystery, or simply the mystery (cf. Col. 2.2, 4.3).

THE PASCHAL MYSTERY

Indeed, the Church locates the center of the whole Christian religion in the paschal mystery. Christ redeemed mankind "principally by 85 the paschal mystery of His blessed passion, resurrection from the dead, and glorious ascension, whereby 'dying, he destroyed our death and, rising, he restored our life' " (SC 5).[2]

Only by realizing that in the liturgy the victory and triumph of Christ's death are made present, can we understand two statements of the Second Vatican Council which might otherwise seem unintelligible: "The liturgy is the summit toward which the activity of the Church is directed; at the same time it is the font from which all her power flows" (SC 10), and, "It is the primary and indispensable source from which the faithful are to draw the true Christian spirit . . ." (SC 14). Such claims are true only because the liturgy continues and makes present the paschal mystery of Christ.

The Unfolding of God's Plan

The paschal mystery is the heart of God's saving plan for us. This 93 plan, of which Christ is the center and summit, unfolds gradually in the history of God's dealings with man and reaches its climax in bringing all things into one in Christ, uniting "all things in Him, things in heaven and things on earth" (Eph. 1.10).

What appeared at the time as a cruel and unjust execution is placed by the Epistle to the Hebrews in its true perspective, in a cosmic liturgical setting. Calvary is seen as a towering mountain, a sanctuary where a new High Priest offers a sacrifice for all the nations of the world. The 89 naked and crucified Servant, now replacing Aaron, appears as the High Priest of mankind according to the order of Melchizedek (cf. Heb. 7; Gen. 14.18). "But when Christ appeared as a high priest of the good things that have come, then through the greater and more perfect tent (not made with hands, that is, not of this creation) He entered once for all into the Holy Place, taking not the blood of goats and calves but His own blood, thus securing an eternal redemption. . . . For Christ has en-

---

[2]The interior quotation is from the Preface for Easter in the Roman Missal.

tered, not into a sanctuary made with hands, a copy of the true one, but into heaven itself, now to appear in the presence of God on our behalf" (Heb. 9.11-12, 24).

284   The Book of Revelation also describes this liturgy as the climax of history. "And between the throne and the four living creatures and among the elders, I saw a Lamb standing, as though it had been slain. . . . 'Worthy is the Lamb who was slain, to receive power and wealth and wisdom and might and honor and glory and blessing!' " (Rev. 5.6, 12). So Jesus crucified, then rising in the glory of the resurrection and ascending into the sanctuary of heaven, offers an acceptable sacrifice in a universal liturgy that joins all men to one another as they are united by Christ to Himself and the Father.

CHRIST IN SACRAMENT

This liturgy, this single sacrifice that redeems all, this most perfect act of worship, is then given to the Church. "Rightly, then, the liturgy is considered as an exercise of the priestly office of Jesus Christ" (SC 7).

91 In this liturgy Jesus Himself is the Source of every sacrament, or every visible sign of salvation. He *is* mankind's encounter with God. He is the Word made flesh (cf. John 1.14). He shows us in His Person, by the humanity He has assumed, what sacrament is: God giving His life to men, God acting redemptively on man through His visible creation. Jesus further extended this principle when He established His Church, the

117 fundamental sacrament, in which men of flesh like Himself, in fact His brethren, are marked by the formative influence of the hidden Spirit. The other sacraments are means whereby Christ reaches out to mankind, and whereby the Church also, joined to Him as His Body, extends His healing and sanctifying action to all His members.

The word "sacrament" comes from the Latin word for the Greek "mysterion," the mystery of God in Christ in which St. Paul sees the vast unfolding plan and action of God among men (cf., e.g., Col. 1.26). In this mystery, Christ poured into the Church, the great sacrament issued from Him, all the riches of grace and truth gained through His death and resurrection.

THE SEVEN SACRAMENTS

118   Through the sacraments the faithful cling to Christ, and draw from Him this grace and life. The Church declares that in the New Law there

are seven sacramental rites instituted by our Lord Jesus Christ.[3] These 173
seven are: Baptism, Confirmation, Holy Eucharist, Penance, the Sacrament of the Anointing of the Sick, Holy Orders, and Matrimony.

Each of these rites has a visible, material element or elements, like bread, wine, water, oil, or visible human actions. These material elements are illumined by sacred words to become signs of faith and instruments of Christ's own saving action on mankind. The visible sign of each sacrament symbolizes the gift of grace conferred by Christ in that sacrament.

These seven sacraments, then, are actions of Christ and of His Church. They are symbols and signs that man is blessed by God and saved by Christ's redeeming mercy. They are signs of faith by which man clings in worship to Christ to share the fruits of His paschal gift; they are instruments by which Christ, through the liturgical acts of His Church, in fact confers the graces symbolized by the sacraments.

The Material Signs

Jesus shows at once His power and His compassion in meeting our human needs and aspirations, and in doing this in a way we can see and understand. He further shows wisdom and understanding in choosing elements that are almost universally recognized by the religious spirit of man as having a character of quasi-sacredness; and this because of their connection with life, whose source is God.

Sacraments are gifts of Christ by which He confers divine life and 172 exercises divine power through expressive signs adapted to the nature of men. In the sacraments Christ reaches out to all men of every place and in every area. In His earthly life Christ shared our finite limitation to one place and one time. Through the sacraments the glorified Christ puts aside these limitations and draws us by visible signs appropriate to our condition to the new world of eternal life, already present but hidden. His sacramental action will continue everywhere until all His promises are fulfilled.

Sacramental Encounter

Our sacramental encounter with God through Jesus Christ is a veiled encounter. Nonetheless, it is also revealing, because the sacra-

---

[3]Cf. Council of Trent, Session 7, March 3, 1547, *Decree on the Sacraments,* canon 1 on the sacraments in general (DS 1601).

mental elements symbolize the character of God's action upon us. Water symbolizes cleansing and life. Bread and wine signify nourishment. Oil means healing and strength. And what they signify, according to Catholic teaching, is what Christ brings about through them. Hence, even though our meeting with God in the liturgy is veiled, it is nonetheless real. Through it we are drawn in all of the sacramental rites into the mystery of the Lord's death and resurrection and ascension.

250   In every sacrament men rise to God in praise, petition, and thanksgiving. At the same time, God comes to men bearing life and other gifts. Each liturgy is, as a prayer of the Christmas season expresses it, a "marvelous exchange."[4]

LITURGICAL CELEBRATION

Because sacraments are symbolic actions with very real effects, care must be taken to administer them validly, that is, in such a way that the full sign is present and its purpose is achieved.

Sacraments have conditions for validity. The sacraments are signs of faith and acts of obedience to Christ, and one may not arbitrarily choose signs other than those He appointed and entrusted to His Church. It is for the Church to state the conditions of validity for sacraments. This the Church does. For example, the Church, faithful to Scripture, insists that baptism can be validly administered only with water, not with other liquids, and that only bread and the fruit of the vine, not other materials, can be validly used in the Eucharist.

If in good faith a minister should fail to administer sacraments validly, God is able to supply in other ways the needs of those who seek Him. Still, a sacrament itself is simply not administered if the conditions established by Christ personally or through His Church are not fulfilled.

Sacraments are sacred actions, and the human minister should celebrate them with great faith and charity. As the Church has always taught, however, the validity of a sacrament does not depend on the 117 worthiness of the minister. It is not from the goodness or power of human ministers that the faithful hope to draw the fruits of salvation, 172 but from Christ Himself, who is always the principal minister of the sacraments.

Certain human dispositions, made possible by grace, are necessary

---

[4]Liturgy of the Hours, Feast of Solemnity of Mary, the Mother of God, the Octave of Christmas (January 1), first antiphon at vespers.

for valid reception of a sacrament. A context of faith and a personal willingness to accept Christ and receive the gift must be present in any adult who wishes to receive a sacrament effectively.

The Church is responsible for reverent care of the sacraments. It makes laws for their licit celebration and for their proper reception, so that the reverence due these gifts and the good of the faithful may be preserved. Thus the Church may insist on reasonable requirements of place and circumstances for these acts of public worship.

Each sacramental liturgy should be fully celebrated as an act of worship. "Pastors of souls must therefore realize that, when the liturgy 265 is celebrated, more is required than the mere observance of the laws governing valid and licit celebration. It is their duty also to insure that the faithful take part knowingly, actively, and fruitfully" (SC 11).

The sacramental rites, then, are not to be handled mechanically, but with faith and with joyful celebration. Past, present, and future come together in the joyful celebration of each rite. Every sacrament recalls the paschal mystery in which Christ won redemption; each symbolizes a grace He now confers; the sacraments point always toward the fullness of eternal life.

SACRAMENTALS

Jesus Himself, as we have already observed, designated the basic 271 material signs around which the sacramental celebrations revolve. The Church reaches further into the material universe and appropriates many other objects, indeed potentially all, into the direct service of God and also as signs in His worship. These the Church calls sacramentals, distinguishing them by name so that they will not be confused with the divinely appointed sacrament-signs. They differ in this, that the spiritual efficacy of sacramentals depends on the faith and devotion of the users, whereas the sacraments are, as it were, arms of the Savior Himself by which He extends His action throughout place and time to give life, to bless, to renew, to heal, and to multiply the bread of life.

Many of the secondary signs — for example, the altar, the font, the sacred vessels — are also drawn directly into worship, supplementing the primary signs, indeed forming with them a constellation of signs for each sacrament whereby the meaning of the sacrament may be revealed, expressed, and shared by the worshipers. It is the task of a full, conscious, and active participation to explore, even to exploit, these signs.

273

IN SUM: THE GRAIN OF WHEAT

A description of the paschal mystery was given by the Lord Himself on the eve of His death and resurrection. "The hour has come for the Son of Man to be glorified. Truly, truly, I say to you, unless a grain of wheat falls into the earth and dies, it remains alone; but if it dies, it bears much fruit" (John 12.23-24). Jesus Himself is the Grain of Wheat who dies in order to "bear much fruit." This fruit, issuing from the paschal mystery, comes to us in the sacramental liturgies.

"He who loves his life loses it, and he who hates his life in this world will keep it for eternal life" (John 12.25). So the paschal mystery becomes a way of life for all the followers of Jesus. "While we live we are always being given up to death for Jesus' sake," says St. Paul, "so that the life of Jesus may be manifested in our mortal flesh" (2 Cor. 4.11). And it is to the sacramental liturgies, especially to the Eucharist, that we bring our own daily dyings and risings to be drawn into the paschal mystery of the Savior. In this way we can also say with the Apostle: "In my flesh I complete what is lacking in Christ's afflictions for the sake of His body, that is, the church" (Col. 1.24).

•   •   •

Questions related to the material in this chapter:

1. What do we mean when we speak of Christ's "presences" in the liturgy? In what ways is He present?

2. What is the central theme of the paschal mystery?

3. What are the seven sacraments instituted by Christ?

4. In what way are the sacraments instruments of Christ and of His Church?

5. What are some of the visible or outward signs used in the sacraments?

6. Does the validity of a sacrament depend on the worthiness of the minister?

7. What are the sacramentals?

8. We say that the spiritual efficacy of sacramentals depends on the faith and devotion of the users. How do sacraments differ from sacramentals in this regard?

27

The Eucharist — Center of Life

The Eucharist is at the heart of the Church's life. Rich in symbolism and richer in reality, the Eucharist bears within itself the whole reality of Christ, and mediates to us His saving work.

This chapter has two major parts. The first treats of the Eucharist and its central role in Christian life, of how it is the sacrifice of the new covenant and our saving Food, of its rich effects, and of Christ's real presence in the sacrament. The second major part treats of holy orders, the sacrament in which men are consecrated to serve the Eucharistic ministry.

The Eucharist

CENTER OF CHRISTIAN LIFE

The center of all Christian life is Christ Himself. By His incarnation 22 and His work of redemption we are healed, and called to share a new 169 life, a life that binds men together as children of God and sharers in the life of the Trinity.

It is for this very reason that the Eucharist is the center and crown of Christian life. For in the Eucharist Christ gives Himself to us, and we lay hold of Him.

The graced relationship begun in baptism and strengthened in confirmation is ordered to union with the Eucharistic Christ and a sharing in His saving sacrifice in the Mass. The Eucharist is the "medicine of immortality"[1] which complements the healing effects of penance and the anointing of the sick. Holy orders confers a priesthood devoted to the altar of the Eucharist. Marriage symbolizes the union of Christ and Church which is the fruit of the Eucharist.

---

[1]St. Ignatius of Antioch, *Epistula ad Ephesios* 20.2 (MG 5.661).

NEW SACRIFICE OF THE NEW COVENANT

Because the Eucharist is the most sacred presence of Christ and His
269 paschal mysteries in the Church, it is both the "source and summit" (PO
5) of all the Church's ministries and apostolates. It threads a beauty,
meaning, and purpose through all the varied activities involved in loving God, ourselves, and our fellow human beings. It offers a contact
with the transcendent on which man can orient himself in the cosmic
and timeless dimensions of his existence. In celebrating the Eucharist
with and in Christ, men are not only offered a share in His life, they are
"invited and led to offer themselves, their labors, and all created things
together with Him" (PO 4).

56-57   *Foreshadowed in Old Testament*

In the ages before Christ's incarnation, God enabled men to seek
Him and to find mercy. From the first pages of Genesis onward, we see
that the initiative to "share" was clearly and consistently God's. Again
and again God called men to sacred worship in which they might share
His presence and His mercy.

With both Noah (cf. Gen. 8.20, 9.9) and Abraham (cf. Gen. 15.9, 18)
covenants were made in the context of a food-sacrifice. Later, when
their descendants refused to respect these covenants, God did not abandon them. Rather He entered into the greatest of the Old Testament alli-
ances in the complexus of events known as the Exodus. Again, the covenant was associated with a sacred meal.

Historically, the great Exodus covenant was completed only with
the giving of the Law on Mount Sinai. Here the people received their
obligations under the covenants, and Moses sealed the agreement by
sprinkling an altar of sacrifice with calves' blood. Half the blood he
sprinkled on the people with these words: "Behold the blood of the covenant which the LORD has made with you in accordance with all these
words" (Exod. 24.8).

The whole series of saving events was ritually preserved in the annual repetition of the Passover meal in what was called a "memorial
feast." As generation after generation shared the paschal lamb and the
unleavened bread, fathers told their children of the wonders Yahweh
had worked on behalf of His chosen people. In this "memorial feast"
they understood and celebrated far more than a community festival. In
this meal the people of God knew they were with their Lord, and they
renewed the covenant He had made with them.

276

At the Last Supper the Lord instituted a new memorial sacrifice. 87 The true "Lamb of God" (John 1.29) was about to be slain. By His cross and resurrection He was to free not just one nation from bondage, but all mankind from the more bitter slavery of sin. He was about to create a new people of God by the rich gift of His Spirit. There was to be a new law of love, a new nearness to God, a new promised land. All was to be new, when God fulfilled the promises of the centuries in the paschal mysteries. It was right, then, that there should also be a new memorial sacrifice, in which through all the ages till the final fulfillment men might be united to the saving deeds of this hour.

Jesus first carried out the rubrics of the Passover ritual. But in this holy night He spoke of the new gifts to come, of which the treasures of the past were only shadows and images. He promulgated the new law of the new covenant (cf. John 15.12). He spoke of the saving work He was about to do for them out of loving obedience to the Father (cf. John 14.31) and out of love for us (cf. John 15.13). Then He made that redemptive sacrifice present in the institution of the Eucharist, in the memorial rite He would command them to perform always in His memory.

During the supper, at one of the ceremonial eatings of the unleavened bread, Jesus "took bread, and blessed, and broke it, and gave it to the disciples and said, 'Take, eat; this is My body' " (Matt. 26.26). Picking up a ceremonial cup of wine, He gave thanks and passed it to His disciples, saying: "This cup which is poured out for you is the new covenant in My blood" (Luke 22.20). Finally, He commanded them: "Do this 287 in remembrance of Me" (1 Cor. 11.24).

Like the Passover meal, this memorial sacrifice of the new law is both sacrifice and sacred meal. "Both sacrifice and sacrament pertain inseparably to the same mystery. In an unbloody re-presentation of the sacrifice of the cross and in application of its saving power, the Lord is 87 immolated in the sacrifice of the Mass when, through the words of consecration, He begins to be present in a sacramental form under the ap- 284 pearances of bread and wine to become the spiritual food of the faithful."[2]

As with many of the sacrifices of the ancient world, Christ's covenantal sacrifice was completed by the shedding of blood. Jesus died

---

[2]Pope Paul VI, Encyclical, *Mysterium Fidei* (September 3, 1965) n. 34.

only once and shed His blood only once, but, because of the command for a memorial, that Blood is made available for all time.

THE EUCHARIST AND THE CHURCH

In describing the life of the early Church, Christian writers of that time gave special attention to the Eucharist. For the Eucharist was the community's essential celebration; it signified, and kept most real, the presence of Christ in the community. In the Acts of the Apostles, St. Luke says of the converts at Jerusalem that they "devoted themselves to the apostles' teaching and fellowship, to the breaking of bread and the prayers" (Acts 2.42).

275

The phrase "breaking of bread" appears also elsewhere in the New Testament (cf. Acts 2.46; 20.7, 11; 27.35; 1 Cor. 10.16) and in the oldest nonscriptural liturgical instructions we know of.[3] In describing the Church's activity in such terms, the writers were already witnessing to the essentially ecclesial nature of the Eucharist.

The liturgical form of Eucharistic worship developed in many places at the same time. There naturally arose a variety of forms, which reflected the cultures of the various faith communities as well as the different theological insights and devotional preferences of their people.

In the western half of the Roman empire this variety eventually merged into a basic unity in the Latin rite. In the East a variety of regional heritages was preserved. The two approaches resulted in a liturgical richness which the universal Church guards and treasures (cf. OE 1-6).

Unity of Faith

With all the variety of ceremony in the Church there is the wonderful uniformity of belief in the single reality which is celebrated. Together, the crucifixion and resurrection of Jesus are responsible for our redemption: "Jesus our Lord . . . was put to death for our trespasses and raised for our justification" (Rom. 4.24-25). Unlike the repetitious sacrifices of the Old Law, the single sacrifice of Jesus' obedient death was completely sufficient in itself. As the Epistle to the Hebrews stresses, He did not have to "offer Himself repeatedly, as the high priest enters the Holy Place yearly with blood not his own; for then He would

---

[3]Cf. *Didache* 14.1.

have had to suffer repeatedly since the foundation of the world. But as it is, He has appeared once for all at the end of the age to put away sin by the sacrifice of Himself" (Heb. 9.25-26).

The One Sacrifice

Jesus does not die and rise again every time the Eucharistic liturgy is enacted, but His one sacrifice is made present to men in every cele- 269 bration of Mass.

At Mass, as upon the cross, Jesus is the chief Priest and also the Victim, giving unending and infinite praise and satisfaction to the Fa- 89 ther. But in the Mass His Church joins Him in the sacrifice. With Him the Church also performs the role of priest and victim, making a total offering of itself together with Him.[4]

Christ commanded His apostles to celebrate this sacrifice. This is a sacred task: to act in the person of Christ, to be His minister, to speak 288 words that make present the living Christ and renew the paschal mysteries. This can be done only at the will of Christ, by those whom He has empowered so to act as His ministers by calling them and sealing them in the sacrament of holy orders.

Mass Offered for All

Priests are called to offer the Eucharistic sacrifice to the Father, with Christ, in the Holy Spirit, for the living and the dead, for the salvation of all, for the many needs of the people of God. Because the Eucharistic sacrifice is the supreme act of worship, it can be offered only to God.

A Mass may be offered on the occasion of a saint's feast, and give incidental honor to the saint. But the sacrifice of Christ is offered only to 252 God, for He alone is worthy of this perfect adoration and praise. Masses may be offered for the needs of an individual person, living or deceased, but no Mass can be offered exclusively for such a limited intention. Every Mass is offered chiefly by Christ, and His ministerial priest must share His universal saving purposes. The Mass is offered to glorify God, to bring salvation to all, to make present and accessible the limitless riches of Christ.

Often the faithful ask that a Mass be said for a special intention of theirs. Ordinarily they give a financial offering when they make such a

---

[4]Cf. Sacred Congregation of Rites, Instruction, *Eucharisticum Mysterium* (May 25, 1967) n. 3.

request. When a Mass offering or stipend is given that a Mass be said for a special intention, it is in truth only a plea that part of the fruits of the Mass might come to one who is loved in Christ. A Mass offering or stipend is to be understood as an expression of a desire on the part of those who give it to participate more intimately in the Eucharistic sacrifice by adding "to it a form of sacrifice of their own by which they contribute in a particular way to the needs of the Church and especially to the sustenance of its ministers."[5]

Holy Communion

It is the privileged responsibility of the celebrant of each Mass to distribute the Sacrament to himself and the people. He may be assisted by other ordained ministers (bishops, priests, deacons) if they are available, or, when necessary, by auxiliary ministers (acolytes or specially appointed lay persons).

The Eucharist as received sacramentally is called "Holy Communion." The name is appropriate, since, as the word "communion" indicates, it is the sharing of a gift God gives to all; it is a coming into close union with Christ, and with one's brothers and sisters in Him.

277   Because of its intimate connection with the sacrificial aspect of the Mass, Holy Communion is most fittingly received by those who are present. Ordinarily, Holy Communion is to be received only once a day. On certain occasions and in certain exceptional circumstances, however, the faithful are permitted to receive Holy Communion a second time on the same day.[6] Catholics of the Latin rite have normally received the Eucharist only under the form of bread, though there are many occasions and circumstances in which they may receive under the forms of both bread and wine. Whether one receives under one species or both, one receives the whole Christ in Holy Communion.[7] This is true since, in the Sacrament, it is the living, risen Christ who is present whole and entire under the appearance of bread, and also under the appearance of wine.

---

[5]Pope Paul VI, Apostolic Letter on Mass stipends (June 13, 1974).
[6]Cf. Sacred Congregation for the Discipline of the Sacraments, Instruction, *Immensae Caritatis* (January 29, 1973).
[7]Cf. Council of Constance, Session 13, June 15, 1415, *Decree on Communion under the Species of Bread Only* (DS 1198-1200); Council of Trent, Session 21, July 16, 1562, *Doctrine on Communion under Both Species and Communion of Children,* ch. 1 and canons 1-3 (DS 1726-1727, 1731-1733).

Participation

The ministerial priest, acting in the person of Christ, brings about the Eucharistic sacrifice and offers it to God in name of all the people. The faithful, too, by virtue of their "royal priesthood" (cf. 1 Peter 2.9), join in the offering (cf. LG 10). They do this not only by the reception of Holy Communion, but by fully exercising their status as members of the Mystical Body, offering the victim and themselves not only through the hands of the priest but also with him.[8]

"The celebration of Mass is the action of Christ and the people of God hierarchically assembled. . . . It is of the greatest importance that the celebration of the Mass, the Lord's Supper, be so arranged that the ministers and the faithful may take their own proper part in it and thus 272 gain its fruits more fully. For this Christ the Lord instituted the eucharistic sacrifice of his body and blood and entrusted it to his bride, the Church, as a memorial of his passion and resurrection. The purpose will be accomplished if the celebration takes into account the nature and circumstances of each assembly and is planned to bring about conscious, active, and full participation of the people, motivated by faith, hope, and charity. Such participation of mind and body is desired by the Church, is demanded by the nature of the celebration, and is the right and duty of Christians by reason of their baptism."[9] 306

NECESSITY OF COMMUNION

Jesus Himself stressed our need to receive Communion. "Unless you eat the flesh of the Son of man and drink His blood, you have no life in you" (John 6.53).

The divine precept does not state how often one must receive Communion. The Church commands the faithful to receive Communion at least once a year, between the beginning of Lent and the end of the Easter season each year.[10] The Church speaks also of the duty to receive Communion when one is in the danger of death.[11] The faithful are in fact encouraged to participate in the Mass and to receive Communion frequently, even daily (cf. LG 42).[12]

---

[8]Cf. Roman Missal, General Instruction, n. 62.
[9]Roman Missal, General Instruction, nn. 1-3.
[10]Cf. *Code of Canon Law,* canon 396.
[11]Cf. *Code of Canon Law,* canon 864.
[12]Cf. *Code of Canon Law,* canon 863.

To receive this sacrament worthily, one must be a baptized Catholic in the state of grace and believe what the Church teaches about the sacrament. One conscious of having committed a mortal sin must make 348 a sacramental confession before approaching the Eucharist.[13] If one who has sinned gravely has a pressing need to receive the Eucharist and has no opportunity to confess, he should first make an act of perfect contrition;[14] and subsequently, when it becomes possible, he should make a sacramental confession.

242   It is not merely Church law that demands that one who approaches this sacrament be in the state of grace. The New Testament reminds us of the grave duty we have to receive worthily (cf. 1 Cor. 11.27-29).

As an outward and communal sign of this respectful awareness of who it is we receive in the Eucharist, and as a penitential preparation, the Church directs us to abstain from food and drink except water one hour before receiving Holy Communion. For the sick and elderly, a fast of a quarter of an hour is sufficient. For those near death, there is no requirement to fast. Drinking water and taking medicine do not break the Eucharistic fast.

Baptism also readies a person to communicate by conferring membership in the Church. Since the entire Eucharistic service is the most characteristic and important activity of the Church, it is an expression of a common belief, not only in the presence of Christ in the Eucharist, but in all that the Church is and teaches in the name of Christ. Fully participating in the sacrificial banquet is itself an act of faith; through it Christians confirm and strengthen the belief that unites them to God and to one another.

162   It is because of this signification that non-Catholics may receive Communion in the Catholic Church only under exceptional circumstances. The local Catholic bishop is to pass judgment in each such case.

SYMBOL AND REALITIES

270   Sacraments are outward signs instituted by Christ that symbolize what they effect and effect what they symbolize. This is true in a special

---

[13]Cf. Council of Trent, Session 13, October 11, 1551, *Decree on the Most Holy Eucharist,* ch. 7 (DS 1647).
[14]Cf. *Code of Canon Law,* canon 856.

way of the Eucharist when the faithful receive the sacrament at the Table of the Lord.

Eucharist as Food

The most obvious sign of this sacrament is the image of nourishment. The elements used in the Passover meal were staples of the Palestinian diet in Biblical times. Bread was available to everyone, the most common of foods. Wine was served as the normal table beverage even in the homes of the poor.

The Eucharist brings about the nourishing effect it symbolizes. This is achieved through the presence of Jesus Himself and the bestowal of 286 grace on those who receive Him according to their individual needs and the needs of the community. Insofar as we have been wounded by sin, Christ and His power work in a remedial way; to the extent that we are making progress in holiness, He strengthens and fosters our growth.

Symbol of Unity

The Eucharist symbolizes also the unity of the Church. Christ prayed for that unity at the first Eucharistic sacrifice (cf. John 17.20-21). The bread and wine He used were themselves symbols of unity; the family of God is to be gathered into one, as many grains of wheat are brought together to make bread and many grapes are brought together to make wine.

Unity is also symbolized by community sharing in the one Bread which is Christ. "Because there is one bread, we who are many are one body, for we all partake of the one bread" (1 Cor. 10.17).

By the sacrament of the Eucharist "the unity of the Church is both 122 signified and brought about" (UR 2). The unity of the Church, the Mystical Body of Christ, is effected chiefly by love. "The liturgy inspires the faithful to become 'one in peace and love'[15] when they have tasted to their full of the paschal mysteries; it prays that we may 'put into action in our lives the baptism we have received with faith.'[16] The renewal in the Eucharist of the covenant between the Lord and man draws the faithful into the compelling love of Christ and sets them afire" (SC 10).

The union that worthy reception of Communion strengthens is first

[15]Roman Missal, Prayer after Communion in the Easter Vigil Mass.
[16]Roman Missal, Opening Prayer for Monday within the Octave of Easter.

of all personal union with Christ. But through union with Him we are bound together with one another, and thus made able to bear fruit for one another in works of love.

Eucharist and Eternal Life

A third symbolism is that of our heavenly inheritance.

270 The entire Eucharistic service should symbolize the kingdom of God in its final fulfillment. Then the community of the faithful, gathered around the throne of the Father with their loved ones, will join with overwhelming gladness in Christ's perpetual praise and receive, as Abraham was once promised (cf. Gen. 15.1), God Himself as their everlasting reward.

In the earthly celebration there is an anticipatory experience of all these elements. Its peace, beauty, and order, though always imperfect in this life, are still a foreshadowing of the conditions of heaven.

351 Participation at Mass not only unites us with the living Church on earth but also with those who have gone before us marked with the indelible character of faith.

Most wonderfully of all, we experience a foretaste of the greatest reward, the presence of God within us. In the Eucharist we see Him, albeit indistinctly with our weak faith, as in the dark metal mirrors of antiquity; yet it is the same Lord now whom we shall see in heaven "face to face" (1 Cor. 13.12).

REAL PRESENCE

The faith of the Church about the presence of Jesus in the Eucharist under the appearances of bread and wine goes back to the preaching of Jesus Himself recorded in the Gospel of St. John. In the Eucharistic discourse after the multiplication of the loaves (cf. John 6.22-71), our Lord contrasted ordinary bread with a Bread that is not of this world but which contains eternal life for those who eat it.

"I am the bread of life. . . . I am the living bread which came down from heaven; if any one eats of this bread, he will live for ever; and the bread which I shall give for the life of the world is My flesh" (John 6.48, 51).

The immediate reaction of the crowd to this claim was a mixed one. Some found this promise too much to believe. Others, including the Twelve, did accept it. Even though such a notion was for them as much as it was for those who rejected it something beyond their personal experience, they gave their assent to His words because they recognized Jesus to be the Holy One of God and they trusted in His assurance more than in their own senses (cf. John 6.69).

On one point, however, the two groups were in clear agreement. All of the hearers understood that Jesus was making a statement that was to be taken quite literally. Nor did He wish it to be understood in any other way. As Christian commentators have noted repeatedly, when the unbelievers walked away Jesus did not retract the promise or try to change their understanding of His words. He did not call them back to say He had been speaking poetically or metaphorically.

Presence in Fullest Sense

The presence of Jesus in the Eucharist is not the only form of His presence within the Church, but the wonder of His Eucharistic presence is unique. Certainly He is also with the Church in a special way as the 268 Church believes, prays, and does works of mercy, and in its faith; He is with the bishops and priests of the Church when they preach God's word, govern His people, and administer His other sacraments. But the sacramental presence of Jesus which is brought about in the Mass has special claim to the description "real presence" — not because the other types of presence are not "real," but because it is "presence in its fullest sense."[17] The other six sacraments are rites in which the faithful encounter Christ in His action and power. Only the Eucharist, however, *is* Jesus Christ.

It is a supernatural mystery that the Person who becomes fully present at Mass is the same risen Savior who is seated at the right hand of the Father. He does not have to leave heaven to become present on earth.

The same is true when many Masses are celebrated simultaneously. What changes is not Jesus, but the number of places in which He is present. When the Eucharistic liturgy is celebrated throughout the world, as it is daily "from the rising of the sun to its setting" (Mal. 1.11), Jesus is not multiplied; nor is He diminished when His sacred Body and Blood are consumed in Holy Communion.

Meaning of Eucharistic Presence

The Eucharistic presence of Jesus is so rich in meaning that it can be spoken of in many ways. When the words of consecration are spoken

[17]Pope Paul VI, Encyclical, *Mysterium Fidei* (September 3, 1965) n. 39.

285

over the bread and wine, there is a great change in meaning or significance, a "transsignification." That which had meant to us only earthly food and drink now means far more, and speaks to us of the presence of Jesus. There is also a change in the purpose of what we see, a "transfinalization." The purpose of earthly bread is to minister to natural bodily life; when the words of Jesus have touched this visible gift in the Eucharist, its whole thrust and dynamism are different. It has become a Food that nourishes the life of God in us and strengthens us for eternal life.

But deeper than all these changes, underlying them and their foundation, is the change in being, the "transsubstantiation." The appearance of bread and wine "take on this new signification, this new finality, precisely because they contain a new reality."[18] Faith is concerned deeply with this reality: Jesus *is* here. He is present not merely spiritually, by His knowledge, His care, His activity, but He is present "in a unique way, whole and entire, God and man, substantially and permanently."[19]

When His priest says His sacred words over the gifts, the bread and wine "have ceased to exist," and it is "the adorable Body and Blood of the Lord Jesus that from then on are really before us under the sacramental species of bread and wine."[20]

The change that occurs when Christ becomes sacramentally present in the Eucharist is enduring because it is so radical, so real a change. After the consecration Jesus remains bodily present as long as the appearances of bread and wine remain.

ADORATION OF THE BLESSED SACRAMENT

Faith in the enduring presence of Christ in the Blessed Sacrament prompted the gradual development of devotions to Christ in the Eucharist even apart from Mass.

In the earliest centuries of the Church the chief reason for preserving the Sacred Species was to assist those unable to attend the liturgy, especially the sick and the dying.

With the passage of time, reverent reflection led the Church to

329
137

---

[18]Pope Paul VI, Encyclical, *Mysterium Fidei* (September 3, 1965) n. 46.
[19]Sacred Congregation of Rites, Instruction, *Eucharisticum Mysterium* (May 25, 1967) n. 9.
[20]Pope Paul VI, *Professio Fidei* ("The Credo of the People of God," June 30, 1968).

enrich its Eucharistic devotion. Faith that Jesus is truly present in the sacrament led believers to worship Christ dwelling with us permanently in the sacrament. Wherever the sacrament is, there is the Christ who is our Lord and our God; hence He is ever to be worshiped in this mystery.[21] Such worship is expressed in many ways: in genuflections, in adoration of the Eucharist, in the many forms of Eucharistic devotion that faith has nourished.

The Blessed Sacrament is at times removed from the tabernacle in which it is ordinarily kept, and placed upon the altar for adoration. Usually the Host is placed in a monstrance. These periods of exposition are sometimes extended into Holy Hours. Catholic parishes often celebrate Eucharistic Days, or the Forty Hours Devotion, in which the Sacrament is exposed upon the altar continuously for a full day or longer, to intensify the Eucharistic life of the parish. When such exposition is terminated, the priest raises the Sacred Host before the people in blessing. From this closing act has come the name "Benediction of the Blessed Sacrament."

In some dioceses and certain religious communities perpetual adoration is maintained before the continuously exposed Host. But every Catholic Church is a place in which the faithful are invited to worship the present Christ. Visits to the Lord in the tabernacle are still another form of devotion to the Real Presence that the Church warmly commends.

Holy Orders

ORIGIN OF PRIESTLY OFFICE

On the same first Holy Thursday on which He instituted the sacrament of the Eucharist, Christ conferred priesthood on the apostles: "Do this in remembrance of Me."

In instituting the sacrament of the Eucharist He created what would be a living re-presentation of His own death and resurrection. At the same time He charged some to see that this sacred mystery would be performed thenceforth in His memory. Thus the origin of holy orders

147

---

[21]Cf. Pope Paul VI, Encyclical, *Mysterium Fidei* (September 3, 1965) nn. 56-62.

lies in the will of Christ and His explicit acts on that first Holy Thursday.

315   On the first Easter, the risen Christ breathed on His new priests and gave them the power to forgive sins: "Receive the Holy Spirit. If you forgive the sins of any, they are forgiven; if you retain the sins of any, they are retained" (John 20.22-23).

The new priesthood established by Christ was a "visible and external priesthood," and "Sacred Scripture shows, and the tradition of the Catholic Church has always taught, that this was instituted by the same Lord our Savior, and that the power of consecrating, offering, and administering His Body and Blood, as also the power of forgiving and retaining sins, was given to the apostles and their successors in the priesthood."[22]

IDENTIFICATION WITH CHRIST

Central to an understanding of how Christ's work is transmitted to His Church is the notion of participation in the person and actions of Christ. Such participation touches the very life of Christ as shared through grace. By ordination a believer is chosen from among the faithful to share more fully in Christ's priestly mission.

When a person is ordained a priest, he becomes a sign of God's presence and power in the world. His consecration represents Christ's total self-emptying, and also prefigures the day when Christ's kingdom will be fully realized. Since the priest is intimately identified with Christ, his priesthood is in some way a permanent part of his being.

The priest's union with Christ is expressed by exercising the unique power which permits him to perpetuate Christ's work (cf. LG 10). This work is the essential work of the apostles: proclaiming the Gospel, gathering together and leading the community, remitting sin and anointing the sick, celebrating the Eucharist, exercising Christ's 133 work of redeeming mankind, and glorifying God. In brief, those ordained to the priesthood are "sharers in the functions of sanctifying, teaching, and governing."[23]

---

[22]Council of Trent, Session 23, July 15, 1563, *Doctrine on the Sacrament of Order*, ch. 1 (DS 1764).
[23]Second General Assembly of the Synod of Bishops, *The Ministerial Priesthood* (1971) Part One, n. 4.

The source of all priestly existence and activity is Christ. Through the priest Christ makes His own priestly life and work present here and now.

The priest is differentiated from all other members of the Church precisely by the way in which he is identified with Christ's unique work. The Church notes how certain powers identified with carrying on the work of Christ were handed on to others. St. Paul clearly was conscious of his acting by Christ's mission and mandate (cf. 2 Cor. 5.18-20, 6.4). In the New Testament we see this mandate being passed on, with the obligation that it be handed on further (cf. 2 Tim. 1.6; Titus 1.5). In one case there is a solemn warning: "Do not be hasty in the laying on of hands" (1 Tim. 5.22). The two Epistles to Timothy and the Epistle to Titus express the sacramental aspects of the laying on of hands, and they point up the fact that ordination is not just a call to community service, but a consecration.

Permanence of Priesthood

The priestly consecration is such that it cannot be lost. Once ordained a priest, a man remains a priest forever. The sacrament of holy orders touches the very being of the recipient: he belongs to Christ in an 308 enduring way. "This special participation in Christ's priesthood does not disappear even if a priest for ecclesial or personal reasons is dispensed or removed from the exercise of his ministry."[24]

To accept ordination is to make a permanent commitment. But at times the Church does permit priests to cease exercising their ministry. For serious reasons the Church may dispense them from the special priestly obligations, as that of celibacy and that of praying daily the Liturgy of the Hours. To some people it may seem strange that the Church can permit a priest to leave his priestly commitment and enter marriage, while it does not permit a person in an unhappy marriage to leave that commitment and marry again. But the cases are different. The Church 335 may dispense from its own law of priestly celibacy; it does not have the power to dispense from Christ's prohibition of divorce and remarriage. There is some likeness in the cases, however; and all in the Church

---

[24]Second General Assembly of the Synod of Bishops, *The Ministerial Priesthood* (1971) Part One, n. 5.

should pray that in every vocation, even in these times of widespread rootlessness, a spirit of faithfulness may grow.

Sacramental Ministry

A priest is preeminently a means of sacramental contact with Christ. The Christian meets God in the sacraments. And it is through the priest that Christ maintains His sacramental presence.

The priest is called to act in the very person of Christ. In the sacrament of penance he says: "I absolve you. . . ." And in the Eucharistic sacrifice: "This is My Body. . . . This is My Blood. . . ." In anointing the sick, the priest continues in a special manner Christ's healing mission. By administering the sacraments the priest builds up community of faith. By bringing human life into contact with divine life, he continues and extends Christ's work of establishing God's kingdom among men.

PRIESTHOOD OF CHRIST SHARED IN DIFFERENT WAYS

330   All members of the Church share one faith and one mission. But the nature of a member's participation in the mission depends on the member's sacramental life and calling. By baptism every Christian is joined 305 to Christ and made a sharer in His divine life and mission. The sacrament of orders, however, makes one participate in Christ's mission in a unique way; it makes the recipient an authentic, authoritative, and 89 special representative of Christ. For Christ at the Last Supper instituted the ministerial priesthood as a distinct sacrament, and the priesthood of the ordained is diffferent and distinct from the common priesthood of the faithful.

Ministries within the Church

All mission with the Church is rooted in Christ's original sending of the apostles to teach His way to all men (cf. Matt. 28.19; Mark 3.14). 164 All Christians share this task.

The Holy Spirit uses all ministries to build up the Church as a reconciling community for the glory of God and the salvation of men (cf. Eph. 4.11-13). In the New Testament ministerial actions are varied and functions and titles are not all precisely defined. Explicit emphasis is given, however, to the proclamation of God's word, the safeguarding of doctrine, the care of the flock, and the witness of Christian living. By the time of the Epistles to Timothy and to Titus and the First Epistle of St. Peter, some ministerial functions are more clearly discernible. This suggests that as the Church matured the importance of certain functions caused them to be located in specific officials of the community. Here we can already see elements which remain at the heart of what we today call "ordination." The laying on of hands by a bishop seals a man as a priest. This ceremony in its essence is found in the pages of Scripture.

New Testament and Now

In the Church today the sacrament of orders has three hierarchical grades, or orders: bishops, priests, deacons. Such offices were distinct in the infant Church, as we learn from the writings of the earliest Fathers of the Church.[25] In the New Testament itself there is frequent mention of bishops ("overseers"), priests ("elders"), and deacons (cf., e.g., Phil. 1.1; Titus 1.5-7). However, the Greek words for bishop and priest seem at times to have been used interchangeably. It is not altogether clear from the books of the New Testament that in ordaining their first associates to the ministerial priesthood the apostles distinguished the office of priest from that of bishop. It is possible that the distinction of orders appeared as the Church developed and it became useful to have not only ministers enjoying the fullness of the sacramental priesthood, that is, bishops, but also assistants to them, ministers having a real but more limited participation in the same priesthood. But the three orders of bishop, priest, and deacon did emerge in the early Church and have continued in it ever since.

As the Church developed, men continued to do divine things, things that men may not do except with the authorization of God. The Church taught that Christ had called men to do these things, because He had chosen apostles and sent them upon a mission that was to endure until He comes again. Those the apostles chose to carry on their work 125 were confirmed in office by Christ and the Holy Spirit.

Thus it is an essential part of the faith of the Church that there is a continuity in mission. As Christ sent the apostles, so the apostles in His name chose associates and successors, and they in turn laid hands on 12b others in Christ's name. By the guidance of the Spirit of Christ the hier-

---

[25]Cf., e.g., St. Ignatius of Antioch, *Epistula ad Magnesios* 6.1 (MG 5.668) and *Epistula ad Trallianos* 3.1 (MG 5.677).

archical priesthood emerged in the Church, and it continues at His will (cf. LG 18-22).

Orders are found in their fullness in bishops, in a secondary manner in priests, and finally in the diaconate.

Bishops and Apostolic Succession

124   Bishops are successors of the apostles. By the will of Christ they carry on a task first done by the apostles, and they are needed always in the Church. Apostolic succession, then, is a reality found in bishops, who trace their mission back to the apostles, and to Christ.

Bishops are to the Church today what the apostles were to the early Christian community. Bishops are ordained to be the focal point of the local church and its source of unity. This unity appears especially when they offer the Eucharistic sacrifice in the midst of their priests and people. Bishops are ordained only by other bishops (cf. LG 21), and long-standing venerable tradition in the Church restricts to them also the ordination of priests and deacons. Bishops are also the ordinary ministers of the sacrament of confirmation, and, as the source and sign of the unity of the Christian community on the local level, they are the leaders first in worship and the official and authentic liturgists and the principal teachers within their dioceses.

The Church teaches "that by divine institution bishops have succeeded to the place of the apostles as shepherds of the Church, and that he who hears them, hears Christ, while he who rejects them, rejects Christ and Him who sent Christ (cf. Luke 10.16)" (LG 20).

Priests

Bishops share their priestly orders with others. Priests "are called to share in the priesthood of the bishops and to be molded into the likeness of Christ, the supreme and eternal Priest. By consecration they will be made true priests of the New Testament, to preach the Gospel, sustain God's people, and celebrate the liturgy, above all, the Lord's sacrifice."[26]

288   Priests are ordained to continue the saving action of Christ in and through the sacraments. A priest gathers the faithful for the Eucharistic sacrifice which only a priest can offer in the person and in the place of Christ. He forgives sins in the sacrament of penance, again acting in the

---

[26]Roman Pontifical, Rite of Ordination of Priests, n. 14.

292

name and person of the Lord. His other specifically priestly functions are preaching, praying for the Church, anointing the sick, and developing within men the divine life received in baptism by the administration of the other sacraments (cf. PO 2).

The priesthood must be viewed in the context of Christ and His Church. It is the Church which has primary responsibility for continuing Christ's work. Each bishop in charge of a local church is responsible for the sacramental life of his flock. He is in charge of a certain area of the Church, and within that area, usually a diocese, he is obliged to see that faith and Christian order are maintained. In charging others to help him, he gives them permission to exercise the orders they have received. When a priest is given this permission, he is said to "receive faculties." By his ordination a priest becomes a proper minister of the sacraments. But to perform priestly work, especially to hear confessions and to preach, he must also receive permission from the bishop in the area in which he is to function.

Women in the Ministry

The service of women in the Church has enriched the Christian community from earliest times. A number of women served Jesus in His ministry (cf. Luke 8.1-3), and Mary, His mother, shared in the saving 150 work of Jesus more intimately than any other human person. The Church has always been blessed with women saints. In the life of the Church women have been involved in countless indispensable ways, in teaching, in care of the sick and the poor, in administration, and in other areas.

But women have never been ordained priests or bishops in the Church. Even the Blessed Virgin, whose role in the Church is more 153 sublime than that of any other human person, was not called to any priestly office.

The early Church, which so vigorously proclaimed, against the social pressures of the time, that men and women have equal dignity before God, still did not call women to the priesthood. In the sacramental order, in which symbol is of deep importance, it is argued that a male priest is required to act in the person of the male Christ.

"The Catholic Church has never felt that priestly or episcopal ordination can be validly conferred on women. ... This practice of the Church therefore has a normative character: in the fact of conferring priestly ordination only on men, it is a question of an unbroken tradition throughout the history of the Church, universal in the East and in the West, and alert to repress abuses immediately. This norm, based on Christ's example, has been and is still observed because it is considered to conform to God's plan for His Church."[27]

Deacons

The diaconate is traditionally traced back to the apostles and to a time when the infant Church needed an expanded ministry. "Therefore, brethren, pick out from among you seven men of good repute, full of the Spirit and of wisdom, whom we may appoint to this duty. . . . These they set before the apostles, and they prayed and laid their hands upon them" (Acts 6.3, 6). The existence of the diaconate as a distinct office in the Church is often noted in Scripture (cf. Phil. 1.1; 1 Tim. 3.8-13) and is confirmed by the witness of the first Fathers.[28] Like the bishopric and the priesthood, the diaconate is a sacramental order and of divine institution;[29] it has an enduring place in the Church of Christ.

Already in the time of the apostles the richness of the ministry of the diaconate is suggested. Deacons "serve at table," notably at the table of the Eucharistic meal. They are ministers of the charity of the Church (cf. Acts 6.1-4). They are witnesses to the faith, and defenders of it.

In the first centuries of the Church the office of deacon was a permanent one of great importance in the community. There was a gradual decline in the scope of its ministry and influence. At length it became in the Western Church an order exercised by an individual for only a brief time; it was an office filled by one who intended shortly thereafter to become a priest. The Second Vatican Council called for a renewal of the permanent diaconate (cf. LG 29), so that this ancient vocation of service could again shine in the Church.

295 The Latin Church has decided in our time to permit married men to become deacons. Still the ancient witness to celibacy attached to holy orders remains. Anyone accepting the office of permanent deacon, if he is single, promises in the name of Christ not to marry; and if he is al-

---

[27]Sacred Congregation for the Doctrine of the Faith, *Declaration on the Question of the Admission of Women to the Ministerial Priesthood* (October 15, 1976), nn. 1 and 4.

[28]Cf. St. Justin Martyr, *Apologia* 1.65 (MG 6.428); St. Ignatius of Antioch, *Epistula ad Philadelphenses* 4 (MG 5.700).

[29]Cf. Council of Trent, Session 23, July 15, 1563, *Doctrine on the Sacrament of Order,* chs. 2-3 (DS 1765-1766).

ready married, he commits himself not to marry again should his wife die before him.

The ancient services of the deacon are continued in the Church today, with added tasks appropriate to our time. The deacon assists at the liturgy; he distributes Communion, and he baptizes. He proclaims the Gospel and preaches. Deacons are invited to assist in many tasks of the Church: in catechesis, in caring for the poor, and in ministering to the sick (though it is the task of the priest to administer penance and to anoint the sick). It is the deacon's office to assist bishop and priest in all the tasks of caring for Christ's flock.

VOCATION AND PRIESTLY QUALITIES

Only those who are called by Christ should enter the priesthood. 232 Christ directs His call, or vocation, to those He wishes. Young men are said to have the "signs" of a vocation if they are blessed with the health, the intellectual ability, and the strengths of character required for the priesthood, and if they find in their hearts a desire to do priestly work for God's glory and the salvation of men. But the individual may only offer his service to the Church. The inner inclination must be confirmed by an ecclesiastical call. The Church has the task of confirming the reality of the vocation, and in Christ's name it ordains those selected. The choice is always Christ's. "You did not choose Me, but I chose you" (John 15.16).

No one can demand ordination. The imposition of hands in the sacrament of orders is not a recognition of merit or a response to individual preference. It is the recognition of God's special call and the Church's unique role in salvation.

Celibacy

When speaking of the sacrifices a man might make in order to follow Him, Christ spoke of those who would give up wives and homes for the sake of the Gospel (cf. Matt. 19.29). From the first days of the Church there were priests who were celibate; that is, who did not marry, so that they might give their lives and hearts even more undividedly to the service of Christ (cf. 1 Cor. 7.32-35, 9.5). Different practices developed in different parts of the Church. In the Eastern Church it was customary to permit the ordination of married men; in the West it became the practice to ordain only those who felt they were able and willing to live celibate lives for Christ. Neither in the East nor in the West was a man permitted to marry after he had received holy orders.

236   Celibacy is loved in the Church for many reasons. It makes the
232 priest more like Christ. St. Paul noted that it gives one great freedom in the service of Christ, and it deepens personal attachment to Him (cf. 1 Cor. 7.32-35). Moreover, the Church desires priests who preach the
91 duty to bear the cross and to be obedient to God's commands even in the most difficult circumstances, to live in such a way that it is obvious that they are making great personal sacrifices for the Gospel. Priestly celibacy has also been called an eschatological sign, a sign pointing toward eternal life, for one who lives a celibate life in the world is living in a style appropriate to the reality of the next life, in which there will be no marrying (cf. Mark 12.25), and so manifests his faith in eternal life.

The requirement of celibacy is one the Church has power to relax should it judge this appropriate. But it is no arbitrary requirement. The New Testament message and the experience of the Church have shown how fruitful for the people of God has been this charism lived by its priests.

Life of Prayer

The priest should be a man of prayer. On the day of ordination, the
265 candidate receives the special obligation to recite daily the Liturgy of the Hours. The Church thus appoints its priests to a ministry of praise, adoration, petition, and thanksgiving. They are a "voice" of the Church petitioning our heavenly Father to bless the whole world.

Meditation and reflection on what he is and what he is called to be should be part of every priest's life. Without deep spiritual convictions, without a spirit of prayer and sacrifice, he cannot lead the flock entrusted to his care to God.

Witness

The priest's identification with Christ is clearly not limited to the dispensing of the sacraments in His name. The mission of the priest is also to represent Christ to the world and to be active in completing
137 Christ's work in the world. In Christ's name he is to serve the word of God, bearing witness and evangelizing in His name, and to lead the Christian community and build Christian unity.

All these tasks of the priest are aspects of one integrated ministry.

To preach Christ's message, to make His saving work present in the sacraments, and to build community in His name must all be parts of his ministry. Priests are to carry out the whole mission entrusted to them by Christ.

Service of Authority

In order to bring about unity, a priest is endowed with authority. Both evangelization and sacramental life demand a *diaconia* (service) of authority. The Church is the context for this priestly authority, and the Church's well-being limits and guides the exercise of it. Priestly authority at all times must work in harmony with the Church's purpose for the spiritual good of men and their unity in the Church. 126

The exercise of the *diaconia* of authority falls into two categories: the teaching of truth with authority, and the directing of the community in the path of unity. The first requires that the priest authoritatively interpret the word of God for his people in ways appropriate to his day. The second is centered in the priest's mission to maintain and build Christian community, acting with the authority conferred by Christ's wish that all may be one (cf. John 17.11).

Politics and the Priest

The work of the priest should affect notably the social and political life of the community. The priest is both a part of the political community and a spokesman for some of its most cherished principles. In his preaching and in other situations he should make clear the moral imperatives contained in the Gospel message that concern the social order. Like all Christians, the priest has a responsibility to help make the political community just. But the means a priest would use are ordinarily different from those appropriate for the layman, whose more immediate role it is to sanctify earthly structures. The extent of priests' engagement in secular political activity must be limited, and guided by the judgment of their bishops.[30] Similarly, while priests should preach on the public duties of Christians, they should not abuse their preaching role by insisting on a particular political, social, or economic option when there is more than one option in harmony with the Gospel.[31] 232

---

[30]Cf. Second General Assembly of the Synod of Bishops, *The Ministerial Priesthood* (1971) Part Two, n. 2.
[31]Cf. Second General Assembly of the Synod of Bishops, *The Ministerial Priesthood* (1971) Part Two, n. 2.

Proclaiming the Gospel

A priest must continually announce the coming and presence among men of the kingdom of God. He is to pass on to others in word and deed the good news that he has received. Priestly witness takes
137 place within the Church. It participates in the authenticity of the Church's witness, because, through the bishop, a priest shares in the call of the Church to spread the message.

The first "witnessing" task of the priest is to proclaim the Gospel. In accepting this task and carrying it out, a priest participates in the mission of Christ as the Truth, the Light of the world. Thus he brings men to faith, upon which they depend to reach God.

The priest must testify not only to the Person of Jesus Christ, but to the content of the faith, carrying the words of life to those who are to believe and have no other way of coming to them, and testifying to the truth by words and acts.

In this aspect of his priesthood, the priest reflects the work of Christ. Jesus, speaking of His role as the witness of the Father, said He did nothing of His own authority, but said only that which He had been taught by the Father (cf. John 8.28). The priest as witness should absorb the message and remain obedient to it, passing it on as it is. The mission remains the same: to testify to the truth of God as revealed, that through the truth all may live.

·   ·   ·

Questions related to the material in this chapter:

1. Why is the Eucharist the center of Christian life?

2. What do we mean when we say that the Eucharist is the new sacrifice of the new covenant? How is it foreshadowed in the Old Testament?

3. When and in what setting did Christ institute the sacrament of the Eucharist?

4. The Eucharist is both sacrifice and sacred meal. How does this compare with the Passover meal?

5. Was the Eucharist celebrated in the early Church?

6. If Jesus sacrificed Himself once for all, how can we say that the Eucharist is a sacrifice?

7. To whom is the Eucharistic sacrifice offered? What do we mean when we say that a Mass is offered for a special intention?

8. Why is a ministerial priest necessary for celebration of the Eucharist?

9. What is Holy Communion? Are we obliged to receive Holy Communion?

10. What are the requirements for worthy reception of Communion?

11. In what sense is the Eucharist our food?

12. What do we mean when we say that the Eucharist both signifies and brings about the unity of the Church? Does it unify us also with the saints in heaven?

13. How is Jesus really present in the Eucharist? How does His presence in the Eucharist differ from His presence in the other sacraments?

14. Do Eucharistic devotions apart from Mass have any real worth or significance?

15. When did Christ confer priesthood on the apostles?

16. Is holy orders a sacrament?

17. In what ways do we speak of a priest's "identification" with Christ and with Christ's work?

18. Sometimes we see or hear statements to the effect that So-and-So "has left the priesthood." What is wrong with statements of that sort?

19. When we say that it is through the priest that Christ maintains His sacramental presence, what do we mean?

20. Is there any significant difference between the common priesthood of the faithful and the ministerial priesthood, the priesthood of the ordained?

21. The sacrament of orders has three hierarchical grades, or orders. What are these and how are they distinguished?

22. What do we mean when we say a priest "receives faculties"?

23. What is the Church's position with regard to women and the priesthood?

24. We say that no Catholic has a *right* to orders. Why is this?

25. What are "signs" of a vocation to the priesthood, and what is required for confirmation of this vocation?

26. What is the significance of priestly celibacy?

27. What do we mean when we speak of a priest's "service of authority"?

28. What are the duties of a priest in proclaiming the Gospel?

28

Sacraments of Initiation

Three of the sacraments — baptism, confirmation, and the Eucharist — are concerned with Christian initiation: "The three sacraments of Christian initiation closely combine to bring the faithful to the full stature of Christ and to enable them to carry out the mission of the entire people of God in the Church and in the world."[1]

The Eucharist, which is the center of all sacramental life, has already been treated at length in the preceding chapter. In this chapter we discuss the sacraments of baptism and confirmation.

Baptism

SALVATION HISTORY AND BAPTISM

We may best approach the sacrament of baptism through the Holy Saturday Vigil liturgy, which is the masterpiece of the Church's liturgical-catechetical teaching art. It goes beyond an abstract presentation of the Church's teaching by drawing on the prophetic symbolism of the 56 Old Testament, which in turn leads to the teaching of the New Testament. Then all is brought together in a rite which richly expresses the meaning of baptism.

The first scriptural reading of the vigil liturgy is the creation story from the Book of Genesis (cf. Gen. 1.1-2.2). It illustrates the power of God, culminating in the creation of human life. This narrative of divine 46 power is seen here as a symbol of what St. Paul will call a "new cre- 98 ation," the creation effected by Jesus Christ through His passion and death. "Therefore, if any one is in Christ, he is a new creation; the old has passed away, behold, the new has come" (2 Cor. 5.17). "For neither circumcision counts for anything, nor uncircumcision, but a new cre-

[1]Sacred Congregation for Divine Worship, *Rite of Baptism for Children,* published by authority of Pope Paul VI, May 15, 1969, General Introduction, n. 2.

ation" (Gal. 6.15). This new creation actually takes place at the climax of the vigil — in baptism.

The second reading (Gen. 22.1-18) recounts Abraham's faith as shown in his readiness to sacrifice his son Isaac. This is a foreshadowing of Christ's sacrifice, from which baptism, like all the other sacraments, receives its power.

The third reading (Exod. 14.15-15.1) tells of the deliverance of the Jews at the Red Sea. This is linked with the account of the paschal sacrifice, anticipated on Holy Thursday.

The water is at once destructive, in Genesis, part of the wasteland and darkness, and also the source from which life arises. This double symbolism of water — death and life, destruction and salvation — becomes ever clearer in the history of Noah, which is alluded to in the fourth reading (Isa. 54.5-14). Water is used by God to destroy His enemies and save His friends.

The remaining readings (Isa. 55.1-11; Bar. 3.9-15, 32-44; Ezek. 36.16-17a, 18-28) are from the prophetic writings and point to the spiritual effects of baptism, still celebrating God's wonderful use of water, as Jesus would use it afterwards: "The water that I shall give him will become in him a spring of water welling up to eternal life" (John 4.14).

Thus the stage was set for "when the time had fully come" (Gal. 4.4). When John the Baptist made his appearance in the Judean desert, he proclaimed a "baptism of repentance for the forgiveness of sins" 79 (Mark 1.4). Jesus Himself, going down into the waters of the Jordan, brings this long, dramatic sequence of water-events to completion. Sinless Himself, He leads His people from sin through the waters of baptism to a new covenant with the Father.

By the waters of baptism, sin and evil are destroyed and we rise to a new life, sharing in the resurrection of Jesus. "You have put off the old nature with its practices and have put on the new nature . . ." (Col. 3.9). Indeed, "our old self was crucified with Him so that the sinful body might be destroyed, and we might no longer be enslaved to sin" (Rom. 6.6).

The Baptismal Liturgy

Against this background of salvation history culminating in Christ, we can appreciate the baptismal liturgy. The vigil itself begins with a Light Service. From a new fire, the paschal candle is lighted; it stands for the risen Christ, His wounds now glorified. While the candle is carried in procession to the sanctuary, the light is gradually diffused as first the celebrant, then the ministers, and finally all others in the congregation light their candles from the paschal candle. The Easter Proclamation 96 (*Exsultet*) is sung, all rejoicing in the victory of God's light at this climax of salvation history. Then come the scriptural readings described above.

The emphasis now turns to the joy of the resurrection. Altar candles are lighted, the Gloria is sung, church bells are rung. All is ready for baptism. First, the water is blessed with a prayer that sums up the salvation history just heard in the readings. The paschal candle is lowered into the water. Through the risen Christ, whom the candle signifies, the font will now become life-giving. The font, the womb of the 105 Church, will bring forth children of God, as once more the Spirit of God is "moving over the face of the waters" (Gen. 1.2).

The baptismal promises are now pronounced. Then follows a profession of faith. Finally there is the baptism itself. Those baptized are then anointed with chrism, recalling Christ's anointing by the Spirit, which is now shared by the new Christian. This foreshadows and anticipates the anointing of confirmation, which may take place here. The baptized are thus admitted to God's covenanted people and will now be allowed to share in the "holy priesthood, to offer spiritual sacrifices acceptable to God through Jesus Christ" (1 Peter 2.5). The ceremony is completed by investing those who have been baptized with a symbolic white garment, the token of their baptismal innocence. They now are ready to share in the Eucharist in which we celebrate and renew the death and resurrection of the Lord.

Lent

Lent is a period for the instruction of catechumens, but it is a period 91 for the baptized as well. The baptized Christian is encouraged to approach each Easter as one should when solemnly preparing for baptism.

All acts of penance are part of that total conversion called for by baptism, a whole inner renewal leading one to think, judge, and arrange one's entire life under the impulse of the charity revealed to us in Christ. Acts of penance without this inner spirit are lifeless.

Christian penance traditionally involves prayer, fasting, and works of charity. Fasting and abstinence are encouraged in Lent, but Church law does not require a great deal of us in this regard. Specific regulations vary in different countries. In the United States of America,

302

for example, all Fridays of Lent are days of abstinence, that is, days on which no meat is to be eaten; and Ash Wednesday and Good Friday are days of fast as well as abstinence. On fast days one is to abstain from solid foods except at the one full meal and the two smaller meals permitted. Fasting binds those between the ages of 21 and 59; those who have reached the age of fourteen are bound by abstinence. For sufficient reasons, the faithful may judge themselves excused or seek a dispensation from these particular regulations. But we can never be excused from the duty of doing penance.

Easter Customs

Some have observed that although Easter is the greatest Christian feast, Christmas is in fact celebrated with greater joy. The reason seems plain. Christmas has more human resonances. There are family gatherings and reunions, children take the center of the stage, gifts are exchanged. To accomplish something like this for Easter, we need more than theological explanation. If a parish community could be brought to recognize Easter as the annual celebration of the baptism and first communion of all the parishioners, then there might also be rejoicing and family gatherings, with sponsors as well as parents and grandparents.

RITE OF BAPTISM

Baptism is in fact celebrated not only at Easter but at all times of the year. Still the spirit of the paschal mystery must always penetrate its celebration. Baptism may be administered either by immersing the candidate three times in the baptismal water, or by pouring water over his head three times. While the water is applied, the celebrant speaks the baptismal formula: "N., I baptize you in the name of the Father, and of the Son, and of the Holy Spirit." The water and the words symbolize the new life of the Trinity to which one is called, by sharing in the death 115 and resurrection of Christ.

Bishops, priests, and deacons are the ordinary ministers of baptism Anyone, however, even a non-Christian, can validly administer this sacrament by performing the rite with the serious intent to baptize in accord with the mind of the Church. Every Catholic should be able to administer this sacrament should an emergency demand this

Each baptismal candidate should have at least one godparent. The godparent should be a mature person, a Catholic living the faith, one

303

who is able to fulfill a role of spiritual concern for the one baptized. In special circumstances, as in the case of children of mixed marriages, a baptized and believing Christian of a separated community may serve as an additional godparent or Christian witness.[2]

A Christian name, ordinarily the name of a saint, is to be given at baptism. Ideally, the saint whose name is chosen should become well known to the one baptized, as a patron and friend.

EFFECTS OF BAPTISM

235   By baptism men "are plunged into the paschal mystery of Christ: they die with Him, are buried with Him, and rise with Him . . ." (SC 6). The ritual adds: "Far superior to the purifications of the old law, baptism produces all these effects by the power of the mystery of the Lord's passion and resurrection."[3] What are "all these effects" comprehended in the paschal mystery?

Dying with Christ

In our review of the Old Testament signs of baptism we saw that
301 water is at once destructive and life-giving. So in baptism there is a destructive process: "Those who are baptized are engrafted in the likeness of Christ's death. They are buried with him. . . ."[4] St. Paul explains: "We know that our old self was crucified with Him so that the sinful body might be destroyed, and we might no longer be enslaved to sin" (Rom. 6.6).

By cleansing us from sin, the waters of baptism set us on a new way of life. When an adult is baptized his sins are forgiven even as he receives the new life of grace; for divine grace, in virtue of Christ's pas-
171 sion and death, has a forgiving and healing effect. Accordingly, baptism remits original sin and, for those baptized after infancy, also all personal sins which are sincerely repented of.

Since original sin involves all the members of our race, in this respect infants as well as adults must "die" with Christ and come to a new life of grace.

Although the guilt of original sin is removed, some of its effects

---

[2]Cf. *Rite of Baptism for Children,* General Introduction, nn. 8-10.
[3]*Rite of Baptism for Children,* General Introduction, n. 6.
[4]*Rite of Baptism for Children,* General Introduction, n. 6.

remain. This inclination to sin remains in those who have been reborn in baptism. It is "left for us to wrestle with," but it "cannot harm those who do not consent but manfully resist through the grace of Jesus Christ."[5] This "wrestling," this agonizing struggle with our own desires, involves a lifelong sharing in the dying of Jesus. God permits us to undergo this struggle that we may more fully share in the great work of our own redemption.

Rising with Christ

The baptized die with Christ only to rise with Him and share His life: "They are buried with him, they are given life again with him, and with him they rise again. For baptism recalls and effects the paschal mystery itself, because by means of it men and women pass from the death of sin into life."[6] It is the risen life of Christ we share.   171

Baptism makes us members of the Church. But to become a member of the Church is to be radically changed; it is to be grafted on the vine (cf. John 15.4-6) and joined vitally to the Body of Christ. Through an all-pervading bond of life we become members of God's covenanted people. All this is effected in the paschal mystery: "This cup which is poured out for you is the new covenant in My blood" (Luke 22.20).

Children of God

"Baptism, the cleansing with water by the power of the living 242 Word, makes us sharers in God's own life and his adopted children."[7] Baptism is both a rising with Christ and a new birth. But that we become children of God through baptism is told to us by Jesus Himself: "Truly, truly, I say to you, unless one is born of water and the Spirit, he cannot enter the kingdom of God" (John 3.5).

Since Jesus Christ is "the only Son of God" (John 3.18), we receive 62 our status by "adoption" (Gal. 4.5). Still, as St. John assures us, this adoption is no legal fiction, as when children are legally adopted: "See what love the Father has given us, that we should be called children of God; and so we are" (1 John 3.1). Offspring share the nature of their

---

[5]Council of Trent, Session 5, June 17, 1546, *Decree on Original Sin*, n. 5 (DS 1515).
[6]*Rite of Baptism for Children*, General Introduction, n. 6.
[7]*Rite of Baptism for Children*, General Introduction, n. 5.

parents. If we are truly children of God, we must in some way share in
169 the nature and the life of God. Scripture assures us that we do: "He has
granted to us His precious and very great promises, that through these
you may escape from the corruption that is in the world because of passion, and become partakers of the divine nature" (2 Peter 1.4).

A Royal Priesthood

The first Epistle of St. Peter is largely a meditation on baptism, its
effects, and its practical implications. St. Peter here speaks of baptism,
by which all become worshipers of God in Spirit and in truth: "You are a
chosen race, a royal priesthood, a holy nation, God's own people, that
you may declare the wonderful deeds of Him who called you out of
darkness into His marvelous light. Once you were no people but now
you are God's people" (1 Peter 2.9-10). The apostle is recalling Exodus
where the Jewish people were spoken of as a royal priesthood (cf. Exod.
19.6) although only the Levites were specially designated for divine service.

In a similar way, while a new order of priests, sharing Christ's High
281 Priesthood, has been instituted to continue and renew His sacrifice, all
the baptized are now called to join in worshiping God fully, consciously,
and actively.

BAPTISM OF INFANTS

The Church has solemnly defined the validity of infant baptism.[8] In
fact, Church law commands Catholics to have their children baptized as
soon after birth as is reasonably possible.[9]

Almost from the beginning, if not from the very beginning of
Christianity, infant baptism was practiced when whole families were
baptized. Origen, writing in the third century, expressly states that the
Church's tradition of baptizing infants came from the apostles.[10] St.
Augustine cites the universal practice of infant baptism as evidence of
the Church's traditional belief in original sin.[11]

---

[8]Cf. Council of Trent, Session 7, March 3, 1547, *Decree on the Sacraments*, canon 13 on
the sacrament of baptism (DS 1626).

[9]Cf. *Code of Canon Law*, canon 770.

[10]Cf. Origen, *In Romanos Commentarii* 5.9 (MG 14.1047).

[11]Cf., e.g., St. Augustine's *Contra Iulianum Opus Imperfectum* 1.50 (ML 45.1073).

The theological reason for infant baptism is given by Jesus Himself: "Truly, truly, I say to you, unless one is born of water and the Spirit, he cannot enter the kingdom of God" (John 3.5). There could be no stronger statement of the need for baptism. After the resurrection Jesus summarized the whole history of God's salvific power working through water when He placed men under the obligation of receiving baptism: "Go into all the world and preach the gospel to the whole creation. He who believes and is baptized will be saved; but he who does not believe will be condemned" (Mark 16.15).

A child born of Christian parents is introduced by baptism into the covenanted people of God. He is given a place, not only in his family, 220 but in the community of the Church, and also in the universe; he is provided with a purpose, a key to the meaning of life, and a place in the economy of salvation in which these can be realized.

The parents, in bringing their child to be baptized, are also acting as members of God's covenanted people; they are exercising their royal priesthood by introducing their child into God's holy nation.

THE NECESSITY OF BAPTISM

The Church, heeding the words of the Gospel (cf., e.g., John 3.3, 5), teaches that no one can enter the kingdom of heaven unless he is baptized.[12]

This insistence on the need for baptism for salvation may seem puzzling to many. Does it not follow that salvation is impossible for those who have never heard of Christ or baptism? This is by no means a new question. Nor is the answer new. Not all baptism is sacramental baptism with water. There is also "baptism of blood" and "baptism of desire."

Baptism of blood is received by dying for Christ. The Holy Innocents (cf. Matt 2.16-18) received such a baptism, as did the early catechumens who were martyred for Christ.

Baptism of desire has a far wider scope. It is most clearly present in those who explicitly wish to be baptized but who die before their intention can be carried out. Moreover, the desire for baptism does not have 131

---

[12]Cf., e.g., Council of Florence, Bull, *Exsultate Deo* (November 22, 1439) (DS 1314); Council of Trent, Session 6, January 13, 1547, *Decree on Justification,* ch. 4 (DS 1524) and Session 7, March 3, 1547, *Decree on the Sacraments,* canon 5 on the sacrament of baptism (DS 1618).

to be explicit. Even those who through no fault of their own do not know Christ and His Church may be counted as anonymous Christians if their striving to lead a good life is in fact a response to His grace, which is given in sufficient measure to all (cf. LG 16).

THE BAPTISMAL CHARACTER

The Church teaches that baptism, like confirmation and orders, imprints a permanent character or sign.[13]

In order to understand the spiritual reality which the word "character" here expresses symbolically, we must note a significant difference between these sacraments and the others. The other sacraments may be received more than once, but baptism, confirmation, and orders may not. There is a reason for this. Apart from the grace which they confer, 289 which can be lost through sin, the sacraments of baptism, confirmation, and orders also have a lasting effect. This endures even if the recipient sins gravely. It remains in eternity.

The character points to the stability and permanence of the Church. It cries out that God's gifts are enduring, and that He will continue to work His mercy in and through those He has chosen. "You are Christ's; and Christ is God's" (1 Cor. 3.23).

Christ marks out His own. He has chosen us. We belong to Him. The baptismal character is the sign at once of the Christian's permanent vocation, of his call by Jesus Christ, and, in the first place, of God's initial and undiscourageable love.

Confirmation

DIVINE ORIGIN OF CONFIRMATION

Confirmation (like the anointing of the sick and matrimony) is a 325 sacrament which we first learn about in New Testament passages that speak of its use in the Church's liturgy. The Gospels contain no direct teaching on it, as they do on the Eucharist, baptism, and penance. When we first hear of this sacrament in the New Testament, it is already being

---

[13]Council of Trent, Session 7, March 3, 1547, *Decree on the Sacraments,* canon 9 on the sacraments in general (DS 1609).

administered — Christ having already ascended — in the infant Church.

"Now when the apostles at Jerusalem heard that Samaria had received the word of God, they sent to them Peter and John who came down and prayed for them that they might receive the Holy Spirit; for it had not yet fallen on any of them, but they had only been baptized in the name of the Lord Jesus. Then they laid their hands on them and they received the Holy Spirit" (Acts 8.14-17).

That we learn of confirmation through its liturgy is significant. This highlights the importance of liturgy as a means of knowing and transmitting religious teaching.[14]

ANOINTING IN SCRIPTURE

To the laying on of hands described in the Acts of the Apostles there was added an anointing with oil. The oil of olives was a valued product in Palestine as in most of the ancient world. Because of its many uses it was also rich in significance. It was a food condiment, a beauty preparation, a medicine, an unguent for athletes and, mixed with perfume, for refreshment after bathing; and it was a sign of joy. It was the ordinary fuel for lamps, even in the sanctuary. A special sacred oil for anointing was prepared at the direction of Moses (cf. Exod. 30.25 f.). Aaron was anointed as high priest, and then Aaron's sons (cf. Lev. 8.12, 30). Later Samuel anointed Saul as king, then David (cf. 1 Sam. 10.1 f., 16.13 f.).

Since Jesus in the line of David was the Messiah, He would certainly be anointed. So Isaiah had foretold (cf. Isa. 61.1), and this was the very prophecy that Jesus read and commented upon in teaching at Nazareth (cf. Luke 4.18).

SACRAMENT OF THE HOLY SPIRIT

Thus oil came to symbolize the coming of the Spirit, as a sharing of the Gift sent first to the apostles.

105

In the administration of the sacrament olive oil perfumed with balsam is used (although other suitable plant oils and other fragrances are acceptable, according to availability). In consecrating this chrism, the bishop recalls that it takes its name from Christ, who is the Messiah, the

---

[14]Cf. Pope Pius XII, Encyclical, Mediator Dei (November 20, 1947) nn. 47-48.

"Anointed One." He goes on to pray that those who receive the sacrament may be given "the fullness of royal, priestly, and prophetic power." With chrism the Christian is, so to speak, Christified.

104   Confirmation exists to extend to the Church of every time and place the Gift of the Holy Spirit sent to the apostles on Pentecost. The Holy Spirit is the gift of Christ.

Marvels accompany the Spirit's coming — the mysterious wind, the tongues of fire, the gift of tongues, the bold proclamation, and the numerous conversions. But perhaps the most notable effect was the transformation of this frightened group of men into inspired and fearless witnesses to their Lord's resurrection: "Their voice has gone out to all the earth, and their words to the ends of the world" (Rom. 10.18; cf. Ps. 19.5).

Confirmation is thus the sacrament whereby the apostles and their successors, by the laying on of hands and anointing with chrism, com-
107 municate to the whole Church and all its members the gift of the Spirit received at Pentecost. It is Pentecost extended throughout the world, perpetuated, and made ever present in the Church. It is a call to spread the kingdom of Christ, to spread the message of salvation.

Although any priest is authorized, as need urges and the Church delegates him, to administer the sacrament of Confirmation, there is a special propriety in its being conferred by a bishop: "The original minister of confirmation is the bishop. Ordinarily the sacrament is administered by the bishop so that there will be a more evident relationship to the first pouring forth of the Holy Spirit on the day of Pentecost. After they were filled with the Holy Spirit, the apostles themselves gave the Spirit to the faithful through the laying on of their hands. In this way the reception of the Spirit through the ministry of the bishop shows the close bond which joins the confirmed to the Church and the mandate of Christ to be witnesses among men."[15]

SACRAMENT OF CHRISTIAN MATURITY

In the early centuries of the Church, confirmation was administered soon after baptism. It became part of the Holy Saturday Vigil service following baptism and preceding the Eucharist. Baptism, although a rebirth and a new creation, was assumed to require completion by the

---

[15]Sacred Congregation for Divine Worship, *Rite of Confirmation,* published by authority of Pope Paul VI, August 22, 1971, Introduction, n. 7.

Spirit. Those who have been baptized still need the further pledge of guidance, inspiration, courage, and growth.

Some would wish to see in confirmation a sacramental sign of coming to spiritual maturity or of adult commitment to Christ. In this they are supported by the New Testament examples of confirming adults. They also seem to be supported by the teaching that confirmation confers strength and belongs to Christian growth.

On the other hand, precisely because confirmation is a sacrament of initiation following baptism, Eastern Catholics confirm even infants 160 after their baptism. Others are concerned that confirmation, because it is a sacrament of initiation, should at least precede full participation in the Eucharist, which is the climax of initiation. Some liturgical considerations therefore seem to favor early confirmation; some psychological factors seem to urge postponement until at least the threshold of maturity.

The Holy See has left the matter somewhat open. The *Rite of Confirmation* states that with regard to children in the Latin Church "the administration of confirmation is generally postponed until about the seventh year" yet allows that it may, for pastoral reasons, be postponed to "a more mature age."[16] If we see the Christian life as a whole, progressing from rebirth to mature manhood in Christ (cf. Eph. 4.13), there is no difficulty in regarding confirmation, even when administered in adolescence or later, as a sacrament of initiation.

LASTING EFFECTS OF CONFIRMATION

Confirmation implies growth, and it is a continual challenge to the recipient to cultivate growth. Life is required for this growth, and the re- 246 cipient must be in the state of grace. Yet confirmation cannot be counted on to produce instantaneous growth; nor is it intended to do this. As one of the sacraments which are administered to a person only once, and whose effect is therefore permanent, confirmation confers a permanent character. This is shown by the words with which it is administered: "Be sealed with the gift of the Holy Spirit."

Growth in the Spirit

As Pentecost follows Easter and is the fruit of the paschal mystery, so confirmation makes Pentecost permanent in the Church and in the

---

[16]*Rite of Confirmation*, Introduction, n. 11.

104 lives of its members. The Holy Spirit is God's unrepented gift; one who receives this gift becomes a "temple of the Holy Spirit" (1 Cor. 6.19). Even if one strays from the fold, the seal remains, an ever-present invitation to return.

Meanwhile, as the feast of Pentecost brings to completion one part of the liturgical year and dominates the liturgical time that follows it, so does the Spirit rule the lives of those who have received this first of God's gifts. His presence is life, and life is growth. St. Paul describes this growing process as issuing from "the mystery": "This mystery, which is
169 Christ in you. . . . Him we proclaim, warning every man and teaching every man in all wisdom, that we may present every man mature in Christ" (Col. 1.27-28).

Growth in the Christian life, precisely because it is a life, cannot be programmed. Here is the difficulty of taking confirmation as a rite of adult commitment. Grace indeed brings about growth. Yet growth also depends on many personal factors, and even perhaps on the experience of spiritual crises, to bring about a realization of what it means to be a child of God and a temple of the Holy Spirit. The grace of confirmation, though it does not immediately effect such full personal realization, can help to bring it about.

To Witness and Defend the Faith

Christ Himself associated the gift of the Holy Spirit and the Christian apostolic mission. "You shall receive power when the Holy Spirit has come upon you; and you shall be My witnesses . . . to the end of the earth" (Acts 1.8). The Church declares that those who have received this special strength of the Holy Spirit in confirmation "are more strictly obliged to spread and defend the faith both by word and by deed as true
233 witnesses of Christ" (LG 11). The call of the laity to apostolic tasks in the world, and to their role in shaping the kingdom on earth, is related to this sacrament. For the laity, "strengthened by the power of the Holy Spirit through confirmation, are assigned to the apostolate by the Lord Himself" (AA 3).

CONFIRMATION AND THE PASCHAL MYSTERY

Confirmation, like all the other sacraments, derives its efficacy from the paschal mystery of the Lord's death and resurrection. This is indicated in that "ordinarily confirmation takes place within

Mass. . . ."[17] But even if confirmation is celebrated apart from Mass, its source is still the paschal mystery.

No Christian can grow to maturity in Christ without accepting His invitation: "If any man would come after Me, let him deny himself and take up his cross daily and follow Me" (Luke 9.23). With St. Paul we must be able to say, "I have been crucified with Christ," if we also wish to say, "It is no longer I who live, but Christ who lives in me" (Gal. 2.20). 91

Isaiah had already told us how the Holy Spirit who dwells in us works through His gifts. "There shall come forth a shoot from the stump of Jesse, and a branch shall grow out of his roots. And the Spirit of the LORD shall rest upon Him, the spirit of wisdom and understanding, the spirit of counsel and might, the spirit of knowledge and the fear of the LORD" (Isa. 11.1-2). Wisdom, understanding, counsel, fortitude, knowledge, piety, and fear of the Lord are commonly known as the gifts of the Holy Spirit. 243

Finally, the indwelling Spirit will produce in those receptive to His presence what are known as the fruits of the Holy Spirit: charity, joy, peace, patience, benignity, goodness, long-suffering, mildness, faith, modesty, continency, and chastity (cf. Gal. 5.22-23).

•   •   •

Questions related to the material in this chapter:

1. What are the sacraments of Christian initiation?

2. The rite of baptism is a ritual passage from the death in sin to life in Christ. How is this expressed in the liturgy of the Easter vigil on Holy Saturday night?

3. What is Lent? Why is Lent a suitable time for preparing for baptism and for renewal of our baptismal pledges?

4. Are fasting and abstinence the only forms of Christian penance?

5. What is the formula used in baptizing?

6. Who are the ordinary ministers of baptism? Can others baptize, and what is required?

7. What are the principal effects of baptism?

---

[17]Rite of Confirmation, Introduction, n. 13.

313

8. Why do Catholic parents have their children baptized as soon after birth as is reasonably possible?

9. Is baptism necessary for salvation?

10. What is "baptism of blood"? What is "baptism of desire"?

11. We say that baptism imprints a permanent character or sign. What does this mean?

12. Is confirmation a distinct sacrament instituted by Christ?

13. Why is confirmation called the "sacrament of the Holy Spirit" and "sacrament of Christian maturity"?

14. Who administers the sacrament of confirmation?

15. At what age are persons confirmed?

16. What are the effects of confirmation?

29

Sacraments of Healing

"Those who approach the sacrament of penance obtain pardon from the mercy of God for offenses committed against Him, and at the same time are reconciled with the Church, which they have wounded by their sins, and which by charity, example, and prayer seeks their conversion. By the sacred anointing of the sick and the prayer of her priests, the whole Church commends those who are ill to the suffering and glorified Lord, asking that He may lighten their suffering and save them (cf. James 5.14-16)" (LG 11).

In this chapter we discuss the sacraments of penance and anointing of the sick, each of them a sacrament of healing instituted by Christ our Physician.

Penance

GOSPEL SIGNS

Jesus promulgated the sacrament of penance on Easter, thus showing clearly how it arises from the paschal mystery of His death and rising.

"On the evening of that day, the first day of the week . . . He breathed on them, and said to them, 'Receive the Holy Spirit. If you forgive the sins of any, they are forgiven; if you retain the sins of any, they are retained' " (John 20.19-23). Thus was the sacrament of penance instituted.[1]

". . . Our Savior, Jesus Christ, when he gave to his apostles and their successors power to forgive sins, instituted in his Church the sacrament of penance. Thus the faithful who fall into sin after baptism may be reconciled with God and renewed in grace."[2]

---

[1]Cf. Council of Trent, Session 14, November 15, 1551, *Doctrine on the Sacrament of Penance,* ch. 1 (DS 1670) and canon 3 on the sacrament of penance (DS 1703).
[2]Sacred Congregation for Divine Worship, *Rite of Penance,* published by authority of Pope Paul VI, December 2, 1973, Introduction, n. 2.

Earlier, as is recorded in the Gospel of St. Matthew, Jesus had anticipated this gift. To Peter, who had just professed Him to be the Messiah and who was rewarded by being made the firm foundation of the Church, He said: "I will give you the keys of the kingdom of heaven, and whatever you loose on earth shall be loosed in heaven" (Matt. 16.19). A little later, after the promise to Peter, He extended this power of binding and loosing to "the disciples" (cf. Matt. 18.18).

192

Through the centuries the Church has exercised this authority to forgive sins. The sacrament of penance, the liturgical rite in which the Church does this, has had a variety of forms. But Catholic faith has always believed that Christ continues to forgive sins in His Church.

THE SACRAMENTAL SIGN

The sign appropriate for the sacrament of forgiveness can be grasped by reflecting on the kind of sickness cured in the sacrament of penance. In penance two things happen. The sinner is restored with healing grace to share in the divine life, as signified by the young man raised to life at Nain (cf. Luke 7.14), and is welcomed back by the Father, like the prodigal son (cf. Luke 15.20-24). At the same time, the sinner is reinstated in the community, and again shares at the community Eucharistic table. God can forgive sins secretly, but it is appropriate for the sinner to be reconciled outwardly, visibly, with the Church community. The community itself is healed as the penitent is healed.

82

A Saving Tribunal

An analogy for this healing of sickness which affects both the individual and the community is found in the manner society deals with its offenders, through a judicial process. The Council of Trent uses this image in developing the theology of penance and distinguishing this sacrament from baptism. It explains and justifies this approach by appealing to the power of the keys granted to St. Peter.[3] Moreover, the teaching of Trent, and of the Church today, is that "absolution is given by a priest, who acts as judge."[4] Indeed, in the manner of a judge the

---

[3]Cf. Council of Trent, Session 14, November 25, 1551, Doctrine on Sacrament of Penance, chs. 2 (DS 1671) and 5 (DS 1679).
[4]Sacred Congregation for the Doctrine of the Faith, Sacramentum Paenitentiae ("Pastoral Norms concerning the Administration of General Sacramental Absolution," June 16, 1972). Cf. Council of Trent, Session 14, November 25, 1551, Doctrine on the Sacrament of Penance, ch. 6 (DS 1685) and canon 9 on the sacrament of penance (DS 1709).

316

priest — except in the case of penitents in danger of death — must have jurisdiction from the local bishop in order to absolve.[5] The *Rite of Penance* states: "Confession requires in the penitent the will to open his heart to the minister of God, and in the minister a spiritual judgment by which, acting in the person of Christ, he pronounces his decision of forgiveness or retention of sins in accord with the power of the keys."[6]

The words with which Christ instituted the sacrament ("If you forgive the sins of any . . .") also contain the authority to judge. As sinners, we need divine forgiveness. Jesus has indicated the sacramental tribunal as His way to forgiveness and reconciliation — a way that in healing the individual sinner also heals the injured community. 316

Judgment of Mercy

The sacrament of penance is an unusual tribunal. The guilty party, the penitent, accuses himself and approaches the Lord in sorrow, admitting guilt before His representative. The priest, who is Christ's minister in penance, listens to the confession in the name of the Lord, to discover in the penitent's openness, sorrow, and will to conversion the grounds for a judgment of forgiveness. It is for Christ that the priest hears the confession of guilt; the words spoken to him there are therefore guarded by the most solemn obligation of complete secrecy. It is in the name of Christ that the priest speaks the judgment of the Savior's mercy: "I absolve you from your sins, in the name of the Father, and of the Son, and of the Holy Spirit."

This judicial form of penance reminds us that God's word also provides a continuing judgment throughout our days of pilgrimage.

Similarly, in the sacrament of penance, we have, as we move along our pilgrim way, a tribunal of mercy in which judgment is not punitive or final, but healing and redemptive.

PERSONAL REPENTANCE

Sins are not forgiven in any automatic way. For full and perfect forgiveness of sins, three acts are required from the penitent as parts of the sacrament. These are contrition, confession, and satisfaction.[7]

---

[5]Cf., e.g., *Rite of Penance,* Introduction, n. 9b.
[6]*Rite of Penance,* Introduction, n. 6b.
[7]Cf. *Rite of Penance,* Introduction, n. 6. Cf. also Council of Trent, Session 14, November 25, 1551, *Doctrine on the Sacrament of Penance,* ch. 3 (DS 1673) and canon 4 on the sacrament of penance (DS 1704); Sacred Congregation for the Doctrine of the Faith, *Sacramentum Paenitentiae* (June 16, 1972).

Contrition

Contrition, or sincere sorrow for having offended God, is the most important of the three acts required of the penitent. Contrition is indeed but the other face of love; it is love rejecting all that destroys or threatens it. Hence contrition is placed first, as love must always be given first place (cf. 1 Cor. 13.13).

There can be no forgiveness of sin if we do not have sorrow, that is, if we do not regret our sin, resolve not to repeat it, and turn back to God. Sorrow must be interior, from the heart, not merely expressed on the lips. Sorrow should be supreme: the conversion to God means putting Him in the first place and resolving that, aided by His grace, one shall prefer nothing else to Him. Our sorrow must be universal: we must be sorry for all grave or mortal sins, sins that exclude one from the friendship of God.

Sorrow for all our sins, even the lesser ones, is urged. Certainly one must have sincere sorrow for whatever sins one hopes to have forgiven.

Contrition is called "perfect contrition" if the motive of sorrow is true love for God, if the individual is sorry because he has offended the God whom he chooses to love above all things. Contrition is called "imperfect" if it is based on some other motive of faith, if, for example, one is sorry because one believes God, knows God is just and faithful to His word, and knows one will be rightly punished by God if one does not turn away from sin to serve Him.

Because it is an act of love of God and fruit of God's grace calling one to repentance, an act of perfect contrition can at once restore to the friendship of God one who has fallen into serious sin. But, except in very extraordinary circumstances, one who has separated himself from Christ and the family of faith by grave sin is seriously obliged to receive the sacrament of penance before receiving the Eucharist.[8]

Sorrow for sin implies a resolve not to fall back into sin. While the individual cannot be certain that his frailty will not betray him again, his present resolve must be honest and realistic. He must will to change, to be faithful to his Lord, to take realistic steps to make faithfulness possible.

------

[8]Cf. *Code of Canon Law,* canon 856; Council of Trent, Session 13, October 11, 1551, *Decree on the Most Holy Eucharist,* ch. 7 (DS 1647).

Confession

The Church teaches that it is necessary by divine law to confess to a priest each and every mortal sin — and also circumstances which make sin a more serious kind of mortal sin — that one can remember after a careful examination of conscience.[9] Sins committed before baptism do not have to be confessed, for in baptism all sins of the past are forgiven. Moreover, a mortal sin which has been once confessed and for which absolution has been received need not be confessed again. 304 324

Devout penitents frequently are guilty of no grave sins; but they may fruitfully bring before Christ with sorrow the venial sins that mar their lives and limit their charity, taking care to have true sorrow for the sins they do confess.

Satisfaction

The Church believes that there are "temporal punishments" for sin. This means that the just and merciful God requires that the penitent sinner atone for his sins; he will receive punishment for them either in this life or after death in purgatory, unless he has taken punishment upon himself by deeds of penance.

The penitent, then, must complete his penitential act by making some satisfaction for his sins, by doing a "penance" imposed by the priest. The penance imposed in earlier days was often severe. Today the penance is usually the recitation of certain prayers assigned by the priest after the penitent has confessed his sins.

Our sins are more serious than we realize, and our deeds of penance are often slight. To assist us in our frailty, the Church also makes possible indulgences for the faithful. An indulgence is a remission before God of all (plenary indulgence) or part (partial indulgence) of the temporal punishment due to sins that have already been forgiven.[10] 302

---

[9]Cf. *Rite of Penance*, Introduction, n. 7a; Council of Trent, Session 14, November 25, 1551, Doctrine on the Sacrament of Penance, canon 7 on the sacrament of penance (DS 1707); Sacred Congregation for the Doctrine of Faith, *Sacramentum Paenitentiae* (June 16, 1972).

[10]Cf. Pope Paul VI, Apostolic Constitution, *Indulgentiarum Doctrina* (January 1, 1967) Norm 1. This document, in AAS 59 (1967) pp. 5-24 and also in *Enchiridion Indulgentiarum* (Vatican Press 1968), explains the history and theology of indulgences fairly fully. Cf. also Council of Trent, Session 25, December 4, 1563, *Decree on Indulgences* (DS 1835).

To gain an indulgence, one must say the prayer or do the good deed to which the Church attaches the indulgence. By a kind of spiritual leverage as it were, a relatively slight act of piety on the part of the individual brings upon him a great mercy.

THE "LABORIOUS BAPTISM"

The Council of Trent, citing St. Gregory of Nazianzus and St. John of Damascus, stated that the sacrament of penance "has rightly been called by the holy Fathers 'a laborious kind of baptism.' "[11] It is called a kind of baptism because it restores baptismal holiness, and "laborious" because it cannot do this "without many tears and labors on our part."

Penance does really restore or renew baptismal holiness. When this holiness has been lost, it can be recovered in the sacrament of penance. A Catholic who has committed grave sin is obliged to ask forgiveness for it in this sacrament. One should do so promptly. Church law requires confession of sins once a year,[12] though, strictly speaking, this particular law does not bind those who would have no grave sins to confess.

But penance is also useful to renew baptismal innocence, that is, to return it to full splendor, even when there are only venial sins or faults committed amidst the moral struggles of everyday living.[13]

Penance and Children

The idea of a "laborious baptism" for children suggests a practical program to prepare them for the sacrament of penance.

An early introduction to penance will help the child make personal the choice implicit in his baptism. That baptism was a conversion, a turning to Christ; the first confession can be an early help in making that basic conversion more personal and free. The child should make his first confession before receiving first Communion.[14]

304

---

[11]Council of Trent, Session 14, November 25, 1551, Doctrine on the Sacrament of Penance, ch. 2 (DS 1672). Cf. St. Gregory of Nazianzus, Oratio 39.17 (MG 36.356); St. John of Damascus, De Fide Orthodoxa 4.9 (MG 94.1124).

[12]Cf. Code of Canon Law, canon 906.

[13]Cf. Rite of Penance, Introduction, n. 7b.

[14]On this paragraph, cf. Sacred Congregation for the Clergy, General Catechetical Directory (April 11, 1971) Addendum, nn. 2 and 5; Sacred Congregation for the Clergy and Sacred Congregation for the Discipline of the Sacraments, Declaration, Sanctus Pontifex (May 24, 1973).

"The suitable age for the first reception of these sacraments (of penance and the Eucharist) is deemed to be that which in documents of the Church is called the age of reason or of discretion. This age 'both for Confession and for Communion is that at which the child begins to reason, that is, about the seventh year, more or less. From that time on the obligation of fulfilling the precepts of Confession and Communion begins.' "[15]

The Community Dimension

Viewing the sacrament of penance as a second baptism enables us also to realize that it is indeed part of the public liturgy of the Church. Today, in approaching penance anew as reconciliation with the commu- 161 nity as well as with God, and perhaps within a communal service, the parallel with baptism offers a perspective for seeing penance as belonging to the liturgical celebration of the whole Church community. 323

COMMUNAL PENANCE

To show more clearly that penance is a genuine liturgical celebration, it may be celebrated as an act of community worship, which forms the context of private confession. 319

Something more is needed, however, if there is to be genuine public penance liturgy. There must also be a sense of the communal and ecclesial dimension of sin. In the early Church sinners guilty of some grave sins were excommunicated, required to do public works of penance, and were reconciled to God through the Church on Holy Thursday by returning to the Eucharist. Even in private confession there is a residue of this public penance. Penitents publicly join the line of people waiting to confess. Meanwhile they must, if guilty of grave sin, exclude themselves from Communion until they return to the life of grace within the Church through the sacrament of penance. Their reconciliation with God and community is completed when they return publicly to the Eucharistic table.

---

[15]Sacred Congregation for the Clergy, General Catechetical Directory (April 11, 1971) Addendum, n. 1, quoting from Sacred Congregation for the Sacraments, Decree, Quam Singulari (August 8, 1910) n. 1 (DS 3530).

To acknowledge, even to become aware, that our sins have a community dimension is not always easy, and perhaps not very pleasant for many in an era marked by highly individualistic thinking. By public penance we do not escape personal responsibility; we in fact enlarge the area of our awareness of responsibility for the sins of the society of which we are a part.

Social Dimensions of Sin

Within this wider context, all particular sins except those directly against God, such as blasphemy, are offenses against God's law precisely because they injure one's neighbor or oneself. Even those which directly harm only oneself have a potential for disturbing community harmony. The last seven commandments of the Decalogue are concerned with our neighbor. If I steal, for example, I injure my neighbor and cause privation to him and his family. I also lower the level of openness and mutual confidence in the whole community, and in a sense I diminish the pulse and flow of life in the Body of Christ. This is true even of "secret" sins against the ninth and tenth commandments, which also have reference to my neighbor. Even blasphemy and other sins against the first three commandments can cause scandal. In a word, my personal and even secret sins can have extensive consequences in the community.

Moreover, certain evils, while involving personal guilt, especially sins of omission, have a communal dimension. An example here is racism. As a web that enmeshes all, it involves us all in its consequences.

The same is true of all widespread social injustices. Although few of us may be involved in large and dramatic ways, a very great many of us are in some measure responsible. The Synod of Bishops in 1971 spoke of the "serious injustices which are building around the world of men a network of domination, oppression, and abuses which stifle freedom and which keep the greater part of humanity from sharing in the building up and enjoyment of a more just and fraternal world"; the world is marked by a "grave sin of injustice."[16]

The follower of Christ will consider his social responsibilities and the social dimensions of sin in his examination of conscience.[17]

---

[16]Second General Assembly of the Synod of Bishops, 1971, *Justice in the World*, Introduction and Part II.

[17]Cf. the outline examination of conscience in *Rite of Penance*, Appendix III.

322

CELEBRATING THE SACRAMENT

The sacrament of penance may be administered in two ways, either within a communal ceremony or in an individual one. Even the communal ceremony guards important personal elements of the sacrament: the individual penitent confesses his sins in private and there is individual absolution. And even the individual form guards certain public elements, as an act of the Church's liturgy must.

The Ancient Practice

The early Christians also confessed their sins privately, although within a community celebration. The real difference between ancient and modern practice, however, is that some early Christians felt they could receive the sacrament of penance only once, and it was only with difficulty that they came to feel penance could be received more often. There developed a tendency to defer absolution until the approach of death.

The Celtic monks broke through this difficulty by making popular private and frequent confession, first in their monasteries, then outside, and finally in their missionary journeys to the Continent as Europe strove to recover from the barbarian invasions. For the tortured in conscience, penance became a sacrament not only of healing but of continuing mercy. For the devout, it became a means of deepening their conversion and promoting their growth in the Spirit.

The New Rite

The *Rite of Penance* joins ancient and modern practice in a new ceremony of reconciliation. Private administration of the sacrament, while retaining its judicial character, continues also to offer its merciful healing. It may do this within the setting of a communal service, which is now recommended. "Communal celebration shows more clearly the ecclesial nature of penance."[18] Such celebrations acknowledge the social dimension of sin and the need to be reconciled to the community as one 321 returns to God.

The individual ceremony also has certain advantages. The ceremonies suggested for it, such as the reading of a scriptural passage by the priest or by the penitent and the priest's extension of his hands over the head of the penitent while saying the words of absolution, can add even

---

[18]*Rite of Penance,* Introduction, n. 22.

323

more dignity to its celebration. The individual ceremony has considerable flexibility, and provides an opportunity for combining spiritual direction and pastoral guidance with the administration of the sacrament. Yet it is also an ecclesial act, a reconciliation with the Christian community.

When for extraordinary reasons groups of people are not able to confess their sins individually, they may in some circumstances receive sacramental forgiveness by a communal absolution. Such communal absolution, however, may be given only when there is a "grave need," which is to be determined by the local bishop, "who is to consult with the other members of the episcopal conference."[19] Unless prevented by some good reason, those who receive communal absolution should go to confession before receiving absolution again.[20] Unless it is morally impossible for them to do so, they are obliged to go to confession within a year.[21]

Whether the sacrament of penance is administered in individual ceremony or within a communal celebration, the deepest joy of the guilty is in their deliverance from the sin in a new passover that frees them from the grossest kind of servitude. They come forth from the sacrament, their turning to God complete, in the gladness of a clear conscience and restored justice, with the exhilarating prospect of a fresh start. Once more they are a "new creation," once more for them "the new has come" (2 Cor. 5.17).

Anointing of the Sick

CHRIST AND THE INFIRM

80   Our Lord has compassion on the infirm. He revealed Himself to John as the Messiah simply by saying: "The blind receive their sight and the lame walk, lepers are cleansed and the deaf hear, and the dead are raised up, and the poor have good news preached to them" (Matt. 11.5). In the parable of the great dinner, the servants were commanded, "Go out quickly to the streets and lanes of the city, and bring in the poor and maimed and blind and lame" (Luke 14.21). Many of His works were cures of the sick; and we have seen in the preceding section how

---

[19]Cf. Rite of Penance, Introduction, nn. 31-33.
[20]Cf. Rite of Penance, Introduction, n. 34.
[21]Cf. Rite of Penance, Introduction, n. 31.

He Himself, as well as the evangelists, deliberately used these works as signs of a spiritual healing (cf. Mark 2.10-11).   316

ANOINTING IN SCRIPTURE

Jesus not only taught His disciples to be compassionate, but He also told them who should be the special objects of their compassion.

Meanwhile, as the apostles assisted Him in His mission, "He called to Him His twelve disciples and gave them authority over unclean spirits, to cast them out, and to heal every disease and every infirmity" (Matt. 10.1). A similar commission was given to them after the resurrection: ". . . they will lay their hands upon the sick, and they will recover" (Mark 16.18). In an earlier passage in the Gospel of St. Mark we read: "And they cast out many demons, and anointed with oil many that were sick and healed them" (Mark 6.13). This is the first allusion to the sacrament of the anointing of the sick.[22]

In His Church Christ wished all to care for the sick. The ministry to the sick is an obligation of every Christian. In a special way, however, Christ charged His priests to anoint the sick while praying over them in a sacramental gesture that would be more properly a deed of His own 270 personal care (cf. James 5.14).

As with the sacrament of confirmation, we first see the actual 308 anointing of the sick in the early Church described in the Epistle of St. James. "Is any among you sick? Let him call for the elders of the church, and let them pray over him, anointing him with oil in the name of the Lord; and the prayer of faith will save the sick man, and the Lord will raise him up; and if he has committed sins, he will be forgiven" (James 5.14-15). This passage is cited by the Council of Trent when it declares that "this sacred anointing of the sick was instituted by Christ our Lord as truly and properly a sacrament of the New Testament. . . ."[23]

SACRAMENT OF THE SICK

The sacrament of anointing of the sick is, as the words of St. James make clear, for the sick and infirm.

---

[22]Cf. Council of Trent, Session 14, November 25, 1551, *Doctrine on the Sacrament of Extreme Unction,* ch. 1 (DS 1695).

[23]Council of Trent, Session 14, November 25, 1551, *Doctrine on the Sacrament of Extreme Unction,* ch. 1 (DS 1695).

Accordingly, "there should be special care and concern that those who are dangerously ill due to sickness or old age receive this sacrament."[24] Relatives and friends of the sick have a responsibility in charity to assist them in calling the priest, or to help get them ready to receive the sacrament worthily, especially in the case of graver illnesses.

During some centuries there was a tendency to reserve this sacrament only for those seriously ill, even quite near death, and the sacrament came to be called "extreme unction," that is, "last anointing." The Church has made it clear that it wishes this sacrament for the sick to be more generously available.

328   Thus there is no need to wait until a person is at the point of death. To determine whether there is a dangerous illness, a prudent judgment is all that is needed; there is no need for scrupulosity.[25] "The sacrament may be repeated if the sick person recovers after anointing or if, during the same illness, the danger becomes more serious."[26] Moreover, "a sick person should be anointed before surgery whenever a dangerous illness is the reason for the surgery."[27]

"Old people may be anointed if they are in weak condition although no dangerous illness is present. Sick children may be anointed if they have sufficient use of reason to be comforted by this sacrament." The faithful "should be encouraged to ask for the anointing and, as soon as the time for the anointing comes, to receive it with complete faith and devotion, not misusing this sacrament by putting it off." Also, people who are unconscious or who have lost the use of reason may be anointed "if, as Christian believers, they would have asked for it were they in control of their faculties." A priest is not to anoint "a person who is already dead." If there is a doubt as to death, the priest may administer the sacrament conditionally.[28]

THE COMMUNITY DIMENSION

Sickness is a crisis of life, both for the individual and for the community to which he belongs.

The *Rite of Anointing and Pastoral Care of the Sick* provides a sub-

---

[24]Sacred Congregation for Divine Worship, *Rite of Anointing and Pastoral Care of the Sick,* published by authority of Pope Paul VI, December 7, 1972, Introduction, n. 8.
[25]Cf. *Rite of Anointing* . . ., Introduction, n. 8.
[26]*Rite of Anointing* . . ., Introduction, n. 9.
[27]*Rite of Anointing* . . ., Introduction, n. 10.
[28]On this paragraph, cf. *Rite of Anointing* . . ., Introduction, nn. 11-15.

stantial and expressive liturgy. It begins with a greeting, introduction, and penitential rite (which may be replaced by sacramental penance). A Liturgy of the Word follows. Suitable readings are suggested. Friends and relatives can add a communal dimension; they may assist in the readings, as also in prayers and singing. There may be a homily, after which the sacrament is conferred. First, there is the laying on of hands — that characteristic scriptural gesture of blessing — by all the priests who are participating. Then the anointing by the minister of the sacrament of the recipient's forehead and hands, or, in case of necessity, of the forehead only or another part of the body. This anointing is also a laying on of hands, now with the blessed oil.

The sacramental sign is especially this anointing, together with the prayer that accompanies it.[29] This prayer speaks of salvation and resurrection with the wise ambiguity of St. James, and it treats the sacrament as the gift of the Holy Spirit, who is also God's first gift to the Church through the paschal mystery.

The oil used for the anointing is olive oil, although the use of another oil may be authorized if olive oil is not available. Ordinarily the oil is blessed by the bishop at the Chrism Mass on Holy Thursday, a custom that also recalls how this sacrament derives its power from the paschal mystery.

The ceremony of anointing of the sick concludes with a special prayer for the sick, followed by the Lord's Prayer, perhaps the reception of Communion, and a blessing.

THE SACRAMENTAL GRACE

The fruit of this sacrament is indicated in these words of St. James: ". . . and the prayer of faith will save the sick man, and the Lord will raise him up." The ambiguity here is simply the result of the way biblical man looks at sickness, as distinct from our modern way. He sees it, not merely as a physical reality, but as situated in man's actual condition of sin. Further, he does not distinguish clearly between body and 49 soul, but sees man as a unity; the healing is intended for the whole man.

Pope Paul VI, quoting the Council of Trent, explains and summarizes the effects of the sacrament: "This reality is in fact the grace of the Holy Spirit, whose anointing takes away sins, if any still remain to be taken away, and the remnants of sin; it also relieves and strengthens

---

[29]*Rite of Anointing . . .*, n. 76.

the soul of the sick person, arousing in him a great confidence in the divine mercy; thus sustained, he may easily bear the trials and hardships of his sickness, more easily resist the temptations of the devil 'lying in wait' (Gen. 3.15), and sometimes regain bodily health, if this is expedient for health of the soul."[30]

The sacrament of penance should precede the anointing,[31] and it would be gravely wrong to receive the sacrament of anointing of the sick while one is knowingly guilty of grave sin. If the person to be anointed is unconscious and in grave sin, but is prepared by prior acts of faith and hope and right fear of God so that he is properly disposed to receive the gifts of a sacrament, the sacrament of anointing of the sick brings forgiveness of even serious sin.

318 The sacrament draws those who receive it into that interior penance, that *metanoia,* which leads into the mystery of Christ. That such a sacrament has been instituted shows also that suffering does not of itself bring salvation; if our suffering is to be a means of healing, the Lord Himself must associate it with His death and resurrection. As St. James indicates, that is the distinctive sacramental grace of the anointing of the sick.

In all his weakness and in all his trust, the sick person encounters the healing power of the Lord's death and resurrection in this sacrament. The Lord "saves" him and "raises him up."

SICKNESS AND THE PASCHAL MYSTERY

326 The Second Vatican Council, in speaking of the anointing of the sick, showed how sufferings caused by sickness may be drawn into the paschal mystery. The whole Church, said the council, exhorts the sick "to contribute to the welfare of the People of God by associating them-
91 selves freely with the passion and death of Christ" (LG 11).

Anointing of the sick, whether or not it heals the body, becomes a remedy for the spirit in which all events are drawn together in a hopeful and joyous experience of life even in its hardships. "So we do not lose heart. Though our outer nature is wasting away, our inner nature is being renewed every day. For this slight momentary affliction is prepar-

---

[30]Pope Paul VI, Apostolic Constitution, *Sacram Unctionem Infirmorum* (November 30, 1972). Cf. Council of Trent, Session 14, November 25, 1551, *Doctrine on the Sacrament of Extreme Unction,* ch. 2 (DS 1696).
[31]Cf. *Rite of Anointing . . .,* n. 65.

ing for us an eternal weight of glory beyond all comparison . . ." (2 Cor. 4.16-17).

THE SACRAMENT OF THE DYING

Eventually all physical remedies fail. In the cycle of life in man's 343 present condition, life begins, grows, matures, declines, and ends in death. Although anointing should be given at the onset of dangerous illness or in the weakness of old age, the Church allows the sacrament to be administered again if there has been a recovery and relapse or if the danger becomes more serious. If the sickness continues or deepens, the invalid may and should receive the Eucharist regularly.

Communion received by the dying is called Viaticum, "Food for 286 the journey," here the spiritual food one takes for his last journey. In death, sign gives way to Reality; but on the journey the Eucharistic sign containing Reality is the most appropriate provision, which is the very meaning of the word Viaticum. Soon, however, the bonds of the sign will burst and Reality will be seen "face to face" (1 Cor. 13.12). 360

Even "death is swallowed up in victory" (1 Cor. 15.54), and only in death does the Christian retrieve all past losses and reap a hundredfold and receive everlasting life (cf. Matt. 19.29). The ordeal of sickness, losses and privations through various trials, and accumulating diminishments of aging, are so many little deaths, mystical deaths, as writers have called them, losses foreshadowing the final separation through death from all that is here loved. Yet in this final and complete loss, all is retrieved. In every Eucharist we say that "we wait in joyful hope for the coming of our Savior, Jesus Christ." The last, the complete healing, is the resurrection.

•　　•　　•

Questions related to the material in this chapter:

1. Why are the sacraments of penance and anointing of the sick called "sacraments of healing"?

2. When we speak of the sacrament of penance as a "tribunal" and a "judicial process," what do we mean?

3. What words does the priest speak in giving absolution? Why does he speak in the first person: "I absolve . . ."?

329

4. What is required of the penitent in the sacrament of penance?

5. What is the difference between "perfect contrition" and "imperfect contrition"?

6. What is an "indulgence"?

7. What is Church law on frequency of confession?

8. In what sense may penance be called "a laborious kind of baptism"?

9. With regard to the young, what is the suitable age for instruction in and first reception of the sacrament of penance?

10. What are ways the sacrament of penance may be celebrated? How do these acknowledge the social dimension of sin and the communal aspect of reparation?

11. Does the Church recommend regular and frequent confession? Why?

12. What does Scripture tell of anointing of the sick?

13. Does a person have to be at the point of death to receive the sacrament of anointing of the sick? Why, for example, should one receive the sacrament before surgery if a dangerous illness is the reason for the surgery?

14. What are the effects of the sacrament of anointing of the sick?

15. What is "Viaticum"?

30

Christian Marriage:
Christ and Human Love

The sacramental sign of marriage is expressed in a pledge of enduring commitment. The love of husband and wife for each other signifies God's eternal love for mankind and the love that binds together Christ and His Church.

In this chapter we discuss covenant love in marriage, the relation of virginity and marriage, and the threefold good of marriage: offspring, fidelity, and the sacrament. Also treated here are the problem of broken marriages, the actions taken by the Church to guard the married state, and the vocation of married persons to holiness.

COVENANT LOVE IN MARRIAGE

In the Old Testament, marriage was not sacred in our sense, nor was it celebrated with a religious ceremony. Yet marriage was preordained by God, who established it at the climax of creation. 44

As there are two accounts of creation, so there are two accounts of the institution of marriage. Each indicates an element of the meaning of marriage, and both themes are joined throughout the history of marriage down to the present. In the first creation account, procreation is stressed (cf. Gen. 1.27-28). In the other account, the companionship of man and woman comes to the fore (cf. Gen. 2.20-24).

God's ancient design of faithful monogamy was not preserved — because of "your hardness of heart," as Jesus was to say to the Pharisees (Matt. 19.8).

Nevertheless, exclusive attachment was prized in the Old Testament. While the wife was subject to her husband, she was no mere chattel, as with the pagans.

THE NEW COVENANT

Both the Song of Songs and Tobit introduce us into Jewish households after the exile. At this time, too, the sages who wrote the Wisdom literature were praising monogamy and urging fidelity in marriage (cf. Prov. 5.1-23, 6.20-35). Malachi wrote: "So take heed to yourselves, and let none be faithless to the wife of his youth. For I hate divorce, says the LORD the God of Israel" (Mal. 2.15-16). He here also speaks of marriage as a covenant, comparing it to the covenant of God with Israel.

The climax of this long saga of love covenant and marriage, and the point at which marriage becomes a sacrament in the New Covenant, is 220 noted in St. Paul's Epistle to the Ephesians: "Husbands, love your wives, as Christ loved the church and gave Himself up for her, that He might sanctify her, having cleansed her by the washing of water with the word, that He might present the church to himself in splendor, without spot or wrinkle or any such thing, that she might be holy and without blemish. Even so husbands should love their wives as they do their own bodies. He who loves his wife loves himself. For no man ever hates his own flesh, but nourishes and cherishes it, as Christ does the church, because we are members of His body. 'For this reason a man shall leave his father and mother and be joined to his wife, and the two shall become one.' This is a great mystery, and I mean in reference to Christ and the church" (5.25-32).

Marriage, then, is a sacrament. It is a covenant between a man and a woman, committing them to live with one another in a bond of married love whose charter was established by God. This covenant is a symbol of the undying covenant love established by Christ with His Church in the paschal mystery. It is an encounter with Christ which makes effective the graces it signifies, the graces needed to make human love enduring, faithful, and fruitful, and so a suitable image of the love between Christ and His Church.

MARRIAGE AND VIRGINITY

Although St. Paul is a striking witness to the sanctity of marriage, 236 he also commends warmly another way of life, that of virginity or celibacy (cf. 1 Cor. 7.32-34).

We have here indicated an alternate form of Christian life. A life of Christian virginity may be lived in a religious community or in the midst of secular responsibilities. For those called to such a life, virginity offers a richer freedom to give themselves more exclusively to the Lord. Virginity is a forceful way of expressing faith in eternal life while "the form of this world is passing away" (1 Cor. 7.31).

Those joined in sacramental marriage are a visible sign of God's

332

love for the Church and of God's love for mankind. They remind us all of God's love, and of the fact that all love comes from God, for "God is love" (1 John 4.16), and should lead back to God. Celibates on their part, while renouncing marriage, do not renounce love: they are rather witnesses in a special way to that greater love of Christ, of which marriage itself is a sign. They are reminders to all that married love, sacred as it is, is transitory as a means to that perfect love of God and one 295 another that we are to strive for and to have perfected in eternal life. Both married love and perfect chastity should direct the heart toward eternity and love fulfilled. The married and celibate vocations, then, far from being opposed to each other, support each other within the basic Christian vocation to seek holiness in love.

THE THREEFOLD GOOD OF MARRIAGE

"In marriage, let the goods of marriage be loved: offspring, fidelity, and the sacrament."[1] In these few words St. Augustine crystallized the teaching of faith on the purposes of matrimony, the goods for which God established and sanctified it.

Conjugal Love

"The first natural tie of human society," says St. Augustine, "is 218 man and wife."[2] The Second Vatican Council calls marriage "a commu- 207 nity of love" (GS 47). Mutual fidelity, at its minimum and considered negatively, forbids intercourse with anyone other than one's married partner; thus it is a bulwark to protect conjugal love.

Mutual and loving fidelity presupposes the fundamental equality of the partners in marriage. "Firmly established in the Lord, the unity of marriage will radiate from the equal personal dignity of wife and hus- 217 band, a dignity acknowledged by equal and total love" (GS 48). Nor can this equality be taken for granted even today. One of the Church's first tasks, in order to make Christian marriage possible, was to secure this basic personal equality. The words of Jesus recorded in the Gospel laid the foundation for this by teaching what was then a revolutionary idea, namely, that the mutual duties of husband and wife are the same: "Whoever divorces his wife and marries another, commits adultery

---

[1]St. Augustine, *De Nuptiis et Concupiscientia* 1.17.19 (ML 44.424).
[2]St. Augustine, *De Bono Coniugali* 1 (ML 40.373).

against her; and if she divorces her husband and marries another, she commits adultery" (Mark 10.11-12).

St. Paul carried this principle of equal rights into the home: "For the wife does not rule over her own body, but the husband does; likewise the husband does not rule over his own body, but the wife does. Do not refuse one another except perhaps by agreement for a reason, that you may devote yourselves to prayer" (1 Cor. 7.4-5).

The Fathers and theologians, and the Second Vatican Council, sometimes speak of conjugal love as friendship. "Friendship" may seem to some a weak word for so close a union; but "friendship" is in fact a rich concept. In sincere friendship the tie of love is enduring, for it is not based on the hope of gratification from personal traits that can fade with time, but on the free and firm commitment of each to pursue the good of the other, for the other's sake.[3] To speak of married friendship is to recognize the fundamental equality of the husband and wife, and, therefore, the possibility of intimate sharing of life not only on the physical level but also on the level of mind and spirit.

Offspring

The Second Vatican Council has reaffirmed in our time that the procreation of children is a basic good of marriage. This good cannot be assailed without harming conjugal love. The distinctive traits of marriage are ordered to the good of offspring. Married love must be faithful and enduring precisely to unite husband and wife in a love of such strength and personal concern that they can suitably carry out the duties of parents. "Marriage and conjugal love are by their nature ordained toward the begetting and educating of children. Children are really the supreme gift of marriage . . ." (GS 50). This in no way detracts from the other purposes of marriage. "Hence, while not making the other purposes of matrimony of less account, the true practice of conjugal love, and the whole meaning of family life which results from it, have this aim: that the couple be ready with stout hearts to cooperate with the love of the Creator and the Savior who through them will enlarge and enrich His own family day by day" (GS 50).

This does not mean that parents should bring children into the world irresponsibly. As we have noted in an earlier chapter, Christian couples may indeed rightly reflect on the number of children they can

---

[3] Cf. St. Thomas Aquinas, *Commentarium in Librum III Sententiarum,* q. 27, a. 2, c.

wisely bring into this world, taking into account here all relevant factors. At the same time, however, they will rule out any and all forms of 210 artificial birth control.

"God is love" (1 John 4.8). Because He is love, He has created us. His love is so vast, so limitless, that He pours it forth into creation. It is to be expected, then, that in willing to share His love with men, He would also will to share with them the creative power of His love. "Parents should regard as their proper mission the task of transmitting human life and educating those to whom it has been transmitted. They should realize that they are cooperators with the love of God the Creator, and are, so to speak, the interpreters of that love" (GS 50).

The Sacrament

The third good or blessing of marriage is sacramentality. Marriage is a covenant of indissoluble love. It is a sacred sign recalling and drawing upon the perpetual love between Christ and His Church. Like that covenant, a consummated sacramental marriage is entirely indissoluble. It endures until death.

The ministers of the sacrament of matrimony are the matrimonial partners themselves. The priest assisting at a marriage "must ask for and obtain the consent of the contracting parties" (SC 77). The consummation of the marriage seals it in a personal and mutual self-surrender of sexual union.

"Marriage arises in the covenant of marriage, or irrevocable consent, which each partner freely bestows on and accepts from the other. This intimate union and the good of the children impose total fidelity on each of them and argue for an unbreakable oneness between them. Christ the Lord raised this union to the dignity of a sacrament so that it might more clearly recall and more easily reflect his own unbreakable union with his Church."[4]

The Church teaches that marriage, even as a natural institution, cannot be dissolved by the will of the partners or by any human authority.[5] The Church does teach that by divine law marriage demands such faithfulness, and that only special divine authority can legitimately dissolve such a bond.

---

[4]Sacred Congregation of Rites, Rite of Marriage, published by authority of Pope Paul VI, March 19, 1969, Introduction, n. 2.

[5]Cf. Council of Trent, Session 24, November 11, 1563, Doctrine on the Sacrament of Matrimony (DS 1797-1799, 1807); Pope Pius XI, Encyclical, Casti Connubii (December 31, 1930) (DS 3712, 3724). Cf. GS 48-49; AA 11.

In some cases God does permit the dissolution of a purely natural bond of marriage, that is, one not contracted by two baptized persons. In the case of married unbelievers, one of whom becomes a Christian, the Church may permit the Christian to remarry, if the unbelieving spouse refuses to live peacefully with him or her. The Church has so understood the words of St. Paul (cf. 1 Cor. 7.12-16), and has judged that in such cases God gives it the right to dissolve a nonsacramental marriage. This right is called the Pauline privilege. The Church, starting from this principle and recalling the "power of the keys" given to it, continues where conditions warrant to dissolve the natural, nonsacramental marriage in favor of the faith.

But the Church has firmly proclaimed and always taught that a sacramental marriage between Christians in which there has been true matrimonial consent and consummation is absolutely indissoluble except by death of one of the partners. A sacrament recalling Christ's undying love for the Church, it is expressed in a binding tie that must endure for life.[6]

SPECIAL MARRIAGE QUESTIONS

In no area of life with all its problems do people suffer grief and anxiety more than in broken marriages. Catholics are not exempt from the pressures that make for such difficulties; the number of those divorced and perhaps remarried outside the Church presents a grave and urgent pastoral problem.

The Church, faithful to the word of Christ that excludes divorce (cf. Matt. 19.3-12; Mark 10.1-12), does not and cannot permit divorce and remarriage as a solution to these problems.[7] Precisely because it is not dissoluble, married couples are assisted in their efforts to overcome the grave obstacles that can threaten any married life.

Still the Church does, when there are grave reasons for this, permit the separation of married partners from common life together.[8] Such cases, however, never justify any claim to a right to dissolve the sacramental marriage bond, or a right to enter on a new marriage.

---

[6]See note 5.

[7]Cf. Council of Trent, Session 24, November 11, 1563, *Doctrine on the Sacrament of Matrimony*, especially canons 7 and 8 (DS 1807, 1808).

[8]Cf. *Code of Canon Law*, canon 1131; Council of Trent, Session 24, November 11, 1563, *Doctrine on the Sacrament of Matrimony*, canon 8 (DS 1808).

Some apparent marriages that "fail" were in fact never true marriages. No real marriage covenant was established if one or both of the 235 partners failed to give, or was incapable of giving, free consent; or if one or both did not intend a real marriage, a bond of faithful love at least in principle open to offspring. If for any reason an apparent marriage was not a genuine marriage from the start, it may be possible to obtain from the Church an official acknowledgment of that fact, that is, an annulment, or, more exactly, a decree of nullity.

Since divorce is forbidden by Christ, the Church wishes to guard carefully entrance into the married state. Normally Catholics can be married validly only in the presence of a priest and witnesses.[9] The priest assisting at a marriage, who is to be the bishop or pastor of the place or his delegate, has the responsibility to see that the couple is in fact free to marry, that they receive sufficient instruction to realize the importance and dignity of the sacrament they are to receive, and that they are aware of the purposes and meaning of marriage, and are entering into a genuine marriage covenant.

Impediments

To guard the married state, the Church has also the right to proclaim the existence of, and to establish, impediments to marriage. As teacher, the Church proclaims the existence of certain barriers. For example, it teaches that impotence, when it precedes the marriage and is permanent, makes a marriage invalid by the very law of nature,[10] and 181 that the same natural law excludes the possibility of a valid marriage between certain very close relatives. Other impediments the Church itself establishes to guard the faithful and to protect the sacredness of marriage. From these latter impediments the Church can, of course, dispense in appropriate circumstances.

An impediment is a circumstance which because of divine or ecclesiastical law causes a marriage to be either invalid or illicit. Those impediments which make an attempted marriage invalid or null, that is, 145 which prevent it from being a true marriage at all, are called diriment impediments. Among these are lack of sufficient age, impotence as described above, a preexisting marriage bond, prior reception of holy orders or prior assumption of a solemn vow of chastity by one of the

---

[9]Cf. *Code of Canon Law,* canon 1094.
[10]Cf. *Code of Canon Law,* canon 1068.

partners, certain close degrees of relationship, and certain prior crimes.[11] The attempted marriage of a Catholic with an unbaptized person without a prior dispensation is also declared invalid.

Other impediments established to protect the married state are called "impedient impediments." A marriage celebrated in spite of such an impediment would be a true and valid marriage, but the Church forbids such marriages — except in circumstances in which, for sufficient reasons, it grants a dispensation. Before granting a dispensation, the Church seeks to see to it that the dangers to a successful marriage that often arise from differences in faith are resolved, by taking steps to guard the faith of the Catholic partner for which the Church has special responsibility, and to provide for the proper instruction to assist each of the partners.

Invalid Marriages

A Catholic who is knowingly a partner in an invalid marriage is in reality and before God not married to his or her apparent spouse. Hence
209 performance of the marriage act within that union is not a sacred and holy seal of married love, but really a wrongful use of sex. Some solution is always possible, even in the most difficult cases. At times one must accept a considerable amount of self-denial and bear the cross generously; but God's grace is able to make even difficult burdens bearable. Those seeking a good conscience in these matters must remember that their consciences are to be formed in the light of Church teaching. Every solution that is reached must be entirely faithful to the command of Christ that consummated and sacramental marriages can in no way be dissolved or treated as though they can be.[12]

THE MARRIED VOCATION

Although indissolubility undergirds conjugal love, it does not exhaust the meaning of the marriage covenant. The Church "is believed to
121 be holy in a way which cannot fail. For Christ . . . loved the Church as His bride, delivering Himself up for her, so that He might sanctify her (cf. Eph. 5.25-26). . . . Therefore, in the Church all . . . are called to holiness" (LG 39).

---

[11]Cf. Code of Canon Law, canons 1035-1080.
[12]Cf. Congregation for the Doctrine of the Faith, Letter to Bishops of the United States of America (April 11, 1973).

338

The Second Vatican Council spoke of how that principle embraces those who enter the sacramental covenant: "Married couples and Christian parents should follow their own proper path to holiness by faithful love, sustaining one another in grace throughout the entire length of their lives. They should imbue their offspring, lovingly welcomed from God, with Christian truth and evangelical virtues. For thus can they offer all men an example of unwearying and generous love, build up the brotherhood of charity, and stand as the witnesses to and cooperators in the fruitfulness of Holy Mother Church. By such lives, they signify and share in that very love with which Christ loved His Bride and because of which He delivered Himself up on her behalf" (LG 41).

MARRIAGE AND THE PASCHAL MYSTERY

Christ's love for the Church is the pattern for married love. Christ's love was a sacrificial love, and it included suffering where necessary. "Greater love has no man than this, that a man lay down his life for his friends" (John 15.13). Such also is the love, for one another as well as for Himself, that He expects of His followers.

Now it is this sacrificial love which is the exemplar of Christian marriage and the sacrament, the mystery, the foreshadowing, through which Christ blesses the married couple. To love each other faithfully until death, they must learn to forgive each other and to bear crosses well. In raising a family, with all the joys and all the heartaches that implies, they will be required to give of self.

St. Paul exhorted: "Husbands, love your wives as Christ loved the church and gave Himself up for her . . ." (Eph. 5.25). Thus the married couple are in a special way plunged into the mystery of the Lord's death and resurrection; through this sacrament their love shares in the saving mystery of Christ and signifies its final perfection in the Church fully realized. This is why Christian marriage must be indissoluble, literally unto death.

The celebration of marriage "normally should be within the Mass."[13] This also signifies its issuance from the paschal mystery. In the wedding Mass, the Liturgy of the Word "shows the importance of Christian marriage in the history of salvation and the duties and responsibility of the couple in caring for the holiness of their children."[14]

---

[13]*Rite of Marriage,* Introduction, n. 6.
[14]*Rite of Marriage,* Introduction, n. 6.

Then in the Liturgy of the Eucharist, in which salvation history rises to its climax, the now-married couple enter the sacramental source of the paschal mystery and "eat this bread and drink this cup" to "proclaim the Lord's death until He comes" (1 Cor. 11.26). Even in its ceremony, the Church seeks to enshrine and consecrate marriage by her most sublime possession, the mystery of the faith.

*   *   *

Questions related to the material in this chapter:

1. What is the difference between marriage as seen in the Old Testament and marriage in the New Testament?

2. How do we explain the apparent paradox of a teaching that describes marriage as a sacrament and yet recommends virginity?

3. What are the "goods" of Christian marriage?

4. When we speak of the fundamental equality of husband and wife, what do we mean?

5. Children are the supreme gift of marriage. Does this mean that Catholic couples have an obligation to seek to have as many children as possible?

6. Who are the ministers of the sacrament of matrimony? What is the role of the priest?

7. Can the Church dissolve a sacramental marriage between Christians in which there has been true matrimonial consent and consummation?

8. Why must the Church reject the idea of divorce?

9. What is an "annulment" or "decree of nullity"?

10. What are "impediments" to marriage and what is their effect?

11. What do we mean when we say that Christ's love for the Church is the pattern for married love?

Part Four

IN CHRIST:
FULFILLMENT
OF ALL

31

The Death of a Christian

"It is appointed for men to die once, and after that comes judgment" (Heb. 9.27).

At the end of time, when Christ will come to pass judgment on all men, and when those who have died will rise again, the redemption of man will be brought to its total fullness. But this world, and his time of trial, ends for each man with death. In this chapter we speak of death, of the judgment which follows it, and of purgatory, hell, and heaven.

DEATH

Death has many meanings for the Christian. In a sense death is en- 46 tirely natural. But it is also seen in faith as a punishment for sin. Christian death is seen also as a sharing in the paschal mystery, a personal sharing in Christ's death so that one may share also in His resurrection.

Death Is Natural

There is "a time to be born, and a time to die" (Eccle. 3.2). Death is natural to man. Our lives are measured by time, in which we change; we grow old, and death seems even appropriate after a full life. "And the dust returns to the earth as it was, and the spirit returns to God who gave it" (Eccle. 12.7).

The natural reality of death gives an urgency to our lives. Remem- 177 brance that we are mortal serves also to remind us that we have but a limited time in which to shape good and meaningful lives.

Result of Sin

But death is also a penalty for sin. "As sin came into the world through one man and death through sin, and so death spread to all men 53 because all men sinned" (Rom. 5.12; cf. Wisd. 1.13, 2.23-24; Rom. 5.21, 6.23; James 1.15). Because of sin man suffers "bodily death, from which man would have been immune had he not sinned" (GS 18).

343

Death, then, appears to us not merely as a liberator from the burdens and limitations of earthly life, but as something fearful, the "last enemy" that will be destroyed by the all-embracing redemption of Christ (cf. 1 Cor. 15.26).

Transformed by Christ

Christ Himself shared the most bitter aspects of human death, and the Gospel accounts show in Him both anxiety and deep tranquility in the presence of death. Certainly death is not the evil which we should fear most. Even when we find death most mysterious and frightening, we are reassured by the firm testimonies of God.

"Do not fear those who kill the body of life but cannot kill the soul" (Matt. 10.28). Something of man, most proper to him, can yet live when the flesh that is part of man's reality is dissolved in death. The soul of man is not the whole of man, the temporary occupant as it were of an 42 alien body. Rather, the soul is the living principle of a man, created to give life to his body. After bodily death, this living principle continues to exist. For this reason St. Paul could confess his longing to be "away from the body and at home with the Lord" (2 Cor. 5.8). Still, to be "away from the body" is to not be a full person.[1] The departed in Christ look forward to "the resurrection of the body."[2]

REVELATION AND THE MEANING OF DEATH

Over the long periods of salvation history revelation concerning the significance of death became progressively more complete. In the 137 centuries since public revelation was completed there has been a progressively fuller understanding of this revelation.

Old Testament

In the Old Testament there is a definite awareness of the relationship between sin and death (cf. Gen. 2.16-17, 3.3, 19). There is general assurance that life and death are in the hands of God. But in earlier times there was no clear recognition that significant personal life continued after man's years on earth. Death was considered to bring reli-

---

[1] Cf. St. Thomas Aquinas, *Summa Theologica* I, 29, 1 ad 5.
[2] The Apostles' Creed.

gious activity to a close. The place into which the dead descended was called Sheol, a place of obscurity over which God continued to reign, but for which God seemed not to have much concern (cf. Ps. 6.5; Isa. 38.17-19). Because death seemed to offer man little or no comfort in terms of his fulfillment or his relationship with God, a long life on earth was viewed as a special divine favor.

Apocalyptic literature (e.g., Dan. 12.1-4) gave a new understanding of the meaning of death to the believer. God would rescue at least some men from death. "Many of those who sleep in the dust of the earth shall awake; some to everlasting life, and some to shame and everlasting contempt" (Dan. 12.2).

Wisdom literature gave an even brighter picture of human immortality. "But the souls of the righteous are in the hand of God, and no torment will ever touch them. In the eyes of the foolish they seemed to have died . . . but they are at peace. For though in the sight of men they were punished, their hope is full of immortality" (Wisd. 3.1-4).

New Testament

In New Testament times Christ was seen as the Conqueror of death. The early Christian community did not focus its reflections so much on death as on the awaited triumphal return of Christ, at which time "death shall be no more" (Rev. 21.4). The emphasis in its hope for salvation was communitarian: Christians looked for the coming of Christ that was to bring to fulfillment the lives of all His people. Hence in early New Testament times there was no great preoccupation with the death of the individual.

Faith in Christ's coming in glory remained, but as years passed and many believers died, it became clearer that the repeated warnings about the unpredictable hour of His coming were no guarantee that any living person could be certain that he would live to see it.

Concern for those who had died, and for themselves, led the living faithful to reflect more earnestly on the mystery of death. Remembrance of such words as those of Christ to the dying thief on the cross (cf. Luke 23.43) and those of Paul in his longing to be "away from the body and at home with the Lord" (2 Cor. 5.8; cf. Phil. 1.23) helped guide the Church as it reflected on death with the assistance of the Holy Spirit. The warning that Christ would come as unexpectedly as a thief (cf. Matt. 24.43-44; Luke 12.39-40; 2 Peter 3.10; Rev. 16.15) began to be understood as equally true of His coming to the individual at death. The individual life,

345

like that of the community, had to be a looking forward to Christ's coming, a life lived in constant preparedness for that event.

Only gradually, then, did a fuller understanding of faith's teaching on last things emerge. The sacramental life of the Church clarified its insight. Reception in the sacramental signs of Him whom they looked forward to greeting as their Savior intensified the longing of the faithful to be with the Lord, and helped the community to realize more fully the personal dimensions of the mystery of salvation.

In later centuries the Church's teaching on the condition of the individual after his death and before the final resurrection at the end of time was solemnly defined.

PARTICULAR JUDGMENT

Implicit in the defined teaching of the Church is the teaching that the death of an individual marks the end of his period of trial. For he is then no longer a pilgrim, and no more will he sin or earn merit. God's judgment comes upon him. Explicitly defined are the teachings that those who die in the state of grace but in need of some purification enter heaven after that purgation or cleansing is completed. Also explicitly defined is the teaching that those who die in actual mortal sin enter their unending punishment promptly after death.[3]

The Church has constantly taught that each individual will appear before God after death to receive judgment, and then begin either eternal happiness or eternal punishment, unless he died in grace but in need of further purgation.[4] The fact of this particular judgment, the judgment of each individual after death, is not explicitly defined. The teaching is, however, implicitly contained in the Church's definition concerning the fact that the reward or punishment of the individual begins promptly after the individual's death. It is suggested also in St. Paul's expression of a desire to die and to be with Christ (cf. Phil. 1.21-23; 2 Cor. 5.6-9). The teaching of the Second Vatican Council contains implicit references to the particular judgment when it says that already, before the final
351 resurrection, some of Christ's disciples "have finished with this life and

---

[3]Cf. Second Council of Lyons, Session 4, July 6, 1274, *Profession of Faith of Emperor Michael Paleologus* (DS 856-858); Pope Benedict XII, Constitution, *Benedictus Deus* (January 29, 1336) (DS 1000-1002); Council of Florence, Bull, *Laetentur Caeli* ("Decree for the Greeks," July 6, 1439) (DS 1304-1306). Cf. LG 48-49, 51; GS 17.
[4]See the references cited in note 3.

are being purified" and some "are in glory, beholding 'clearly God Himself triune and one, as He is' " (LG 49).[5]

God's judgment is not to be thought of as simply a judicial procedure.

Each individual is at the moment of his death all that he has made himself to be by his free acceptance or free rejection of the divine call and gifts. He is thus related to God and to the whole of creation at that moment in a decisive way. God's judgment clearly indicates to the individual what he has made himself to be, and it gives him the place for which he has fitted himself. In the light of divine judgment the individual recognizes and affirms what he has merited and has become. Those who have been justified in Christ and have died in the Lord experience God's judgment after death as a completion, a fulfillment of all their human efforts during life.

PURGATORY

Some die in grace in the friendship of God, but burdened with venial sins and imperfections, or before they have done suitable penance 252 for their sins. The Church teaches that the souls of these are cleansed in purgatory of these last hindrances to their entry into the vision of God. Their communion with the faithful on earth is not thereby broken. The living can bring comfort and alleviation to those in purgatory by their intercessions, by "Masses, prayers, almsgiving, and other pious works which, in the manner of the Church, the faithful are accustomed to do for others of the faithful."[6]

The word "purgatory" is not in the Bible, nor is the doctrine of purgatory explicitly taught there. But the ancient belief in purgatory is deeply grounded in what Scripture explicitly teaches about divine judg- 137 ment, on the need for holiness to enter the vision of God, and on the reality of divine temporal punishment for sins which have been forgiven.

The works of the Fathers have many references not only to the ex-

---

[5]The internal quotation is from the Council of Florence, Bull, *Laetentur Caeli* ("Decree for the Greeks," July 6, 1439) (DS 1305).

[6]Second Council of Lyons, Session 4, July 6, 1274, *Profession of Faith of Emperor Michael Paleologus* (DS 856); Council of Florence, Bull, *Laetentur Caeli* ("Decree for the Greeks," July 6, 1439) (DS 1304). Cf. Council of Trent, Session 22, September 17, 1562, *Doctrine on the Most Holy Sacrifice of the Mass*, ch. 2 (DS 1743) and canon 3 (DS 1753), and Session 25, December 3, 1563, *Decree on Purgatory* (DS 1820); etc. Cf. also LG 51, which explicitly reaffirms these teachings.

istence of purgatory, but also the fact that the faithful departed can be
279 helped by the prayers of the living, especially by the Sacrifice of the
Mass.[7] Ancient inscriptions as well show that the Mass was offered for
the departed in the earliest centuries of the Church. Very much aware
of the bonds that link us with those who have died in Christ, the Church
never ceases to remember and pray for the departed (cf. LG 50).

The Pains of Purgatory

St. Augustine says the "fire" of purgatory will be "more severe
than anything a person can suffer in this life."[8] The precise nature of the
sufferings in purgatory, however, has never been defined by the
350 Church. Certainly the greatest pain of purgatory is that of separation
from God. The soul in purgatory now realizes far more than it ever
could before the infinite goodness of God, and it suffers from knowing
that it is for a while impeded from the beatific vision by obstacles of its
own making.

Although the soul suffers, it is in peace, for it is now utterly certain
of salvation, and it knows that God wills this "purgation" for it out of
great love.

Beyond the soul's great sense of longing for God, the nature of the
punishment in purgatory is not known to us. The ordinary teaching of
the Church is that there is some positive punishment in addition to the
pains of deprivation, but there is no definitive teaching on the exact nature of this punishment.

LIMBO

Since the thirteenth century "limbo" (from the Latin limbus, meaning "border" or "hem") has been used to designate a place or state that
some persons in exceptional circumstances would come to after death.
Infants who die without being baptized are guilty of no personal sin;
neither, however, have they received saving grace in sacramental baptism, or, so it would seem, in free personal responses to grace offered in
other ways. The Church has never made any official pronouncement on
306 the reality or nature of limbo; but it does teach that baptism in some
form is required for salvation.

---

[7]Cf., e.g., St. Ephraem, Testamentum 72; St. Cyril of Jerusalem, Catechesis 23 (myst.
5). 9-10 (MG 33.1116); St. Epiphanius, Adversus Haereses Panarium 75.8 (MG 42.513);
St. John Chrysostom, In Epistulam ad Philippenses Homilia 3.4 (MG 62.203); St. Augustine, Enchiridion 110 (ML 40.283), etc.

[8]St. Augustine, Enarratio in Psalmum 37(38) 3 (ML 36.397).

Many contemporary scholars have suggested that God will provide for the eternal salvation of these persons, enabling them in some way to obtain grace by a baptism of desire before death. Revelation does not give any certainty on this point. God remains infinitely merciful, but the gifts of grace are entirely gratuitous, and we are not certain that the mercy He shows them will include the gift of supernatural beatitude.

HELL

Following the example of Christ, the Church has in all centuries warned the faithful of the "sad and lamentable reality of eternal death."[9]

There is an essential relationship between hell and the mystery of evil, and ultimately between hell and man's freedom. A refusal to be- 193 lieve in hell is a refusal to take God seriously, and also a refusal to take seriously man and his freedom and his responsibility to do good.

Old Testament

In the earliest stages of salvation history there was no real perception of the reality of hell as it came to be understood in later revelation. "Sheol" was conceived of as the place where both the good and the bad reside after death, having there a shadowy, unsatisfactory form of existence. The revelation that "Sheol" would be a place of punishment for the wicked came only gradually. With it came fuller understanding of the responsibility people have for what they do.

In time there was a growing understanding of the kind of punishment appropriate for sin. Early in the Old Testament period punishment was conceived in materialistic images, in terms of trials, illnesses, and brevity of life. Only gradually did it become clear that the deeper punishment is implicit in the very nature of sin: that to reject God is to separate oneself from the infinite Goodness for which the heart truly hungers (cf. Ps. 63.1).

New Testament

Christ spoke often of hell. When He spoke of "hell . . . the unquenchable fire" (Mark 9.43; cf. Matt. 25.31; Luke 16.22), He spoke in

---

[9]Sacred Congregation for the Clergy, *General Catechetical Directory* (April 11, 1971) n. 69. For early creedal recognitions of the everlasting reality of hell, cf. the affirmations commonly known as the "Faith of Damasus" (DS 72) and the so-called "Athanasian Creed" (DS 76).

compassion, to warn men away from this ultimate tragedy (cf. Mark 9.43-50), this "second death" (Rev. 21.8) with its permanent separation from the everlasting life in God for which man was made (cf. Matt. 25.31). Christ spoke forcefully in the images used in that time, of "hell, where their worm does not die, and the fire is not quenched" (Mark 9.47-48; cf. Isa. 66.24). In using these images Christ was not giving a literal description of hell, for the evil of separation from God cannot be adequately described. But Christ wished to call to conversion, and to warn that those who deliberately persist in malice will come to total ruin.

Frequently the New Testament refers to the punishments of hell as unending (cf. Matt. 25.46; Mark 9.43-48; 2 Thess. 1.9; Rev. 14.9-11). This entered into the ordinary teaching of the Church from the beginning. Some early theologians, notably Origen in the third century, took the position that all sinners, including even Satan, will eventually be brought to salvation. This and similar views, however, the Church has always decisively rejected, as incompatible with revealed truth, and the Church has solemnly confirmed the doctrine that punishment in hell is eternal.[10]

Nature of Punishment

There are two chief elements in the punishment of hell. Christ's words, "Depart from Me, you cursed" (Matt. 25.41), indicate what is by far the most bitter part of hell: eternal separation from the God in whom alone man can have the life he longs for. The damned also suffer pains of sense, caused by "the eternal fire" (Matt. 25.41) of which Scripture speaks.

The Church does not define the nature of that fire, but it does teach that the punishment of the damned is not only that of loss (corresponding to their turning away from God), but also a suffering caused by created realities (corresponding to their turning toward finite things in evil ways). With these there is also the endless pain of remorse, of unredeeming self-hatred, for "their worm does not die" (Mark 9.48; cf. Isa. 66.24).

---

[10]The Origenistic position was rejected by a Synod at Constantinople in 543 (DS 411); cf. also Second Council of Constantinople, Session 8, June 2, 553 (DS 433). The doctrine of eternity of hell was solemnly taught by the Fourth Lateran Council, November 1215, *The Catholic Faith* (DS 801).

Justice and Mercy

The punishment of hell is great, but is in no way excessive. Faith 31
teaches that God is just and merciful, that no one is punished more
harshly than he deserves. No one goes to hell as one predestined there 40
by God,[11] but only by deliberately and knowingly doing grave evil and
persisting in it to the end. Deeds done without real freedom, or without
sufficient understanding of their malice, do not merit the eternal damnation given to those who die in actual mortal sin.

The mystery of hell remains disturbing. Men ought to dread the
thought that persons created for eternal life could shape their wills to
unending rejection of God. But it is our comfort that the Son of God 89
chose to die on the cross to save from such punishment all who would be
willing to come to everlasting life.

ETERNAL LIFE

The Christian who unites his own dying with the death of Jesus
sees death as coming to Him and as an entering into eternal life.

The Church teaches that those who die in grace will enter into the
presence of Jesus and the beatifying vision of the Blessed Trinity.
Should they die in venial sin, or still have penance to do for forgiven
sins, there may first be a time of purification. But those who die in faith
and love may die with great peace. They are entering into life (cf. LG 48).

The Church, to be sure, makes a clear distinction between the
events that occur when the individual Christian dies and those which
will occur when Christ comes on the last day as Lord and Judge of all.
But in each case there is a coming of Christ to His own, and an entrance
into life. Already at the death of the individual what may be called the
"relative fullness" of eternal life begins for those who are rightly disposed. For already they enter into companionship with Christ, His
mother, and the blessed, and in glory behold God Himself as He is (cf.
LG 49).

Communion of Saints

The death of the individual has ecclesial significance. For the
Church is not only the family of those living in faith here on earth. It is 284

---

[11]Cf. Second Council of Orange, 529 (DS 397); Council of Trent, Session 6, January 13,
1547, Decree on Justification, canon 17 on justification (DS 1567).

351

a communion of saints. It reaches into eternity, embracing also all who are being purified to enter the blessed vision and all who are already rejoicing in the beholding of God's glory (cf. LG 49). Our union with those we love "who have gone to sleep in the peace of Christ is not in the least interrupted" (LG 49). Their entrance into life has not ended their relevance to us. Through their entrance into life we too are brought nearer to God (cf. LG 49).

356   Their blessedness is not yet totally fulfilled, for they await the final resurrection and the sharing of that flesh which is part of their being in the joy of eternal life. But the essential core of beatitude is already and 360 irrevocably theirs. They have come to see and to possess their God in the blessed vision.

They not only enjoy the blessedness of God's immediate presence, the indescribable happiness of knowing and loving God as He knows 151 and loves Himself, but they also contribute to the building of the kingdom by praying for their brothers and sisters in Christ who are still here on earth (cf. LG 49). Their happiness is intensified by the realization that they can influence the salvation of those whom they know and love. They perceive in glory the absolute goodness of God, and they share with the great "cloud of witnesses" (Heb. 12.1) the perfect peace of Christ as they await with joyful longing the final resurrection and final judgment when all will be made perfect in God.

•   •   •

Questions related to the material in this chapter:

1. What meaning does death have for the Christian?

2. What do we mean when we say that death is a penalty for sin?

3. Does any part of us actually live on after bodily death?

4. Do the Old and New Testaments show a progressive understanding of the significance of death?

5. What does the Church teach about particular judgment, the judgment of each individual after death?

6. What is purgatory? Why does the Church pray for the dead?

7. Is there any official Church teaching with regard to limbo?

8. What is hell? Does the Church teach that punishment in hell is eternal?

9. What do we mean when we say that the death of the individual has ecclesial significance? What is the communion of saints?

32

The Fulfillment of All

"Here we have no lasting city, but we seek the city which is to 190 come" (Heb. 13.14). Christian faith is not waiting for a final catastrophe to mark the end of time; rather, it looks forward with confidence to God's total deliverance of His people into perfect freedom and complete fullness of life.

In this chapter we discuss the elements that enter into this crowning of God's work in Christ: the end of history as it now is, and the transformation of the world by God; Christ's second coming, the resurrection of the body, the final judgment, and the life to come.

THE END IS THE BEGINNING

Everlasting life is not a joy or blessedness unrelated to the labors 191 and love manifest in history. It is that for which this world was made, the fullness of life "prepared for you from the foundation of the world" (Matt. 25.34).

God's plan for creation began to be fulfilled in the very act of His creating. The final triumph of God's heavenly victory has its seeds in this world.

This is one reason why man's work in this world has such impor- 40 tance and dignity. Human efforts to put intelligence and care into the service of divine love, and into the remaking of this world, are elements in the building up of God's kingdom.

God did not create man to be a merely passive recipient of His mercies. He calls men to a greater glory. God made man in His image, that by His grace men might freely work with God in history, doing His deeds, and by His mercy themselves assisting in building up fruits of 174 their labor that will never perish.

Transformation of the World

To say that this world will end is not to say that it will be utterly annihilated. It is the world as we know it that is passing away (cf. 1 Cor. 7.31; 1 John 2.17). For the world itself is to be radically transformed.

20   The material world itself will in a certain sense participate in the paschal mystery. It too will have a death or destruction that leads to rich renewal. Some passages of Scripture stress the dying aspect of this transition. "The elements will be dissolved with fire, and the earth and the works that are upon it will be burned up" (2 Peter 3.10). But, as the sacred author of that passage goes on to say: "We wait for new heavens and a new earth" (2 Peter 3.13; cf. Isa. 65.17; 66.22). St. Jerome speaks with the voice of Catholic tradition when he says in his commentary on Isaiah: "He did not say that we shall see different heavens and a different earth, but the old and ancient ones transformed into something better."[1] St. Thomas Aquinas writes of the enduring gift of creation: " 'God has formed all things that they might have being' (Wisd. 1.14) and not that they might revert to nothingness."[2]

Equally to be remembered is the promise of positive fulfillment of material creation when, in the last days, God's own saving action will bring to glorious completion all His mercies, and all the works that the just have done in His name. "The creation itself will be set free from its bondage to decay and obtain the glorious liberty of the children of God" (Rom. 8.21).

We do not know exactly how this world will be transformed, and we cannot adequately imagine the future shape of present realities. But we do know that there is a certain permanence to our temporal activity. The ultimate factor in this permanence is love, that which "never ends" (1 Cor. 13.8).

The Transforming Love of God

191   What is built on selfless, benevolent love will not pass away. It is our most important contribution to the transforming work of Christ. And like His love, it will remain. Selfless love is our contribution to the final reality, the "new creation." Toward that we labor by seeking to transform the world now by works of love.

"Behold, I stand at the door and knock; if any one hears My voice and opens the door, I will come in to him and eat with him, and he with Me. He who conquers, I will grant him to sit with Me on My throne, as I Myself conquered and sat down with My Father on His throne" (Rev. 3.20-21).

---

[1] St. Jerome, *In Isaiam* 18.65 (ML 24.644).
[2] St. Thomas Aquinas, *Quaestiones Quodlibetales* 4.4.

It is Christ who speaks, and He calls Himself "the Amen, the faithful and true witness, the beginning of God's creation" (Rev. 3.14). In Jesus the divine promises have been realized; in His humanity there already shines the glory that God will give on the last day to those who are His adopted sons and daughters in Christ.

But the new creation is described also in more social terms. "I heard a great voice from the throne saying, 'Behold the dwelling of God is with men. He will dwell with them, and they shall be His people, and God Himself will be with them; He will wipe away every tear from their eyes, and death shall be no more, neither shall there be mourning nor crying nor pain any more, for the former things have passed away. . . . It is done! I am the Alpha and the Omega, the beginning and the end. To the thirsty I will give water without price from the fountain of the water of life' " (Rev. 21.3-4, 6).

Here we find the fulfillment of the Old Testament promises. All of man's ancient enemies, death, pain, sorrow, are removed. Men's deep- 49 est longings, their thirst for an infinite good, will be satisfied. God, who is with His people even now, will be with them then in a far richer way. Then indeed we shall be made utterly different, for we shall see God as He is (cf. 1 John 3.2), not "in a mirror dimly," but "face to face" (1 Cor. 13.12).

What we shall be and have in eternal life is, however, already in its seed present in those who love Christ, who live in faith, hope, and love. Though we are but wayfarers, in a pilgrim Church, we have already within us the beginnings of eternal life. Already we have been set free from the despair and the blindness of not knowing God; already His life gives energy to us in the gifts of grace. Already we are signed with the Holy Spirit, the "guarantee of our inheritance" (Eph. 1.14).

THE PAROUSIA

Catholic faith has always looked forward with confident hope to the final coming of Christ in glory. The early Christians' "Marana tha," Aramaic for "Our Lord, come!" (1 Cor. 16.22; cf. Rev. 22.20), was an expression of their eager desire to see the final triumph of Christ's saving work. Christ indeed comes to His people in many ways, but they looked for that definitive coming of His that would crown all His mercies, end all sorrows, and bring His people to the fulfillment of all their hopes.

The awaited coming of Christ in glory is called the "Parousia." The word literally means presence or arrival; the ceremonial entry of a king or triumphant conqueror into a city was called a "parousia." The coming of Jesus, the Lord and Savior of all, will be the most joyful and triumphant of all. In His Parousia He will be universally recognized as Lord of all. On that day those who have believed in Him and served Him will be proved right; His glorification will be the beginning of the "life of the world to come."[3]

The Time of Parousia

We do not know when Jesus will come in glory. Some scriptural passages suggest it is imminent (cf., e.g., Matt. 10.33; Luke 21.32; 1 Thess. 4.13-18), while others caution against concluding that it is at hand (cf. 2 Thess. 2.1-6; 2 Peter 3.3-9).

126 Even as the early Christians longed and hoped to see His coming, they planted the Church in many places and provided for the future years. For they knew that all time is short in comparison with eternity, that with the Lord a thousand years are "as one day" (2 Peter 3.8). The actual time of Parousia is known only to God, but it will come unexpectedly, "like a thief" (2 Peter 3.10).

The expectation of Christ's coming is indeed a longing for a fulfillment that is to come. But it is also a revelation of a kingdom present even now in those who share by grace in the saving work of Christ (cf. John 12.31; 2 Cor. 5.17, 6.2). The Parousia will bring to completion what already is, for we are God's children now (cf. 1 John 3.2). The central

94 event in history is not the last day, but the resurrection of Jesus. When He rose from the dead, the "end of the ages" (1 Cor. 10.11) had already begun. In the Parousia the full glory of Christ's rising will shine forth. Its power will extend to His disciples, raising them from the dead. Its splendor will renew the whole universe, making "all things new" (Rev. 21.5).

THE RESURRECTION OF THE BODY

98 Intimately associated with Christ's Parousia is the resurrection of the dead.

45 Catholic teaching on what a man is, and on the breadth of his hope, and on the power of Christ's resurrection, demands faith in man's rising

[3]Roman Missal, The Order of Mass, Profession of Faith.

again. All men, both those who are saved and those who have rejected salvation (cf. John 5.29), will rise again with their own bodies. Those who have died will no longer be dead. The Church "firmly believes and steadfastly teaches" that "on the day of judgment all men will appear before the tribunal of Christ with their own bodies, to give an account of their deeds."[4]

Faith in our resurrection is inseparable from faith in Jesus' resurrection. For He is the new Adam; He rose not for His own sake, but as our Head, as the pattern for our rising and as the life-giving source of our new life. "Now if Christ is preached as raised from the dead, how can some of you say that there is no resurrection of the dead? But if there is no resurrection of the dead, then Christ has not been raised; if Christ has not been raised, then our preaching is in vain and your faith is in vain" (1 Cor. 15.12-14).

All Christian life, even now on earth, is a sharing in the resurrection; but our rising with Him will be fulfilled in the resurrection on the last day.

Then will be fulfilled the promise of Christ: "I am the resurrection and the life; he who believes in Me, though he die, yet shall he live" (John 11.25). For He is the Author of life (cf. John 1.4) and the living Bread come down from heaven so that those who eat of it might have ev- 284 erlasting life (cf. John 6.50).

The doctrine of the final resurrection reminds us again of what a man is, of the fact that man is not simply a spirit. It is the whole person, flesh enlivened by spirit, who accomplishes the tasks to which we have been called by God; it is the whole person who is called to life forever 44 with God.

The Same Flesh Transformed

In the final resurrection our bodies will be transformed. We do not know precisely how. But of this we are certain: "This perishable nature must put on the imperishable, and this mortal nature must put on immortality" (1 Cor. 15.53). Then shall we rejoice in the fulfillment of the ancient promises, and the last enemy, death, will be definitively conquered, "swallowed up in victory" (1 Cor. 15.54; cf. Isa. 25.8).

---

[4]Second Council of Lyons, Session 4, July 6, 1274, *Profession of Faith of Emperor Michael Paleologus* (DS 859). Cf. Fourth Council of the Lateran, November 1215, *The Catholic Faith* (DS 801). Cf. LG 48.

Christ's resurrection from the dead is the pattern for our rising. The Gospels recognize the mystery and glory of His new life, but they emphasize two points. One is the element of identity. The risen body of 96 Jesus is that very body in which He suffered and died on the cross. "See My hands and My feet, that it is I Myself" (Luke 24.39). The other point 98 is that His risen body is transformed. He "became a life-giving spirit" (1 Cor. 15.45).

So also, then, will all men who rise to new life in Christ be transformed. Each will rise as the same person he was, in the same flesh made living by the same spirit. But his life will be richly enlarged and deepened.

Bodily resurrection, implying the transformation of the whole man, will be the beginning and in a real sense the source of the definitive happiness of the community of believers in Christ.

GENERAL JUDGMENT

32   "When the Son of man comes in His glory . . . before Him will be gathered all the nations, and He will separate them one from another as a shepherd separates the sheep from the goats. . . . Then the King will say to those at His right hand, 'Come, O blessed of My Father, inherit the kingdom prepared for you from the foundation of the world' " (Matt. 25.31-34).

The general judgment will not be simply a collective summing up of all the particular and individual judgments of men after their deaths. For this last judgment will be far more than a judicial passing of sentence 191 upon the good and the evil. In and through this judgment God will establish the heavenly community, the ultimate stage of His kingdom. In judging, He will bring all to completion.

There men will be judged by their deeds of love. "I was hungry and you gave Me food, I was thirsty and you gave Me drink" (Matt. 25.35). Men will be judged according to their relationship to Christ. Not only those who know Him explicitly in the light of clear faith, but all men, at least in obscure but real ways, are affected in this life by His saving power. He invites all to respond freely to His saving love, and He invites all to life. To love Him is to keep the great command of love, to love God with the whole heart and to love the neighbor in whom He dwells. At the last judgment, then, each man will be judged by the love he has shown Christ in our midst.

Christ as Judge

It is God who judges. The final judgment of all men will be shared 61 in by the three Persons of the Trinity, each in a way befitting His role in redemption. Because it is through the incarnate Word that the Blessed Trinity has saved us, it is Christ as man who is presented as the supreme Judge of men. "He is the one ordained by God to be judge of the living and the dead" (Acts 10.42). This will be the crowning act of Christ as Savior. Through it He will complete His work as Redeemer, because through it He will bring about His Father's will that all might be made one, that they might be gathered into the final kingdom.

Christ's goodness will shine even in the condemnation of those who have rejected God, who have said no to the love that is the center and crown of existence, who have refused to build up the kingdom of justice, mercy, and peace. Christ's just sentence will recognize and confirm their own deliberate and definitive rejection of God. His holiness will be exalted by the manifest fairness of His condemnation of those who have freely chosen not to respond to that Love which called them to 170 a life to which they could come only freely. The condemned will be bitterly aware that it is they themselves who have freely rejected the saving mercy of their Lord.

The centrality and lordship of Christ will shine in the hour of judgment; so also will His boundless love for the Father and His will to draw us to that first Source of all that is good.

ETERNAL LIFE

To enter heaven is not simply to go to a particular place. Heaven is more a way of being, a sharing in divine life and joy, than a place. Still, for human beatitude, place is not entirely irrelevant. Jesus has risen bodily, and where His living humanity is it is good for those who love 96 Him to be. We do not know where heaven is, but we do know that God is able to provide for the bodily creatures He has made a splendor to adorn their glorious life in Him.

The scriptural expectation of "new heavens and a new earth" (2 Peter 3.13; cf. Isa. 65.17; 66.22; Rev. 21.1) seem to suggest that in the age to come the whole renewed universe will be heaven to those who have loved God and dwell in His light.

To enter heaven is to reach the fullness of life for man. Even here, in this present life, we share in divine life by faith, hope, and love. But

359

353 our eternal life in time is only a seed, a promise; it imperfectly expresses and points us toward that fullness of life we shall have in heaven. Then, when faith is no more, because we shall see God as He is, and when we no longer hope, because the promises of God will be completely fulfilled, and when we love with a gladness no one will take from us (cf. John 16.22), then we shall live with the fullness of eternal life for which we were made.

God Is Our Beatitude

217   Those who come to eternal life will enjoy every manner of blessing, but the heart of their joy will be the possession of God Himself.

No longer shall we see Him merely by faith, but we shall see Him "face to face" (1 Cor. 13.12). "We shall be like Him, for we shall see Him as He is" (1 John 3.2). Those who enter eternal life "see the divine essence intuitively and face to face, with no creature acting as a medium of vision for what they see, but with the divine essence showing itself to them plainly, clearly, and openly," and by so grasping and rejoicing in
239 the immediately present reality of God they are "truly happy and have life and eternal rest."[5]

To possess God in that way is far more than simply to "see" Him or to know Him. As His infinite life is His knowing and loving and His rejoicing in infinite goodness, so God brings those who come to eternal life to share intensely in His inner life. "Enter into the joy of your master" (Matt. 25.21).

Then we shall understand why we have been called by God to love,
110 as we see in the Blessed Trinity the pattern of all love. Then we shall see what it is to be a person, and how being a person is being called to community and the giving of self. The inner life of the Trinity is personal self-giving. The Father communicates Himself totally to the Son, giving Him all that He has and is, while remaining the Father. The Father and the Son in boundless love communicate Their whole being to the Spirit, giving Him all that He has and is, while remaining distinct from Him. In the glory of God's kingdom we shall not only see the eternally generous love of the Trinity; we shall be invited to be shaped by it as fully as possible. We shall taste Their joy in giving ourselves fully to the Father, Son, and Holy Spirit, and to one another, when God has strengthened and transformed our love.

---

[5]Pope Benedict XII, Constitution, *Benedictus Deus* (January 29, 1336) (DS 1000).

Our Native Land

Then only shall we cease to be pilgrims and strangers (cf. Heb. 11.13), and we shall know that we have come to the land where we are fully at home. Our period of exile (cf. 1 Peter 1.17) will be ended when we have come to the Life to which our whole heart can give itself in gladness. Then shall we begin to know one another fully, in the light of God, and love one another entirely. We shall remember and understand all the experiences and trials of this life without regret, infinitely grateful that God has enabled us to serve Him freely and has crowned His first gifts with the second life that exceeds all our longing. 174

Each shall be perfectly happy in knowing and loving the Blessed Trinity and all his brothers and sisters in Christ. But though each will 217 have all the understanding and joy he can bear, the gladness of the blessed will differ according to the measure of each one's love (cf. 1 Cor. 15.41-42). Some are rewarded in clarity of vision "more perfectly than others according to their respective merits."[6] But this difference is known and rejoiced in without jealousy, for each is filled with all the gladness he is capable of.

To this life, which we now understand so poorly, Christ earnestly invites us. Now, in time, He calls out to us through the promptings of His Holy Spirit and the voice of His Bride, the Church. "The Spirit and the Bride say, 'Come.' And let him who hears say, 'Come.' And let him who is thirsty come, let him who desires take the water of life without price" (Rev. 22.17).

.   .   .

Questions related to the material in this chapter:

1. Is there any relation between this world of history and the world to come? Do the good things of this world have lasting value?
2. What do we mean when we say that the world we know will be transformed?
3. Christian faith looks forward to Christ's second coming. His final coming in glory will be at the end of time, His Parousia. When will this occur?

---

[6]Council of Florence, Bull, *Laetentur Caeli* (July 6, 1439) (DS 1305).

361

4. When Christ comes again in glory, the dead will rise again. Is "resurrection of the body" to be understood symbolically or literally? Will the dead rise in their own bodies? Will these bodies be in any way transformed?

5. In what way will the end of time and bodily resurrection be a beginning rather than an end?

6. At the general judgment, the final judgment of all at the end of time, who will be judge?

7. What is heaven? Do we know where heaven is? Are those in heaven truly happy?

8. Why is it appropriate to speak of heaven as "our native land"?

APPENDIXES

The Bible

Throughout this catechism we have referred to the Bible and to particular sections within it. Even though it is now commonly published as a single volume, the Bible actually consists of a collection of sacred writings, or scriptures, composed over the course of many centuries. They are entirely exceptional writings, which the Church recognizes in faith as God's special message to those whom He calls. All of the Church's teaching and preaching must be nourished and regulated by Holy Scripture. "For in the sacred books, the Father who is in heaven meets His children with great love and speaks with them; and the force and power in the word of God is so great that it stands as the support and energy of the Church, the strength of faith for her sons, the food of the soul, the pure and perennial source of spiritual life. Consequently, these words are perfectly applicable to Sacred Scripture: 'For the word of God is living and efficient' (Heb. 4.12) and it is 'able to build up and give the inheritance among all the sanctified' (Acts 20.32; cf. 1 Thess. 2.13)" (DV 21).

Inspiration and Inerrancy

Other groups besides Christians possess and revere collections of religious literature, but the distinguishing characteristic of the Bible is its divine inspiration. Acting as the principal Author, God moved ("inspired") the human authors of the Scriptures to understand and freely will to write precisely what He wished them to write. Being God's word in this unique fashion did not keep the Scriptures from being cast in a rich variety of literary forms ranging from intricate and mystical psalm prayers to highly interpretative and often poetically formulated styles of religious historical narratives. Though common in the ancient Near East and as accurate as our contemporary equivalents, these literary forms can at times be very enigmatic to modern readers. Yet, because it is divine as well as human, the Bible achieves the varieties of communication peculiar to each of these forms free from any error regarding that which the divine Author wished specifically to express.

The dual traits of inspiration and inerrancy have been recognized and taught by the People of God since even before the Bible was completed. Corresponding to these qualities of the text of Scripture, the Church possessed the ability in faith first to distinguish and then to preserve and use the various parts or "books" of what came to be called the Bible. These divinely inspired works were produced over a period of more than a thousand years.

The official or standard list of these inspired writings is still referred to by the Greek word "canon," a word used among the early Christians and meaning a measuring standard or rule. The Canon of Scripture is divided into two main sections, called the Old Testament and the New Testament, and these contain the books written before and after the life of Jesus respectively. This terminology derives from the testaments or contractual agreements dominating the relationship between God and His people ratified at Sinai (the Mosaic Covenant) and at the Last Supper (the New Covenant).

Content and Arrangement

There is no universally accepted sequence which the Old Testament canon follows, although the most frequent pattern places historical materials first (within this class the first five books of the Old Testament form a special set, often called the Pentateuch, or the Mosaic books, or the *Torah,* the Law), followed by so-called wisdom or sapiential literature, and then prophetic or exhortational writings. When this division is used, the books of the Old Testament (some of which have alternative names) are typically listed in the following order:

The Pentateuch
    Genesis
    Exodus
    Leviticus
    Numbers
    Deuteronomy

The Historical Books
    Joshua (Josue)
    Judges

Ruth
1 Samuel (1 Kings)
2 Samuel (2 Kings)
1 Kings (3 Kings)
2 Kings (4 Kings)
1 Chronicle (1 Paralipomenon)
2 Chronicles (2 Paralipomenon)
Ezra (1 Esdras)
Nehemiah (2 Esdras)
Tobit (Tobias)
Judith
Esther
1 Maccabees (1 Machabees)
2 Maccabees (2 Machabees)

The Wisdom Books

Job
Psalms
Proverbs
Ecclesiastes (Qoheleth)
Song of Songs
Wisdom
Sirach (Ecclesiasticus)

The Prophets

Isaiah (Isaias)
Jeremiah (Jeremias)
Lamentations
Baruch
Ezekiel (Ezechiel)
Daniel
Hosea (Osee)
Joel
Amos
Obadiah (Abdias)
Jonah (Jonas)
Micah (Michaeas)
Nahum
Habakkuk (Habacuc)
Zephaniah (Sophonias)
Haggai (Aggeus)

Zechariah (Zecharias)
Malachi (Malachias)

A standardized order of the New Testament books is more commonly found. It begins with the four accounts of events in the life of Jesus called Gospels. The word "gospel" means "good news," a term Christianity has applied from earliest times to its Founder's presence and deeds and their saving effects. All four canonical Gospels present the "good news" in this basic sense. Differences in the evangelists' choice of material and manner of retelling it (vocabulary, sequence, inclusion of details, and the like) evidence the different readerships for which the Gospels were originally designed as well as the theological emphases of their human composers. The fifth book in the New Testament canon is the Acts of the Apostles, in which we have an historical record of the first decades of the Church. Next are the Epistles, letters of instruction and correction written to the first Christian communities by their apostolic pastors. Varying in length from the sixteen chapters of the Epistle to the Romans down to the few sentences of the Second and Third Epistles of St. John, they preserve a treasure of details about the joys and problems of the first-century Church. The last book of the New Testament, and hence of the Bible, is Revelation, known also as the Apocalypse. This is a highly symbolic depiction of the final triumph of Christ, the punishment of His adversaries, and the establishment of the just in heaven to praise and share the divine glory. The New Testament canon, then, is as follows:

Gospels: Matthew
Mark
Luke
John
The Acts of the Apostles
Epistles: Romans
1 Corinthians
2 Corinthians
Galatians
Ephesians
Philippians
Colossians
1 Thessalonians
2 Thessalonians

1 Timothy
2 Timothy
Titus
Philemon
Hebrews
James
1 Peter
2 Peter
1 John
2 John
3 John
Jude
Revelation (Apocalypse)

For a period of time shortly before the rise of Protestantism in the sixteenth century certain critics questioned the canonical authenticity or divine inspiration of some parts of the Bible. To some extent at least this was a revival of questions raised in some quarters centuries earlier. The Council of Trent (Session 4, April 8, 1546) resolved any doubts in this area for Catholics by declaring that all the books of the Old and New Testaments (as listed above) were equally inspired in their entirety, a declaration reaffirmed by both the First and Second Vatican Councils. One surviving residue of the historical disagreement is reflected in Catholic authors' references to the sections that had been called into question as "deuterocanonical," while some or all of the same material is usually labeled "apocryphal" by other church groups which exclude some or all of it from their Bibles or include the parts they consider noncanonical in separate appendixes. The word "deuterocanonical" means literally "of or pertaining to a second canon." The Council of Trent did not establish a new list of the books of the Bible, but rather it formally confirmed the canonicity of all parts of the list fixed in tradition more than a thousand years earlier. The deuterocanonical parts of the Bible are Tobit, Judith, 1 Maccabees, 2 Maccabees, Wisdom, Sirach, Baruch, and parts of Esther and Daniel, and, in the New Testament, Hebrews, James, 2 Peter, 2 John, 3 John, Jude, and Revelation.

Interpretation and Use

Just as it has the exclusive ability to distinguish which writings constitute the Bible, the Church alone possesses the means to understand and interpret Scripture infallibly. Since God chose a literature and culture already separated from us by more than nineteen centuries, continual research into the world of the human authors and their contemporaries is the indispensable cost of further insight into the sacred text. To help those without special training to read this literature, the Catholic Church has long insisted on the tradition that editions of the Bible include notes explaining unusual or disputed passages.

Moreover, because God and His Self-revelation infinitely transcend and surpass us, His help is an absolute necessity if we are to expand our horizons, so limited by sin, apathy, and human nature itself. The use of the Bible by groups or individuals remains an occasion for God's continuous grace and enlightenment to those who avail themselves of its riches. This is why the Church so strongly urges that studying and praying from the Bible be the lifelong project of every Christian. The Catholic reads and studies the Scriptures always within the Family and Spirit of the Church. "Sacred tradition and Sacred Scripture form one sacred deposit of the word of God, which is committed to the Church. . . . The task of authentically interpreting the word of God, whether written or handed on, has been entrusted exclusively to the living teaching office *(Magisterium)* of the Church, whose authority is exercised in the name of Jesus Christ. This teaching office is not above the word of God, but serves it, teaching only what has been handed on, listening to it devoutly, guarding it scrupulously and explaining it faithfully in accord with a divine commission and with the help of the Holy Spirit; it draws from this one deposit of faith everything which it presents for belief as divinely revealed. It is clear, therefore, that sacred tradition, Sacred Scripture and the teaching authority *(Magisterium)* of the Church, in accord with God's most wise design, are so linked and joined together that one cannot stand without the others, and that all together and each in its own way under the action of the one Holy Spirit contribute effectively to the salvation of souls" (DV 10).

Appendix II

The General Councils of the Church

A general or ecumenical council is an assembly of the bishops of the Church gathered together to consider and make decisions on ecclesiastical matters: on the doctrine, discipline, liturgy, and life of the Church. Decisions of a general council are binding on all members of the faithful. Church law, reflecting the teaching on the role of Peter in the Church, requires that a general council be called by and be approved by the Holy Father. No assembly of bishops can be a general council unless it is convoked by, or its convocation is approved by, the Roman Pontiff; no decrees or actions of a general council are effective and binding unless they are approved by the Roman Pontiff.

There have been twenty-one general councils. These are listed below with their dates. The first eight general councils were held in the Greek-speaking East; all subsequent ones have been held in the West. The first general council was held in Nicaea in the year 325; the most recent was held at the Vatican in 1962-1965. The spacing of the general councils in the history of the Church has varied widely. There were two general councils in the fourth century, two in the fifth, one in the sixth, one in the seventh, one in the eighth, one in the ninth, none in the tenth or eleventh, three in the twelfth, three in the thirteenth, one in the fourteenth, two in the fifteenth, two in the sixteenth, and then none until the latter half of the nineteenth century. A mere sixteen years separated the ninth and tenth general councils; more than three centuries elapsed between the nineteenth and twentieth.

1. First General Council of Nicaea, 325.
2. First General Council of Constantinople, 381.
3. General Council of Ephesus, 431.
4. General Council of Chalcedon, 451.
5. Second General Council of Constantinople, 553.
6. Third General Council of Constantinople, 680-681.
7. Second General Council of Nicaea, 787.
8. Fourth General Council of Constantinople, 869-870.
9. First General Council of the Lateran, 1123.
10. Second General Council of the Lateran, 1139.

11. Third General Council of the Lateran, 1179.
12. Fourth General Council of the Lateran, 1215.
13. First General Council of Lyons, 1245.
14. Second General Council of Lyons, 1274.
15. General Council of Vienne, 1311-1312.
16. General Council of Constance, 1414-1418.
17. General Council of Basel-Ferrara-Florence, 1431-1445.
18. Fifth General Council of the Lateran, 1512-1517.
19. General Council of Trent, 1545-1563.
20. First General Council of the Vatican, 1869-1870.
21. Second General Council of the Vatican, 1962-1965.

Fathers and Doctors of the Church

Christian writings contain frequent references to "Fathers of the Church" and "Doctors of the Church." The two terms are not synonymous, but to some extent they overlap in meaning. Both are titles applied to certain ecclesiastical writers. Both refer to teachers, witnesses of authentic Christian tradition.

From a very early date the title "father" was applied to bishops as witnesses of the Christian tradition. Bishops were teachers, and this was in accord with the concept of teachers as fathers of their students. We find this in St. Paul, who wrote to the Corinthians: "For though you have countless guides in Christ, you do not have many fathers. For I became your father in Christ Jesus through the gospel" (1 Cor. 4.15). In time the term came to be used in a more comprehensive sense, being extended to ecclesiastical writers who were not bishops but who were accepted as representative of the tradition of the Church. St. Jerome, for example, was not a bishop, but was numbered by St. Augustine among the Fathers. Already in the early centuries of the Church, the teaching of the earlier Fathers was being cited by later Fathers as proof of the authentic faith.

Today the title "Fathers of the Church" is applied only to those writers who combine four necessary qualifications: orthodoxy of doctrine, holiness of life, ecclesiastical approval, and antiquity. Each of these qualifications is to be considered in a broad sense. The ecclesiastical approval required may be either explicit, formally expressed by the Church magisterium, or implicit, that is, evident in the practice and custom of the Church.

The patristic era, the time of the Fathers, is not an age precisely determined by fixed dates. While in one sense the apostles themselves were "Fathers of the Church," the patristic era as a literary period is held to begin with the first noncanonical (that is, non-Scripture) Christian writings. The authors of these writings which have survived from the first and early second centuries are sometimes called the "Apostolic Fathers," indicating that they had personal contact with apostles or were instructed by disciples of the apostles. The term "Apostolic Father" was not known in the early Church. It is a term introduced by scholars in the seventeenth century and has been used for St. Clement of Rome, St. Ignatius of Antioch, St. Polycarp of Smyrna, Hermas, Papias of Hieropolis, and the unknown authors of the *Epistle of Barnabas*, the *Epistle to Diognetus*, and the *Didache*.

The patristic age is generally considered to end with St. John of Damascus (d. 749) in the East, and, in the West, with St. Gregory the Great (d. 604) or St. Isidore of Seville (d. 636), though some would extend the period to include St. Bede the Venerable (d. 735).

Near the end of the thirteenth century, Pope Boniface VIII declared that he wished St. Ambrose, St. Jerome, St. Augustine, and St. Gregory the Great to be known as "outstanding teachers (doctors) of the Church" (*egregii doctores ecclesiae*). These four saints are also called "the great Fathers of the Church." The four "great Fathers of the East," all also designated Doctors of the Church, are St. Basil the Great, St. Gregory of Nazianzus, St. John Chrysostom, and St. Athanasius.

Although some Fathers of the Church are also Doctors of the Church, "antiquity" is not required for one to be declared a Doctor of the Church. In addition to orthodoxy of doctrine and holiness of life, Doctors of the Church are recognized for the eminence of their learning and the excellence of their teaching. A further requirement is explicit proclamation as a Doctor of the Church by a pope or general council.

The number of Doctors of the Church now stands at 32. The first saints to be so designated were those noted above as declared such by Pope Boniface VIII, in 1295. The latest to be declared Doctors of the Church, in 1970 by Pope Paul VI, and the first female saints to be so designated, are St. Teresa of Avila and St. Catherine of Siena.

Catholic Prayers

In this appendix we include some of the most cherished prayers of the Church that are found often on the lips of Catholics.

Our Father

> Our Father, who art in Heaven,
> hallowed be Thy name;
> Thy kingdom come;
> Thy will be done on earth as it is in heaven.
> Give us this day our daily bread;
> and forgive us our trespasses
> as we forgive those who trespass against us;
> and lead us not into temptation,
> but deliver us from evil. Amen.

Sign of the Cross

The Sign of the Cross is a simple and profound prayer. In part it is an action or gesture. One marks oneself with the cross to show faith in Christ's saving work. A cross is described on the body by the right hand moving from the forehead to the breast, and then from shoulder to shoulder. In the Western Church the cross stroke is made from left to right; in the Eastern Church from right to left. While tracing the sign of the cross, one says: "In the name of the Father, and of the Son, and of the Holy Spirit." This formula, which recalls the words of Christ sending His apostles to teach and baptize (cf. Matt. 28.19), expresses here an act of faith in the Blessed Trinity.

Glory Be to the Father

> Glory be to the Father,
> and to the Son, and to the Holy Spirit.
> As it was in the beginning,
> is now, and ever shall be,
> world without end. Amen.

Hail Mary

Hail Mary, full of grace,
the Lord is with you;
blessed are you among women,
and blessed is the fruit of your womb, Jesus.
Holy Mary, Mother of God,
pray for us sinners,
now and at the hour of our death. Amen.

The Rosary

The rosary is a popular form of prayer that combines meditation on the mysteries of faith with the recitation of vocal prayers. A "decade" of the rosary corresponds to each of the fifteen mysteries commemorated in the rosary. Ten Hail Marys are said for each decade; they are preceded by an Our Father and followed by a Glory Be to the Father. While reciting a decade of the rosary, one is to meditate on the particular mystery for that decade and on its meaning for our life. The entire rosary is divided into three chaplets: the joyful, the sorrowful, and the glorious mysteries. To "say a rosary" commonly means to pray one such chaplet of five mysteries. Commonly a chaplet is preceded by the recitation of the Apostles' Creed and of an Our Father and three Hail Marys, offered as a petition for an increase of faith, hope, and love. The Church has long recommended this form of prayer as a convenient and effective way of meditating on the great mysteries of our salvation.

The Joyful Mysteries

1. The Annunciation.
2. The Visitation of Mary to Elizabeth.
3. The Nativity.
4. The Presentation of Jesus in the Temple.
5. The Finding of Jesus in the Temple.

The Sorrowful Mysteries

1. The Agony of Jesus in the Garden.
2. The Scourging at the Pillar.
3. The Crowning with Thorns.
4. The Carrying of the Cross.
5. The Crucifixion.

The Glorious Mysteries

1. The Resurrection of Jesus.
2. The Ascension of Jesus into Heaven.
3. The Descent of the Holy Spirit upon the Apostles.
4. The Assumption of Mary into Heaven.
5. The Coronation of Mary as Queen of Heaven.

The Apostles' Creed

I believe in God, the Father almighty, Creator of heaven and earth.

And in Jesus Christ, His only Son, our Lord; who was conceived by the Holy Spirit, born of the Virgin Mary, suffered under Pontius Pilate, was crucified, died, and was buried. He descended into hell; the third day He arose again from the dead; He ascended into heaven, sits at the right hand of God the Father almighty; from thence He shall come to judge the living and the dead.

I believe in the Holy Spirit, the Holy Catholic Church, the communion of saints, the forgiveness of sins, the resurrection of the body, and life everlasting. Amen.

Acts of Faith, Hope, and Love

Faith

O my God, I firmly believe that You are one God in three Divine Persons, the Father, the Son, and the Holy Spirit. I believe in Jesus Christ, Your Son, who became man and died for our sins, and who will come to judge the living and the dead. I believe these and all the truths which the Holy Catholic Church teaches, because You have revealed them, who can neither deceive nor be deceived. Amen.

Hope

O my God, trusting in Your infinite goodness and promises, I hope to obtain pardon of my sins, the help of Your grace, and life everlasting, through the merits of Jesus Christ, my Lord and Redeemer. Amen.

Love

O my God, I love You above all things, with my whole heart and soul, because You are all-good and worthy of all my love. I love my neighbor as myself for love of You. I forgive all who have injured me, and I ask pardon of all whom I have injured. Amen.

Act of Contrition

O my God, I am heartily sorry for having offended You, and I detest all my sins, because I dread the loss of heaven and the pains of hell, but most of all because they offend You, my God, who are all-good and deserving of all my love. I firmly resolve, with the help of Your grace, to confess my sins, to do penance, and to amend my life. Amen.

Morning and Evening Prayers

Morning Offering

O my God, I adore You, and I love You with all my heart. I thank You for having created me and saved me by Your grace, and for having preserved me during this night. I offer You all my prayers, works, joys, and sufferings of this day. Grant that they may be all according to Your will and for Your greater glory. Keep me from all sin and evil, and may Your grace be with me always. Amen.

Evening Prayer

O my God, I adore You, and I love you with all my heart. I thank You for having created me and saved me by Your grace, and for having preserved me during this day. I pray that You will take for Yourself whatever good I might have done this day, and that You will forgive me whatever evil I have done. Protect me this night, and may Your grace be with me always. Amen.

Grace at Meals

Before Meals

Bless us, O Lord, and these Your gifts, which we are about to receive from Your bounty. Through Christ our Lord. Amen.

After Meals

We give You thanks, almighty God, for these and all the gifts which we have received from Your bounty. Through Christ our Lord. Amen.

Prayers for the Dead

Sacred Scripture reminds us that it is good to pray for the dead (cf. 2 Macc. 12.39-45). We have a special obligation to ask God's mercy on those of our parents, family members, relatives, friends, and benefactors who have gone from this world and await the final judgment of God. The Book of Psalms has a beautiful prayer (cf. Ps. 130) that the Church has long used in prayers for the departed. Christian prayers for the dead usually end with the Eternal Rest, a plea for God's mercy.

Eternal rest grant unto them, O Lord,
and let perpetual light shine upon them.
May they rest in peace. Amen.

Index

Augustine, St., 26, 60, 140, 150, 151, 155, 159, 174, 186, 306, 333, 348, 373, 374

authority, in the Church, 124-130, 145-146; of pope over universal Church, 127-128; of bishop in diocese, 129-130; service of, 297; public, civil, 218-220, 224-225; the need for universal public authority, 226-227

baptism, 111, 118, 119, 131, 146, 149, 172, 271, 272, 275, 282, 293, 300-308; salvation history and, 300-303; rite of, 303-304; formula of, 303; minister of, 303; godparents, 303-304; effects of, 304-306; cleanses from sin, 305-306; makes children of God, 304, 319; imprints permanent seal, 308; gives apostolic vocation, 233; necessity of, 307-308; infant, 306-307; of desire, 307-308; of blood, 307; provides sacramental bond of unity, 160

Basil the Great, St., 374

beatitudes, the, 244

Bede the Venerable, St., 374

Benedict, St., 238

Benedict XII, pope, 346, 360

Benedict XV, pope, 137

Bethlehem, 59

Bible, 365-370; books of and order, 366-369; deuterocanonical parts of, 369; heritage of Old Testament of, 156; origin in the Church of New Testament writings of, 139; inspiration of, 56-57, 104, 125, 139, 165-166, 369; inerrancy of, 26, 104, 306; interpretation of, 36, 37, 139, 369-370; reading and study of, 56-57, 370; see also Scripture

birth control, 210-212, 334-335

bishops, Christ acts in, 133; successors of the apostles, 126, 130, 137, 292; receive "sure gift of truth," 138; are authentic teachers, 129, 137, 141; college of, 128-129, 137, 145; in ecumenical councils, 128-129; in dioceses, 129-133; ordain, 292; ordinary ministers of confirmation, 292; see also Synod of Bishops

blasphemy, 197, 322

Blessed Sacrament, adoration of, 286-287; see also Eucharist

body, sacredness of the, 42; resurrection of the, 43, 344, 356-358

Boniface VIII, pope, 374

bread, symbol of unity, 283; unleavened, 277

brethren, separated, 130-131, 158-162

Bride of Christ, the Church, 121; see also Church

Buddhism, 163

councils *(continued)*

Vatican II: citations of Vatican II documents appear throughout the catechism text
Vienne: 209, 372
counsels, the Gospel, 235-238
covetousness, capital sin, 246
creation, in Genesis, 36, 42; doctrine of, 34-35; in, through, and for, 65-66; man in springtime of his, 44-47; invisible, 35, 41
creed, creeds, 103, 122, 123; Apostles', 34, 93, 257, 344; of Nicaea I, 63; of Constantinople I, 21, 63, 114, 122; Athanasian, 109, 349; Faith of Damasus, 349; of Mass, 21, 97, 101, 103, 356
Cyprian, St., 121, 131
Cyril of Alexandria, St., 62, 63
Cyril of Jerusalem, St., 348

Dante, 32
David, 309
deacons, 294-295
death, human, 24; the "last enemy," 344; revelation and meaning of, 344-346; ecclesial significance of, 351-352; particular judgment after, 346-347; eternal, hell, 349-351
Decalogue, the, 183
deposit of faith, preserving the, 136; Scripture and tradition form one sacred, 139
despair, sin of, 197
devil, devils, 54, 246
diaconia of authority, 126, 297
Didache, 192, 278, 374
diocese, entrusted to bishop, 129-130; authority in, 129-130
discernment of spirits, 107
dispensations, from marriage impediments, 338
Divine Office, 262, 264-265; "work of God," 238; *see also* Liturgy of the Hours
docetism, 72
Doctors of the Church, 373-374
doctrine, irreformable formulations of, 142; differences in expressions of, 160; development of, 137
"Dormition," feast of Mary's, 154
Duns Scotus, John, 76

Hail Mary, 256, 376

heaven, 20; perfect fulfillment, 21; to be merited, 20; beatific vision, eternal life, 351-352, 359-361; perfect happiness in, 361

hell, 343, 349-351; Old Testament concepts, 349; in New Testament, 349-350; no one predestined to, 351; eternal punishments of, 349, 350

heresy, heresies, 114, 141, 158-159; what heresy is, 158-159, 197

Hermas, 374

Herod, 88

hierarchy, Church, 124-130; scriptural foundation of, 125-126

hierarchy of truths, 109

Hinduism, 163

Holy Communion, see Communion

holy days of obligation, 146

Holy Hours, 287

Holy Office, 131, 193, 209, 214, 257

Holy Saturday Vigil, 300-302, 310

Holy Spirit, 101-108; gradual revelation of, 101-103; in faith and doctrine, 103; inspired Scripture, 104, 139; promised by Christ, 101, 103; sending of the, 103, 112; coming on Pentecost, 104; mission of, 107-108; and the Church, 104-105; "soul" of the Church, 104; guides the Church, 108; Paraclete, 103; Counselor, 103, 111; Sanctifier, 105; in the faithful, 101, 105-107; gifts of, 105-107, 243-244, 313; fruits of, 244, 313; devotion to, 103-104

Holy Thursday, 301, 321

homosexual acts, 207, 209

hope, virtue of, 190-192; and self, 190; and this world, 190-191; act of, 377; sin against, 197

human race, unity of, 42

humility, virtue of, 198

"hypostasis," 63

Ignatius Loyola, St., 238

Ignatius of Antioch, St., 121, 275, 294, 374

ignorance, invincible, 180; culpable, 180-181

Immaculate Conception, 76; definition of, 76

impediments, marriage, 337-338

impotence, 337

incest, 207

indwelling, divine, 240, 241-242, 313

indulgences, 319-320

Jesus Christ (continued)

120, Prince of Shepherds, 127; Physician, 315; Founder of the Church, 21, 117, 118; Teacher, 17, 113, 171, 248; the Way, 83; the Way, Truth, and Life, 21, 153; Model and Teacher of prayer, 248; Exemplar of life, 171

Jews, Christian relations with, 157-158; see also Israel, Judaism

Job, 50-51

John XXIII, pope, 180, 182, 213, 216, 218, 222, 223, 224, 226

John, St., apostle, 88

John Chrysostom, St., 348, 374

John of Damascus, St., 154, 250, 320

John the Baptist, St., 70, 71, 79, 80, 301

Jordan, 79

Joseph, St., 70, 102, 154-155; patron of universal Church, 155

joy, Christian, 231

Judaism, 156-158; see also Israel, Jews

judgment, particular, 346-347, 351; the final, 352, 353, 358

justice, divine, 53; in political community, 225-226; need to be concerned with, 226-228; education for, 225-226; cardinal virtue, 243

justification, 240-241

Justin Martyr, St., 294

keys of the kingdom, 125-126, 127, 316; Peter granted power of the, 146, 316

Kyrios, 98

laity, vocation of, 232-235; special obligation for renewal of temporal order, 233; and the apostolate, 233-235, 312

language, faith and human, 134

Last Supper, 87, 89, 103, 121, 125, 241, 277, 290

La Verna, 238

law, divine, 180; of reason, 177; natural, 176, 177, 181-182, 202; binding force of natural, 181-182; the Torah, the Pentateuch, 316; of Christ, 184; of new covenant, 277; marriage, 146; Church, 197, 282, 320; precepts of the Church, 145-146; Canon Law, 146; unjust laws do not bind, 224; see also commandments, Code of Canon Law

laying on of hands, in ordination, 289, 291; in confirmation, 309 310; in anointing of the sick, 327

Lazarus, 51

Leo I, pope, St., 64, 74, 128
Leo IX, pope, St., 209
Leo XIII, pope, 51, 104, 115, 182, 242, 244
Lent, 302-303
life, dignity of each human, 201-206; transmission of, 206-212; social, in society, 216-228; economic, 221-223; ways of living a Christian, 230-239; lay Christian, 232-235; religious, 235-238; God gives us new, 169-171; a free gift, 170; elements of the new, 171-172; acquiring and living the new, 172-174; sharing the divine, 240-247; life eternal, *see* heaven
limbo, 348-349
liturgy, what it is, 262-263; exercise of priestly office of Christ, 263; Christ present in, 268-269; each of the seven sacraments is part of, 270-271; characteristics of liturgical prayer, 265-266; Eucharistic sacrifice is highest form of, 263-264; liturgical celebration, 272-273
Liturgy of the Eucharist, 264, 339
Liturgy of the Hours, 264-265, 296; *see also* Divine Office
Liturgy of the Word, 254, 264, 327, 339
Lord's Prayer, *see* Our Father
Lourdes, 152
love, Christian, 184, 192-200, 231; life of the Trinity is model of, 193; conjugal, 209, 333-334
lust, 195, 198; capital sin, 246
lying, 213-215; *see also* truth

Macedonianism, 114
magisterium, Church, 140-145; ordinary, 140-141; extraordinary, 141-144; papal, 142-144; task of authentically interpreting Scripture and tradition entrusted exclusively to, 139, 370
Magnificat, 71
man, creation of, 36; crown and glory of creation, 42; image of God, 34, 42, 43; body and soul, 42-43; created in full friendship of God, 36; in holiness, freedom, and peace, 52; sin of, 52-54; after Adam, born in sinful state, 52; sins only by free choice, 54; freedom of choice of, 43-44, 185-186; tasks of, 47; death and immortality of, 44; eternal life with God is proper destiny of, 39
Manresa, 238
"Marana tha," 355
marriage, Christian, 332-340; threefold good of, 333-336; children are supreme gift of, 208, 334; ministers of, 335; indissoluble, lifelong,

marriage *(continued)*

235-236; sex in, 207-212; and virginity, 332-333; and the paschal mystery, 339-340; symbolizes union of Christ and the Church, 275, 332; the married vocation, 338-339; impediments to, 337-338; invalid, 338; annulment, decree of nullity, 337; sins against marital values, 209-211

Martha, 51

Martin V, pope, 214

martyrs, martyrdom, 123, 204, 205, 307

Mary, 63, 69-77, 102, 118, 149-155; handmaid of the Lord, 71; full of grace, 71; did not incur original sin, 76, 149; virginity of, 74-75; her mediation and intercession, 151-152; *see also* Annunciation, Assumption, Immaculate Conception

Mass, 87, 103, 253, 254, 262, 263, 264, 265, 266, 275, 279, 280, 281, 285, 313, 339; Christ the Chief Priest and also Victim, 279; participation in, 284; duty to attend on Sundays and holy days, 146, 197; for whom offered, 279; Mass stipends, 279-280; efficacy of Masses for the departed, 347-348; Chrism Mass, 327; *see also* Eucharist

masturbation, 209

meditation, 250, 258, 259

Melchizedek, 269

metanoia, 328

miracles, Christ's, 80-81, 98; purpose of Christ's, 80; gift of, 106

missionary task, the Church's, 164

modalism, 114

monks, Celtic, 323; of the desert, 257; Egyptian, 254

morality, freedom and, 176, 178, 185-186; the Christian nature of, 186; objective norms of, 180; "new," 191; sexual, 207-212

Moses, 55, 156, 183, 276, 309

Moslems, 162, 163

murder, 201, 202

"mysterion," 270

mysteries, divine, grasped only by faith, 110; not contrary to human reason, 110

Mystical Body of Christ, *see* Church

Nain, 316

nation state, limitations of, 226-227

natural law, *see* law

Nazareth, 59, 79, 309
Nestorius, Nestorian, 72
Noah, 276, 301
nullity, decree of, 337

oath, 214; false oaths, 197
obedience, Gospel counsel of, 235; consecrated, 237; in the Church, 145-146; in the family, 221; to civil laws, 224; obedience of faith, 188, 234
Office, see Divine Office, Liturgy of the Hours
oil, olive, 327; blessed, 327; anointing with, 309, 327
omnipotence, God's, 31
omnipresence, God's, 31
omniscience, God's, 30
orders, holy, 147, 197, 230, 271, 275, 287-298; institution of, 287-288; imprints permanent character, 289, 308; celibacy and, 295-296; women and, 293-294
ordinary, diocesan, 129, 130
Origen, 306, 350
Orthodox Churches, 159-160
Our Father, 251, 256, 327, 375; the perfect prayer, 248

Palestine, Palestinian, 81, 309
parables, Christ's use of, 81-82
Paraclete, see Holy Spirit
Parousia, 355-356; time of, 356
paschal mystery, 101, 303, 327, 328, 332, 354; passion and resurrection inseparably joined in, 90; and sacramental life, 268-274; confirmation and, 312-313; marriage and, 339-340; sickness and, 328-329
Passover, meal, 276, 277, 283; ritual, 277
Paul IV, pope, 75
Paul V, pope, St., 46
Paul VI, pope, 41, 52, 85, 129, 142, 149, 153, 163, 183, 190, 207, 210, 211, 216, 219, 228, 234, 237, 257, 262, 277, 280, 285, 286, 287, 300, 310, 315, 319, 326, 328, 335
Pauline privilege, 336
peace, obligation to be concerned with pursuit of world, 227-228; fruit of Holy Spirit, 313
Pelagius, 159
penance, sacrament, 243, 271, 292, 315-324, 328; institution of, 315;

392

penance *(continued)*

judicial form of, 316-317; acts required of penitent (contrition, confession, satisfaction), 317-320; administration of, 323-324; the "laborious baptism," 320; preparation of children for, 320-321
Pentateuch, 366
Pentecost, 101, 103, 104, 107, 150, 310, 311, 312
People of God, *see* Church
perfection, universal call to, 230
perjury, 197, 214
Peter, St., apostle, 80, 88, 127, 128, 140, 141, 142, 143, 146, 309, 316; Christ's promises to, 125-126; given power of the keys, 316-317
Philip, papal legate, 128
Pilate, 88
Pius V, pope, St., 193
Pius VI, pope, 53
Pius IX, pope, 76, 214
Pius X, pope, St., 152
Pius XI, pope, 203, 211, 218, 220, 335
Pius XII, pope, 35, 36, 43, 64, 104, 116, 121, 128, 137, 145, 152, 154, 194, 206, 210, 211, 222, 237, 242, 265, 309, 374
pluralism, types and limits of, 38
political community, 223-226; need for authority in, 224
Polycarp of Smyrna, St., 374
Pontifical Bible Commission, 78
pope, 126, 127, 140, 146, 153; successor of Peter, primacy of, 127-128; special teaching office of, 142-143; infallibility of, 143-144; encyclicals of, 144-145; *see also* individual entries
poverty, Gospel counsel of, 235; professed, 236
prayer, prayers, 248-255, 256-267, 375-378; types and purposes of, 250-251; growth in, 261; memorization of, 257, 266; mental, 258-261; private and liturgical, 256-267; private ordered toward liturgical, 263; excellence of liturgical, 263; to whom we pray, 151, 252-253; of petition, 251-252, 252-253; learning to pray, 266 teaching prayer to children, 266-267; prayers of the blessed in heaven, 251
Prayer of the Faithful, at Mass, 251
precepts of the Church, 146
predestination, 39-40, 170, 351
presumption, 199
pride, capital sin, 246

priest, priests, 130, 145, 153; share in the priesthood of the bishops, 292-293; identification with Christ and His work, 289; receive "faculties," 293; as judge, 316-317; and life of prayer, 296; politics and the, 297

priesthood, shared in different ways, 290-295; of the faithful, 281, 290, 302, 306, 307; distinct role of ministerial, 290; vocations to, 295; service of authority, 297; permanence of, 289-290

property, private, 221-222, 223

prophecies, Old Testament, 55, 56, 97-98, 244, 301, 309; Christ is fulfillment of, 49

prophecy, gift of, 100-107, 199-200

prophets, God speaks through, 55; teaching of the, 55-56; used human language, 134

Protestantism, 160, 369

providence, God's, 39, 49, 57, 181-182, 204

prudence, cardinal virtue, 243

purgatory, 343, 347-348; pains of, 348; prayers for souls in, 252, 347-349

qāhāl, 120

racism, 322

reason, faith and, 34, 36-37; can come to certain knowledge of God, 27-28; law of, 177

Red Sea, 301

redemption, mystery of the, 89-90; foretelling of, 54-56; completed and continuing, 90; Mary's "anticipatory," 76; Mary's role in our, 150

Reformation, 75, 160

religious freedom, 164-165, 212

resurrection, Christ's, 93-99; mystery of the, 93-94; predestined from beginning of creation, 97-98; historical fact, 93; importance of fact of, 96-97; power of the, 98-99; foundation of Christian life, 99; central event of history, 356

resurrection of the body, 352, 353, 356, 357, 358

revelation, gift of living God, 25; gradual, 34, 101-104, 110-111; end of apostolic age ended time of new, 136

Roman Missal, 21, 44, 90, 97, 101, 251, 269, 281, 356

osary, 153, 257, 376-377

Sabellianism, 114

sacramentals, 273

sacraments, 118, 262; seven, 117-118, 264, 270-272; outward signs in-
stituted by Christ to give grace, 172-173; symbolize what they effect,
effect what they symbolize, 282; Christ present in, 268; basically ac-
tions of Christ, 272-273; the Church as sacrament, 117-118
Sacred Congregation for the Clergy, 109, 266, 320, 321, 349
Sacred Congregation for Divine Worship, 300, 310, 315, 326
Sacred Congregation for the Discipline of the Sacraments, 279, 320
Sacred Congregation for Doctrine of the Faith, 111, 142, 162, 205, 294,
316, 317, 319, 338
Sacred Congregation of Rites, 229, 286, 335
sanctification, 240-241, 242
Sanhedrin, 95
Satan, 54, 89, 238, 350
Scripture, and tradition form one sacred deposit of the word of God, 139,
370; canon of, 366-369
secular institute, 235
separated brethren, 130-131, 158-162
sex, importance of, 207-212; in marriage, 207-209; sins against marital
values, 209-211
Shema, 248
Sheol, 98, 349
Sign of the Cross, 257, 375
Simon Magus, 159
sin, 171, 193-196, 214, 242, 245, 246, 322; original, 52, 76; original sin
not incurred by Mary, 76, 149; worse than any physical evils whatever, 204; venial, 193, 196, 319, 320; mortal, 193-195; 242-243, 245,
319; fundamental option, 195-196
sloth, capital sin, 246
socialization, 217-218; goal and purpose of social institutions, 45,
216-217
soul, of man, 42-43, 206, 327, 344; each created individually, 43; does
not exist before body, 43; continues to exist after death, 43; "saving
one's soul," 44
Spirit, see Holy Spirit
stipend, Mass, 279-280
Subiaco, 238
subsidiarity, principle of, 218, 221-222, 223, 227
superstition, 197
Synod of Bishops, institution of, 129; Second General Assembly of, 226,
289, 297

temperance, cardinal virtue, 198, 243
Teresa of Avila, St., 238, 374
theandric works, 67
Theotokos, 72, 73, 74, 76
Thomas, St., apostle, 97
Thomas Aquinas, St., 43, 51, 73, 86, 182, 185, 249, 250, 334, 344, 354
Torah, 366
transcendence, God's, 32
Trinity, 109-116; three distinct Persons, coequal, coeternal, 109; mystery of God in Himself, 110; central mystery of faith, 109, 110-111, 184-185
truth, value of, 212-215; duty to pursue religious, 212-213; duty to seek and to speak, 213; hierarchy of truths, 109

unbelief, mystery of, 26-27
United States National Conference of Catholic Bishops, 72, 146, 152, 206, 209, 226, 257, 267

vespers, 264-265
Vincent of Lerins, 137
virginity, Mary's, 69, 74-75; life of Christian, 332-333; and marriage, 331, 332-333; for Christ is vocation of "surpassing excellence," 237
vocation of man, 47; Christian, 230-239; the married, 332-333; the lay, 232-235; to priesthood, 295-298; religious, 230, 235-238
vows, religious, 236-237, 265

war, acts of, 202, 203-204; causes of, 227; condemnations of total, 202; arms race, 226-228, 322
water, symbolism of, 300-301
William of Ware, 76
wine, 283
witness, to faith, obligation to bear, 161, 233
women, dignity of, 45; in ministry, 293-294
Word, the eternal, *see* Jesus Christ
world, damaged by sin, 17, 240; marked by injustice, 322; Christian hope for, 190-191; to be transformed, 353-354

Yahweh, 150, 276

Zechariah, 70, 102